Advanced Research and Trends in Human-Computer Interaction

Volume I

Advanced Research and Trends in Human-Computer Interaction
Volume I

Edited by **Stanley Harmon**

CLANRYE INTERNATIONAL

New Jersey

Published by Clanrye International,
55 Van Reypen Street,
Jersey City, NJ 07306, USA
www.clanryeinternational.com

Advanced Research and Trends in Human-Computer Interaction: Volume I
Edited by Stanley Harmon

International Standard Book Number: 978-1-63240-024-6 (Hardback)

Printed in the United States of America.

Contents

Preface

Human-computer interaction is a field that involves the study, planning, design and use of the process of interaction between people or users and computers. The term 'human-computer interaction' was established around the 1980s. The term can be simplified through the fact that unlike other tools with only limited and one dimensional uses, a computer has many uses and these functions take place in an open-ended dialog between the user and the computer. It is an interdisciplinary field of study with foundations in computer science, behavioural science, media studies, design, and several other arenas. It studies how computers and people interact with each other and to what extent computers are developed for such successful interactions. There are many ways for a user to interact with computers, and the interface used for this interaction between humans and the computers is crucial. Desktop applications, internet browsers, handheld computers, and computer are examples of human-computer interfaces that we use daily. There are constant and rapid developments in this field and they all have ramification on our day to day lives. Thus there is always a demand for graduates who can work towards better and more efficient interfaces.

This book is an attempt to compile and collate all available research on human-computer interaction under one aegis. I am grateful to those who put their hard work, effort and expertise into these research projects as well as those who were supportive in this endeavour.

Editor

Source Detection and Functional Connectivity of the Sensorimotor Cortex during Actual and Imaginary Limb Movement: A Preliminary Study on the Implementation of eConnectome in Motor Imagery Protocols

Alkinoos Athanasiou, Chrysa Lithari, Konstantina Kalogianni, Manousos A. Klados, and Panagiotis D. Bamidis

Lab of Medical Informatics, Medical School, Aristotle University of Thessaloniki (AUTH), 54124 Thessaloniki, Greece

Correspondence should be addressed to Alkinoos Athanasiou, alkinoosathanassiou@gmail.com

Academic Editor: Christos Papadelis

Introduction. Sensorimotor cortex is activated similarly during motor execution and motor imagery. The study of functional connectivity networks (FCNs) aims at successfully modeling the dynamics of information flow between cortical areas. *Materials and Methods.* Seven healthy subjects performed 4 motor tasks (real foot, imaginary foot, real hand, and imaginary hand movements), while electroencephalography was recorded over the sensorimotor cortex. Event-Related Desynchronization/Synchronization (ERD/ERS) of the mu-rhythm was used to evaluate MI performance. Source detection and FCNs were studied with eConnectome. *Results and Discussion.* Four subjects produced similar ERD/ERS patterns between motor execution and imagery during both hand and foot tasks, 2 subjects only during hand tasks, and 1 subject only during foot tasks. All subjects showed the expected brain activation in well-performed MI tasks, facilitating cortical source estimation. Preliminary functional connectivity analysis shows formation of networks on the sensorimotor cortex during motor imagery and execution. *Conclusions.* Cortex activation maps depict sensorimotor cortex activation, while similar functional connectivity networks are formed in the sensorimotor cortex both during actual and imaginary movements. eConnectome is demonstrated as an effective tool for the study of cortex activation and FCN. The implementation of FCN in motor imagery could induce promising advancements in Brain Computer Interfaces.

1. Introduction

Motor imagery (MI) is described as the concept of imagining a motor task without resulting in physical execution. It is the visualization and rehearsal of an imaginary movement [1] as opposed to the actual practice of the movement, which is described by the term Motor Execution (ME). This concept is widely applied in the development of Brain Computer Interfaces (BCIs). BCIs are systems that translate human volition to control of external devices and exploit a person's will to move or to communicate, regardless if that person is able to actually perform such a task due to severe impairments (such as spinal cord injury (SCI), stroke, or amyotrophic lateral sclerosis (ALS)) [2]. Cortical activation during motor

imagery can be recorded with a variety of methods, including functional Magnetic Resonance Imaging (fMRI), which has the optimal spatial accuracy [3], and electroencephalography (EEG), which provides excellent temporal accuracy (on the order of milliseconds) [2]. EEG in particular has been extensively applied, as it is an inexpensive, widely available, and relatively simple method that can be applied to real-life scenarios [2].

The brainwaves can be extracted by the EEG easily and in real time and play a crucial role in BCI applications. The mu-rhythm has been identified as an EEG feature that corresponds to movement volition and is usually examined in motor imagery studies [4]. Its physiological role is not yet clearly defined, though it is associated with the inhibition of the movement [5]. The amplitude of the mu-rhythm typically decreases when the corresponding motor areas are activated and is most accurately recorded over the primary sensorimotor cortex [5]. Its exact range is not firmly defined, but it generally overlaps with the alpha rhythm (8–12 Hz) [6] and possibly with a part of the lower beta band [4]. Mu-rhythm (also known as sensorimotor rhythm (SMR)) is commonly studied using Event-Related Desynchronization/Synchronization analysis (ERD/ERS), where ERD usually denotes the activation of cortical areas, while ERS denotes a decrease in excitability and information processing [7].

BCIs continue to develop over the past five years becoming more user friendly, accurate, and efficient [8], while they still carry certain drawbacks that need to be addressed [9]. However, ERD/ERS of the EEG mu-rhythm provides spatially static neuroelectric information of brain regions that are activated during tasks. ERD/ERS analysis does not convey the information of how these regions communicate with each other [10]. Brain activity is distributed spatiotemporally, and brain functional networks are formed through this distribution. The behavior of such networks provides important physiological information for understanding brain functions and dysfunctions [11]. The relatively new concept of brain functional connectivity [11] promises to play a key role in neurosciences, allowing researchers to study the organized behavior of brain regions beyond the standard cortical source estimation, mapping, and localization of activity [12]. The estimation of functional cortical connectivity aims at describing the interactions between differently organized and specialized cortical regions as patterns depicting dynamics of information flow between those regions [10].

A conceptual definition of functional connectivity is stated as a "temporal correlation between spatially remote neurophysiological events" [10, 13]. Several approaches have been proposed for the estimation of this correlation, known as connectivity metrics. Latest approaches, such as the Directed Transfer Function (DTF) and the Adaptive Directed Transfer Function (ADTF), rely on the key concept of Granger causality between time series [14]. The mathematical background of these methods lies beyond the scope of this paper, but—on a very short account—the lack of reciprocity between two times series, one of which results to the other, provides the direction of the information flow between each pair of elements [15].

In our work, a classic paradigm of cue-paced motor imagery is deployed in healthy young volunteers. Our goal is to investigate the implementation of functional connectivity on Brain Computer Interfaces and Motor Imagery protocols and to examine the possibility of classifying the motor volition accurately and fast by functional connectivity analysis. For this purpose, we used the novel MATLAB toolbox, eConnectome [16]. The solutions to the inverse problem were provided by the toolbox together with the activation maps on cortical level. We currently present the preliminary results of implementing functional connectivity analysis on motor imagery by exploiting the open eConnectome toolbox.

2. Materials and Methods

In the current study 7 healthy right-handed subjects participated (4 male and 3 female); mean age of 28.1 (range 23–37). The procedure was accurately explained beforehand, and all subjects gave their written consent prior to the experimental procedure. None of the subjects had any experience in the concept of motor imagery prior to their participation. The setup of the experiment and part of the analysis has been analytically described in our previous work [17]. Each subject performed four motor tasks: (a) real hand movement (biceps-flexion of the forearm), (b) imaginary hand movement, (c) real foot movement (quadriceps—stretch of the lower leg), and (d) imaginary foot movement. Each task was repeated 95 times, divided into five sets of 19 trials each. There was 1-minute rest between sets and 5-minute rest between tasks. During trials, the subjects were presented with visual feedback on a computer screen (the word "move"), which constituted the cue to perform the relevant task. The cue of the visual feedback was recorded with an optic fiber placed on the computer screen serving as the trigger channel synchronous to the EEG recording. A Nihon-Kohden (Japan) EEG and an active electrode cap (EASYCAP, Germany) were used. EEG was recorded by 17 electrodes (CP3, CP1, CPz, CP2, Cp4, C5, C3, C1, Cz, C2, C4, C6, FC3, FC1, FCz, FC2, and FC4), placed in accordance with the 10-10 international electrode system. The recording electrodes were referenced with LPA and RPA mastoid electrodes. The impedance threshold was set below 5 kOhm. The electrode setup corresponds to the skull area above the sensorimotor cortex.

Following signal extraction, further processing is described in two parts. Initially, the extracted signals were processed with an ERD/ERS of mu-rhythm EEG paradigm in mind. This paradigm of cue-paced motor imagery [17], is presented here as an intermediate step that serves to instigate our research towards functional connectivity. The second part, consisting of source depiction and functional connectivity of the extracted signals, deploys different processing methodology, as we describe accordingly. Signal preprocessing and analysis was performed in MATLAB (Mathworks Inc.), using EEGLAB toolbox [18] and eConnectome toolbox [16].

For ERD/ERS analysis, we chose to focus on 7 electrodes (CP1, CPz, CP2, C1, Cz, C2, FC1, FCz, and FC2), those more relevant to the primary motor cortical areas of hand and foot. Filtering was performed using EEGLAB [16] at 8–15 Hz (mu-rhythm, possibly including a fraction of the lower beta band) [4]. Independent Component Analysis (ICA) was used to remove ocular artifacts. Epochs were set from 800 msec prestimulus to 2200 msec poststimulus.

Following preprocessing, Event-Related Desynchro-nization/Synchronization (ERD/ERS) values of the mu-rhythm were calculated. Each subject's 95 epochs for each task were first divided in five sets of 19 epochs and then were averaged across sets. For each of the five sets, as well as for each of the seven focus electrodes, ERD/ERS was computed at three poststimuli intervals (100–400 msec, 400–700 sec, and 700–1000 msec) towards −300–0 msec prestimulus, to account

Source Detection and Functional Connectivity of the Sensorimotor Cortex during Actual and Imaginary Limb Movement: A Preliminary Study on the Implementation of eConnectome in Motor Imagery Protocols

3

for different reflexes of the subjects. This resulted in matrices of $7 \times 5 \times 3$ size, containing the ERD/ERS values for each subject. In order to test for similarities between the ERD/ERS values during the real movements and ERD/ERS values during the imaginary ones, Student's t-tests were performed. Moreover, the ERD/ERS values during the imaginary foot movements were compared to their counterparts during the imaginary hand movements to reveal any differentiation. For all statistical tests, the level of significance was set to 0.05.

Source imaging and functional connectivity on the source level were applied taking into account all 17 electrodes. The area covered by the electrodes can be anatomically corresponded to the primary motor area, primary somatosensory area, and premotor cortex of the brain. In order to append those signals recorded at the surface of the skull to specific Brodmann areas of the cortex though, the solutions to the "inverse problem" have to be calculated. eConnectome handles this part using the Cortical Current Density (CCD) source model [19]. The toolbox provides a high-resolution cortical surface model segmented and reconstructed for visualization from MRI images of the Montreal Neurological Institute and a scalp surface that forms the sensor space. These are generic realistic head models designed to provide improved accuracy in cortical source estimation [20]. Cortical regions of interest (ROIs), corresponding to Brodmann areas, are predefined (by the eConnectome software) and available to compute estimated cortical sources. The user has also the choice to define custom regions of interest, a feature that we explored in our study.

Preprocessing involved filtering at 8–15 hz, and ICA using EEGLAB [16] and epochs were set from 800 msec prestimulus to 2200 msec poststimulus. At this point, one further step was decided, in order to compute the average of all (95) epochs for each subject—rather than in sets of 19 (as was done for the ERD/ERS analysis). This produced a dataset of four EEG sets for each of the seven subjects. Each of these four sets consisted of the average of 95 trials during each task: Foot Motor Execution (FME), Foot Motor Imagery (FMI), Hand Motor Execution (HME), and Hand Motor Imagery (HMI). Using the EEG module of eConnectome [21], for each subject, we compared ROI activation of FME versus FMI, HME versus HMI, as well as FME versus HME, and FMI versus HMI. The average of each task trials for each subject was chosen over individual epoch analysis, in order to minimize the effect of random occurrences and artifacts to the imaging of cortical activation. Similarly, it is suggested that the causality relations between cortical networks appear to be independent from the frequency band analyzed [10]. Thus, we opted to estimate source activation for the narrow frequency band that we used for mu-rhythm ERD/ERS analysis and connectivity was computed for the band of mu-rhythm (8–12 hz), aiming for better comparability of results and reduction of computational workload.

Directed Transfer Function (DTF) was used for the estimation of functional connectivity relationships between cortical areas of the human brain [16]. DTF is a connectivity metric based on the multivariate autoregressive (MVAR) modeling [22]. It was applied on the whole -800 to 2200 msec interval for the range of 8–12 Hz (mu or

TABLE 1: Real/imaginary statistical similarity and hand/foot discrimination percentages of subjects using t-test comparisons ($P > 0.05$) of ERD/ERS values: our subjects showed high performance in Foot and Hand Motor Imagery but low source discrimination.

Real/imaginary similarity	
Hand	85.71%
Foot	71.41%
Hand/foot discrimination	
Real	28.57%
Imaginary	14.28%

alpha rhythm). For a single representative subject, the functional connectivity of the sensorimotor cortex during motor execution and imagery for both foot and hand movements was analyzed and further compared. During this investigation, we custom defined ROIs on the sensorimotor cortex, correlating to primary hand and foot motor areas (M1), hand and foot sensory areas (S1), and supplementary motor areas (SMAs). The selected subject was the one with the highest performance in both FMI and HMI, as defined by no differentiation between imaginary and real ERD/ERS patterns in the majority of focus electrodes and time intervals. Connectivity patterns were visualized at both the cortical surface and the EEG sensor level, on a model using the standard 10-10 electrode system [23].

3. Results

3.1. Event-Related Desynchronization/Synchronization (ERD/ ERS) Analysis. Regarding the ability to perform motor imagery, four out of seven subjects performed equally well in both FMI and HMI, activating their cortex during imaginary movements in the same patterns as in real movements ($P > 0.05$) in all of the three time intervals as reported previously by our group [17].

Regarding the ability to statistically discriminate between hand and foot movements, in two out of seven subjects, ERD/ERS of the mu-rhythm was unable to provide hand-foot discrimination in either MI or ME. For two subjects, hand-foot discrimination (for both MI and ME) was poor, both spatially (7 electrodes) and temporally (3 time intervals). For further two subjects, the discrimination between foot and hand ME was possible across most electrodes and time intervals. Finally, one subject produced distinctive ERD/ERS patterns for foot and hand MI, while this was not the case for ME.

The results of ERD/ERS statistical analysis, published in a previous paper [17] and presented here in a summary (Table 1), encouraged us to further investigate MI movements in terms of functional connectivity.

3.2. Cortical Source Imaging. The distinction between different cortical sources' activation is facilitated with the visualization of the inverse problem solutions (computed with Current Cortical Density) that provide the corresponding cortical activation maps. In all subjects, as expected, visual discrimination between foot and hand activation

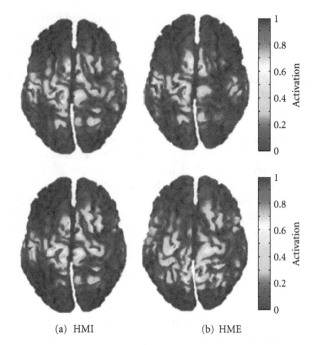

(a) HMI   (b) HME

FIGURE 2: Cortical source activation maps for one subject during (a) Hand Motor Imagery (HMI) and (b) Hand Motor Execution (HME). Each row represents a different poststimulus instance, and the variance in activation patterns can be observed.

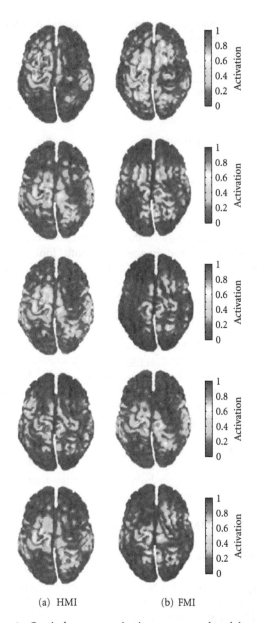

(a) HMI   (b) FMI

FIGURE 1: Cortical source activation maps produced by eConnectome after solving the inverse problem using Current Cortical Density. Poststimuli instances for 5 subjects during (a) Hand Motor Imagery (HMI) and (b) Foot Motor Imagery (FMI). Different activation patterns can be observed for different subjects, but in all of them, the hand and foot imagery are discriminated.

in real movements is apparent. Moreover, in five out of seven subjects, the discrimination becomes possible between imaginary foot and hand movements as well (Figure 1). As also shown in Figure 1, not all subjects activate the relevant cortical sources in the same pattern, especially during imaginary movement. It can be observed that during imaginary movements, there is greater involvement of the ipsilateral hemisphere. Moreover, activation patterns are not static during the whole epoch (the average of 95 epochs of each task), but different instances produce different patterns for each subject in both MI and ME tasks (Figure 2).

Although activation is similar during MI and ME, generally imagery produces lower levels of activation, at both scalp and cortical area (Figure 3). Finally, it can be observed that activation of supplementary motor areas (SMAs) varies and is more intense during foot motor for all subjects. This is demonstrated at Figure 4 for subject 1, but similar patterns stand for the rest of the subjects.

3.3. Functional Connectivity. For this part of our analysis, one representative subject was chosen, as described in Section 2. All figures hereafter concern this particular subject. Functional connectivity can be studied either at the scalp surface (electrode plane) or at the cortical surface (regions of interest plane). Figure 5 depicts connectivity at the electrode plane, at different instances for one subject. Different connectivity patterns can be recognized at different temporal instances, but there are some that prevail across the whole task as shown in the second and the third rows of Figure 5. In HME, a strong outflow current is produced from electrode C1 towards electrodes corresponding to both hemispheres of the sensorimotor cortex (Figure 5(a)). eConnectome provides the option to portray information flow between all channels or the single highest outflow, inflow, or information exchange. This outflow is maximal towards CP4 and FC2 in most examined instances. On the contrary, in HMI, this strong outflow is not as obvious, although when each electrode is examined, the same prevalence of C1 can be found. In HMI, information flow is portrayed to be maximal from electrode C1 towards electrode FC2 and from electrode FC1 towards electrode C4 (Figure 5(b)).

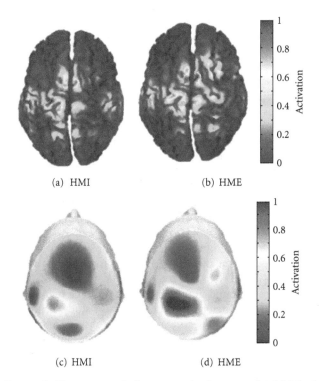

(a) HMI   (b) HME

(c) HMI   (d) HME

FIGURE 3: First row: cortical source activation maps for (a) Hand Motor Imagery (HMI) and (b) Hand Motor Execution (HME). Second row: scalp area activation maps for (c) HMI and (d) HME. All images are from a single subject, and a lower level of activation can be observed in imagery as compared to the corresponding instance during execution.

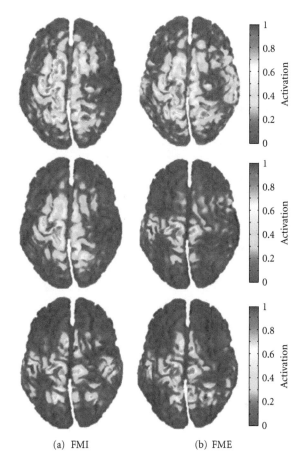

(a) FMI   (b) FME

FIGURE 4: Cortical source activation maps for one representative subject during (a) Foot Motor Imagery (FMI) and (b) Foot Motor Execution (FME). The activation of supplementary motor areas (SMAs) varies in different poststimulus instances (rows) and can be observed to be more intense during FMI.

On the cortical surface, after solving the inverse problem, functional connectivity can be studied either using the predefined regions of interest (cortical ROIs defined by eConnectome, corresponding to Brodmann areas) or using custom-defined ROIs on the dynamic activation maps produced by source imaging. Initially, the primary hand motor areas were defined in both hemispheres, and then Directed Transfer Function (DTF) was computed. Figure 6 depicts a strong information flow between primary hand motor areas, directed from the contralateral (to the moving hand) towards the ipsilateral area. This flow is almost identical in power amplitude in both motor execution and motor imagery. To test whether that was a result of defining only primary motor areas, another ROI corresponding to primary right foot sensory cortex (the purple-colored area in Figure 6(b)) was defined, but no information flow was detected. In Figure 7, the cortical network produced by Hand Motor Imagery consists, additionally, of the SMAs and the primary hand sensory areas. In this case, information flow is stronger from the SMAs towards the ipsilateral primary hand motor area, showing the important regulative role of those cortical sources in the imagination (preparation) of a movement [10]. The activation time series of the ROIs of this small cortical network, consisting of primary hand motor and sensory areas and SMAs, is presented in Figure 8. Finally, another small cortical network was tested,

this time consisting of primary foot motor areas and SMAs. The information flow from the SMAs is present in this network too, directed to the contralateral primary foot motor area. In addition, there is a high output information exchange between the SMAs of both hemispheres as shown in Figure 9.

4. Discussion

The sensorimotor cortex, during the practice of motor imagery tasks, has been proven to produce similar patterns of activation with actual motor execution tasks [4, 6], something our work also confirms [17]. Cortex activation is found to be less intense during motor imagery as compared to motor execution, which is shown by ERD/ERS amplitude as well as by source activation maps produced by eConnectome. Mu-rhythm detection and ERD/ERS analysis achieve high performance (over 85% for Hand Motor Imagery in our experiment) and are considered to be a suitable modality for accurate and fast classification of human motor volition. However, ERD/ERS analysis does not facilitate the discrimination between different sources'

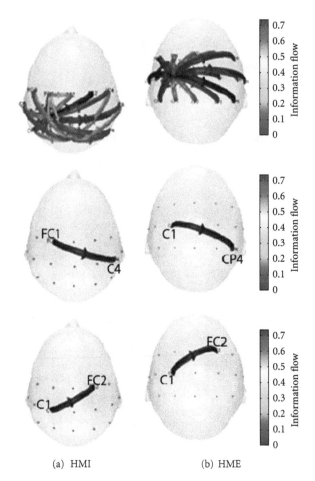

(a) HMI   (b) HME

FIGURE 5: Functional connectivity patterns at the electrode plane for one representative subject during (a) Hand Motor Imagery (HMI) and (b) Hand Motor Execution (HME). First row: information exchange between all channels. Second and third rows: maximal information exchange.

activation. On the contrary, the production of cortical source activation maps, such as those produced by eConnectome, can be greatly effective in source discrimination. As has been proposed by BCI experts, design of motor restoration systems should be based on a self-paced (asynchronous) approach [24]. Our results agree with this viewpoint, as each subject tended to produce unique patterns of brain activity, regarding electrodes and time intervals of activation [17]. The study of functional connectivity at both the scalp and the source level can help further understanding of each subject's unique patterns, providing information on "communication" exchange between electrodes and cortical sources.

The mu-specific approach was induced by certain reasons. Concerning sensorimotor-related rhythms, it is proposed that mu- and beta-rhythms are couple-phased and should not be combined as independent control features [25]. Also, it is suggested that causality relation between cortical networks is not maximally present in any specific frequency band [10]. Taking those viewpoints into account

allowed us to focus on a narrow band of brain activity, reducing computational workload, while at the same time without resulting in sacrifice of information. Our brain connectivity findings tend to confirm novel studies in the area [10, 15, 21] regarding the highly dynamic nature of functional connectivity networks [15]. Such studies report small-world topologies [11] in brain networks, a characteristic that seems to play a crucial role regarding neurophysiological organization and behavior of the cortex [26, 27] during motor execution and imagery. Furthermore, in the current study, eConnectome revealed the SMAs as a clearly defined nested network exchanging information with primary motor regions, a finding we appreciate to be coherent with the regulative role of SMAs during the planning of a movement [10]. Through the use of eConnectome, we were able to study specific cortical regions of interest and the way they interact in motor execution and motor imagery tasks of the hand and the foot.

There are several limitations that have to be mentioned, including some that are not specific to our study. Primarily, the low number of subjects along with the absence of patients does not allow us to safely generalize our findings and conclude an effective BCI approach for mobility restoration. Moreover, regarding connectivity analysis, we have to mention again that in the view of the feasibility analysis aimed at in this paper, only exploratory results are reported herein, based on the investigation of ME and MI performance for one subject. However, we reiterate that this study dealt with the feasibility and usefulness of BCI and connectivity integration rather than with specific neurophysiological findings. There are many changes in brain activation and functional connectivity that come with severe impairment [8, 10]. As such, the inclusion of patients in such research is crucial in order to produce useful conclusions.

Regarding our method, the absence of electromyographic (EMG) signal recording is crucial to further analysis, since the trials were not accurately time locked, and the contamination because of muscular artifacts could not be eliminated. Also, a higher number of EEG sensors would have resulted to better spatial resolution, and in order to efficiently study connectivity, we ought to have a recording of higher spatial resolution (more electrodes, possibly placed in accordance with 10–5 international system [23]). However, an increased number of EEG sensors have been identified to produce unwanted (false) small-world topologies [11], since uncorrelated electrodes would be more easily influenced by strong focal signals. Practicality reasons also demand that a possible BCI-FCN integration should deploy a rather small number of electrodes in order to facilitate portability and usage in real-life scenarios. The optimal compromise between portability and spatial resolution is something that has yet to be researched.

Finally, the selection of the connectivity metric is proven to be critical for the formation of the brain functional networks [28], and a more reliable interpretation of measured activations and information flow could be obtained by comparing results from different connectivity metrics. Furthermore, eConnectome includes specific multivariate metrics (DTF and ADTF) that are not proven to be

Source Detection and Functional Connectivity of the Sensorimotor Cortex during Actual and Imaginary Limb Movement: A Preliminary Study on the Implementation of eConnectome in Motor Imagery Protocols

7

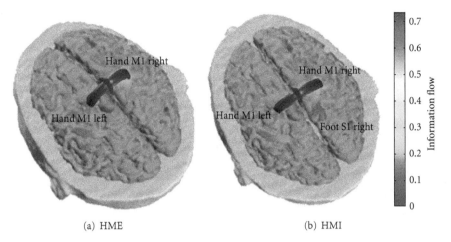

(a) HME   (b) HMI

FIGURE 6: Identical high Information outflow from the cortical ROI corresponding to hand area of motor cortex contralateral to movement towards the same ipsilateral area during (a) Hand Motor Execution (HME) and (b) Hand Motor Imagery (HMI).

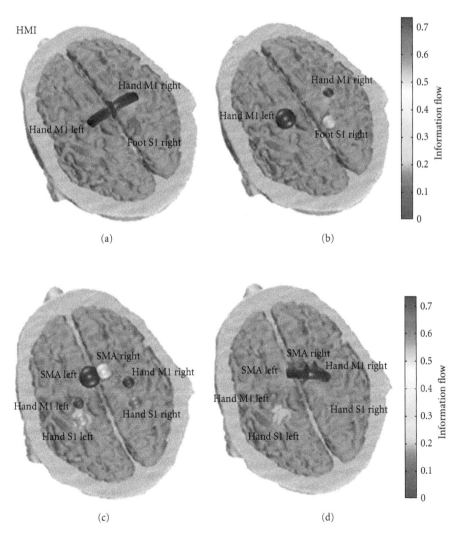

FIGURE 7: FCN during Hand Motor Imagery (HMI) of one representative subject. (a) Information exchange between primary hand motor areas, (b) information outflow from the same areas, (c) information outflow from SMAs, and (d) the highest information exchange was shown to occur between the two SMAs and the ipsilateral primary hand motor area. The size of the spheres is proportional to the outflow, which is also obvious from the chromatic scale.

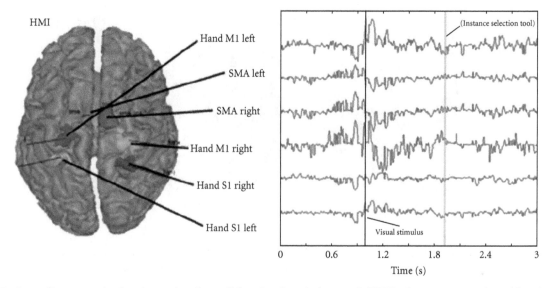

FIGURE 8: Regions of interest activation time series of a small functional cortical network (FCN) of one representative subject during Hand Motor Imagery (HMI).

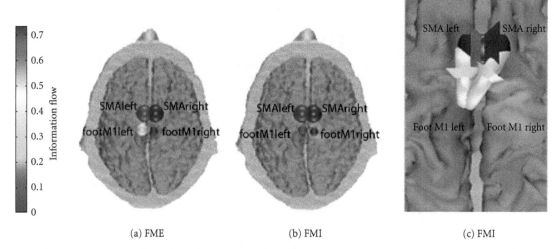

FIGURE 9: FCNs of one representative subject during foot motor tasks. Information outflow from SMAs and primary foot motor areas during (a) Foot Motor Execution (FME) and (b) Foot Motor Imagery (FMI). (c) Information exchange of those areas during Foot Motor Imagery (zoom in).

specifically more suitable for BCI approaches than other connectivity metrics. The integration of connectivity in Brain Computer Interfaces seems far from being immediately feasible. It has to be stressed that DTF cannot yet be performed in real time. The prospect of real-time application of a connectivity metric in a BCI application would also require a time-adaptive metric, such as the ADTF, which seems more suitable for such a use. However, ADTF needs even more computational workload and time to be performed than the DTF. The real-time environment that is crucial for rehabilitation or commercial BCI approaches cannot yet benefit from connectivity analysis, though this is a limitation that time and technological progress is expected to eventually solve [29].

In conclusion, it is our conviction that the study of functional connectivity in the context of Brain Computer Interfaces applications, although not yet a mature solution, has a lot to offer in terms of neurophysiological integration and understanding and the design of intuitive high-performance self-paced systems. eConnectome is an appropriate toolbox to be used in order to test and enhance the effectiveness of Motor Imagery protocols and Brain Computer Interface systems in a research environment. In our study, this toolbox enabled us to extensively study and detect expected similarities and differences in cortical activation, as well as depict simple FCNs between a small number of highly important cortical regions of interest. eConnectome is demonstrated to be able to facilitate the study of functional connectivity, providing easy-to-use tools and graphical interpretations of cortical activity and information exchanges. Further evaluation and experiments involving healthy and patient subjects need to be performed in order to fully implement FCN findings in typical BCIs. We cannot emphasize enough the breakthroughs that can occur in the field of motor restoration; however, we can only capture the need towards the design of appropriate software and tools to precipitate the integration of the two fields of research.

References

[1] J. Decety and D. H. Ingvar, "Brain structures participating in mental simulation of motor behavior: a neuropsychological interpretation," *Acta Psychologica*, vol. 73, no. 1, pp. 13–34, 1990.

[2] A. Athanasiou and P. D. Bamidis, "A review on brain computer interfaces: contemporary achievements and future goals towards movement restoration," *Aristotle University Medical Journal*, vol. 37, no. 3, pp. 35–44, 2010.

[3] R. Sitaram, A. Caria, R. Veit et al., "FMRI brain-computer interface: a tool for neuroscientific research and treatment," *Computational Intelligence and Neuroscience*, vol. 2007, Article ID 25487, 10 pages, 2007.

[4] G. Pfurtscheller and C. Neuper, "Motor imagery activates primary sensorimotor area in humans," *Neuroscience Letters*, vol. 239, no. 2-3, pp. 65–68, 1997.

[5] S. Arroyo, R. P. Lesser, B. Gordon, S. Uematsu, D. Jackson, and R. Webber, "Functional significance of the mu rhythm of human cortex: an electrophysiologic study with subdural electrodes," *Electroencephalography and Clinical Neurophysiology*, vol. 87, no. 3, pp. 76–87, 1993.

[6] C. Neuper, R. Scherer, S. Wriessnegger, and G. Pfurtscheller, "Motor imagery and action observation: modulation of sensorimotor brain rhythms during mental control of a brain-computer interface," *Clinical Neurophysiology*, vol. 120, no. 2, pp. 239–247, 2009.

[7] E. V. C. Friedrich, D. J. McFarland, C. Neuper, T. M. Vaughan, P. Brunner, and J. R. Wolpaw, "A scanning protocol for a sensorimotor rhythm-based brain-computer interface," *Biological Psychology*, vol. 80, no. 2, pp. 169–175, 2009.

[8] J. Zhou, J. Yao, J. Deng, and J. P. A. Dewald, "EEG-based classification for elbow versus shoulder torque intentions involving stroke subjects," *Computers in Biology and Medicine*, vol. 39, no. 5, pp. 443–452, 2009.

[9] V. Morash, O. Bai, S. Furlani, P. Lin, and M. Hallett, "Classifying EEG signals preceding right hand, left hand, tongue, and right foot movements and motor imageries," *Clinical Neurophysiology*, vol. 119, no. 11, pp. 2570–2578, 2008.

[10] L. Astolfi, H. Bakardjian, F. Cincotti et al., "Estimate of causality between independent cortical spatial patterns during movement volition in spinal cord injured patients," *Brain Topography*, vol. 19, no. 3, pp. 107–123, 2007.

[11] A. A. Ioannides, "Dynamic functional connectivity," *Current Opinion in Neurobiology*, vol. 17, no. 2, pp. 161–170, 2007.

[12] F. Varela, J. P. Lachaux, E. Rodriguez, and J. Martinerie, "The brainweb: phase synchronization and large-scale integration," *Nature Reviews Neuroscience*, vol. 2, no. 4, pp. 229–239, 2001.

[13] K. J. Friston, "Functional and effective connectivity in neuroimaging: a synthesis," *Human Brain Mapping*, vol. 2, no. 1-2, pp. 56–78, 1994.

[14] C. W. J. Granger, "Investigating causal relations by econometric models and cross spectra methods," *Econometrica*, vol. 37, pp. 424–438, 1969.

[15] F. de Vico Fallani, L. Astolfi, F. Cincotti et al., "Cortical functional connectivity networks in normal and spinal cord injured patients: evaluation by graph analysis," *Human Brain Mapping*, vol. 28, no. 12, pp. 1334–1346, 2007.

[16] B. He, Y. Dai, L. Astolfi, F. Babiloni, H. Yuan, and L. Yang, "eConnectome: a MATLAB toolbox for mapping and imaging of brain functional connectivity," *Journal of Neuroscience Methods*, vol. 195, no. 2, pp. 261–269, 2011.

[17] A. Athanasiou, E. Chatzitheodorou, K. Kalogianni, C. Lithari, I. Moulos, and P. D. Bamidis, "Comparing sensorimotor cortex activation during actual and imaginary movement," in *Proceedings of the 12th Mediterranean Conference on Medical and Biological Engineering and Computing (MEDICON '10)*, vol. 29 of *IFMBE Proceedings*, pp. 111–114, Chalkidiki, Greece, May 2010.

[18] A. Delorme and S. Makeig, "EEGLAB: an open source toolbox for analysis of single-trial EEG dynamics including independent component analysis," *Journal of Neuroscience Methods*, vol. 134, no. 1, pp. 9–21, 2004.

[19] A. M. Dale and M. I. Sereno, "Improved localization of cortical activity by combining EEG and MEG with MRI cortical surface reconstruction: a linear approach," *Journal of Cognitive Neuroscience*, vol. 5, no. 2, pp. 162–176, 1993.

[20] P. A. Valdés-Hernández, N. von Ellenrieder, A. Ojeda-Gonzalez et al., "Approximate average head models for EEG source imaging," *Journal of Neuroscience Methods*, vol. 185, no. 1, pp. 125–132, 2009.

[21] F. Babiloni, F. Cincotti, C. Babiloni et al., "Estimation of the cortical functional connectivity with the multimodal integration of high-resolution EEG and fMRI data by directed transfer function," *NeuroImage*, vol. 24, no. 1, pp. 118–131, 2005.

[22] C. Wilke, L. Ding, and B. He, "Estimation of time-varying connectivity patterns through the use of an adaptive directed transfer function," *IEEE Transactions on Biomedical Engineering*, vol. 55, no. 11, pp. 2557–2564, 2008.

[23] R. Oostenveld and P. Praamstra, "The five percent electrode system for high-resolution EEG and ERP measurements," *Clinical Neurophysiology*, vol. 112, no. 4, pp. 713–719, 2001.

[24] R. Scherer, A. Schloegl, F. Lee, H. Bischof, J. Janša, and G. Pfurtscheller, "The self-paced graz brain-computer interface: methods and applications," *Computational Intelligence and Neuroscience*, vol. 2007, Article ID 79826, 9 pages, 2007.

[25] D. J. Krusienski, G. Schalk, D. J. McFarland, and J. R. Wolpaw, "A μ-rhythm matched filter for continuous control of a brain-computer interface," *IEEE Transactions in Biomedical Engineering*, vol. 54, no. 2, pp. 273–280, 2007.

[26] F. Pichiorri, F. De Vico Fallani, F. Cincotti et al., "Sensorimotor rhythm-based brain-computer interface training: the impact on motor cortical responsiveness," *Journal of Neural Engineering*, vol. 8, no. 2, Article ID 025020, 2011.

[27] S. H. Jin, P. Lin, and M. Hallet, "Reorganization of brain functional small-world networks during finger movements," *Human Brain Mapping*, vol. 33, no. 4, pp. 861–872, 2012.

[28] F. Wendling, K. Ansari-Asl, F. Bartolomei, and L. Senhadji, "From EEG signals to brain connectivity: a model-based evaluation of interdependence measures," *Journal of Neuroscience Methods*, vol. 183, no. 1, pp. 9–18, 2009.

[29] T. Li, J. Hong, and J. Zhang, "Electroencephalographic (EEG) control of cursor movement in three-dimensional scene based on small-world neural network," in *Proceedings of the IEEE International Conference on Intelligent Computing and Intelligent Systems (ICIS '10)*, vol. 3, pp. 587–591, Xiamen, China, October 2010.

2

Comparing Horizontal and Vertical Surfaces for a Collaborative Design Task

Brianna Potvin, Colin Swindells, Melanie Tory, and Margaret-Anne Storey

Department of Computer Science, University of Victoria, Engineering/Computer Science Building (ECS), Room 504, P.O. Box 3055, STN CSC, Victoria, BC, Canada V8W 3P6

Correspondence should be addressed to Melanie Tory, mtory@cs.uvic.ca

Academic Editor: Antonio Krüger

We investigate the use of different surface orientations for collaborative design tasks. Specifically, we compare horizontal and vertical surface orientations used by dyads performing a collaborative design task while standing. We investigate how the display orientation influences group participation including face-to-face contact, total discussion, and equality of physical and verbal participation among participants. Our results suggest that vertical displays better support face-to-face contact whereas side-by-side arrangements encourage more discussion. However, display orientation has little impact on equality of verbal and physical participation, and users do not consistently prefer one orientation over the other. Based on our findings, we suggest that further investigation into the differences between horizontal and vertical orientations is warranted.

1. Introduction

Although considerable effort has been devoted to the design of tabletop interfaces, the tasks and situations for which they are preferable to vertical displays are less certain. Marshall et al. [1] argue that there is a need for more studies investigating how interfaces encourage or inhibit group participation. One aspect worthy of consideration is orientation: horizontal versus vertical. While vertical displays are known to be effective for presentations [2], some researchers have argued that horizontal displays might support more seamless interactions among small groups for collaborative tasks [2, 3]. Consequently, substantial effort has been placed on designing effective interfaces and applications for tabletop displays.

There are surprisingly few studies that explicitly compare how horizontal and vertical displays influence collaborative work. The studies that do make this comparison are highly varied in terms of their configuration (task, number of users, input, etc.), making it difficult to draw conclusions for any particular configuration. As researchers working with both horizontal and vertical displays, we were curious about how the display orientation influences group participation. We focus particularly on dyads (pairs of participants) working on a software design task. This is a very common task in software engineering and is often performed by pairs or small groups [4]. Our choice of task was also motivated by current interest in building digital tools to support early-stage software design [5–7]; however, the results may be relevant to dyads performing other types of open-ended tasks on shared displays.

By examining the differences between horizontal and vertical displays, we expect to influence groupware design and the choice of display orientation for particular tasks. At the outset of our study, we expected to observe benefits for horizontal displays in terms of group participation, but surprisingly, we did not. Our results indicate that vertical displays may encourage more face-to-face contact among dyads (i.e., they glance at each other's faces more often), and side-by-side arrangements of people may encourage more discussion, at least when users are standing, which was the configuration used in our study.

In the next section, we describe previous studies and their findings and relate these to our experimental design. We then describe our study objectives and hypotheses (Section 3), our methods (Section 4), followed by results (Section 5), discussion (Section 6), and an outlook to future work (Section 7).

2. Related Work

2.1. Shared Displays. Design considerations for shared displays have been studied extensively. Scott et al. [3] provide an overview of design suggestions specific to horizontal displays. In this section, we summarize some of the key findings from this body of research.

Observations of groups working together on shared displays have revealed that people frequently switch between loosely and closely coupled styles of work [8]. Research shows that even during loosely coupled work, maintaining awareness (e.g., what is being worked on by whom, and how your actions will affect others) is critical to ensure efficient and effective team coordination [9]. Supporting awareness is even more critical when team members are working at different locations. Another important factor for many applications is territoriality. Distinguishing between personal and shared work territories mimics the way people work naturally and supports transitions between individual and shared work [10]. The positioning of users relative to each other and to the display also impacts collaboration. For example, Hawkey et al. [11] found that collaboration was perceived to be more effective and more enjoyable when two users were both positioned close to a large display. Also, numerous papers have considered technological challenges and design considerations for multidisplay environments (e.g., [12–14]).

Studies of how people use whiteboards and other large nondigital drawing surfaces are also relevant. People's interactions with such surfaces have been studied in many different contexts, but these studies have usually not considered the effect of the surface orientation. For example, Walny et al. characterized the visual constructs that people use on whiteboards and derived design implications for information visualization tools. Tang [15] studied interactions with shared drawing surfaces for a group design task but focused on categorizing people's physical actions in the drawing space and the function of those actions. Tang et al. [16] examined how whiteboards facilitate transitions between tasks and different modes of activity, particularly for asynchronous group work. Perhaps most relevant to our study, Damm et al. [6] conducted two field studies examining how software developers use whiteboards to design software using UML (Unified Modeling Language). They found that approximately 80% of the drawings were formal UML diagrams and the remaining 20% were informal or incomplete drawings. They also made several specific recommendations for the design of interactive UML diagramming tools. While these and other whiteboard studies contribute to our understanding of how people use surfaces collaboratively, they do not directly address the differences between horizontal and vertical displays.

2.2. Studies Comparing Horizontal and Vertical Displays. Few studies have focused on explicitly comparing horizontal and vertical displays. Table 1 situates our study among previous experiments that compared horizontal and vertical surfaces. We note that in most cases, display orientation was not the only or main factor of interest. (A second study presented in [17] examined the effects of the arrangement of users around a horizontal display, which is also relevant to our findings.) In some of these studies, orientation was confounded with other factors (e.g., sitting versus standing [2, 17], digital versus nondigital [18]). In another related study, only a single pen was used [2], thus perhaps making it easier to share in the horizontal condition where the pen can be placed in the center of the table. Our study eliminates these confounds by having participants stand in both conditions and by allowing participants to write simultaneously with multiple pens. Table 1 also demonstrates that our study is consistent with previous work in terms of group size and number of groups studied.

The studies summarized in Table 1 have a wide variation in tasks, input, data, group size, and so forth. This makes it difficult to draw overall conclusions about the advantages and disadvantages of different orientations and to predict which would best encourage participation in a pair-based design task. Nonetheless, in the remainder of this section, we identify commonalities among these findings, which we then use to motivate our hypotheses in the next section.

One fairly well-supported finding is that more equal physical interaction takes place with tabletop interfaces. Studies have reported that asymmetrical roles tend to develop with vertical displays, whereby one user becomes the primary interactor or "scribe" [2]. Difficulty in switching control of the display is likely the largest factor in systems where control must be explicitly passed from one user to another [2, 18]. For example, in a single-pen system, the need to explicitly pass a pen with a vertical display (rather than placing it in a central location on a horizontal display) was observed to reduce people switching control of the display [2]. In addition, seated participants may be reluctant to get up and walk to a distant display. Multitouch tables have been found to encourage equitable physical interaction [20, 21] and more physical gestures [2, 17]. Our study extends earlier results by examining whether greater equality of physical participation on horizontal surfaces still holds true when control does not need to be explicitly passed, and when all users are standing, so they do not need to get up in order to interact.

A greater amount of discussion has also been reported with horizontal displays as compared to vertical [2, 17] displays. This can likely be attributed to the fact that adults generally prefer holding conversations face to face or in corner seating arrangements [3].

Equal participation of all users in a collaborative task is often desirable, since a dominant individual may stifle discussion, generation of ideas, and sharing of relevant information [20]. Thus, a display orientation that encourages equal verbal participation may be advantageous. However, Marshall et al. [20] and Rogers et al. [21] both found that display orientation had little influence on this outcome. Although multitouch tabletop displays led to more equitable physical interaction, this equality did not extend to verbal participation. Dominant users continued to dominate the conversation, while quiet users continued to be quiet.

We have heard informal claims that horizontal displays support better face-to-face contact among small groups, but experimental evidence on this topic is quite sparse. Some

TABLE 1: Summary of horizontal and vertical display orientation studies (H: horizontal, V: vertical).

Study	Digital (D) or nondigital (ND)	Input	Task	Orientation-dependent data?	Artifacts created or used?	Sit or stand	Group size	Number of groups
RL04 [2]	D	Single pen	Travel itinerary planning	Yes	Both	H—sit V–sit except interactor	3	8
IHK∗05 [17]	ND	Pens	Route planning	No	Used	H—sit V—stand	2	6
PRR09 [18]	1 D (H), 3 ND (V, other)	ND–pens D–multitouch	Concept mapping	Yes	Created	Free form	9-10	4—one per condition
PS08 [19]	D	Multiple mice, laser pointers	Target acquisition	No	Used	Free form	1, 2, 3	12
Our study	ND	Pens	Software design	Yes	Created	Stand	2	10

evidence comes from Lindley and Monk [22]: participants seated in a face-to-face arrangement around a desktop computer gazed at each other more often than those seated in a presenter/audience arrangement. Similarly, Inkpen et al. [17] found that participants seated at right angles at a horizontal display looked at each other significantly more often than when seated side by side or across from each other. However, they did not find a significant difference between horizontal and vertical displays when participants were arranged side by side. The fixed seating arrangements and the difference of sitting at the horizontal display versus standing at the vertical display may have influenced these results. In contrast, our study avoids a sit/stand confound and does not constrain participant arrangements around the horizontal display.

Though less relevant to our work, it is worth mentioning that horizontal and vertical displays have also been compared for individual work tasks. For example, Morris et al. [23] compared horizontal and vertical displays (as well as paper and tablets) for a reading and summarization task, finding that no single display was best for all parts of the task. For instance, the vertical displays were strongly preferred for writing, but strongly disliked for annotation. In a field study of horizontal and vertical displays in personal office environments, Morris et al. [24] found that the horizontal display was used less than the vertical one and was used in a more peripheral way. Both of these studies identified ergonomic problems of horizontal displays and suggested that for individual work it should be possible to angle a horizontal display like a drafting table. Müller-Tomfelde et al. [25] found a similar result: most participants in their study preferred interacting with a tilted workspace over a fully horizontal workspace during a distributed collaboration task. Note that in this situation, only one user was interacting with each display, so it is not clear whether these results would extend to collaboration on a shared display.

3. Objective and Hypotheses

We aimed to answer the question, "*How does a horizontal surface differ from a vertical surface when used by dyads for*

a constructive design task?" We chose to focus on a design task because people commonly collaborate around shared displays when brainstorming and refining design ideas. By *constructive design*, we mean design that involves actively creating a visual representation of the design, as compared to modifying an existing representation or working abstractly without any visual representation. We also focus on data that has an orientation, again for external validity, as most design information has a preferred viewing orientation.

Our study tested the following hypotheses:

(H1) *Greater Face-to-Face Contact (i.e., More Glances at a Partner's Face) with Horizontal.* Since users can arrange themselves face to face around a horizontal display, they will look at each other more often.

(H2) *More Discussion with Horizontal.* Horizontal displays will encourage more discussion due to the face-to-face arrangement, as found in related studies.

(H3) *Equality of Participation in Discussions will not Differ Between Orientations.* Prior experiments tested the conjecture that face-to-face arrangements would encourage more equal verbal participation, but found this to be untrue [20, 21].

(H4) *Increased Equality of Physical Interactions with Horizontal.* Physical accessibility of the tabletop surface may encourage equal interaction. Vertical displays may encourage defined interactor/audience roles, and audience members may be reluctant to approach the surface to take control [2].

4. Methods

Pairs of skilled software designers collaboratively designed a UML-based software architecture on both horizontal and vertical whiteboards. We chose this task domain because software designers frequently work in pairs or small groups to design software on whiteboards, and there are several current research efforts to design electronic whiteboards for UML diagram design. The task was also a challenging design problem involving knowledge creation often seen in the real world. To avoid constraining participant activities based on a particular software tool, input technology, or software controls, participants used nondigital whiteboards and standard whiteboard markers. Although this makes the task a noncomputerized one, we felt that this approach offered the greatest flexibility to users so that the resulting natural behaviours could be used to inform the design of digital whiteboard systems. There is an established history in computer-supported cooperative work in studying nondigital settings prior to designing digital support technologies (e.g., [16, 17]). Dyads were chosen over slightly larger groups for simplicity in terms of recruitment and analysis, and because most interactions with whiteboards involve groups of 2 to 3 people [26]; however, future work should examine larger groups since group size is known to influence group dynamics [27].

4.1. Participants. Ten pairs of Computer Scientists participated in the study (5 pairs of students from a university setting and 5 pairs of software professionals from industry). All 20 participants (15 males and 5 females) were experienced developers. Industry professionals were mostly entry-level software developers, but this group also included a team lead, a senior software architect, and a product analyst. All participants had previous knowledge of UML, but their practical experience with it varied from a little use in past university courses to regular use on most software projects. Participants ranged in age from 22 to 51 ($M = 32.4$, $SD = 8.5$). Participants had either normal or corrected vision. Each participant was compensated with a $20 gift certificate.

4.2. Apparatus. As shown in Figure 1, participants sketched UML diagrams on two 48″ × 36″ whiteboards: one mounted to a wall in landscape format, with its bottom edge 39″ from the ground, and the other on a tabletop 35″ from the ground. Each participant was given a dry erase marker (one red, one blue) and an eraser brush. Participants stood around the whiteboard in both vertical and horizontal conditions. We focused on standing configurations to eliminate any sit/stand confound between display orientations, to ensure that participants could move around freely, and because people often stand around vertical whiteboards when brainstorming UML software designs.

Video footage captured participants' interactions on the whiteboard and with each other. Two cameras were used: for the vertical condition, one camera was placed behind the participants and one off to the side; for the horizontal condition, cameras were placed on opposite sides, above and away from the table. A still image of each whiteboard was taken at the end of each session.

4.3. Tasks. Each pair was instructed to design two software systems using standard UML class diagrams. They were given a requirement document containing functional system requirements, recommended classes, and use case diagrams. The two tasks were chosen to be similar in complexity (as evaluated by an experienced software developer). Task 1 was

a restaurant order management system and Task 2 was a hospital patient management system.

4.4. Procedure. Each session took approximately 60 minutes. Participants completed the following pretrial, trial, and posttrial activities.

(i) Pretrial. Participants were briefed, signed a consent form, and filled out a pretrial questionnaire that contained demographic questions, questions about previous UML experience, and (for industry participants) questions about their use of whiteboards at work and their current job responsibilities. The briefing included a 5-minute refresher summary of UML syntax.

(ii) Trial. Participants started with Task 1 in one display configuration, were offered a 5-minute break, and then performed Task 2 in the other configuration. Horizontal and vertical configurations were counter-balanced for order. Pairs were given up to 20 minutes for each task.

(iii) Posttrial. The session concluded with a posttrial questionnaire that asked questions about which task and surface each participant preferred.

4.5. Measures. We primarily measured counts and durations of activities, determined through manual video coding. Specific activities that we coded are described in the results section.

One of our goals was to measure the relative participation (verbal and physical) by the two individuals. To measure this, we use an index of inequality, I, previously used by Marshall et al. [20] I varies from zero (perfect equality; all participants contribute equally) to one (perfect inequality; only one participant contributes). I is robust to small numbers of participants and is normalized for the number of participants per group, enabling comparison across studies with different group sizes. It was calculated for each group and condition using (1), where N is the group size; E_i is the expected cumulative proportion of events if each participant contributes equally; and O_i is the observed cumulative proportion of events, starting with the participant who contributed least:

$$I = \frac{(1/N) \sum_{i=1}^{N} (E_i - O_i)}{(1/2)(1 - 1/N)}, \quad (1)$$

when $N = 2$, $I = 2(0.5 - O_1)$, where O_1 is the observed proportion for the participant who contributed less.

5. Results

We organize our results according to the four hypotheses. We also report user preferences for orientation and task. Q-Q plots suggested that all data were normally distributed. When Mauchly's test of sphericity indicated that it was necessary, we used a Huynh-Feldt correction for repeated measures ANOVA.

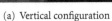

(a) Vertical configuration   (b) Horizontal configuration

FIGURE 1: Participants working in vertical and horizontal configurations.

For horizontal displays, some of our results presumably depend on the arrangement of users around the table. We classified the arrangements as side-by-side, opposite one another, or kitty-corner (facing perpendicular directions). Total time spent in each configuration was video coded. Side-by-side and kitty-corner were both substantially used, but opposite was used only rarely. Only two groups remained side-by-side 100% of the time. Average percent time in each configuration was side-by-side $M = 53.6\%$, opposite, $M = 7.7\%$, and kitty corner, $M = 38.6\%$.

For each hypothesis, we first examined the overall results comparing horizontal to vertical and then broke down the horizontal results by arrangement. The opposite arrangement was excluded due to its rare use. For the arrangement analysis, we adjusted for the different amounts of time spent in each arrangement by calculating results on a per-minute basis.

5.1. H1: Face-to-Face Contact.
H1 stated that participants would glance at each other's faces more often in the horizontal condition. To investigate this, we coded (from video) all of the times when each participant looked at the other's face. Since many of the looks consisted of a quick glance that would be difficult to time, we counted the looks rather than attempting to code their duration.

Figure 2 shows the unexpected result that participants looked at each other's faces significantly more often in the vertical orientation than the horizontal orientation, $t(19) = 3.2$, $p = 0.005$.

The number of looks per minute was higher for vertical than for both horizontal arrangements (side-by-side and kitty corner), as shown in Figure 3. Repeated measures ANOVA revealed a significant difference ($F(2, 38) = 9.8$, $p < 0.001$, $\eta_p^2 = 0.34$). Bonferroni-corrected post hoc tests showed that horizontal side-by-side was significantly different from vertical ($p = 0.001$).

5.2. H2: Total Discussion.
H2 stated that there would be more overall discussion in the horizontal condition. We coded the duration of verbal utterances from each participant and summed these for each condition to examine the total overall amount of conversation. Mean values for horizontal and

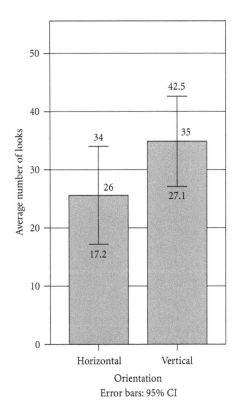

FIGURE 2: Average number of looks (per person).

vertical orientations were very similar (see Figure 4). To gain a better understanding of this similarity, we calculated differences from the mean as shown in the boxplots of Figure 5. The similarity suggests that horizontal and vertical are likely equivalent, though more participants would be needed to test this statistically.

With the horizontal display, time talking varied with the user arrangement (see Figure 6). Perhaps surprisingly, there was more talking per minute when side-by-side as compared to kitty-corner, and this was also higher than side-by-side with a vertical display. Repeated measures ANOVA showed an overall significant effect ($F(1.3, 24.9) = 20.2$, $p < 0.001$, $\eta_p^2 = 0.52$). Bonferroni-corrected post hoc tests showed that all pairs were significantly different ($p < 0.008$).

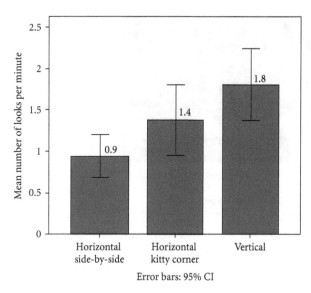

FIGURE 3: Average looks per minute (per person).

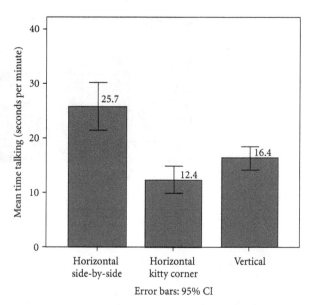

FIGURE 6: Average time talking per minute (per person).

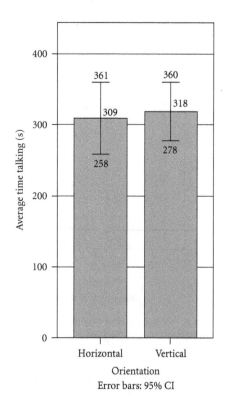

FIGURE 4: Average time talking (per person).

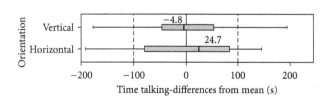

FIGURE 5: Equivalence of talking times, shown as differences from the mean.

5.3. H3: Equality of Verbal Participation. Prior evidence [20, 21] indicated that relative contributions of each participant to discussion would not be influenced by the orientation. To examine this, we first calculated the proportion of speaking time by the less talkative person in each condition. We used this value to calculate the index of inequality. Figure 7(a) shows these data. Vertical had slightly greater equality (lower value), but the difference was not statistically significant. With the horizontal display, there was greater equality with side-by-side ($M = 0.22$) than with kitty corner ($M = 0.34$), but this difference was also not significant.

5.4. H4: Equality of Physical Participation. H4 stated that participants' physical interactions would be more equal in the horizontal condition. To examine this, we coded the durations of drawing and erasing and calculated the proportion of interactions done by the person who inter-acted the least. We then used this proportion to calculate the index of inequality. Figure 7(b) shows that equality was slightly greater with the horizontal orientation, though this difference was not statistically significant. Inequality of physical participation also did not vary significantly with horizontal arrangement (side-by-side versus kitty corner).

5.5. Orientation and Task Preference. Preference for the conditions was equally split: 10 participants preferred hor-izontal surface orientation and 10 preferred vertical surface orientation. This echoes results found elsewhere [17] for preference of horizontal and vertical surfaces. Preference for the two tasks was close to equally split (8 preferred task 1, 11 preferred task 2, and 1 had no preference). There was a strong correspondence between the preferred task and preferred orientation (75% agreement), so it is unclear which is the most important factor influencing preference.

Analysis of the poststudy questionnaire results gives some further insight. Regarding the display conditions,

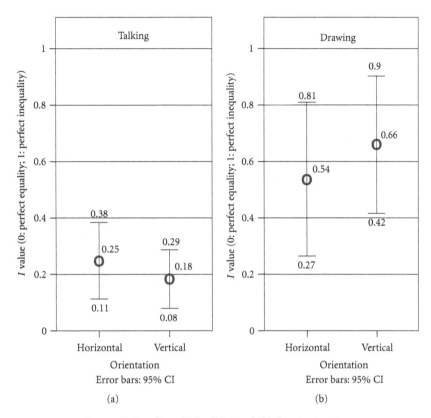

FIGURE 7: Equality of (a) talking and (b) drawing/erasing.

most participants referred to ergonomics: they preferred the display that they felt was easiest on their head and neck position, or that facilitated writing or drawing. However, which display did this best was not consistent between participants. For example, one participant who preferred horizontal wrote, "I'm short! lol. I thought it was easier to stand with someone and communicate by pointing." whereas one who preferred vertical wrote, "I'm short, it's easier to access the wall mounted board". Regarding the tasks, we found that the two tasks were not perfectly equivalent. The restaurant scenario was conceptually simpler for many participants. Some preferred this simplicity while others preferred a greater challenge. Others expressed a preference based on which topic interested them the most. All participants gave separate reasons for their preference of task and display, suggesting that the correlation may be accidental, or that if the issues are conflated, it is at a subconscious level (e.g., it is possible that a more comfortable working position influenced them to subconsciously like the task more, or vice versa).

6. Discussion

Our experiment calls into question many assumptions we made regarding advantages of horizontal displays. Most importantly, face-to-face contact was found to be significantly greater with vertical displays, not horizontal (opposite of H1). This occurred despite the fact that participants spent over 46% of their time standing in face-to-face

configurations with the horizontal condition. We had expected these face-to-face arrangements to enable more glances between participants. However, our observations and poststudy questionnaire responses suggest that looking at the other person was more cumbersome in the horizontal condition. With vertical, the board and the other person's head were at a similar height, so looking at the person required only turning one's head horizontally. With the horizontal board, however, looking at the other person typically involved turning one's head horizontally as well as looking up. This suggests that when users are standing, face-to-face contact may be easier with vertical displays. Results may of course differ for seated configurations. Height of the table may also have an impact; a higher table might make face-to-face contact easier but would probably also make writing more difficult. As expected, there were a greater number of looks with the horizontal condition when users stood in a kitty corner arrangement as compared to side-by-side. This reaffirms earlier results [17]. Both were still less than the vertical condition, however.

These results demonstrate that horizontal displays alone do not cause more face-to-face contact, contradicting a common assumption about interactive surfaces. Thus a horizontal display should not be chosen purely for this reason, and other factors need to be taken into consideration. In fact, at least if users will be standing, face to face contact may be easier with a vertical display, which also has the added benefit of all users seeing the same perspective. This result might be counterintuitive to some designers.

Our results did not support H2. Horizontal and vertical may be equivalent overall in terms of total discussion time; the strong similarity suggests that it may be worthwhile to conduct a more rigorous test of equivalence with more participants. It was interesting to see that significantly more discussion took place when users were side-by-side with the horizontal board, as compared to kitty corner or side-by-side with the vertical board. Rodden et al.'s [28] findings for trade show that displays might explain this; they found that side-by-side arrangements could ease social awkwardness and encourage shy people to talk. It is also possible that users moved to a side-by-side arrangement when talking, to gain a common perspective. However, our observations suggest that changes in arrangement were usually motivated by writing: participants moved in order to write somewhere that was hard to reach, or moved out of the way so the other person could write.

Our study did not show evidence of a significant difference between horizontal and vertical orientation for equality of physical or verbal participation (H3 was supported but H4 was not supported). Additional participants may reveal a significant difference, but it appears to be small.

We do note that our evaluations of discussion looked only at overall quantity; we did not consider the formality of the discussion nor the quality of ideas generated. Although there was no observable quality difference in the final design solutions, there is still some possibility of differences in the quality of discussion between horizontal and vertical configurations. A qualitative analysis could examine the discussion in this way, as well as other differences such as the way in which people collaborated; however, this was beyond the scope of the current work. We did qualitatively examine the resulting UML diagrams, looking for differences such as software design quality, diagram structure, and types and location of strokes placed by each participant (observable through the different coloured pens). However, we found no observable diagram differences between horizontal and vertical conditions.

It is also interesting to note that we did not observe territorial behaviour in our study, unlike reports from previous work [10]. Although participants tended to work in different areas of the whiteboard at any given time, they appeared to have no trouble moving to another area or adding onto a part of the diagram created by their partner. We do not interpret this to mean that territoriality is not important, however. We suspect that the UML diagram was simply treated as a shared representation so that no ownership was implied by creation of its various parts.

Our results must be considered in the context of the choices we made in our experimental setup. We focused on dyads, standing configurations, and a design task with naturally oriented information. Some of the significant differences seen in previous studies that were not seen in our study (despite a similar number of participants) may be attributable to some of these factors. For instance, equality of physical interaction may depend less on the orientation and more on all users being able to easily reach the surface and use it without explicitly taking control from another user. Ergonomics of being able to view the other person around

the tabletop may have been easier in a seated configuration, but this would have introduced a confounding factor and constrained positioning around the display. Additionally, in our study, the orientation of the information may have biased participants to spend more time in a side-by-side arrangement than might otherwise be seen with horizontal displays, though it was interesting that more discussion actually took place in the side-by-side arrangement. Results for digital UML diagrams may differ slightly from our whiteboard-based results since digital UML components can be more easily rotated or moved. However, we suspect that movement would be used mainly to make space for new information and that actions that disrupt the global view (e.g., rotation and movement for the purpose of obtaining a better view) would happen rarely since they would impact the other participant. Finally, it is unclear to what extent the UML design task is similar to other types of design tasks. While we expect that many other design tasks would have similar coupling, division of labour, and coordination characteristics, some of our results may be particular to the software engineering domain that we studied.

Our results should not be taken to mean that one orientation is necessarily better than another, but that the choice of orientation may depend on the task at hand as well as personal preference. It is useful to note that there were fewer differences between horizontal and vertical surfaces than expected; for example, there was no observable difference in the quality of the resulting design work. People were able to adapt, and they found effective ways to work in both configurations. Perhaps the choice of horizontal versus vertical displays is not as important as we might have thought. This finding would be very beneficial to organizations with limited resources, since vertical displays are more commonplace, require less floor space, and are often less expensive than horizontal ones. Or perhaps other factors such as input and physical positioning (e.g., sitting versus standing) have a larger impact on group dynamics than the surface orientation.

7. Conclusion and Future Work

Our results add new empirical evidence regarding how display orientation impacts collaboration. Perhaps our most interesting finding is that looking at a collaborator's face can be awkward when standing at a horizontal display and occurs less often than at a vertical display; vertical displays may be better for standing users in terms of face-to-face contact. In contrast, the most discussion took place when participants stood side-by-side next to a horizontal display. We found no evidence for a difference in equality of physical or verbal participation for horizontal versus vertical conditions, in contrast to some earlier studies. In summary, our findings demonstrate that dyads can work effectively with both vertical and horizontal surfaces. What was most surprising to us was that we did not observe a strong motivation to prefer one orientation over the other. We feel that we need to follow this up with future work, where we would like to investigate the relationships between physical positioning and display orientation by constraining participant's spatial movement and comparing sitting versus standing positions. We would also like to consider tilted displays as a compromise between horizontal and vertical. Additional conclusive findings will help future designers of whiteboard applications that support small groups performing design tasks on both horizontal and vertical displays.

Acknowledgment

This work was supported by the Natural Sciences and Engineering Research Council of Canada (NSERC).

References

[1] P. Marshall, Y. Rogers, and E. Hornecker, "Are tangible interfaces really any better than other kinds of interfaces?" in *Proceedings of the Tangible User Interfaces in Context and Theory Workshop (CHI '07)*, 2007.

[2] Y. Rogers and S. Lindley, "Collaborating around vertical and horizontal large interactive displays: which way is best?" *Interacting with Computers*, vol. 16, no. 6, pp. 1133–1152, 2004.

[3] S. D. Scott, K. D. Grant, and R. L. Mandryk, "System guidelines for co-located, collaborative work on a tabletop display," in *Proceedings of the European Conference Computer-Supported Cooperative Work*, pp. 159–178, 2003.

[4] U. Dekel and J. D. Herbsleb, "Notation and representation in collaborative object-oriented design: an observational study," in *Proceedings of the ACM SIGPLAN Conference on Object-Oriented Programming, Systems, Languages, and Applications (OOPSLA '07)*, pp. 261–280, October 2007.

[5] Q. Chen, J. Grundy, and J. Hosking, "An e-whiteboard application to support early design-stage sketching of UML diagrams," in *Proceedings of the IEEE Symposium Human Centric Computing Languages and Environments (HCC '03)*, pp. 219–226, 2003.

[6] C. H. Damm, K. M. Hansen, and M. Thomsen, "Tool support for cooperative object-oriented design: gesture based modeling on an electronic whiteboard," in *Proceedings of the SIGCHI Conference on Human Factors in Computing Systems (CHI '00)*, pp. 518–525, April 2000.

[7] J. Wu and T. C. N. Graham, "The software design board: a tool supporting workstyle transitions in collaborative software design," in *Proceedings of the Engineering Human Computer Interaction and Interactive Systems*, vol. 3425 of *Lecture Notes in Computer Science*, pp. 363–382, 2005.

[8] A. Tang, M. Tory, B. Po, P. Neumann, and S. Carpendale, "Collaborative coupling over tabletop displays," in *Proceedings of the ACM Conference on Human Factors in Computing Systems (CHI '06)*, pp. 1181–1190, April 2006.

[9] O. Kulyk and G. van der Veer, "Situational awareness support to enhance teamwork in collaborative environments," in *Proceedings of the 15th European conference on Cognitive Ergonomics*, pp. 1–5, 2008.

[10] S. D. Scott, S. M. T. Carpendale, and K. M. Inkpen, "Territoriality in collaborative tabletop workspaces," in *Proceedings of the ACM Conference on Computer Supported Cooperative Work (CSCW '04)*, pp. 294–303, November 2004.

[11] K. Hawkey, M. Kellar, D. Reilly, T. Whalen, K. M. Inkpen et al., "The proximity factor: impact of distance on co-located collaboration," in *Proceedings of the International ACM SIGGROUP Conference on Supporting Group Work (GROUP '05)*, pp. 31–40, November 2005.

[12] S. Bachl, M. Tomitsch, K. Kappel, and T. Grechenig, "The effects of personal displays and transfer techniques on collaboration strategies in multi-touch based multi-display environments," in *Proceedings of the 13 International Conference on Human-Computer Interaction (INTERACT '11)*, vol. 6948 of *Lecture Notes in Computer Science*, pp. 373–390, 2011.

[13] M. Haller, J. Leitner, T. Seifried et al., "The NiCE discussion room: integrating paper and digital media to support co-located group meetings," in *Proceedings of the 28th Annual CHI Conference on Human Factors in Computing Systems (CHI '10)*, pp. 609–618, April 2010.

[14] J. R. Wallace, S. D. Scott, T. Stutz, T. Enns, and K. Inkpen, "Investigating teamwork and taskwork in single- and multi-display groupware systems," *Personal and Ubiquitous Computing*, vol. 13, no. 8, pp. 569–581, 2009.

[15] J. C. Tang, "Findings from observational studies of collaborative work," *International Journal of Man-Machine Studies*, vol. 34, no. 2, pp. 143–160, 1991.

[16] A. Tang, J. Lanir, S. Greenberg, and S. Fels, "Supporting transitions in work: informing large display application design by understanding whiteboard use," in *Proceedings of the ACM SIGCHI International Conference on Supporting Group Work (GROUP '09)*, pp. 149–158, May 2009.

[17] K. Inkpen, K. Hawkey, M. Kellar et al., "Exploring display factors that influence co-located collaboration: angle, size, number, and user arrangement," in *Proceedings of the Human-Computer Interaction Conference (HCI '05)*, 2005.

[18] N. Pantidi, Y. Rogers, and H. Robinson, "Is the writing on the wall for tabletops?" in *Proceedings of the 12th International Conference on Human-Computer Interaction: Part II*, vol. 5727 of *Lecture Notes in Computer Science*, pp. 125–137, 2009.

[19] A. Pavlovych and W. Stuerzlinger, "Effect of screen configuration and interaction devices in shared display groupware," in *Proceedings of the 3rd ACM International Workshop on Human-Centered Computing (HCC '08)*, pp. 49–56, October 2008.

[20] P. Marshall, E. Hornecker, R. Morris, N. S. Dalton, and Y. Rogers, "When the fingers do the talking: a study of group participation with varying constraints to a tabletop interface," in *Proceedings of the IEEE Tabletops and Interactive Surfaces (TABLETOP '08)*, pp. 37–44, October 2008.

[21] Y. Rogers, Y. Lim, W. R. Hazlewood, and P. Marshall, "Equal opportunities: do shareable interfaces promote more group participation than single user displays?" *Human-Computer Interaction*, vol. 24, no. 1-2, pp. 79–116, 2009.

[22] S. Lindley and A. F. Monk, "Social enjoyment with electronic photograph displays: awareness and control," *International Journal of Human Computer Studies*, vol. 66, no. 8, pp. 587–604, 2008.

[23] M. R. Morris, A. J. B. Brush, and B. R. Meyers, "Reading revisited: evaluating the usability of digital display surfaces for active reading tasks," in *Proceedings of the Horizontal Interactive Human-Computer Systems (Tabletop '07)*, pp. 79–86, October 2007.

[24] M. R. Morris, A. J. B. Brush, and B. R. Meyers, "A field study of knowledge workers' use of interactive horizontal displays," in *Proceedings of the Horizontal Interactive Human Computer System (TABLETOP '08)*, pp. 105–112, October 2008.

[25] C. Müller-Tomfelde, A. Wessels, and C. Schremmer, "Tilted tabletops: in between horizontal and vertical workspaces," in *Proceedings of the International Workshop on Horizontal Interactive Human Computer System (TABLETOP '08)*, pp. 49–56, October 2008.

[26] J. Walny, S. Carpendale, N. H. Riche, G. Venolia, and P. Fawcett, "Visual thinking in action: visualizations as used on whiteboards," *IEEE Transactions on Visualization and Computer Graphics*, vol. 17, no. 12, pp. 2508–2517, 2011.

[27] G. Simmel, "The number of members as determining the sociological form of the group," *American Journal of Sociology*, vol. 8, pp. 1–46, 1902.

[28] T. Rodden, Y. Rogers, J. Halloran, and I. Taylor, "Designing novel interactional workspaces to support face to face consultations," in *Proceedings of the New Horizons Conference on Human Factors in Computing Systems (CHI '03)*, pp. 57–64, April 2003.

3

Improved Haptic Linear Lines for Better Movement Accuracy in Upper Limb Rehabilitation

Joan De Boeck,[1,2] **Lode Vanacken,**[1] **Sofie Notelaers,**[1] **and Karin Coninx**[1]

[1] *Expertise Centre for Digital Media, transnational University Limburg, Hasselt University, Wetenschapspark 2, 3590 Diepenbeek, Belgium*
[2] *ICT and Inclusion, K-Point, Katholieke Hogeschool Kempen, Kleinhoefstraat 4, 2440 Geel, Belgium*

Correspondence should be addressed to Joan De Boeck, joan.deboeck@gmail.com

Academic Editor: Kiyoshi Kiyokawa

Force feedback has proven to be beneficial in the domain of robot-assisted rehabilitation. According to the patients' personal needs, the generated forces may either be used to assist, support, or oppose their movements. In our current research project, we focus onto the upper limb training for MS (multiple sclerosis) and CVA (cerebrovascular accident) patients, in which a basic building block to implement many rehabilitation exercises was found. This building block is a haptic linear path: a second-order continuous path, defined by a list of points in space. Earlier, different attempts have been investigated to realize haptic linear paths. In order to have a good training quality, it is important that the haptic simulation is continuous up to the second derivative while the patient is enforced to follow the path tightly, even when low or no guiding forces are provided. In this paper, we describe our best solution to these haptic linear paths, discuss the weaknesses found in practice, and propose and validate an improvement.

1. Introduction

Force feedback applications show their benefits when they are applied in a robot-assisted rehabilitation program [1, 2]. In such a setup, the training can be more finely tailored to the abilities and needs of the patient. At the same time, less assistance of the therapist may be required, allowing at the longer term to abolish the "one therapist for one patient" requirement. The ultimate goal should be to allow patients to perform their training independently without active assistance of the therapist, or even to use the force feedback enabled setup at home while being remotely monitored [3, 4]. It may sound evident that this opens possibilities for cost reduction or an increased training intensity, where the latter at its turn provides better training results [5]. Additionally, several studies suggest that using games in a therapy may improve the patient's motivation [6]. Not necessarily using force feedback, but surely by bringing the computer to the revalidation setup and exploiting the "fun"-factor, this improvement in motivation may be achieved.

Our research lab participated in a pilot study focussing on the training of the upper limbs in Multiple Sclerosis (MS) (MS is an autoimmune disease of the central nervous system, resulting in an increasing loss of force and coordination) patients [7]. As the results were promising, the project was prolonged and the focus was broadened to both MS and CVA (CVA: cerebrovascular accident or stroke is the loss of brain function(s) due to disturbance in the blood supply to the brain, caused by a blockage or a leakage of blood) patients. More information regarding our haptic-assisted rehabilitation approach can be found in [8].

A Phantom haptic device, a HapticMaster and/or a Falcon, were chosen to be used to control several game-like training exercises. The generated forces can be applied to either assist, support, or oppose the patient, according to their individual needs [9].

Assisting Forces. They "assist" the patient in performing a (new) movement. The patient can remain passive and can feel how the movement has to be made.

Supporting Forces. They help the patients, but patients have to perform the movement by themselves. The forces avoid making too large deviations from the intended motion path.

Opposing Forces. They oppose the patient's movement by generating forces opposite to the intended motion (friction, viscosity, etc.), requiring the patient to develop larger force amplitudes.

In the following sections we first introduce our previous work on this topic and illustrate the weaknesses found during further usage. Afterwards we discuss an improvement on our work as well as experimental data to validate and motivate it.

2. Previous Work

During the development of rehabilitation exercises, we noticed that only a few basic haptic effects were necessary. Among them, we identify the ones available in most haptic APIs such as feedback when touching objects, spring forces, or magnetic force fields. However, one important building block is what we call a "linear path" between two or more points in space. One of the important features of such a haptic linear path is that an adjustable spring force *supports* the patient by attracting the cursor to the center of the line. Supplementary, additional forces such as an *assisting* forward force, or an *opposing* friction or viscosity may be useful as well. The current existing implementations, in the most common haptic APIs. (We consider OpenHaptics [10], CHAI3D [11] and H3D [12]), unfortunately are not fully suitable. In what follows, we first shortly indicate the design requirements.

(1) *Continuous Path.* It is required that the haptic simulation is continuous in the first and the second derivative in each point. This is necessary for a smooth haptic rendering with no bumps or oscillations, furthermore allowing the smooth superimposing of additional forces (see item 5).

(2) *Easy to Design.* For the designer of a scene, the interface must be as easy as possible, avoiding complex shapes such as splines, to be entered manually. A simple enumeration of a set of points in space may be suitable, although a naive implementation would conflict with our first requirement.

(3) *Approximate the Given Path.* The interpolated continuous path must approximate the original linear path *as close as possible.*

(4) *Support for Several Devices.* In our rehabilitation project we consider three different haptic devices: the HapticMaster, the Phantom, and the Falcon. Obviously, the same software should apply to all three devices.

(5) *Apply Additional Forces.* For our rehabilitation program it is necessary not only to generate a spring force to the center of the curve. Additional forces, either supporting or opposing (such as a forward force, friction, or viscosity), have to be superimposed, as well.

In [13] we proposed two approaches that meet all of our requirements: one using rounded corners, another using cardinal splines, as is illustrated in Figure 1. Analysis showed that both types had their own benefits and disadvantages. Using both implementations in practice, we found that the cardinal spline solution provided the best results. Therefore, in the scope of this paper, we will limit our discussion to the cardinal spline implementation.

In the next section, we first explain the math behind the original implementation and explain the problem with this implementation. Thereafter, in Section 4, we propose our additional "pull-back algorithm" as an improvement. Finally, in Section 5, we show the results of our solution in a short benchmark.

3. Haptic Lines Implementation

As shown in Listing 1, the designer of a new scene or rehabilitation exercise defines a new path by defining a sequence of points in (3D) space. Using Cardinal splines interpolation [10], the haptic rendering is calculated. Cardinal splines are a subset of Hermite Splines where the tangent control points are defined as a function of the other control points (providing an easier interface to the "designer").

The Cardinal Splines solution guarantees that the continuous curve runs through the control points. Depending on the "tension factor," however, the actual curve can slightly deviate from the line between two successive points (see Figure 1(b)).

Given the points s_1 and s_2 and the tangential lines T_1 and T_2, the tangential line T_n is given by $\alpha \cdot (s_{n-1} - s_{n+1})$. This means that the tangential is parallel with the line between the previous and the next control point. Alpha (α) is the tension factor, typically between 0 and 1, defining how "tight" the curve is in the control points.

The spline curve is then defined by four parametric functions:

$$\begin{aligned}
h_1(t) &= 2t^3 - 3t^2 + 1, \\
h_2(t) &= -2t^3 + 3t^2, \\
h_3(t) &= t^3 - 2t^2 + t, \\
h_4(t) &= t^3 - t^2.
\end{aligned} \tag{1}$$

An arbitrary point P on the curve is calculated by

$$\vec{P}(x, y, z) = h_1(t) \cdot s1 + h_2(t) \cdot s2 + h_3(t) \cdot s1 + h_4(t) \cdot s2. \tag{2}$$

For a smooth haptic rendering, we need to find the perpendicular projection h' from the position of the haptic device h. The calculation of the minimal distance of a point to the spline can be achieved by solving the equation $\partial P(t)/\partial t = 0$, but this is not trivial [14]. We decided to take a more pragmatic approach and exploit the strong coherence between successive haptic rendering steps by searching for a new local minimum in the neighborhood of the previous projection point.

The pragmatic approach can be applied for all rendering steps, except for the very first one (at startup). In that situation, the entire closest line segment has to be sought for a

```
(1) <Toggle Group DEF="Linear Pad" haptics On="false" graphics On="false">
(2)    <Shape>
(3)    <Appearance>
(4)       <Material emissive Color="0 0 0"/>
(5)       <Line Properties linewidth Scale Factor="5"/>
(6)    </Appearance>
(7)    <Linear Path vertex Count="11" DEF="myPath">
(8)       <Coordinate point="−0.1466667 0.02666667 0,
(9)          −0.1053333 0.078 0,
(10)         −0.005333333 0.07933334 0.0,
(11)         0.018 0.04666667 0.0,
(12)         −0.01066667 0.01866667 0,
(13)         −0.06933333 0.04333333 0,
(14)         −0.07333333 0.1213333 0,
(15)         0.05466667 0.1266667 0,
(16)         0.1166667 0.05333333 0,
(17)         0.1146667 −0.012 0,
(18)         0.072 −0.036 0"/>
(19)    </LineraPath>
(20)    </Shape>
(21)    <Linear Path Forces DEF="myForces" interpolation="splines"
(22)         spring Constant="40"
(23)         aid Constant="1.3"
(24)         viscosity Constant="5"
(25)         static Friction="0.8"
(26)         dynamic Friction="0.5">
(27)       <Linear Path USE="myPath"/>
(28)    </Linear Path Forces>
(29) </Toggle Group>
```

LISTING 1: Listing example of a linear path with some haptic effects.

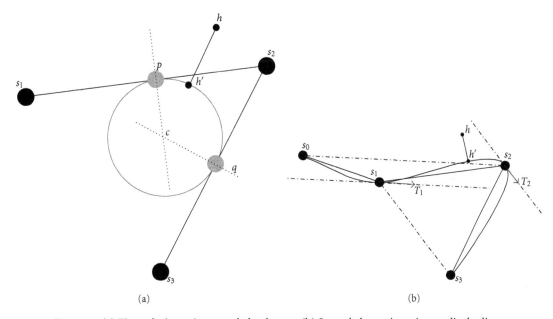

(a)   (b)

FIGURE 1: (a) First solution using rounded polygons. (b) Second alternative using cardinal splines.

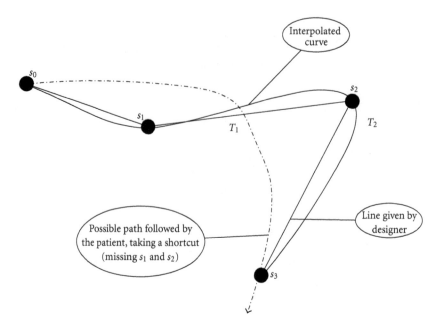

FIGURE 2: Illustration of a possible "shortcut a user can make."

minimum distance. In our implementation, for performance optimization, the spline curve is precalculated in a spline table.

The spline equation is a parametric equation (in t), with t varying between 0 and 1, respectively, corresponding with the start and the end point of a segment. It may be clear that the step size of the samples of t, must be linked to the actual length of a segment; otherwise small segments would be oversampled while longer segments would have a coarser resolution. A reasonable high resolution is important to ensure smooth haptics; otherwise the haptic simulation may suffer from stutter effects. In our implementation, the number of steps is proportional to the Euclidian distance between the control points, or is written as:

$$n_{\text{steps}} = k \cdot |p_n - p_{n-1}|. \tag{3}$$

For example, for the phantom k is determined to be 7000 based on the resolution of the phantom which is 0.03 mm. For the other devices k would be smaller or close to k; therefore we define k as a constant at 7000 for all our haptic devices.

4. Haptic Lines Problem and Improvement

The implementation described in the previous section has as a downside that while the spring forces are low, it may be easy to find "a shortcut" between the beginning and the end of a line. Figure 2 illustrates this shortcoming. It may be clear that in a rehabilitation context; this effect is unwanted, as we want the patient to accurately follow the predefined path. This is particularly true in low-force circumstances where it is (physically) easy to deviate from the path. In this section we will describe an improvement which forces the patient to better keep on the track.

4.1. Pullback Function. The central idea of our solution is to define a continuous function that virtually "pulls back" the perpendicular projection of the cursor on the spline curve based upon the distance of the actual cursor from the curve. The larger the distance is between the cursor and its projection, the more the projection point is pulled back. The new (pulled back) projection point is then used for calculating the feedback forces. Pulling back the projection point increases the attraction forces and introduces a slight resistance force to advance on the path, but even when low or no attraction forces are present, the pullback function will ultimately halt a wrong progression of the user in a continuous way.

4.2. Implementation. Although the general idea is pretty simple, the implementation is less evident. In this section, we will clarify how the function is implemented and how continuity is ensured.

The pullback function is defined as follows (see also Figure 3):

$$G - \left(\left(1 - \cos\left(\frac{\text{dist}}{d} \times \pi \right) \right) \times \frac{m}{2.0} \right), \tag{4}$$

where G is the global spline parameter (see further) on the spline curve (taking all segments into account) and dist is the perpendicular distance of the actual cursor to the curve. d and m are two constants that define the behaviour of the pullback function as will be explained later in this section.

We work with the global distance parameter G, rather than the parametric spline values per segment, as the the pullback function must behave consistently independent of the length of a particular segment. In order to calculate G, in a first step, the current spline parameter (in the current segment) must be converted into a global distance value taking all the past segment lengths into account. The total distance

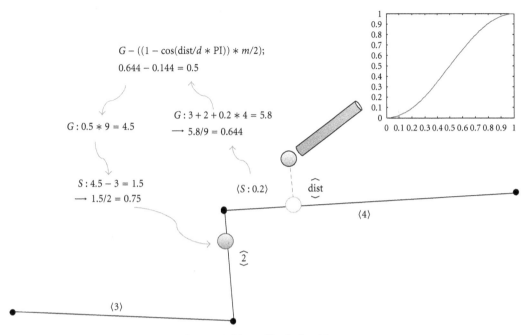

FIGURE 3: The pullback algorithm.

from the beginning of the curve, divided by the total spline length gives us the global distance parameter (G).

The second term in the formula is a sinusoidal function in dist that behaves as shown in the upper right corner in Figure 3. d is a constant that defines the distance at which the pullback function is maximal. When $d >$ dist, the pullback function is kept at its maximum. Hence, when dist approaches from zero to d, the cosine function ensures a smooth and continuous increase.

The parameter m defines the maximum value the projection point is "pulled back". When dist approaches to d, the cosine becomes 0 and the maximum pull back value (divided by 2.0) is applied. Hence, our global distance parameter is lowered by the pullback value.

After applying the equation we reconvert G back into a parametric spline value (taking the lengths of the different segments into account) that gives us the new position onto the haptic line: the *pullback point*.

The explanation above describes the basic algorithm. However, a couple of smaller refinements were necessary in order to make the algorithm work in practice and insure continuity in all cases. Amongst them, some logic takes into account that it is possible for a user to make a shortcut that goes beyond the border of one segment, or even to skip one or more segments.

5. Benchmarking

5.1. Experimental Design. In order to verify our improvement, an evaluation was necessary. However, conducting a standard user study would not provide us with satisfying results. This is because the enhancement described in this paper is to prevent patients to take a shortcut instead of following the defined path; this situation grows only after a patient is fully familiar with the application and has learned to exploit all back doors. Hence, evaluation using naive users would not give us any useful feedback on the quality of our solution.

Therefore, we opted to perform a benchmark test. In this benchmark we deliberately try to search for the shortest path between the start and the end of the curve, not necessarily following the path. This was done using different paths and different parameters, as defined:

(i) four different values for the attractive force to the center of the line (0 N, 50 N, 100 N, 150 N), (these are the values given to the API. The values were empirically chosen in order to have "no," "weak," "medium," and "strong" attraction forces),

(ii) four different pullback strengths, defined by the parameter m (0, 0.033, 0.066, 0.1) (these values are expressed as a percentage of the total curve length),

(iii) two different haptic lines: a highly curved curve and a less curved, as shown in Figure 4.

This results in 16 different benchmarking conditions for the two curves, or 32 conditions in total.

Two of the authors performed the benchmarking, as they are supposed to know the insights of the solution and are better able to find the shortest possible path. In order to ensure that the authors would really strive for the best minimal values, a little competition between the benchmarkers was set up, electing the winner as the one who found the shortest path in the majority of the conditions.

For each of the 32 conditions, each benchmarker was obliged to try for 10 times to find the shortest path, while the result (the ratio between the covered path and the actual length of the path) was shown after each trial. The latter was also logged to file for later analysis.

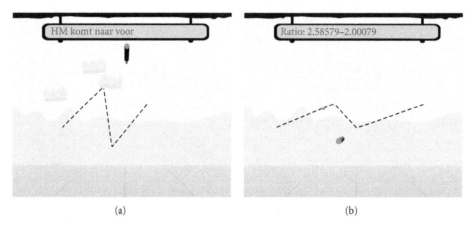

FIGURE 4: The two curves used in the benchmarking test. Curve 1 (a) with a high curvature, curve 2 (b) with much less curvature. Note that the visual representation only shows the straight lines, while the haptic simulation uses the spline interpolation.

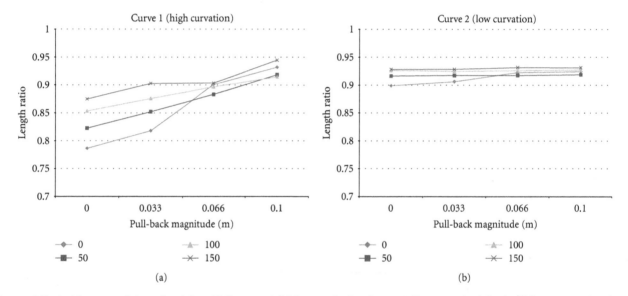

FIGURE 5: Ratio (shortest path/actual path length) for curve 1 (high curvature) and curve 2 (low curvature) for the different attraction forces (colours) and different pull-back values (x-axis).

5.2. Results. The results of the benchmark are given in Figure 5. The graph depicts the lowest ratio (measured distance versus actual distance), measured for a given condition, respectively, for curves 1 (a) and 2 (b). The x-axis contains the different m values for the pullback algorithm; the different graphs show the different attraction forces (no force, low, medium, and high force).

In what follows, we clarify how these graphs can be interpreted.

In Figure 5(a), given the $m = 0$ condition (first column), we get a ratio of $0, 78$ in the no-force condition (lower curvature). This means that one of the benchmarkers could complete the trial by making a movement that was 78% shorter than the actual intended path. In this condition there was no attraction force and no pull back, so we can assume that this is the shortest path that the spline interpolation allows. In Figure 5(b), we see for the same condition a ratio of $0, 90$,

which can be explained by the fact that the intended path is less curved, and hence the possible deviation is smaller.

When looking at the different force conditions (still given $m = 0$), we observe that the more the attraction force increases, the more tightly the original curve must be followed. This may in no means be a surprise, as this is the actual goal of the haptic lines: supporting a patient in practising a given path or movement and keeping them tight to this path. It may be evident that in curve 2 the difference is less pronounced as the path is more straight.

Having a better understanding of how to interpret the graphs, let us now discuss the influence of the parameter m, indicating "how far" the projection on the curve is "pulled back" when the perpendicular distance to the curve is increasing. In Figure 5(a), we see that increasing m forces the user to better follow the original curve in all force conditions. In the situation where $m = 0.1$, the ratio is even almost independent from the attraction force, with ratios between 0.91 and 0.94. For curve 2, the result is obviously less pronounced, but here we also notice that the "no force, no pull-back" condition allows to slightly "bypass" the intended curve, while adding our pull-back algorithm inhibits this behaviour, independent of the attraction forces.

This is exactly the initial intention of our pull-back mechanism: finding a smooth and continuous manner of forcing a user to follow a given path, when attraction forces are low. Moreover, we felt that our solution did not hinder the natural interaction with the system, which was the case in our former rounded corners solution described in [13]. The latter, however, remains to be confirmed by a practical usage in our project.

6. Conclusion

In our current research project, focussing on the upper-limb rehabilitation of MS and CVA patients using force feedback supported exercises, we found that several basic force feedback behaviors were necessary, among which a linear haptic path. Unfortunately current implementations in available APIs do not suite our particular need. In this paper, we described one of our best performing alternatives to implement these curves, based upon Cardinal Splines. In practice, however, we observed that patients getting experienced in the exercises, had the possibility to shorten their path as the attraction force was lowered. Therefore, we proposed a "pull back" algorithm, smoothly pulling back the projection on the curve based upon the distance of the cursor and the curve. In a benchmarking test, we could show that adding a higher pull-back factor makes the user to better follow the intended path, independent of the available attraction forces.

During informal tests, we found that the pull-back function felt natural and did not hinder the interaction. This, however, requires verification in a formal user study, by letting naive users or patients work with our solution during real rehabilitation exercises.

Acknowledgment

This research was partly funded through the INTERREG program (Project 4-BMG-II-1-84 and IVA-VLANED-1.14, Euregio Benelux).

References

[1] J. E. Deutsch, J. Latonio, G. C. Burdea, and R. Boian, "Post-stroke rehabilitation with the rutgers ankle system: a case study," *Presence*, vol. 10, no. 4, pp. 416–430, 2001.

[2] M. K. Holden, "Virtual environments for motor rehabilitation: review," *Cyberpsychology and Behavior*, vol. 8, no. 3, pp. 187–211, 2005.

[3] M. Rosen, "Introduction to special topic issue on technology in neurorehabilitation," *NeuroRehabilitation*, vol. 12, no. 1, pp. 1–2, 1999.

[4] G. Lathan, "Dimensions of diversity in design of telerehabilitation systems for universal usability," in *Proceedings of the Conference on Universal Usability (CUU '00)*, pp. 61–62, ACM, New York, NY, USA, November 2000.

[5] G. Kwakkel, R. van Peppen, R. Wagenaar et al., "Effects of augmented exercise therapy time after stroke: a meta-analysis," *Stroke*, vol. 35, no. 11, pp. 2529–2539, 2004.

[6] S. J. Housman, V. Le, T. Rahman, R. J. Sanchez, and D. J. Reinkensmeyer, "Arm-training with T-WREX after chronic stroke: preliminary results of a randomized controlled trial," in *Proceedings of the IEEE 10th International Conference on Rehabilitation Robotics (ICORR '07)*, pp. 262–268, Noordwijk, The Netherlands, June 2007.

[7] J. de Boeck, G. Alders, D. Gijbels et al., "The learning effect of force feedback enabled robotic rehabilitation of the upper limbs in persons with MS—a pilot study," in *Proceedings of the 5th Enactive International Conference (ENACTIVE '08)*, pp. 117–122, Pisa, Italy, November 2008.

[8] T. de Weyer, S. Notelaers, K. Coninx et al., "Watering the flowers: virtual haptic environments for training of forearm rotation in persons with central nervous deficits," in *Proceedings of the 4th International Conference on Pervasive Technologies Related to Assistive Environments (PETRA '11)*, ACM, Crete, Greece, May 2011.

[9] V. Popescu, G. Burdea, M. Bouzit, M. Girone, and V. Hentz, "Pc-based telerehabilitation system with force feedback," *IEEE Trans Inf Technol Biomed*, vol. 4, no. 1, pp. 45–51, 2000.

[10] Sensable Technologies, OpenHaptics Toolkit, 2011, http://www.sensable.com/.

[11] Chai 3d api, June 2011, http://www.chai3d.org/.

[12] SenseGraphics, H3D API, 2011, http://www.h3dapi.org/.

[13] J. de Boeck, S. Notelaers, C. Raymaekers, and K. Coninx, "Haptic linear paths for arm rehabilitation in MS patients," in *Proceedings of the IEEE International Workshop on Haptic Audio Visual Environments and Games (HAVE '09)*, pp. 42–47, Lecco, Italy, September 2009.

[14] Distance to a bezier curve, June 2011, http://www.tinaja.com/glib/bezdist.pdf.

4

A Combination of Pre- and Postprocessing Techniques to Enhance Self-Paced BCIs

Raheleh Mohammadi,[1] Ali Mahloojifar,[1] and Damien Coyle[2]

[1] Department of Biomedical Engineering, Tarbiat Modares University, Tehran 14115194, Iran
[2] Intelligent Systems Research Centre, University of Ulster, Derry BT48 7JL, UK

Correspondence should be addressed to Ali Mahloojifar, mahlooji@modares.ac.ir

Academic Editor: Christoph Braun

Mental task onset detection from the continuous electroencephalogram (EEG) in real time is a critical issue in self-paced brain computer interface (BCI) design. The paper shows that self-paced BCI performance can be significantly improved by combining a range of simple techniques including (1) constant-Q filters with varying bandwidth size depending on the center frequency, instead of constant bandwidth filters for frequency decomposition of the EEG signal in the 6 to 36 Hz band; (2) subject-specific postprocessing parameter optimization consisting of dwell time and threshold, and (3) debiasing before postprocessing by readjusting the classification output based on the current and previous brain states, to reduce the number of false detections. This debiasing block is shown to be optimal when activated only in special cases which are predetermined during the training phase. Analysis of the data recorded from seven subjects executing foot movement shows a statistically significant 10% ($P < 0.05$) average improvement in true positive rate (TPR) and a 1% reduction in false positive rate (FPR) detections compared with previous work on the same data.

1. Introduction

Brain-computer interface (BCI) is an alternative communication and enabling technology which offers the potential to provide a nonmuscular path for physically impaired individuals to convey messages and commands to the external world [1]. Various applications of BCI for able-bodied individuals have also been investigated [2–4]. Depending on the mode of operation, BCI systems are categorized into two main classes: synchronous (system paced or cue paced) and asynchronous (self-paced). In a synchronous BCI, the earliest type of BCI, the analysis, classification, and output activation of the system are carried out during predefined time intervals controlled by the machine/computer using cues; that is, the onset of the mental activity is known in advance. This mode of interaction is not natural for most typical applications since the system dictates when the user can control the application and must be switched off when the user does not wish to use the system so that control cues are stopped. In contrast, asynchronous or self-paced systems

are more natural for real-life applications since self-paced BCIs allow the user to control the system when desired. These systems have two operational states: intentional control (IC) and no control (NC) [5]. During the IC state the user controls and activates the BCI by intentionally varying their brain signals. NC is the period the user is free to perform any action such as watching TV, reading, relaxing, and eating unless activating the BCI. Continuous classification of the EEG signal is required to reveal the onset of IC or mental activity. The ultimate goal of a self-paced system is detecting the IC states and activating the system in these periods while staying completely inactive during NC periods therefore the percentage of true output activation during IC states, true positive rates (TPR), and false activation during NC states, false positive rates (FPR), determines the self-paced BCI system performance.

One of the most common mental strategies for BCIs is motor imagery because its features are well-defined physiologically. Movement-related potential (MRP) is a response in the EEG signal as a result of particular limb movement which lies in the frequency band below 4 Hz and starts about 1.5–1 sec before the movement onset [6]. In addition, due to the movement or imagination of the movement, EEG signal energy in specific frequency bands and also in specific regions of brain fluctuates producing an event-related desynchronization (ERD) before and during movement and event-related synchronization (ERS) in the beta frequency band after termination of the movement [7]. As ERD/S features are observable in both real and imaginary movement [8, 9] and also more accurate labeling of the EEG signal is possible for real movement asynchronous experiments, real movement data are used for testing new machine learning algorithms in most of the self-paced BCIs [5, 10–19].

Detection of only one movement from the ongoing EEG signal has been considered in self-paced BCI configurations by different BCI groups [5, 10–19]. BCIs capable of detecting only one brain pattern from the continuous EEG signal are referred to as a brain switch and are suitable for controlling different applications.

The first self-paced BCI system, referred to as Low-Frequency-Asynchronous Switch Design (LF-ASD), was proposed in [5] by Mason and Birch and was designed to detect the MRPs in the EEG signal recorded during right index finger movement. A wavelet-like function was applied to extract the features, and a 1-nearest neighbor (1-NN) classifier was used to distinguish the IC and NC classes/states. Several changes such as adding the energy normalization transform in the feature extraction block [10], adding a moving average and debounce window in a postprocessing block for decreasing the FPR [11], subject customization of the feature generator's parameter [12], and incorporating the knowledge of the past paths of features into the system [13] have been applied for improving the performance of the LF-ASD.

In the last design of this switch, Fatourechi et al. [14] proposed an improved version of the LF-ASD by extracting features from three neurological phenomena: movement-related potentials, changes in the power of Mu rhythms, and changes in the power of Beta rhythms to detect the IC states. A stationary wavelet transform followed by matched filtering was applied as a feature extraction method. A set of SVM classifiers were used for each neurological phenomenon classification from the idle state. Although the offline reported results of this paper show significant improvement in LF-ASD performance, the EEG signals are not continuously classified in this research. Another drawback of this design is that the NC periods were recorded in a special situation where the subject was asked to count the number of times that a white ball bounced off the screen [14].

In [15] movement onset detection from 64 EEG channels recorded during right-hand movement was investigated. Using the power spectral density estimated by the Thomson Multiplier Method for narrow-band spectral analysis of each EEG channel and Davis Bouldin Index, the best features were extracted and selected. A naïve Bayes classifier was applied to classify each sample to detect the movement onset. In another work of this group [16], the first fully unsupervised system for self-paced BCIs was suggested. An unsupervised

classification method based on Gaussian Mixture Model (GMM) was applied.

In [17] Qian et al. developed a novel paradigm for a motor-imagery-based brain-controlled switch that was interactive in the sense that the users performed repeated attempts until the switch was turned on. The beta band event-related frequency power from a single EEG Laplacian channel, recorded during the motor imagery of finger movement, was monitored online. When the relative ERD power level exceeded a predetermined threshold the switch was turned on.

Another brain switch designed in [18] proved the suitability of one single Laplacian derivation for detecting foot movement in ongoing EEG. Twenty-nine band pass filters with 2 Hz bandwidth from 6 to 36 Hz with 1 Hz overlap were applied for extracting the band power values of the EEG signal. Two distinct SVM classifiers were used to detect ERD and ERS patterns separately. In the postprocessing block a fixed dwell time and fixed refractory period for all 7 subjects were used to reduce the false detections of the brain switch. Using receiver operating characteristic (ROC) for balancing TP and FP, each SVM classification performance and a combination of the SVM outputs with a product rule were reported. The results demonstrate that the ERS patterns are more successful in detecting the onset of the foot movement in ongoing EEG signal. The result of [19] also proves that ERS phenomena are suitable for realizing a brain switch due to some features such as its subject-specific stability, specificity, and somatotopic organization. According to the above characteristic of ERS, in this paper we only consider ERS as a neurological phenomenon for discriminating foot movement onset from the idle state.

In this paper we improve the onset detection performance of a brain switch designed in [18]. For frequency decomposition of the EEG signal we apply constant-Q filters instead of constant bandwidth filters in self-paced BCI systems. Constant-Q frequency decomposition has previously shown to produce better classification accuracies in determining right- and left-motor imagery in synchronous motor-imagery-based BCI systems [20, 21]. We show that these filters significantly improve the performance of the brain switch and reveal the ERS features in the ongoing EEG signal much better than constant bandwidth filters.

Another innovation proposed in this paper is selecting the optimum postprocessing parameters such as dwell time and threshold for each subject and each combination of train/test runs. Most of the research in self-paced system design has a special postprocessing block for decreasing the FPR. Event-by-event analysis of self-paced BCI systems has been proposed in [22] and for its modification "threshold", "dwell time", and "refractory period" also introduced. In most of the self-paced systems [18, 19] "dwell time" and "refractory period" are fixed for all the subjects, and they report the best results achieved in the test phase by changing the threshold but for online application; all the parameters should be available from the training phase. Therefore a fixed threshold should be selected from the training data of each subject. In this paper "dwell time" and "threshold" are selected in the training phase, and refractory period is fixed for all the subjects. We observed that sometimes the selected threshold and dwell times are very low for the test phase classification output and in this situation the false positive rates increase. Therefore we apply a debiasing block before postprocessing which decreases the FPR by readjusting the classification output based on the current and previous brain states. This block is activated just in special cases which are determined from the training phase because in some cases adding debiasing results in decreasing TPR.

The remainder of the paper is organized as follows. Section 2 outlines data acquisition and the methodology of feature extraction, classification, performance evaluation, and postprocessing parameter selection. Results of using constant-Q filters and optimum postprocessing parameters in the brain switch performance are illustrated and discussed in Section 3; finally conclusions are presented in Section 4.

2. Methods

2.1. Data Description. Our analysis is performed on the data provided by the laboratory of Brain Computer Interface (BCI-Lab), Graz University of technology [18]. Data was acquired from 7 subjects during the execution of a cue-based foot movement. Each subject performed 3 runs with 30 trials on the same day. At the beginning of the trial ($t = 0$) a "+" was presented; then at $t = 2$ the presentation of an arrow pointing downwards cues the subject to perform a brisk foot movement of both feet for about 1-second duration. The cross and cue disappear at $t = 3.25$ s and at $t = 6$ s, respectively. At $t = 7.5$ the trials end. In between trials, a wait period of maximum 1 second occurs (Figure 1(a)). The recording was made using a g.tec amplifier and Ag/AgCl electrodes. The sampling frequency was 250 Hz. Sixteen monopolar EEG channels covering sensorimotor areas were measured. From these data, one small Laplacian derivation [23] over electrode position Cz was computed using orthogonal neighbor electrodes (Figure 1(b)). The surface Laplacian is approximated as follows:

$$V_{Cz}^{Lap} = V_{Cz} - \frac{1}{4} \sum_{k \in S_j} V_k, \qquad (1)$$

where V_{Cz} is the scalp potential EEG of the Cz channel and S_j is a set of four orthogonal neighbor electrodes.

2.2. Feature Extraction. Finding a suitable representative of data which makes the classification or detection of brain patterns easier is the goal of feature extraction. We select an appropriate feature for extracting ERS as a stable and more detectable movement-related pattern from spontaneous EEG signals. The energy increase in specific frequency bands as a result of correlated deactivation of neural networks in specific cortical areas of the brain is referred to as event-related synchronization (ERS). Band power which reveals the energy or power fluctuations of the signal in specific frequency bands is employed in this paper. Since band power features have low-computational requirements, they have been used widely in fast online BCI signal processing in self-paced applications [24–26].

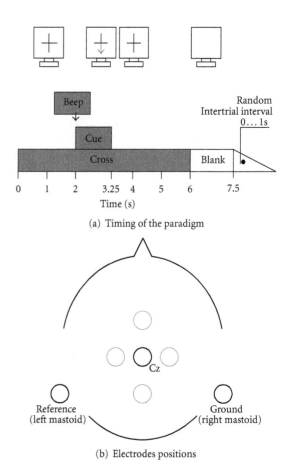

FIGURE 1: Paradigm and electrodes positions. (a) Foot movement timing scheme of each trial, (b) electrodes position (Cz as a Laplacian derivation).

2.2.1. Frequency Decomposition. Frequency decomposition of a signal is done using constant bandwidth or constant-Q (Q is the quality factor) filters. In constant-Q frequency decomposition, the ratio of center frequency to bandwidth for all the filters is the same and equal to Q. In other words, for low frequencies the frequency resolution is better while for high frequencies the time resolution is better. After selecting center frequencies, for different amounts of Q, the bandwidth of each filter is calculated as

$$Bw = \frac{f_c}{Q}, \qquad (2)$$

where Bw is the filter's bandwidth, f_c is the center frequency, and Q is the quality factor of the filter. Different values of Q result in various frequency decompositions of the signal. If Q is selected to be small, the bandwidth of the filters is large. The wideband signal components might be more contaminated with substantial noise in the EEG signal.

For large Q, the bandwidth of the filters is small. In this situation the percentage of overlap of neighboring frequency bands decreases and therefore cannot provide a proper redundancy of signals. In this paper for two different Q ratios ($Q = 2$ & $Q = 3$) we constructed two sets of fifth-order Butterworth bandpass filters with center frequencies at 6, 6.9, 7.8, 9, 10.2, 11.7, 13.4, 15.3, 17.5, 20.0, 22.8, 26.1, 29.8, and 33.5 Hz as suggested in [21] and cover the total range from 6 to 36 Hz. The frequency responses of these filters with $Q = 2$ are illustrated in Figure 2. It is obvious that the filter banks with constant Q may increase the redundancy of information in the feature set. The reasons behind the vast frequency band selection from 6 to 36 Hz are as follows: firstly the significant frequency characteristics of motor-related patterns are in beta (13–30 Hz) and mu (8–12 Hz) rhythm components [27] and secondly the optimal frequency bands of ERS vary among subjects. The ERD/S time-frequency maps of all subjects in Figure 3 show the differences between each subjects' optimum ERS frequency bands. For each subject, ERD/S map using constant-bandwidth filters and constant-Q filters is plotted. Figure 3 has been plotted using the ERDS map toolbox of Biosig [28].

2.2.2. Band Power.

During offline analysis, 28 logarithmic band power features were extracted from time segments of 1 s length to give a comprehensive spectral description of the EEG signals from 6 Hz to 36 Hz. Each segment has 250 samples with an overlap of 125 samples between adjacent segments. The logarithmic band power features were computed with two sets of constant-Q filters (Section 2.2.1). Each time segment of 1-second length was digitally band pass filtered, squared and averaged over all samples within the time segment and transformed with logarithm.

2.3. EEG Data Labeling.

The continuous EEG data is categorized into two classes: baseline and movement. According to the results of [18, 19] the ERS occurring after the end of the motor task is the dominant feature for realizing an asynchronous brain switch. Therefore all the samples were labeled for the classification of ERS against all other brain activities. According to the ERD/S map of the subjects, (Figure 3) the ERS happens mostly in $t = 4\text{-}5$ seconds in each trial. Therefore the samples in $t = 4\text{-}5$ s of each are labeled as movement class or (class 1), and the rest of the samples are labeled as baseline or (class 0). The data labeling is the same as [18].

2.4. Classification.

Support vector machines (SVMs) are supervised learning methods that classify the data by constructing an N-dimensional hyper-plane for a given feature set. Several advantages of SVM are as follows: it has a good generalization property as a result of selecting the hyper-plane which maximizes the margins, SVM is less prone to overtraining, and it is also insensitive to the curse-of-dimensionality.

The Gaussian-kernel-based SVM classifier has been used in self-paced BCI research successfully [14, 18, 19, 29]. The SVM performance depends on the regularization parameter C and the Gaussian kernel bandwidth σ. These parameters should be properly selected in the training phase. The goal is to identify C, σ using training data so that the classifier can accurately classify testing data. We use the libsvm software [30] for implementing the SVM since this software provides the posterior class probabilities in the output.

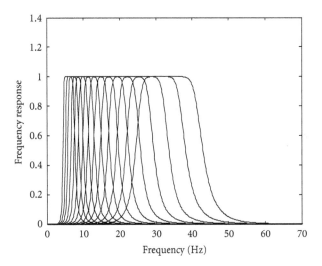

FIGURE 2: Frequency responses of constant-Q filters ($Q = 2$), 14 center frequencies are between 6 to 36 Hz.

2.4.1. SVM Parameter Selection and Training.

For each subject there are 3 runs each consisting of 30 trials. The patterns from 2 runs out of 3 runs are used as training data. For generalization purposes we will report the mean results of three different combinations of train and test runs for each subject. In each combination there are 60 training trials of two runs available for selecting the parameters of SVM. We use a "grid-search" on C and σ with a 10-fold cross-validation. C and σ are varied from 2^{-8} to 2^1 while for each step the values of parameters are doubled. Various pairs of C, σ are tried and the ones with the highest sample by sample true-positive rate and lowest false-positive rate are selected. In order to combine both conditions into a single measure we calculate the Youden index [31] TF for each pair as follows:

$$\text{TF} = \text{TPR} - \text{FPR}. \tag{3}$$

The best C and σ, the pair which maximizes TF, and the whole training set (two runs) are used to train a final SVM [18].

2.4.2. Testing.

The remaining run is used for testing the trained SVM. In order to simulate an online asynchronous system, we continuously compute logarithmic band power features applying a 1-second moving window at the rate of the sampling interval. The SVM classifier calculates the posterior class probability for patterns of the test run (Figure 4).

2.5. Performance Evaluation.

Performance measurement of the online self-paced paradigm is carried out in an event-by-event manner while in the training phase TPR and FPR were measured on the basis of sample by sample analysis. Before event-by-event analysis, the event class posterior probability of classifier was postprocessed using threshold, dwell time, and refractory period [22]. Dwell time is the amount of time that the output signal of the classifier must exceed the threshold to be considered as a control event. When one

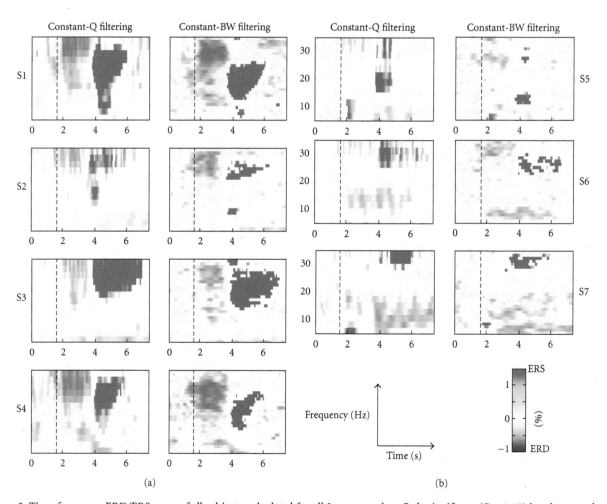

FIGURE 3: Time-frequency ERD/ERS maps of all subjects, calculated for all 3 runs together. Only significant ($P < 0.05$) band power changes in 0–7.5 s and in a frequency range 6–35 Hz are displayed. For each subject, constant-bandwidth filters (b) and constant-Q filters are plotted (a). The significant power decrease (ERD) and power increase (ERS) are displayed in red and blue colors, respectively.

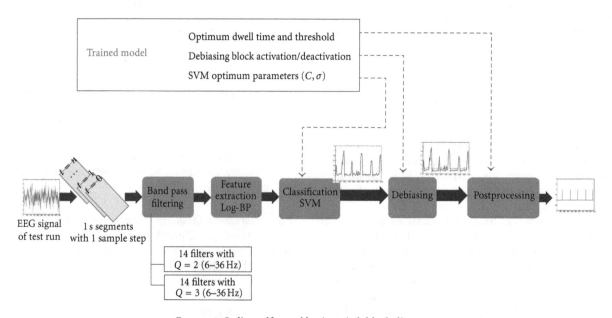

FIGURE 4: Online self-paced brain switch block diagram.

control event is detected, the output signal will be ignored during a refractory period. If the control event is detected in the intentional control (IC) periods of each, it is regarded as a true positive, but any detection out of the IC period is a false positive. For evaluation the time interval from $t = 3$ to 5.5 seconds of each is considered as the IC period. This interval is the same for all the subjects. The refractory period is also fixed for all the subjects and is equal to 750 samples or 3 seconds. The refractory period limits the number of detections of the brain switch and that longer values reduce the number of false activations at expense of lowering the bit rate. The event-by-event TPR and FPR are computed as follows [18]:

$$TPR = \frac{TP}{NTP},$$

$$FPR = \frac{FP}{NFP}, \qquad (4)$$

$$NFP = \frac{\text{total number of samples in test run}}{\text{dwell time + Refractory period}},$$

where TP and FP are the number of true positive and false positive detections, respectively. NTP is the number of IC periods. Since only one detection is allowed in the brain switch design, for this dataset NTP = 30 (30 trials in test run). Figure 5 shows the onset detection of the brain switch during 5 trials of the test run. Determining the threshold and dwell time for each subject and each combination of runs plays a very important role in the final performance of the system in terms of detecting the movement onset.

2.6. Postprocessing

2.6.1. Optimum Threshold and Dwell Time Selection. For simulating the online asynchronous system, all the parameters should be tuned in the training phase. Selection of the threshold and dwell time has a significant effect on the final performance of the system. Therefore in the training phase after selecting the best C and σ, we trained the SVM using the logarithmic band power features of one of the training runs. The log band power of another training run extracted in a 1s moving window was continuously classified by the trained SVM. In this stage, for different values of threshold (varied from 0.1 to 0.5 in steps of 0.01) and dwell time (varied from 30 to 70 samples in step of 5 samples) the event-by-event TPR and FPR were calculated.

The best threshold value in each dwell time corresponds to the point of the ROC curve (TPR versus FPR) closest to line $y = 1 - x$ where the FPR is taken to be horizontal (x-axis) and the TPR is vertical (y-axis). Analysis of a set of ROC curves leads to optimal value selection.

2.6.2. Debiasing. The event class posterior probability used for classification has DC offset which increases the number of false positive detections. In order to decrease the number of false detections in the test phase, each classifier output sample can be debiased using the average of the previous classifier outputs in a window with about 20 seconds size.

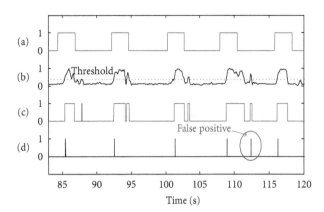

FIGURE 5: (a) IC intervals or true labels of the signal during 5 trials, (b) the posterior probability of movement class and its threshold, (c) predicted labels, and (d) detected onsets after postprocessing using dwell and refractory periods.

The following equation is used for debiasing the classifier output at time instant t [32]:

$$C_t = y_t - \frac{\sum_{i=t-\tau}^{i=t} y_i}{\tau}, \qquad (5)$$

where y_t is the classifier output at time instant t, C_t is the zero mean output, and τ is the number of previous classifier outputs used for averaging. In a case of 20 seconds window size, $\tau = 250 \times 20 = 5000$ samples [32].

2.6.3. Automatic Activation of Debiasing Block. Figure 6(a) shows an example of decreasing the number of FPs using the debiasing block. However, in some cases (Figure 6(b)) debiasing might lead to a decrease in true positive rate. Since the overall mean of the classifier output signal may decrease as a result of debiasing, it is probable that the best threshold selected in the training phase would be high; that is, after debiasing a threshold which is too high it results in low FP but also low TP which is not desirable. Therefore in the training phase we can perform analysis to determine whether the debiasing is required or not for final evaluation. In the training phase for the best threshold and dwell time selection, only half of the trials of the second run are used for determining the optimum postprocessing parameter. The other half of the trials is used for checking the necessity to use the debiasing block in final test session. Using the optimum threshold value and dwell time, TF = TPR − FPR (event-by-event analysis) is calculated for two situations: with debiasing and without debiasing. The higher TF value determines whether to apply the debiasing in test phase.

3. Results and Discussion

The results of onset detection are summarized in Tables 1–4. In all the tables for each subject TPR and FPR values are reported in the form of mean ± standard deviation. As explained for each subject, 3 different combinations of train/test runs are possible. The average of TPR and FPR values of all 3 combinations for each subject is presented in the tables.

TABLE 1: Individual performance using constant-Q filters and constant bandwidth filters for different dwell times (threshold = 0.5).

Subj. ID	Constant-Q filters						Constant Bandwidth filters					
	Dwell = 30		Dwell = 40		Dwell = 60		Dwell = 30		Dwell = 40		Dwell = 60	
	TPR	FPR	TPR	FPR	TPR	FPR	TPR	FPR	TPR	FPR	TPR	FPR
S1	94 ± 10	4 ± 5	94 ± 7	4 ± 4	96 ± 2	3 ± 3	88 ± 7	7 ± 3	89 ± 8	3 ± 4	85 ± 8	4 ± 4
S2	76 ± 4	17 ± 7	70 ± 3	16 ± 6	60 ± 5	6 ± 2	53 ± 9	10 ± 3	35 ± 8	9 ± 5	25 ± 7	6 ± 3
S3	99 ± 2	7 ± 2	99 ± 2	4 ± 1	93 ± 12	3 ± 1	93 ± 6	5 ± 4	94 ± 7	3 ± 3	92 ± 8	2 ± 2
S4	95 ± 5	6 ± 4	93 ± 4	6 ± 4	93 ± 4	4 ± 3	82 ± 7	8 ± 2	75 ± 6	7 ± 1	70 ± 15	4 ± 1
S5	69 ± 8	8 ± 3	65 ± 5	6 ± 3	51 ± 7	4 ± 4	43 ± 15	4 ± 1	36 ± 10	2 ± 3	31 ± 12	2 ± 3
S6	90 ± 4	12 ± 5	87 ± 6	10 ± 3	83 ± 6	6 ± 2	61 ± 10	10 ± 1	49 ± 9	7 ± 4	39 ± 5	5 ± 3
S7	81 ± 12	11 ± 8	79 ± 10	8 ± 6	77 ± 12	5 ± 2	65 ± 10	9 ± 6	54 ± 14	6 ± 4	42 ± 21	6 ± 3
Average	86 ± 7	9 ± 5	84 ± 6	8 ± 4	79 ± 8	4 ± 3	69 ± 10	8 ± 3	62 ± 9	5 ± 4	55 ± 12	4 ± 3

TABLE 2: Individual performance while the dwell time and threshold are automatically selected in training phase, the selected values also are written for each subject in 3 different combinations of runs. Run no. n shows the test run number.

Subjects ID	TPR (mean ± SD)	FPR (mean ± SD)	Dwell time			Threshold		
			Run no. 1	Run no. 2	Run no. 3	Run no. 1	Run no. 2	Run no. 3
S1	95 ± 4	3 ± 3	70	50	60	0.55	0.56	0.29
S2	75 ± 7	**24 ± 16**	30	35	30	0.37	0.5	0.27
S3	99 ± 2	3 ± 3	50	50	40	0.36	0.5	0.15
S4	90 ± 7	6 ± 3	70	30	55	0.44	0.43	0.31
S5	70 ± 12	**23 ± 17**	50	30	30	0.38	0.4	0.25
S6	76 ± 7	5 ± 2	55	70	70	0.48	0.5	0.5
S7	75 ± 11	**9 ± 9**	55	70	40	0.5	0.5	0.41
Average	83 ± 6	10 ± 3						

TABLE 3: Individual performance with optimum threshold value, dwell time, and automatic activation of debiasing.

Subjects ID	TPR (mean ± SD)	FPR (mean ± SD)
S1	94 ± 2	3 ± 4
S2	61 ± 2	9 ± 2
S3	99 ± 2	2 ± 2
S4	89 ± 5	6 ± 4
S5	66 ± 12	7 ± 6
S6	76 ± 7	5 ± 2
S7	76 ± 10	6 ± 4
Average	80 ± 7	5 ± 4

In order to show the effect of using constant-Q filters in improving the performance of the Brain switch, in Table 1 we illustrate the results of applying a set of fifth-order Butterworth filters with constant bandwidth (2 Hz bandwidth and 1 Hz overlap between 6 to 36 Hz) in one column and with constant-Q ($Q = 2$ and $Q = 3$ and 14 center frequencies from 6 to 36 Hz) in another column. The intentional control is 3–5.5 seconds for evaluation, the threshold is 0.5, and the refractory period is equal to 750 samples. For the dwell times equal to 30, 40, and 60 samples, the results are reported in three subcolumns for each type of filter to show the changes of the performance in different dwell times.

According to the results of Table 1 the average TPR achieved by applying constant-Q filter is significantly better than the constant bandwidth approach. In a two-sided non-parametric statistical test, the Wilcoxon signed rank test [33, 34] was used that the improvement is statistically significant ($P < 0.05$).

These results confirm that constant-Q filters are more capable of extracting ERS features from the ongoing EEG signal compared with constant bandwidth filters. The results of constant-Q filtering prove our prediction according to the ERD/S map (Figure 3) using constant-Q filters. According to these maps for all subjects denser ERS is present using constant-Q filters in contrast to a sparse ERS using constant bandwidth filters. One of the nice features of the constant Q filter is its increasing time resolution towards higher frequencies and increasing frequency resolution in lower frequencies which contributes to define more precisely the movement onsets in EEG signal. This characteristic decreases the nonstationary effects of the EEG signal and results in performance improvement specially for some of the subjects which suffers more from nonstationarity. Moreover, the filter banks with constant Q may increase the redundancy of information in the feature set therefore when the subject-specific frequency bands are not applied, the classifier performance can be improved. The results in the remaining tables are therefore reported with constant-Q filters. For different dwell times we report the results to show the effect of choosing optimum dwell time in the final performance of

TABLE 4: Comparison of the results of this paper and results presented in [18].

Subjects ID	Constant-Q filter + dwell time selection		Results of paper [18]	
	TPR (mean ± SD)	FPR (mean ± SD)	TPR (mean ± SD)	FPR (mean ± SD)
S1	98 ± 4	3 ± 3	97 ± 5	3 ± 2
S2	61 ± 2	8 ± 1	61 ± 10	7 ± 2
S3	100 ± 0	3 ± 2	94 ± 5	4 ± 4
S4	96 ± 2	6 ± 2	83 ± 12	4 ± 3
S5	65 ± 9	7 ± 2	54 ± 14	7 ± 2
S6	91 ± 10	6 ± 3	79 ± 12	8 ± 1
S7	83 ± 9	5 ± 2	52 ± 20	6 ± 2
Average	**85 ± 6**	5 ± 2	74 ± 21	6 ± 3

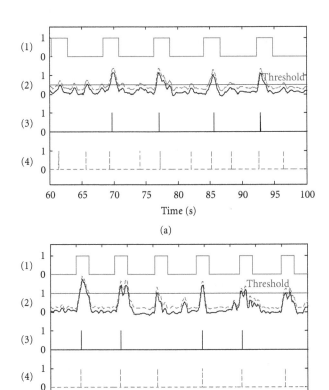

FIGURE 6: An example of comparison between biased and debiased classification output in detecting the onset of the movement: (1) IC intervals, (2) dashed line: biased classification output and straight line: debiased output. (3) Detected onsets using debiased output and (4) detected onsets using biased output. ((a) the case that debiasing improves the performance by decreasing FP detections, (b) the case that debiasing decreases the TPR).

Table 2 shows the results of the brain switch where threshold and dwell time are selected automatically in the training phase as suggested. This automatic selection is done since we cannot select the proper value for these parameters randomly. The mean value of the TPR is satisfactory, but the FPR value of three subjects S2, S5, and S7 are high. The high value of FPR for these subjects shows that the best dwell time and threshold selected using the training data are not necessarily the best ones for the test data because EEG signal is nonstationary. In order to decrease false positive detections the debiasing block can be added to the output of the classifier. As explained in Section 2.6.2, this block is not activated always. The posterior probability of the classifier will be debiased if its effectiveness has been confirmed in the training phase. The results of automatic applying the debiasing block in the output of the classifier are illustrated in Table 3. Although the mean value of TPR has decreased for some subjects the problem of a high number of false detections has been solved using this block. Therefore the automatic selection of the dwell time and threshold value along with automatic activation of the debiasing block results in acceptable performance since the FPR is less than 10% for all the subjects. Although it seems some of the columns of Table 1 (dwell = 60) also result in the same performance, selecting that specific dwell time and threshold which lead to acceptable performance cannot be done randomly, and in some cases random selection of these parameters (dwell = 30 and 40) might result in the high FPR value (FPR > 10%).

In order to prove our claim of improving the performance of the brain switch designed in [18] we compare the results of our method and the reported results of [18] in Table 4. The results of [18] were reported after ROC curve analysis in the test phase. The maximum TPR associated to a FPR < 0.1 had been selected for each combination of runs for each subject. The left side of the Table 4 shows our results calculated after ROC analysis in the test phase while the best dwell time has been selected in the training phase. The right side of Table 4 is the reported results of ERS classification [18]. Comparing the mean TPR and FPR results of the right and left columns, the performance improvement of the brain switch provided by the proposed adjustments is clear. A two-sided nonparametric statistical hypothesis test, Wilcoxon signed rank [33, 34], between the accuracies obtained by the proposed method and those reported in [18], shows a

each subject. In Table 1 the threshold value is also fixed for all subjects. Adjusting the threshold also can improve the results of the classification significantly. Increasing and decreasing the dwell time and threshold value selection can impact the result considerably; therefore for designing a brain switch suitable for online applications, it is recommended that these values are determined in the training phase properly.

significant improvements in the TPR ($P < 0.03$), while the FPR decrease is not statistically significant ($P = 1$).

The differences between the results reported in the Table 4 (left column) and Table 3 originate from threshold value. In Table 3 the results are calculated in only one threshold value selected in the training phase, while the results illustrated in the Table 4 are selected between various results calculated for different threshold values in the test phase with the same criteria of [18] (maximum TPR associated with FPR < 0.1).

In the following we briefly count the differences between the brain switch designed in this paper and in [18] which leads to performance improvement: (1) applying constant-Q filters instead of filters with equal bandwidth provides more separable features between event class and nonevent class. (2) Increasing the refractory period from 2 seconds (500 samples) to 3 seconds (750 samples) has a positive effect on the final performance. Since the summation of the refractory period and dwell time is less than the time duration between two consecutive events, increasing the refractory period does not cause any problem. (3) Automatic threshold value and dwell time selection using training data prepare the system for online application. For the cases with low selected threshold value and short optimum dwell time, debiasing plays an important role in decreasing the number of false detections. Its automatic activation using the training results prevents losing the high true positive rates in the cases of some subjects.

4. Conclusion

The results of this paper illustrate that using constant-Q filters without any optimization of frequency bands for each subject resulted in more separable features of event and nonevent class samples. The automatic selection of dwell time and threshold values in the training session makes the brain switch suitable for online applications. Adding a debiasing block to the classification output signal only in special cases which are predetermined during the training phase also resulted in a more accurate brain switch. Overall, the study shows that combining a range of simple techniques including constant-Q filters, optimum threshold values, optimum dwell time, and automatic activation of a debiasing block improves detection of foot movement in ongoing EEG. Although previous studies have investigated these processes individually, this study provides new evidence to suggest that combining these various techniques can improve self-paced BCI performance. With the proposed combination of methods, no adjustment or collaboration (e.g., threshold setting) is required during the test phase, whereas many other studies require a number of parameters to be adjusted to account for nonstationary changes.

Acknowledgment

The authors are grateful to Professor G. Pfurtscheller and Mr. T. Solis-Escalante of the Laboratory of Brain Computer Interface (BCI-Lab), Graz University of technology, for making their data available.

References

[1] J. R. Wolpaw, N. Birbaumer, D. J. McFarland, G. Pfurtscheller, and T. M. Vaughan, "Brain-computer interfaces for communication and control," *Clinical Neurophysiology*, vol. 113, no. 6, pp. 767–791, 2002.

[2] B. Z. Allison, E. W. Wolpaw, and J. R. Wolpaw, "Brain-computer interface systems: progress and prospects," *Expert Review of Medical Devices*, vol. 4, no. 4, pp. 463–474, 2007.

[3] S. Marcel and J. D. Millán, "Person authentication using brainwaves (EEG) and maximum a posteriori model adaptation," *IEEE Transactions on Pattern Analysis and Machine Intelligence*, vol. 29, no. 4, pp. 743–752, 2007.

[4] R. Scherer, A. Schloegl, F. Lee, H. Bischof, J. Janša, and G. Pfurtscheller, "The self-paced graz brain-computer interface: methods and applications," *Computational Intelligence and Neuroscience*, vol. 2007, Article ID 79826, 9 pages, 2007.

[5] S. G. Mason and G. E. Birch, "A brain-controlled switch for asynchronous control applications," *IEEE Transactions on Biomedical Engineering*, vol. 47, no. 10, pp. 1297–1307, 2000.

[6] C. Babiloni, F. Carducci, F. Cincotti et al., "Human movement-related potentials vs desynchronization of EEG alpha rhythm: a high-resolution EEG study," *NeuroImage*, vol. 10, no. 6, pp. 658–665, 1999.

[7] G. Pfurtscheller and F. H. Lopes da Silva, "Event-related EEG/MEG synchronization and desynchronization: basic principles," *Clinical Neurophysiology*, vol. 110, no. 11, pp. 1842–1857, 1999.

[8] G. Pfurtscheller and C. Neuper, "Motor imagery activates primary sensorimotor area in humans," *Neuroscience Letters*, vol. 239, no. 2-3, pp. 65–68, 1997.

[9] E. Gerardin, A. Sirigu, S. Léhericy et al., "Partially overlapping neural networks for real and imagined hand movements," *Cerebral Cortex*, vol. 10, no. 11, pp. 1093–1104, 2000.

[10] Z. Yu, S. G. Mason, and G. E. Birch, "Enhancing the performance of the LF-ASD brain computer interface," in *Proceedings of the 2nd Joint Engineering in Medicine and Biology, 24th Annual Conference and the Annual Fall Meeting of the Biomedical Engineering Society EMBS/BMES Conference*, vol. 3, pp. 2443–2444, October 2002.

[11] J. F. Borisoff, S. G. Mason, A. Bashashati, and G. E. Birch, "Brain-computer interface design for asynchronous control applications: improvements to the LF-ASD asynchronous brain switch," *IEEE Transactions on Biomedical Engineering*, vol. 51, no. 6, pp. 985–992, 2004.

[12] A. Bashashati, M. Fatourechi, R. K. Ward, and G. E. Birch, "User customization of the feature generator of an asynchronous brain interface," *Annals of Biomedical Engineering*, vol. 34, no. 6, pp. 1051–1060, 2006.

[13] A. Bashashati, S. Mason, R. K. Ward, and G. E. Birch, "An improved asynchronous brain interface: making use of the temporal history of the LF-ASD feature vectors," *Journal of Neural Engineering*, vol. 3, no. 2, pp. 87–94, 2006.

[14] M. Fatourechi, R. K. Ward, and G. E. Birch, "A self-paced brain-computer interface system with a low false positive rate," *Journal of Neural Engineering*, vol. 5, no. 1, pp. 9–23, 2008.

[15] C. S. L. Tsui, A. Vuckovic, R. Palaniappan, F. Sepulveda, and J. Q. Gan, "Narrow band spectral analysis for movement onset detection in asynchronous BCI," in *Proceedings of the 3rd*

International Workshop on Brain-Computer Interfaces, pp. 30–31, Graz, Austria, 2006.

[16] B. A. S. Hasan and J. Q. Gan, "Unsupervised movement onset detection from EEG recorded during self-paced real hand movement," *Medical and Biological Engineering and Computing*, vol. 48, no. 3, pp. 245–253, 2010.

[17] K. Qian, P. Nikolov, D. Huang, D. Y. Fei, X. Chen, and O. Bai, "A motor imagery-based online interactive brain-controlled switch: paradigm development and preliminary test," *Clinical Neurophysiology*, vol. 121, no. 8, pp. 1304–1313, 2010.

[18] T. Solis-Escalante, G. Müller-Putz, and G. Pfurtscheller, "Overt foot movement detection in one single Laplacian EEG derivation," *Journal of Neuroscience Methods*, vol. 175, no. 1, pp. 148–153, 2008.

[19] G. Pfurtscheller and T. Solis-Escalante, "Could the beta rebound in the EEG be suitable to realize a "brain switch"?" *Clinical Neurophysiology*, vol. 120, no. 1, pp. 24–29, 2009.

[20] T. Wang, J. Deng, and B. He, "Classifying EEG-based motor imagery tasks by means of time-frequency synthesized spatial patterns," *Clinical Neurophysiology*, vol. 115, no. 12, pp. 2744–2753, 2004.

[21] N. Yamawaki, C. Wilke, Z. Liu, and B. He, "An enhanced time-frequency-spatial approach for motor imagery classification," *IEEE Transactions on Neural Systems and Rehabilitation Engineering*, vol. 14, no. 2, pp. 250–254, 2006.

[22] G. Townsend, B. Graimann, and G. Pfurtscheller, "Continuous EEG classification during motor imagery—simulation of an asynchronous BCI," *IEEE Transactions on Neural Systems and Rehabilitation Engineering*, vol. 12, no. 2, pp. 258–265, 2004.

[23] B. Hjorth, "An on line transformation of EEG scalp potentials into orthogonal source derivations," *Electroencephalography and Clinical Neurophysiology*, vol. 39, no. 5, pp. 526–530, 1975.

[24] R. Leeb, D. Friedman, G. R. Müller-Putz, R. Scherer, M. Slater, and G. Pfurtscheller, "Self-paced (asynchronous) BCI control of a wheelchair in virtual environments: a case study with a tetraplegic," *Computational Intelligence and Neuroscience*, vol. 2007, Article ID 79642, 8 pages, 2007.

[25] R. Leeb, D. Friedman, R. Scherer, M. Slater, and G. Pfurtscheller, "EEGbased, "walking" of a tetraplegic in virtual reality," in *Proceedings of the Maia Brain Computer Interfaces Workshop—Challenging Brain Computer Interfaces: Neural Engineering Meets Clinical Needs in Neurorehabilitation*, pp. 43–44, 2006.

[26] F. Lotte, Y. Renard, and A. Lécuyer, "Self-paced brain-computer interaction with virtual worlds: a quantitative and qualitative study 'out-of-the-lab'," in *Proceedings of the 4th International Brain-Computer Interface Workshop and Training Course*, 2008.

[27] G. Pfurtscheller and C. Neuper, "Motor imagery direct communication," *Proceedings of the IEEE*, vol. 89, no. 7, pp. 1123–1134, 2001.

[28] A. Schlogl, C. Brunner, R. Scherer, and A. Glatz, "BioSig: an open-source software library for BCI research," in *Towards Brain-Computer Interfacing*, pp. 347–358, MIT Press, Boston, Mass, USA, 2007.

[29] F. Lotte, M. Congedo, A. Lécuyer, F. Lamarche, and B. Arnaldi, "A review of classification algorithms for EEG-based brain-computer interfaces," *Journal of Neural Engineering*, vol. 4, no. 2, pp. R1–R13, 2007.

[30] C.-C. Chang and C.-J. Lin, "LIBSVM: a library for support vector machines," Software, 2001, http://www.csie.ntu.edu.tw/~cjlin/libsvm/.

[31] M. Sokolova, N. Japkowicz, and S. Szpakowicz, *Beyond Accuracy, F-Score and ROC: A Family of Discriminant Measures for Performance Evaluation*, Springer, Berlin, Germany, 2006.

[32] A. Satti, D. Coyle, and G. Prasad, "Continuous EEG classification for a self-paced BCI," in *Proceedings of the 4th International IEEE/EMBS Conference on Neural Engineering (NER'09)*, pp. 315–318, Antalya, Turkey, May 2009.

[33] J. D. Gibbons, *Nonparametric Statistical Inference*, Marcel Dekker, New York, NY, USA, 1985.

[34] M. Hollander and D. A. Wolfe, *Nonparametric Statistical Methods*, John Wiley & Sons, Hoboken, NJ, USA, 1999.

5

Exploring Sensor Gloves for Teaching Children Sign Language

Kirsten Ellis and Jan Carlo Barca

Faculty of Information Technology, Monash University, Clayton Campus, VIC 3800, Australia

Correspondence should be addressed to Kirsten Ellis, kirsten.ellis@monash.edu

Academic Editor: Armando Bennet Barreto

This research investigates if a computer and an alternative input device in the form of sensor gloves can be used in the process of teaching children sign language. The presented work is important, because no current literature investigates how sensor gloves can be used to assist children in the process of learning sign language. The research presented in this paper has been conducted by assembling hardware into sensor gloves, and by designing software capable of (i) filtering out sensor noise, (ii) detecting intentionally posed signs, and (iii) correctly evaluating signals in signs posed by different children. Findings show that the devised technology can form the basis of a tool that teaches children sign language, and that there is a potential for further research in this area.

1. Introduction

Communication involves the exchange of information, and this can only occur effectively if all participants use a common language [1]. Deaf people need an efficient nonauditory means of expressing and interpreting information in order to communicate, and sign language have proven effective in communicating across a broad spectrum of requirements from everyday needs to sophisticated concepts. Australian sign language (Auslan) is the native sign language used in Australia where the research has been conducted, but the work is equally applicable to other signed languages. It is important that intuitive and efficient tools for teaching sign language are available to ensure that hearing impaired people are able to develop extensive social networks with deaf and hearing people. In addition to ensure that deaf people are able to obtain the best possible education and services within the community.

This research investigates if a computer, and an alternative input device in the form of sensor gloves, can be used in the process of teaching children Australian sign language (Auslan). Each sign consists of a number of parts: hand shape, place of articulation, orientation, path of movement, and nonsign components including facial expression [1]. For this research we are focusing on the hand shape component as one important aspect of a sign. We wish to use a computer,

because computers can act as an ideal medium for conveying details of sign language such as hand shapes, location, and hand movements. In addition to this, the learner can work at their own pace, at a place and time that is convenient to them. The learner can target the vocabulary that is relevant to their circumstances and multimedia can provide supplementary information to enhance the learning experience. The computer can also be used to effectively assess the learner's receptive vocabulary. However, traditional computing systems are unable to provide feedback about the accuracy of the learner's expressive signs [2, 3].

A central difference between current research in this area and our work is that current research tends to investigate how sensor gloves can be used for sign language interpretation [4], while we focus on investigating how sensor gloves can be used as a teaching aid. Another central difference is that current research mostly focuses on adults, while we focus on children. We have this focus because to date no research has been completed in the area of using sensor gloves to teach sign language to children, despite the possibilities this technology offers for teaching sign language.

This research paper presents the initial research into the viability for using data gloves in combination with a computer and software to provide feedback to children on the accuracy of their expressive signs. The aspects covered in this paper are a description of the gloves and hardware, how to identify intentionally posed handshapes, and an initial investigation into the viability of evaluating signals from two children with different hand sizes using one set of data gloves. This paper only briefly discusses how the results could be incorporated into a learning system.

We have decided to incorporate sensor gloves into our system design, as this technology has been used in a variety of application areas, which demands accurate tracking and interpretation of sign language. An example is the AcceleGlove technology developed by [5]. In their work, they use a computer and sensor gloves to manipulate a virtual hand, icons on a virtual desktop, and a virtual keyboard through the use of 26 different signs. They also show that computers and sensor gloves can be used to translate sign language into speech or text.

This paper is organized as follows. In Section 1, we provide a brief overview of existing sensor glove technologies. In Section 2, we describe how the sensor glove technology used in this research was devised. In Section 3, we start off by describing how a set of experiments, which investigates if the devised technology (i) can identify intentionally posed signs, (ii) is robust enough to correctly evaluate signs posed by more than one child. In the end of Section 3 we provide an analysis of results from the experiments, and in the final section of the paper we conclude by outlining the potential for further research in this area.

2. Sensor Glove Technologies in Literature

In this section we define what sensor gloves are, and describe some of the existing glove technologies. The hardware components of the gloves will be discussed first. We then go on to describe some of the processing techniques that are used to analyse and interpret data signals that are generated by the gloves.

2.1. Sensor Glove Hardware Described in Literature. Sensor gloves are hand worn devices with inbuilt sensors that can capture information about the movements and positioning of the user's hands. Some of the most widely known sensor glove technologies are the (i) DataEntryGlove [6], (ii) Data Glove [7], (iii) CyberGlove [8], and (iv) AcceleGlove [9].

The DataEntryGlove was presented by Gary Grimes from Bell Telephone Laboratories in 1983, and was the first widely published sensor glove [6, 10, 11]. The DataEntryGlove was originally devised as an alternative to the keyboard, and made it possible to generate 96 printable ASCII characters from 80 different finger positions. The glove was made out of cloth and had flex sensors along the fingers, tactile sensors on the fingertips, and inertial sensors positioned on the knuckle side of the hands. The distribution of the sensors was specified with the aim of recognizing the Single Hand Manual Alphabet for the American Deaf [10]. The DataEntryGlove was researched but was never commercially developed.

Thomas Zimmermann developed the DataGlove in 1987. This glove was constructed of a lightweight fabric glove equipped with optical sensors on each finger, and magnetic sensors on the back of the gloves [7, 11]. The optical sensors

were constructed of optical cables with a small light in one end and a photodiode in the other. When the fingers were bent, the light was reduced in strength before it reached the photodiode. The bending of the fingers could therefore be determined by measuring how much light the photo diode detected. The magnetic sensor measured the rotations of the hand in relation to a fixed reference point [7, 10]. The DataGlove was commercialized by VPL Research and could be purchased at a reasonable price, which lead to widespread use of this glove.

The CyberGlove was developed at Stanford University in 1988 and was specifically designed for the Talking Glove Project, which focused on translating American sign language into spoken English [8, 10, 11]. This glove was made up of a cloth glove with the fingertips and the palm areas removed. This made it possible for users to easily grasp objects and made it possible for deaf-blind users to conduct manual finger spelling while wearing the gloves [8]. The gloves were equipped with a total of 22 flex sensors, which was made out of thin foil mounted onto plastic modules. These sensors were sewn into pockets running over each joint, and could measure flexing of fingers and wrists. The maximum flex that could be detected by a sensor was regulated by adjusting the thickness and elasticity of the plastic modules. The plastic modules were selected in such a way that they of maximized the output signal, and at the same time minimized fatigue of the sensors [8]. Informal experiments have shown that this glove performs in a smooth and stable way, and that it is accurate enough to capture complex and detailed finger and hand gestures [10]. However, according to Sturman, one must calibrate the sensors to each user in order to accurately capture gestures from different hand sizes and hand shapes. The CyberGlove is commercially available from VR logic [12].

The AcceleGlove uses accelerometers and potentiometers to capture finger and hand poses. The accelerometers are placed on the fingers, the wrist, and the upper arm, and are used to provide orientation and acceleration information. The potentiometers are located on the elbow and the shoulder, and provide information about the hand's absolute position with respect to the body [13]. The AcceleGlove also incorporates a wrist button, which allows the user to easily activate and deactivate the glove. To activate the glove the user simply presses the wrist button, and to deactivate it, the user presses the button a second time. This process is repeated for each sentence, in order to assist the system in interpreting the signals correctly.

Before we move on to the next section, it is important to notice that literature points out that signals from sensor gloves have to be converted from an analogue to a digital format before being interpreted by a computer [8]. This process can be conducted with an analogue to digital converter.

2.2. Sensor Glove Software Described in Literature. When the reviewed literature discusses issues related to the software components of glove technologies, the main focus is on how to classify signals. This focus is held because the classification process is central in determining if signs can be correctly identified. The requirements of the target application area determines what method is best suited for classifying the signals (e.g., sometimes it is sufficient to use a classification method that only takes into account the shapes of the hands, while other times it is necessary to use a classification method, which analyses hand shapes, hand locations, and hand movements). One must also determine if one wants to classify static or articulated signs. If one wishes to classify static signs, then it might be necessary to use a classification method that can filter out "transitional signs," which not only are intentionally posed by the user, but rather arise as the fingers and hands move from one pose to another. If the target application area requires classification of articulated signs, then one might have to use a classification method, which takes into account (i) initial hand shapes, (ii) hand orientations, (iii) hand positions, (iv) hand motions, and (v) end hand shapes [14].

Some methods that have been used to successfully classify signals from sensor gloves are (i) neural networks (NNs), (ii) hidden markov models (HMMs), and (iii) template matching. When using NNs or HMMs, one must first construct a network with sufficient nodes and links to capture gestures at an abstraction level, which satisfies the requirements of the application area. Then one must train the network by iteratively processing representative samples of the type of data to be classified. The drawback with using NNs and HMMs, is that significant time and effort is required in order to design and train the networks. It is also hard to search for errors, and to explain the outcome of the classification process [15]. Template matching based classification methods on the other hand, can be devised relatively fast, makes it easy to search for errors, and makes it easy to explain the outcome of the classification process [15]. One form of template matching, which has been successfully used for classifying data from sensor gloves, is referred to as "conditional template matching." "conditional template matching" compares incoming data signals with a prestored library of patterns. This is done by evaluating one component of the signal after another, until the signal has been compared to all the patterns in a library, or a condition is met. Conditional template matching has proven to provide an accuracy of 95% on 175 signs, and this better than results provided by HMMs and NNs [5]. We will therefore use a form of "conditional template matching" in this research.

3. System Design

In this section we will describe the hardware and software components that have been devised throughout this research. We start off by describing the hardware components. Then we continue by describing software components that have been devised to (i) filter out sensor noise, (ii) detect intentionally posed signs, and (iii) evaluate signals in signs posed by different children.

3.1. Hardware. A number of issues had to be considered when we were assembling the hardware for the sensor gloves. Some of these issues are the following.

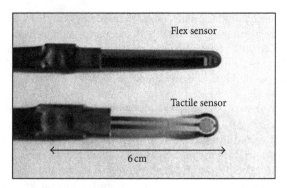

FIGURE 1: A pair of the selected flex and tactile sensors.

(i) What size the gloves had to be, to fit onto the hands of different children?

(ii) How to make the gloves robust enough to ensure that they can withstand the wear and tear, which results from several children putting them on and taking them off?

(iii) What type and number of sensors to select to successfully extract Auslan signs?

(iv) How to attach the sensors to the gloves?

(v) How to convert the analogue signals from the sensor gloves into a digital format, which can be readily interpreted by a computer?

To ensure that the gloves would have a size suitable for a child, we used a pair of children's gloves as a base for the sensor gloves. The selected gloves were made up of robust and stretchy lycra material. We selected gloves with this material to ensure that the sensor gloves would be robust enough to withstand wear and tear, and to ensure that they would have enough stretch to fit the hands of different children.

10 flex and 10 tactile sensors were incorporated into the gloves. These sensors were selected because they would make it possible to detect finger flexion and the touch of fingertips, which is sufficient to register a number of different Auslan signs. A pair of the selected flex and tactile sensors are shown in Figure 1. To make it possible to detect finger flexion and the touch of fingertips correctly, the sensors had to be appropriately distributed onto the gloves. This was made possible by mounting pockets onto the gloves at both the palm and the knuckle side of each finger. The size of these pockets was specified so that they would fit the sensors and keep them in place. When the pockets had been mounted onto the gloves, the flex sensors were slid into the pockets located on the knuckle side of the fingers, while the tactile sensors were slid into the pockets located on the palm side. How the sensors were distributed across the gloves is illustrated in Figure 2. When the sensors had been slid into the pockets, a set of tubes was sewn onto the wrist area of the gloves. Wires from the sensors were then pulled through these tubes to keep them out of the way when the sensor gloves were in use.

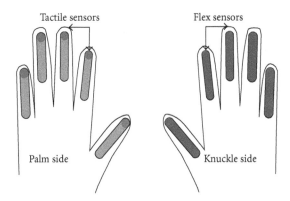

FIGURE 2: How flex and tactile sensors were distributed across the gloves.

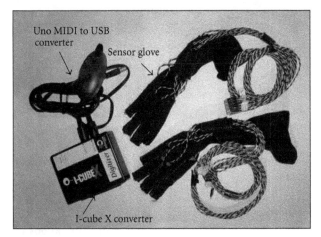

FIGURE 3: Sensor gloves, I-cube X converter, and uno MIDI to USB converter.

The wires from the sensors were then plugged into an I-cube X converter so that sensor signals could be converted from an analogue to a digital format. The I-cube X is a system that enables a large variety of sensors to be connected to the I-cube X box which is a digitizer that converts the signal from the sensor into a digital message [16]. Data from the system can then be accessed via a computer and used to feed into programs that are written in a variety of languages. A third party plug in for Adobe Director was used to develop the children's data gloves. To access the output from the system the MIDI cables from the I-cube X converter was plugged into a uno MIDI to USB converter before the setup was linked to a laptop. The sensor gloves, the I-cube X converter, and the uno MIDI to USB converter is shown in Figure 3.

3.2. Software. The main issues that had to be considered when we were designing the software for the sensor gloves were the following.

(i) How to simplify the data to support fast processing?

(ii) How to identify intentionally posed signs?

(iii) How to correctly evaluate signals in signs posed by different children?

We will provide a quick overview of the raw data from the sensors before we go on to describe the architecture of the software, as this will make it easy to understand why we have employed the particular methods. Data packets with raw data are transmitted from the I-cube X box to the computer every fourth millisecond. These data packets include information about when the data was captured, the wire or channel the data is transmitted through, and the signal strength. Signals from the tactile sensors have a strength that range from zero to 118, where zero corresponds to no pressure, and 118 corresponds to hard pressure. Signals from the flex sensors range from zero to 115, where zero corresponds to no flex and 115 corresponds to maximum flex.

To support fast processing we devised a low-pass filter. This filter removes data signals if the input from all the sensors has a strength below a set threshold. The threshold value was set to 45, which is a value just above the maximum random signal fluctuation observed in the sensor system when the sensors are not stimulated. Signals that are not removed by the low-pass filter are scaled so that the minimum value of all signals is zero, the maximum value of signals from the tactile sensors is 73, and the maximum value of signals from the flex sensors is 70. These signals are then passed on to a classification module. This classification module first labels each data packet according to the finger and sensor the particular stimulus was detected from. This is done by using a mapping model, which relates wires or channels to particular label names. The mapping model is shown in Table 1.

When the data packets have been labeled, they are analyzed to discriminate between intentionally and unintentionally posed signs. This analysis is conducted by evaluating the strength of the sensor signals throughout pulses, which last for two seconds. These pulses have two main phases. We call the first of these phases (which lasts for one second) a "registration phase." In this phase, signals from all the sensors are registered by the software. The second phase (which also lasts for one second) is referred to as a "constant phase." In this phase the signals from the sensors can only fluctuate 30 units above or below the signals detected in the first phase, for input to be recognized as being part of an intentionally posed sign. If sensor signals that have been detected throughout the "constant phase" are stable enough to satisfy this criterion, then they are grouped into an intentionally posed sign and processed further. If some sensor signals fail to satisfy this criterion, then all the detected signals are discarded at the end of the pulse. This process is illustrated in Figure 4. The thick lines illustrate the "registration phases," the thin lines with an X illustrate the "constant phases," and the black dots illustrate the end of each pulse, which is when signals can be grouped into intentionally posed signs. Time is illustrated in seconds along the horizontal axis.

When an intentionally posed sign is detected, it is compared to a library of prestored model signs. This is done to classify the sign, and to determine if it is correctly posed. An intentionally posed sign is regarded as being correctly posed, if it satisfies two criterions. To satisfy these criterions the sensor signals in the intentionally posed sign must

TABLE 1: Mapping model used to label data packets from the sensors.

Mapping model for labeling of data packets				
Channel	1	2	3	4	5
Right hand	Thumb tactile	Thumb flex	Index tactile	Index flex	Middle tactile
Channel	6	7	8	9	10
Right hand	Middle flex	Ring tactile	Ring flex	Little tactile	Little flex
Channel	11	12	13	14	15
Left hand	Thumb tactile	Thumb flex	Index tactile	Index flex	Middle tactile
Channel	16	17	18	19	20
Left hand	Middle flex	Ring tactile	Ring flex	Little tactile	Little flex

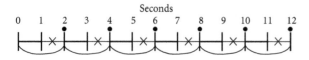

Seconds

— Registration phase
✕ Constant phase
• Is sign intentionally posed?

FIGURE 4: Process of discriminating between intentionally and unintentionally posed signs.

(i) be the *same* as the sensor signals in a model sign, when the signals are expected to be zero.

(ii) *deviate with less than* 30 units from the sensor signals in a model sign, when the signals are expected to be higher than zero. (We allow for these deviations to make the software robust towards slight variations in accents.)

The parameters were specified throughout an empirical trial and error process. Six different model handshapes have been generated. These model signs have been labeled (i) fist, (ii) thumb up, (iii) little finger up, (iv) pointer up, (v) ok, and (vi) cup. How these model handshapes are expressed is shown in Figure 5. The sensor signals that are associated with each of the model signs, and actual sensor signals that have been generated as two children posed these signs, are shown in Table 2.

Model signs and their associated sensor signals are displayed in rows with bold bounding boxes. The sensor signals that were generated when the children posed the signs are displayed in the cells below each model sign. The first of the two values in the cells with sensor signals generated by children, was detected in the "registration phase" of pulses. The second value was detected in the "constant phase." Gray cells contain sensor signals that have been successfully matched with corresponding signals in a model sign. Preliminary analysis shows that the technology has the potential to recognize aspects of intentionally posed signs. When one studies the table further, one also find that the flex and tactile sensors on the ring finger generated data that was most consistent with signals in model signs.

When one studies Table 2 one finds that sensor signals from one or both of the children were correctly matched with

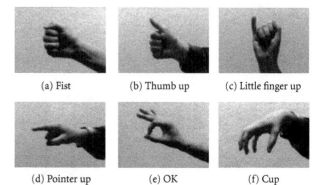

(a) Fist   (b) Thumb up   (c) Little finger up

(d) Pointer up   (e) OK   (f) Cup

FIGURE 5: How the six model signs incorporated into the software should be posed.

a corresponding signal in a model sign in 36 of 60 possible instances. In 15 of these instances, the signals from both children were correctly matched.

We will describe provide a more thorough analysis of the data presented in Table 2 in the following section.

4. Experiments on the Glove Technology

In this section we will describe two experiments, which have been conducted to investigate if the devised technology (i) has the potential to identify intentionally posed signs, (ii) is robust enough to correctly evaluate signs posed by more than one child. We will also explain how the data in Table 2 was collected and used in these experiments. In the end of this section we will describe the results from the two experiments.

4.1. Experiment Design. To properly test the devised technology, we asked three different children one 7-year-old and two 5-year-olds to pose the six-model signs illustrated in Figure 5. This would have enabled us to explore how children at different ages interact with the technology, and how the technology responds to similar and different hand shapes and hand sizes.

However, before we go on to describe the results we have to point out that one of the three participants (one of the children aged 5 years) did not want to interact with the technology in any way. When conducting ethical experiments it is important to give participants the right to refuse to

TABLE 2: Expected and actual input values from sensors in the sensor glove.

| | Model signs and results | | | | | | | | | |
	Thumb tactile	Thumb flex	Index tactile	Index flex	Middle tactile	Middle flex	Ring tactile	Ring flex	Little tactile	Little flex
Fist	*50*	*50*	*30*	*60*	*30*	*60*	*30*	*60*	*30*	*60*
Child 1	34/35	0/0	0/0	0/0	0/0	34/31	31/31	46/60	52/33	0/50
Child 2	35/34	80/77	73/39	0/0	0/0	0/0	0/0	45/48	0/0	79/71
Thumb up	*0*	*20*	*30*	*60*	*30*	*60*	*30*	*60*	*30*	*60*
Child 1	0/0	0/0	33/33	0/0	0/0	0/0	31/31	38/38	0/0	0/0
Child 2	31/31	48/43	73/46	0/0	0/0	0/0	0/0	56/56	0/0	0/0
Little finger up	*50*	*50*	*30*	*60*	*30*	*60*	*30*	*60*	*0*	*20*
Child 1	49/55	0/31	0/0	0/0	31/31	0/0	31/31	105/90	61/42	0/0
Child 2	0/0	0/0	0/0	0/0	0/0	0/0	0/0	65/67	0/0	0/0
Pointer up	*50*	*50*	*0*	*0*	*30*	*60*	*30*	*60*	*30*	*60*
Child 1	37/35	33/33	0/0	0/0	0/0	0/0	0/0	90/35	0/0	0/0
Child 2	0/0	0/0	34/34	0/0	0/0	0/0	0/0	53/75	0/0	0/0
OK	*60*	*30*	*60*	*60*	*0*	*20*	*0*	*20*	*0*	*20*
Child 1	54/50	0/0	88/78	34/33	0/0	0/0	0/0	0/0	0/0	0/0
Child 2	0/0	0/0	36/47	0/37	0/0	0/0	0/0	55/38	0/0	0/0
Cup	*0*	*60*	*0*	*60*	*0*	*60*	*0*	*60*	*0*	*60*
Child 1	0/41	36/100	0/0	0/0	0/0	0/0	0/0	0/0	0/0	0/0
Child 2	0/0	0/0	0/0	36/31	0/0	0/0	0/0	70/76	34/34	0/0

participate at any stage during the experiment as exercised by one child [17]. We were therefore only able to obtain data from two participants (child 1 was 7 years old and child 2 was 5 years old), and only two datasets will therefore be analyzed for each experiment.

At the start of the first experiment we asked the children to put a sensor glove onto the right hand. We then asked them to pose the signs in Figure 5 in a sequential manner, and to hold each sign for a minimum of two seconds, so that we could obtain the data signals detected by the computer at the start and the end of a pulse. The signal information from the start and the end of the pulses were then stored and analyzed. The aim of this analysis was to investigate if the signals are similar enough to detect intentionally posed signs with the pulse concept described in Section 2.2. We regard it as possible to identify if a sign is intentionally posed and if the summed signal values (from sensors on all fingers) captured at the start and the end of a pulse deviates with less than 600 units. We used 600 units as an upper limit because (i) the software has been programmed to regard signs as being intentionally posed, if the signals detected from each sensor at the end of a pulse are less than 30 units smaller or greater than the signal detected at the start of the pulse (these specifications equates to an allowed deviation of 60 units per sensor, and a summed deviation of 600 units for a hand), and (ii) we want to test if these parameters enable us to identify intentionally posed signs.

In the second experiment, we compared the signals captured from different children as they intentionally posed the six hand shapes in Figure 5. This was done to investigate if signals in signs intentionally posed by different children are similar enough to be correctly evaluated with the devised technology. We regard it as possible to correctly evaluate signals in signs posed by different children, if the signals

(i) deviate with less than 30 units below or above the model values, when the model values are greater than zero.

(ii) are not different when the model values are zero.

We use these boundaries because a study of the model signs show that it is possible to discriminate between the six model handshapes in Figure 5, when these constraints are employed. Results from the experiments are presented in the following section.

4.2. Analysis and Results from the Experiment. Results from the experiments described in the last section are presented below. We start off by describing the data that was generated throughout the experiment that investigated if it is possible to identify intentionally posed signs.

4.2.1. Consistency at Start and End of Pulses. To investigate if it is possible to identify intentionally posed signs by using the pulse concept described in Section 2.2, We compared the data signals captured at the start and end of pulses which the children posed the six handhapes presented in Figure 5. The data that was generated is shown in Figures 6 and 7. One can observe that the difference between the summed signal values captured at the start and the end of the pulses are far less than 600 units in all cases. In addition, the difference is less than

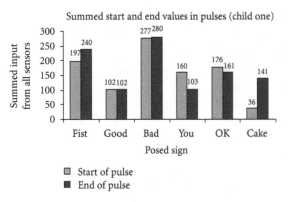

FIGURE 6: Summed signal values registered at the start and the end of pulses as each of the six signs were posed by participant 1.

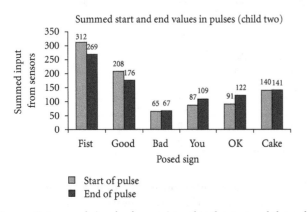

FIGURE 7: Summed signal values registered at the start and the end of pulses as each of the six signs were posed by participant 2.

50 units in four of the six cases, while the greatest difference is 105 units (when the cake sign is posed). The mean difference is 37.16 units. The difference between the signals detected by the computer at the start and the end of pulses as participant two posed the six signs is shown in Figure 7. One can observe that the summed deviations are less than 600 units in all situations also in this case. One can further observe that the maximum deviation is 43 units. The mean deviation is 21.83.

4.2.2. Consistency Across Participants. To investigate if the devised technology is robust enough to correctly evaluate signs from more than one child, we compared the signals registered as the children posed the six hand shapes shown in Figure 5. This allowed us to determine if signals in signs intentionally posed by different children are similar enough to be correctly evaluated with the defined constraints. The number of signal pairs that did, and did not, satisfy the defined constraints when the allowed deviation from a model sign was zero is shown in Figure 8. One can observe that seven of 12 signal pairs satisfied the constraints. One can also observe that five of 12 signal pairs were too different to be able to evaluate both signals correctly, when the current system specifications are used.

The number of signal pairs that did, and did not, satisfy the constraints when the allowed deviation from a model

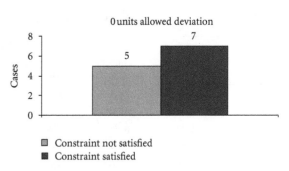

FIGURE 8: Outcome when the allowed deviation from a model sign was zero units.

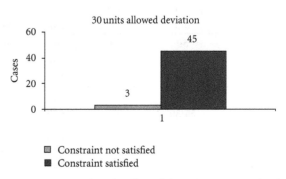

FIGURE 9: Outcome when the allowed deviation was 30 units above or below a model sign.

sign was 30 units below or above the specifications of the model sign is shown in Figure 9. One can observe that 45 of 48 signal pairs satisfied the constraints, and that 3 of 48 signal pairs did not satisfy the constraints in this case.

Results from this experiment show that a total of 52 of the 60 signal pairs, were similar enough to be correctly evaluated. We therefore regard it as being possible to correctly evaluate signals in signs posed by different children. However, the results also show that eight of the 60 signal pairs were so different that it is impossible to correctly evaluate at least one of the signals in the pair by using the current system specifications.

An analysis of why the differences between these eight signal pairs are so great, indicates that the differences arise because the children were unable to wear the gloves in the exact same way. The children had considerable difficulty in putting the glove on the individual fingers and pulling it up to the correct position. The other reason for the differences is that the children were of different age, and therefore had quite different hand sizes. This turned out to be a problem because the sensors ended up being distributed differently onto the hands of the different children.

5. Conclusions

This paper has described how to construct a set of sensor gloves, which could potentially be used as a component in a system that can provide feedback to children learning Auslan sign language from a computer. Experiments showed that the devised technology can (i) identify intentionally posed signs, and (ii) correctly evaluate signals in signs posed by different children. It is therefore worth pursuing this research further and extending the research to address other aspects of sign language including movement, hand orientation, and the location of where the sign is made relative to the body. Furthermore, work should be conducted before the technology can be used to teach children Auslan sign language in an accurate and efficient way. Some of the issues that should be addressed include (i) how to redesign the gloves to reduce the discrepancy between signals registered from different children, and (ii) how to devise a function, which provides intuitive feedback that can be used to guide children in the process of reducing the discrepancy between posed signs and model signs. A learning system could only be developed if the feedback that was given was timely and accurate for a wide range of learners.

References

[1] G. R. Karlan, "Manual communication with those who can hear," in *Manual Communication: Implications for Education*, H. Bornstein, Ed., pp. 151–185, Gallaudet University Press, Washington, DC, USA, 1990.

[2] K. Ellis and K. Blashki, "Children, Australian sign language and the web; the possibilities," pp. 281-287.

[3] K. Ellis and K. Blashki, "The digital playground: kindergarten children learning sign language via multimedia," *AACE Journal*, vol. 15, no. 3, pp. 225–253, 2007.

[4] gizmag, "The acceleglove—capturing hand gestures in virtual reality," September 2003, http://www.gizmag.com/go/2134/.

[5] J. L. Hernandez-Rebollar, N. Kyriakopoulos, and R. W. Lindeman, "A new instrumented approach for translating American sign language into sound and text," in *Proceedings of the 6th IEEE International Conference on Automatic Face and Gesture Recognition*, pp. 547–552, May 2004.

[6] G. Grimes, *Digital Data Entry Glove Interface Device*, AT & T Bell Labs, 1983.

[7] S. Sidney and E. Geoffrey, "Glove talk—a neural-network interface between a data-glove and a speech synthesizer," *IEEE Transactions on Neural Networks*, vol. 4, no. 1, pp. 2–8, 1993.

[8] J. Kramer and L. Leifer, "The talking glove: an expressive and receptive "verbal" communication aid for the deaf, deaf-blind, and Nonvocal," in *Proceedings of the Computer Technology, Special Education, and Rehabilitation Conference*, pp. 335–340, 1987.

[9] J. Hernandez, N. Kyriakopoulos, and W. Lindeman, *The AcceleGlove: A Whole-Hand Input Device for Virtual Reality*, ACM Press, 2002.

[10] D. Sturman and D. Zelter, "A survey of glove-based input," *IEEE Computer Graphics and Applications*, vol. 14, no. 1, pp. 30–39, 1994.

[11] M. Mohandes and S. Buraiky, "Automation of the Arabic sign language recognition using the powerglove," *AIML Journal*, vol. 7, no. 1, pp. 41–46, 2007.

[12] vrlogic, "CyberGlove," March, 2009, http://www.vrlogic.com/html/immersion/cyberglove.html.

[13] R. M. McGuire, J. Hernandez-Rebollar, T. Starner, V. Henderson, H. Brashear, and D. S. Ross, "Towards a one-way American sign language translator," in *Proceedingsof the 6th IEEE International Conference on Automatic Face and Gesture Recognition (FGR '04)*, pp. 620–625, May 2004.

[14] J. L. Hernandez-Rebollar and E. Mendez, "Interactive American sign language dictionary," in *Proceedings of the ACM SIGGRAPH International Conference on Computer Graphics and Interactive Techniques*, p. 26, Los Angeles, Calif, USA, August 2004.

[15] S. Simon and K. Johnson, "Improving the efficacy of motion analysis as a clinical tool through artificial intelligence techniques," in *Pediatric Gait: A New Millenium in Clinical Care and Motion Analysis Technology*, pp. 23–29, 2000.

[16] Infusion Systems, "Infusion systems," June, 2012, http://www.Infusionsystems.com.

[17] K. Ellis, M. Quigley, and M. Power, "Experiences in ethical usability testing with children," *Journal of Information Technology Research*, vol. 1, no. 3, pp. 1–13, 2007.

6

Text Entry by Gazing and Smiling

Outi Tuisku,[1] **Veikko Surakka,**[1] **Ville Rantanen,**[2] **Toni Vanhala,**[1,3] **and Jukka Lekkala**[2]

[1] *Research Group for Emotions, Sociality, and Computing, Tampere Unit for Computer-Human Interaction (TAUCHI), School of Information Sciences, University of Tampere, Kanslerinrinne 1, 33014 Tampere, Finland*

[2] *Sensor Technology and Biomeasurements, Department of Automation Science and Engineering, Tampere University of Technology, P.O. Box 692, 33101 Tampere, Finland*

[3] *ICT for Health, VTT Technical Research Centre of Finland, Tekniikankatu 1, P.O. Box 1300, 33101 Tampere, Finland*

Correspondence should be addressed to Outi Tuisku; outi.tuisku@sis.uta.fi

Academic Editor: Kerstin S. Eklundh

Face Interface is a wearable prototype that combines the use of voluntary gaze direction and facial activations, for pointing and selecting objects on a computer screen, respectively. The aim was to investigate the functionality of the prototype for entering text. First, three on-screen keyboard layout designs were developed and tested (n = 10) to find a layout that would be more suitable for text entry with the prototype than traditional QWERTY layout. The task was to enter one word ten times with each of the layouts by pointing letters with gaze and select them by smiling. Subjective ratings showed that a layout with large keys on the edge and small keys near the center of the keyboard was rated as the most enjoyable, clearest, and most functional. Second, using this layout, the aim of the second experiment (n = 12) was to compare entering text with Face Interface to entering text with mouse. The results showed that text entry rate for Face Interface was 20 characters per minute (cpm) and 27 cpm for the mouse. For Face Interface, keystrokes per character (KSPC) value was 1.1 and minimum string distance (MSD) error rate was 0.12. These values compare especially well with other similar techniques.

1. Introduction

Recently, there have been several attempts to develop alternative human-computer interaction (HCI) methods that utilize eye tracking in combination with another human behavior related measurement. One line of investigation has been to measure signals that originate from human facial expression systems [1–4]. One reason for using facial muscle behavior in HCI has been the fact that the human facial system is versatile when used for communication purposes and whose functionality could serve as a potential solution in HCI systems as well [3]. Pointing and selecting as well as text entry are the most common tasks in HCI, and thus being able to carry them out with acceptable performance can be considered important in order to consider an HCI solution fit for use.

The potential of the human facial system has been already utilized in the context of eye tracking research. For example, eye blinks have been used for selecting objects when gaze direction has been used for pointing [5, 6]. The choice of using use eye blinks results from the fact that video-based eye trackers that image the eyes are able to recognize whether the eyes are opened or closed [5, 7]. The relation to the facial muscle system comes from the fact that eye blinks result from the activation of *orbicularis oculi* facial muscle [8]. While video-based eye trackers track the eyes, computer vision methods can be used to track the eyelids directly [9]. Eye blinks which are used for selection purposes could be mistaken for unintentional eye closure, which in turn can cause unwarranted selection incidents.

The use of facial actions other than blinking can offer more functional solutions in combination with gaze pointing. Other facial muscles that can be used in HCI are, for example, *corrugator supercilii* (i.e., activated when frowning) or *zygomaticus major* (i.e., activated when smiling). In 2004, a real time HCI method was introduced where voluntary gaze direction was used for pointing and voluntarily produced facial muscle activations were used for object selection [3].

Remote eye tracker was used to record the gaze direction and facial electromyography (EMG) was used to measure frowning related facial muscle activations. An overall mean pointing and selection task time of 0.7 seconds was reporter using a relatively simple experimental setup [10]. In comparison to the computer mouse, the results showed that as measured with pointing task times, use of the mouse proved significantly faster than the new technique in the shortest pointing distance. However, with medium and long distances, there were no statistically significant differences between the mouse and the new technique. In a follow-up study, the technique was extended so that two EMG channels (i.e., frowning and smiling related electrical activity) could be used with gaze direction and to then determine which of the two would function better as a selection technique [4]. Findings revealed that smiling functioned faster than frowning; overall mean pointing task times were 0.5 seconds and 0.8 seconds for smiling and frowning, respectively.

San Agustin et al. [2] compared the use of two pointing techniques and two selection techniques. These were the mouse and the gaze for pointing and the mouse click and voluntarily produced changes in facial EMG (i.e., frowning or jaw clenching) for selecting objects. They tested all the four possible pointing and selection combinations with simple tasks. Results showed that the overall mean task time was 0.4 seconds. Gaze combined with facial EMG was the fastest one of the pointing and selection combinations with the task time of approximately 0.35 seconds. Chin et al. [1] used facial EMG for correcting the inaccuracy of the eye tracker as well as for selecting objects. If the cursor was not inside the object when the user gazed at the object, facial muscle activations were used to move the cursor on the object. For example, left and right jaws clench resulted in the cursor to move left and right, respectively. Finally, user selected the target by clenching the whole jaw. This technique resulted in a mean task time of 4.7 seconds. These findings show that combination of gaze direction and facial activity measurement can function very well and effectively for pointing and selecting in HCI. This depends, of course, on the test setup and activations required for facial behavior.

Recently, further studies in developing the technique that combines the use of voluntary gaze direction and facial muscle activations have resulted in a prototype called Face Interface. It is a wearable device that is built in the frames of protective glasses and it consists of both a video-based eye tracker and capacitive sensors for measuring facial activity [11–14]. Capacitive sensors measure the movement of facial tissue instead of the electrical activity of the muscles that the EMG measures. Capacitive measurement has the advantage that it requires no contact with the facial skin, and thus, no preparation of the skin is needed. In addition, it makes a significant difference in respect to the wearability of the prototype. The aim is that the user just wears the prototype and starts to interact with computer.

In the first version of Face Interface, a wired commercial USB web camera was used for imaging the eye. There was no compensation for head movements, and thus, a chin rest was used for preventing involuntary head movements [13]. In the second version, a scene camera was added to help in compensating head movements so that it was used to image the display that was used as a reference for the head-movement compensation. The prototype was also made wireless [12, 14]. In earlier experiments, the functionality of the prototype has been tested using simple Fitts' law style pointing and selecting tasks, so that the task was first to select a home square and then to select a target circle using different pointing distances, pointing angles, and sizes of the targets [10, 15, 16]. In the first experiment, the participants used frowning as the selection technique. It was found that the Face Interface prototype was functional in pointing and selecting tasks. The overall mean pointing task time of 2.5 seconds was reported [13]. In the second experiment participants used either lowering (i.e., frowning) or raising the eyebrows as the selection technique. The results showed an overall mean pointing task time of 2.4 seconds by means of frowning and 1.6 seconds by means of raising the eyebrows. Further, an important finding was that the objects were difficult to point and select on the left and right edges of the display which suggested a design guideline that objects should be larger on the edges of the display than in the middle of the display to make them easier to select [14]. Both of the above studies revealed that the larger targets were easier to select than smaller targets which is similar to other gaze-based or manual pointing studies [17].

All the above new studies have been done with controlled setups that allow calculation of performance metrics using Fitts' law analyses [2–4, 13, 14]. However, little by little testing new interaction techniques need to be extended to more applied (i.e., closer to "real world") tasks. Text entry is such a task that has been widely studied with systems that use only gaze input [18]. In this case, pointing is done by gazing and selection by various dwell time algorithms. Evidently, text entry studies fits well to the research of the Face Interface prototype because it has the same functions (i.e., pointing and clicking). A more direct route to apply these functions for text entry is to use an on-screen keyboard.

Most of the on-screen text entry studies with gaze-based methods have used a traditional QWERTY layout. That is mainly because QWERTY has the advantage that it is familiar for most users [19]. Based on previous research with Face Interface, however, it is clear that a QWERTY layout keyboard with equally sized buttons would not be optimally functional [14]. This is due to the fact that accuracy of eye tracking varies depending on gaze direction, and gazing with the eye closer to the extremities of its rotational range makes the tracking less accurate. This is because the eye tracking camera is often placed in front of the eye and gaze is more precisely tracked based on features on the eye (e.g., pupil) when the gaze is straight towards the camera and the features thus cover more of the image. Also, near the extremities of eye's rotational range the eyelid may occlude part of the pupil making eye tracking less accurate than when the pupil is fully visible [12]. As stated, earlier results showed that pointing was more accurate in the middle of the computer display than at the edges of the screen. This made the target selection at the edges of the screen difficult if the targets were same sized all over the display. In the case of QWERTY on-screen keyboard arrangement, for example, some frequently used letters are situated on the edges of the keyboard (e.g., letter "a" is situated in the left side of the layout) which makes them difficult to point and select [20]. Thus, different types of keyboard layouts are needed to create a better functionality for the Face Interface prototype. An encouraging first result that writing speed could be faster with different keyboard arrangement comes, for example, in a study by Špakov and Majaranta [21]. They designed an optimized keyboard arrangement for on-screen keyboard. Most frequently used letters were placed in the topmost row of the keyboard in order to make them easy and fast to select. Their results showed that the mean writing speeds were 11.1 wpm for QWERTY and 12.18 wpm for the optimized letter placement. Similar results have also been found in different text entry studies [22, 23]. In addition to Face Interface, there are also other wearable eye trackers where an eye camera has been placed in front of the user's eye and they could benefit from new kind of on-screen keyboard layout as well [24, 25]. Also high-end remote eye trackers could benefit from a new kind of layout for an on-screen keyboard [20].

In most eye typing studies, the layout design (e.g., key size and placement) of the keyboard has not been explicitly considered. GazeTalk is one exception [26–28]. The GazeTalk consisted of 11 cells, including a text field and 10 buttons. The size of the buttons was approximately 8 cm × 8 cm and the size of the text field was 8 cm × 16 cm. In the ten buttons, six letters were visible at a time, as well as space, backspace, possibility to select letters from alphabet listing, and eight most likely words. The six visible letters changed after every typed character based on a predictive algorithm, so that if user had typed, for example, "ca", the visible letters that would be predicted as the most probable letters are, for example, t, r, n, u, l, and b. The eight most probable words dynamically changed during typing, similarly as did the six letters. If the visible letters were not what a user wished to type, the next character had to be selected from the alphabet listing. The buttons were selected using a dwell time algorithm. In a longitudinal study with the GazeTalk, the maximum text entry speed for Danish and Japanese text, after thousand typed sentences, was approximately 9.4 words per minute (wpm) and 29.9 cpm, respectively.

Dasher is one alternative for text entry that uses only one modality (e.g., mouse or gaze) [29]. It is a zooming interface which user operates with continuous pointing gestures. At first, the letters are placed in the alphabetical order in a column in the right-hand side of the screen. User should then move the cursor to the place where the desired letter is, for example, by looking at the letter. The area where the desired letter starts to grow and most probable next letters will come closer to the current cursor position. Letter is selected when it crosses a horizontal line in the center of the screen. User should navigate through the letters simply by looking at them. At first glance, the letters may seem to be unorganized because the sizing of the letters is different based on the probability of the next character so that the more probable the next character the larger its size is. This is the problem that may arise when using Dasher for the first time and some people may not understand the logic of Dasher even with long practice. After two and half hours of practice with Dasher, users were able to write text at an approximate rate of 17 wpm. After the first 15-minute session, the average writing speed was approximately 2.5 wpm [30].

As stated above, the keyboard layouts have not been explicitly studied. In most cases, the layout was just pre-designed and then an experiment was run to test the typing speed that could be achieved with it. It is possible that keyboard layout design can be an important factor especially with new alternative interaction techniques. It should be noted that the subjective experiences of the keyboard layout could be a more important factor than the writing speed when deciding which keyboard layout to use because the user might not realize while writing which layout is faster in terms of writing speed. Thus, it is important to compare the possible layouts with each other in one fair method where the places of the letters would not interfere with the evaluation of the layout. It has been common to compare new pointing devices to computer mouse [2, 3]. However, users have a very long experience with mouse pointing, and this makes the comparison of new techniques to mouse somewhat unfair because it is the case that the mouse is very likely to be better than any new techniques. Further, usually it has been the case that the words to be written have been randomized while the letter placement of the keyboard has stayed static [31, 32]. This type of randomization is to certify partly the quality of experimental arrangement and to rule out possible biases resulting from, for example, the use of same order of the words to be written. This does not, however, change the fact when people have used some interaction technique like mouse for over some years the comparison with a new interaction technique will always result in favor of the older technique. When comparing new interaction techniques to traditional ones, the use of randomization could be considered to balance out the advantage the use of traditional pointing device in most cases has. So, randomizing the places of the letters in the keyboard could result in a more fair comparison between a new technique and a traditional one. The randomization can help in balancing out the huge advantage the mouse has over new interaction techniques. Further, randomization can be also a suitable method when comparing different input devices with each other because the places of letters that are learned with one pointing device do not provide advantage to the next condition where another device is used. In terms of text entry rate, it was shown already in the 1980s that random placing of letters do not have an effect on the writing speed, if the random letter arrangement is compared to alphabetically arranged letters [33].

When testing new techniques, objective measures of functionality are imperative. However, it is equally important to measure how the participants rate (i.e., experience) the functionality of these new techniques. There are several possibilities to measure subjective ratings of the techniques. One possibility is to use the semantic differential method which is a combination of associational and scaling procedures [34, 35]. With this method participants can rate their experiences using a set of bipolar scales that can vary, for example, from bad to good or from boring to fun. Ratings along these scales can be done by self-assessment manikin (SAM) or a modification of it. In HCI studies, these types of scales have been frequently used to analyze experiences about new interaction techniques [3, 4, 13, 14].

Using bipolar rating scales, Surakka et al. [3] reported that the use of their technique was rated as faster than the use of the mouse. On the other hand, mouse was rated as easier and more accurate to use. San Agustin et al. [2] reported similar findings as their participants rated the combined technique as faster but less accurate to use than the mouse pointing. Recently, the participants rated the usage of the Face Interface prototype as enjoyable, easy, fast, efficient, and accurate [12]. When comparing the use of different facial activations as the selection technique with bipolar rating scales, the studies have found no difference in ratings between frowning and smiling [4], and frowning and raising eyebrows [14]. In order to deepen the systematically collected ratings, also interviews can be done to get additional information [36].

To summarize, so far the research on Face Interface has been concentrated on simple pointing and selection tasks to test the functionality of the prototype. The natural continuation would then be to extend the task with Face Interface to on-screen text entry. The previous research with Face Interface showed that there are some parts on the widescreen display that were difficult to point and select [14]. To remediate this, three different keyboard layouts were designed and tested. They were all designed so that the sizes of the keys were larger in the edges of the keyboard than in the middle of the keyboard. Another feature that was used was the randomization of letters each time a word was entered to balance out the advantage mouse interaction has over all new interaction methods.

Two experiments were run to investigate the keyboard layout and to compare writing with Face Interface to writing with the mouse. The aim in the first experiment (i.e., layout selection experiment) was to compare three different on-screen keyboard layouts, so that it would be equally easy to select any character from the keyboard. The three designed layouts were then pilot tested with ten participants to see which of the layouts would be most promising to be used in the future. After the experiment, participants rated the used keyboard layouts and a short interview was conducted. In the second experiment (i.e., text entry experiment) the aim was to compare entering text with Face Interface to entering text with computer mouse. The on-screen keyboard layout that was selected as the most prominent to be used with Face Interface in the first experiment and was used in the second experiment. In both of the experiments, the task of the participants was to enter one word at a time, and after the experiment participants rated their experiences on six bipolar scales and were shortly interviewed.

2. Face Interface

Face Interface is an eye-glass like wireless wearable device that combines the use of wearable video-based eye tracker and a capacitive sensor to detect the movement of facial skin resulting from the activation of facial muscles. The third generation Face Interface device is shown in Figure 1.

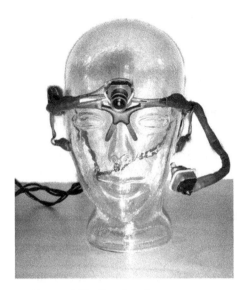

FIGURE 1: The Face Interface prototype.

The prototype device was built on the frames of protective glasses. The head-worn device includes two cameras, one for imaging the eye and the other for imaging the computer screen, an infrared (IR) light emitting diode for illuminating the eye and to provide the corneal reflection, sensors and electronics for detecting facial movements using a capacitive method, and a Class 2 Bluetooth radio (RN-42 by Roving Networks) for serial transmission of the measured capacitance signal. The used cameras were low-cost, commercial complementary metal oxide semiconductor (CMOS) cameras. The eye camera was a greyscale camera with a resolution of 352×288 pixels that was modified to image IR wavelengths, and the scene camera was a color camera with a resolution of 597×537 pixels. The frame rate for both of the cameras was 25 frames per second. The eye camera is placed near the user's left eye and the IR light source was placed right next to it. The scene camera was placed in front of the user's forehead [12, 14]. The facial movement sensors are based on capacitance measurement with a programmable controller for capacitance touch sensors (AD7147 by Analog Devices). The capacitive sensors in the frames were placed in front of both eyebrows and cheeks, and one was placed in front of the forehead.

In addition to the head-worn device, a separate carry-on unit to house some components responsible for the wireless operation was included. The unit included a power supply, four AA batteries, and two wireless analogue video transmitters that used the common free frequencies at 2.4 GHz. The PC computer was connected to a receiving station consisting of two video receivers with a power supply, and two frame grabbers for the video signals. The capacitive signal was received with computer's Bluetooth functionality.

Computer vision library OpenCV version 2.1 [37] was utilized to extract features from the image streams of both eye and scene cameras. Pupil detection was based on the corneal reflection method. The algorithm that was used for pupil detection and corneal reflection detection was the same that Rantanen et al. [12] introduced. Calibration of the eye tracker was done in a similar manner as in the OpenEyes project [38]. Head movements in relation to the computer screen were compensated using a computer vision algorithm. The screen detection algorithm aimed to find the frames of a dark rimmed computer display from the scene camera image and, thus, no separate markers (e.g., colored dots on the borders to be detected) were needed. The algorithm was based on three observations. First, there were one or two highly contrasted edges that separated the display surface from the surrounding background. The screen is typically brightly illuminated and thus lighter than the surroundings. Further, many monitors have a black frame that surrounds the display surface. Thus, there is a sharp contrast between the illumination of the display surface and the surrounding space (e.g., monitor frame or background), and there may also be another edge with high contrast between the dark monitor edge and the background. Second, both the display surface and the monitor frame are typically rectangular, which means that they have four straight corners. Third, the corners of the outer border of the monitor frame are relatively close to the corners of the display surface. These three features were used to rank potential screen candidates to select a best one [39]. For example, a candidate with a dark rimmed border was preferred to one without.

Previously, with Face Interface, only frowning and raising the eyebrows have been used as the selection technique [12–14]. Earlier by using facial EMG, Surakka et al. [4] had compared the use of frowning and smiling as the selection technique and found out that the smiling was a faster selection technique than frowning when voluntary gaze direction was used as the pointing technique. Further, Rantanen et al. [39] found that smiling as the selection technique does not interfere with the accuracy of the eye tracker. On the basis of these findings, Face Interface was updated so that smiling activity can be tracked with capacitive sensors.

3. Layout Selection Experiment

3.1. Methods

3.1.1. Participants. Ten (7 male, 3 female) able-bodied volunteers participated in the experiment. Their mean age was 29.5 years (range 21–44 years). All of them had normal or corrected-to-normal (i.e., with contact lenses) vision. All were native Finnish speakers. To avoid any bias, participants had no knowledge of the design of the layouts.

3.1.2. Apparatus. The Face Interface prototype was used as the pointing and selection device. A $24''$ widescreen display was used and the viewing distance was approximately 60 cm. A computer with Windows XP operating system was used to run the experiment. The software for online processing of the data from the prototype was implemented with Microsoft Visual C++ 2008 [12]. The software translated the obtained information to cursor movements and selections on the computer screen.

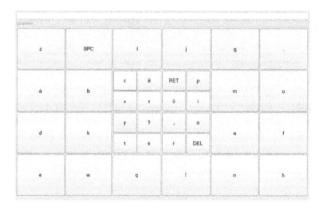

FIGURE 2: Layout 1.

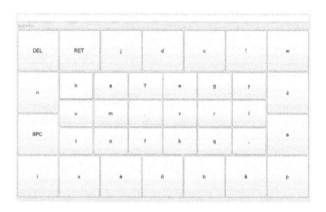

FIGURE 3: Layout 2.

Three different keyboard layouts were designed (see Figures 2–4). Each of them consisted of 36 keys, although, the keys were laid out differently. In every keyboard RET, key represented the Enter key, SPC key represented the space key, and DEL key represents the delete key. In Layout 1 (see Figure 2), the keys in the middle of the screen were made smaller because earlier research has shown that it is easier to select smaller keys in the middle of the screen than on the edges of the screen. In Layout 2 (see Figure 3), keys only on the edges of the keyboard were made larger and smaller keys were used the middle of the keyboard. Finally, in Layout 3 (see Figure 4), the sizes of the keys were gradually increasing from the middle of the keyboard to the edges of the keyboard. Keyboards were implemented in .NET environment using Visual Basic 2008 programming language.

The keyboard layouts (i.e., button placement) were kept static but the places of the letters were randomized every time the participant had entered the requested word and pressed the Enter key. This approach was chosen in order to prevent the possible learning effects of the keyboard layout. Keys were highlighted when the participant's gaze was inside a key. When participant had pressed the key, a "click" sound was played to indicate the selection. Cursor was not visible. The characters that the user typed appeared in the white text box at the top of the keyboard. The grey text box under it showed the word to be written.

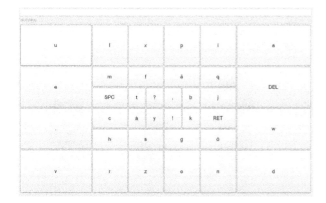

FIGURE 4: Layout 3.

3.1.3. Experimental Task. The task was to write one word (as in other studies [31, 40]) "aurinko" (i.e., sun in English) ten times with each of the three keyboard layouts. The word "aurinko" was chosen from the list of 1000 most common Finnish words and it was chosen because of three reasons: (1) it was a quite long word compared to other common ones such as "ei" (no in English) or "silmä" (eye), (2) because it was a noun, and (3) because each of the characters appeared only once.

The users entered characters by looking at the desired character and smiled in order to select the character. When participants had entered the word "aurinko" once, she or he was instructed to press the Enter key (i.e., the key that had label "RET" on it). After the participant had hit the Enter key, the places of the letters were randomized, and participant was required to look the letters needed to write word "aurinko" again. This procedure was repeated until the participant had written the word ten times. After that, the keyboard disappeared. In total, one participant wrote the word "aurinko" 30 times in total, ten times with each of the keyboard layouts.

3.1.4. Procedure. When a participant arrived in the laboratory, the laboratory and the equipment were introduced to him or her. The participant was asked to sign an informed consent form. The participant was told that the purpose of the experiment was to evaluate three different layouts of on-screen keyboards using gaze direction as the pointing technique and smiling as the selection technique. Then, the prototype was introduced to the participant. The participant wore the prototype and saw live videos from the eye camera and from the scene camera. She or he was instructed to try different head orientations to see how large head movements were possible while still keeping the display visible in the scene camera image. Next, the participant was instructed to try and perform clicks by smiling. After a few successful clicks were produced, the eye tracker was calibrated.

Before conducting the experiment, there was a practice session consisting of 5 trials which were precluded from the actual experiment. In the practice session a keyboard with same equal sized keys was used and participants wrote the word "elokuva" (i.e., movie in English) five times. The participants were told to perform the tasks as fast and as accurate as possible. Then, there was a short relaxation period before the actual experiment. Then the eye tracker was calibrated and the actual experiment started. The order of the used keyboard layouts was counterbalanced. The eye tracker was re-calibrated during the experiment when needed (i.e., approximately 0.2 times per participant on average). After the participant had completed the task with one keyboard layout, she or he was allowed to rest for a while, if necessary.

At the end of the experiment, participant rated the keyboard layout that was used on three different scales: enjoyableness, clarity, and functionality. For the enjoyableness and clarity ratings, they saw the pictures of each of the keyboard layouts lined up in the computer screen in a randomized order. They were asked to select the layout that was most enjoyable and most clear out of the three layouts. If they could not decide, they were allowed to select the "I don't know" option. The order of enjoyableness and clarity ratings were counterbalanced. For the functionality ratings, participants were allowed to interact with each of the keyboards as long as they wished and they were allowed to write anything they liked. After trying out every layout, they were asked which of the three layouts were the most functional in their opinion. Short (semistructured) interview was conducted after participants had rated the layouts in the three specified scales. Completing the whole experiment took approximately an hour per participant.

3.1.5. Metrics. Text entry rate was measured in cpm. The measure of cpm was chosen instead of the often used wpm measure because only one word at a time was to be written. Similar approach was also chosen by Helmert et al. [31]. Error rates were measured in two different ways: the minimum string distance (MSD) error rate and keystrokes per character (KSPC). The MSD error rate was measured with the improved MSD error rates as suggested by Soukoreff and MacKenzie [41]. MSD error rate is calculated by comparing the transcribed text (i.e., the text that was written by the participant) with the presented text, using minimum string distance. The key strokes per character (KSPC) value indicates how often the participants cancelled characters [41]. In a best case scenario KSPC = 1.00, which indicates that each key press has produced a correct character. However, if a participant makes a correction during text entry (i.e., presses Delete key and chooses another letter), the value of KSPC is larger than one. Thus, KSPC measures the accuracy of the text input process. Note that MSD error rate only compares the transcribed text to the presented text, whereas KSPC takes into account the errors produced.

3.2. Results. Data for statistical analyses were extracted from the moment of entering the first character to the selection of Enter character at the end of the word.

3.2.1. Text Entry Rate. Text entry rate for each of the on-screen keyboard layouts is presented in Figure 5. The overall mean text entry rate ± standard error of the means (S.E.M.s.) for Layout 1 was 14.5 ± 1.7 cpm, 14.9 ± 1.4 cpm for Layout 2,

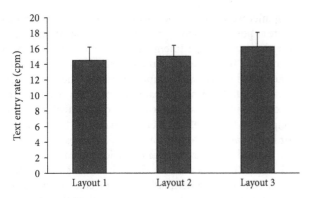

FIGURE 5: Text entry rate by cpm.

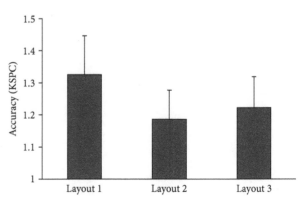

FIGURE 7: KSPC values.

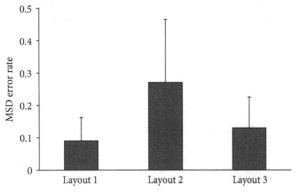

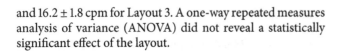

FIGURE 6: MSD error rate.

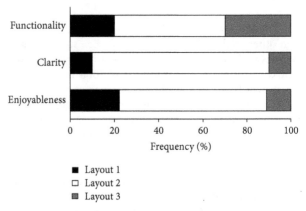

FIGURE 8: Subjective ratings.

and 16.2 ± 1.8 cpm for Layout 3. A one-way repeated measures analysis of variance (ANOVA) did not reveal a statistically significant effect of the layout.

3.2.2. Error Rates. MSD error rates by the layout and task number are presented in Figure 6. The overall mean for MSD error rate $\pm$ S.E.M was 0.09 ± 0.07 for Layout 1, 0.27 ± 0.19 for Layout 2, and 0.12 ± 0.09 for Layout 3. A one-way ANOVA did not reveal a statistically significant effect of the layout.

KSCP values by the layout and task number are presented in Figure 7. The overall mean for KSPC $\pm$ S.E.M. was 1.3 ± 0.12 for Layout 1, 1.18 ± 0.09 for Layout 2, and 1.22 ± 0.09 for Layout 3. A one-way ANOVA showed a statistically significant effect of the layout $F(2, 18) = 4.2$, $P < 0.05$. The post hoc pairwise comparisons were not statistically significant. Based on the results shown in Figure 7, it seemed, however, that the Layout 2 was the most promising in terms of effectiveness.

3.2.3. Subjective Ratings. The results of the ratings of the layouts can be seen in Figure 8. From the Figure 8, it is clear that the participants clearly preferred Layout 2. One participant considered the layouts equally enjoyable.

Overall, participants liked to use the Face Interface technique for text input. After the experiment they gave spontaneous comments such as "this was cool" or "that was fun." One participant commented that the technique feels natural to use and other participant commented that

the use of smiling for selections felt fun. One participant commented that entering text with the prototype felt very easy. Comments about each of the three keyboard layouts were mainly positive. About Layout 1, we got comments such as "it is easy to see many letters at the same time, because the keys are smaller in the middle [of the keyboard]." This was actually noted by two participants. Further, it was commented that Layout 1 is nicely geometrically shaped which makes it enjoyable, and clear. Of Layout 2, participants gave comments such as "the layout was nice to look at", as well as it was said to be "calm". It was also mentioned that it was easy to seek the letters from this layout. Further, one participant said that the equal sizing of the keys in the layout made entering the text enjoyable. Also, it was mentioned that the text entry felt to be the fastest with Layout 2. One participant commented that with Layout 2, it was easiest to find the letters because of the layout was so pleasant looking. One participant said that he preferred Layout 2 because it did not contain small keys, as the other layouts did. It was also noted that from this layout, it was easiest to select the keys (because of their size). Of Layout 3 comments such as "even though it is not really pretty to look at, nor does it seem to be very clear, it is still the most functional layout" were given. The participants motivated their answers by saying that the keys seemed to be just on the right place, and the sizing of the keys was really good. One participant mentioned that it was easy to find the letters from Layout 3 because it "directed" one's gaze naturally (i.e., because of the sort of a spiral-shaped layout).

Some negative comments were given as well. For example, Layout 1 was found to be "hideous" by one participant and "awful" by other participant. On Layout 3, it was mainly mentioned that it was "fuzzy" and it did not seem to have clear logic behind how the keys were placed. Layout 2 was actually the only layout that received only positive comments.

4. Text Entry Experiment

First experiment indicated that the Layout 2 would be the most promising one to be used with Face Interface. Thus, based on the results of Experiment 1, a second experiment was run with Layout 2.

4.1. Methods

4.1.1. Participants. Twelve (4 male and 8 female) able-bodied volunteers participated in the experiment. Their mean age was 24 years (range 18–37). All the participants had normal vision. They were native Finnish speakers and they were novices in using any gaze-based system for controlling computers and same for using Face Interface. However, they were pretty experienced users of computer mouse; that is, their average experience in using mouse was 14.5 years (range 9–20).

4.1.2. Apparatus. The same prototype device was used as in Experiment 1. The keyboard that was used, was Layout 2 selected from Experiment 1 study. Again, the places of letters changed during the experiment to prevent the possible advantage that mouse may have if the letter placement is known (e.g., QWERTY). The mouse that was used was an optical mouse (Logitech Mouse m100). Mouse speed was set to medium level.

4.1.3. Experimental Task. The experimental task was the same as in Experiment 1.

4.1.4. Procedure. When the participant arrived in the laboratory, the laboratory and the equipment were introduced to him/her. The participant signed an informed consent form before the experiment. The participant was told that the aim of the experiment was to compare typing with mouse to the typing with Face Interface prototype using on-screen keyboard. The order of the used pointing device was counterbalanced so that half of the participants started with Face Interface and the other half started with the mouse. Participants performed the experimental task ten times, then there were a short pause and they performed the experimental task again ten times. After participant had conducted the experimental task with one pointing device she or he rated the experience with six nine-point bipolar scales. The scales were general evaluation (i.e., from bad to good), difficulty (i.e., from difficult to easy), speed (i.e., from slow to fast), accuracy (i.e., from inaccurate to accurate), enjoyableness (i.e., from unpleasant to pleasant), and efficiency (i.e., from

inefficient to efficient). The scales varied from −4 (e.g., bad experience) to +4 (e.g., good experience), and 0 represented a neutral experience (e.g., not slow nor fast). Then the same procedure was repeated with the other pointing device. After participant had completed the task with both of the pointing devices, a short interview was completed. Conducting the whole experiment took approximately 60 minutes.

4.1.5. Metrics. Same metrics were used as in Experiment 1.

4.2. Results

4.2.1. Text Entry Rate. Text entry rate for both pointing devices by participant is presented in Figure 9. The overall mean text entry rate ± S.E.M.s for Face Interface was 19.4 ± 1.9 cpm and 27.1 ± 2.8 cpm for the mouse. A one-way ANOVA for the pointing device showed a statistically significant effect of the pointing device $F(1, 11) = 66.8$, $P < 0.001$. A one-way ANOVA for Face Interface showed a statistically significant effect of session $F(1, 11) = 4.9$, $P < 0.05$. For the mouse, the effect of session was not statistically significant.

Figure 10 shows minimum and maximum values for every participant by pointing device. The overall mean maximum values for Face Interface was 33.4 cpm and 48.3 cpm for mouse.

4.2.2. Error Rates. MSD error rate for both pointing devices by participant is presented in Figure 11. The overall mean MSD error rate ± S.E.M was 0.12 ± 0.09 for Face Interface and 0 ± 0 for mouse. A one-way ANOVA for the pointing device showed a statistically significant effect of pointing device $F(1, 11) = 18.6$, $P < 0.01$. One-way ANOVAs for the session were not statistically significant.

KSPC values for both pointing devices by participant are presented in Figure 12. The overall mean KSPC ± S.E.M was 1.1 ± 0.05 for Face Interface and 1.0 ± 0.002 for mouse. The one-way ANOVA showed a statistically significant effect of pointing device $F(1, 11) = 45.9$, $P < 0.001$. One-way ANOVAs for session were not statistically significant.

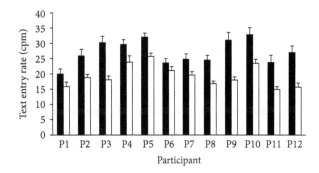

FIGURE 9: Text entry rate for both pointing devices divided by participant.

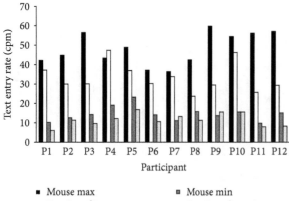

FIGURE 10: Maximum and minimum values for mouse and Face Interface.

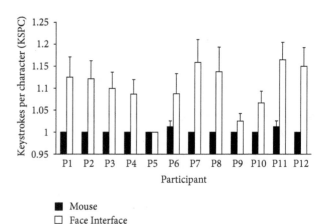

FIGURE 12: KSPC values by participant.

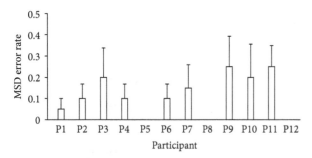

FIGURE 11: MSD error rate by participant.

TABLE 1: Mean ranks of ratings of both techniques.

	Face Interface	Mouse	Mann-whitney U	Significance
General evaluation	10.2	14.8	44.5	n.s.
Difficulty	8.6	16.4	25.0	$P < 0.01$
Speed	9.4	15.6	35.0	$P < 0.05$
Accuracy	7.8	17.2	15.5	$P < 0.01$
Efficiency	9.7	15.3	38.0	n.s.
Enjoyableness	10.3	14.8	43.5	n.s.

4.2.3. Subjective Ratings. Mann-Whitney U test was used for pairwise comparisons because it is commonly used for comparing two independent samples with each other. Mean ranks of subjective ratings are presented in Table 1.

After the experiment a short interview was conducted. First, participants were asked if they could see that the prototype would be used wider in future. All the participants answered yes to that question. They justified their answers by stating, for example, that the use of the prototype was quite easy and the prototype was interesting to use. Participants liked especially the fact that gaze was used for pointing because it was easy and even natural to use. They also

mentioned that the smiling felt natural as the selection technique but it required some time to get to use to it.

Participants were also asked that in what kind of task they would think that the Face Interface prototype could be used in the future. The answers varied between participants. However, some common points could also be found. Nine participants out of 12 answered that disabled people could use this prototype for communicating with other people. They saw the prototype as a promising concept for the disabled people who cannot move their hands. There were many other ideas as well. For example, Face Interface could be used as an alternative for remote control while watching television. Reasoning for using Face Interface as remote control could be that people are getting lazy, and thus, in future, even moving a remote-control with hand may require too much effort and thus, Face Interface could be a potential solution. It was also suggested that this kind of technique could be used in public when interacting with large interactive billboards or tourists could use it when interacting with a map in a strange city. The map could, for example, show sights that are near the place that user is looking and user could then select an attraction that she or he would like to know more. On a similar topic, a lecturer could use this to emphasis some specific point to students from the slides. Further, prototype could be used in a loud spaces, where talking would be impossible, for example, in a factory. Idea that Face Interface could be used while driving a car also came up. That is, there would be a transparent screen in the windshield and the driver could do something with it. One task that was mentioned that Face Interface could be used while playing video games or children could use it when playing.

On the other hand, there were fewer ideas about where Face Interface could not be used. Participants suggested that Face Interface could not be used in tasks that need really high accuracy or where the result is not shown. One such task that was mentioned was the use of PIN code in ATM's. Overall, participants found more tasks that were suitable for Face Interface and less that were not. Four of the participants did not come up with anything where Face Interface could not be used.

The last interview question was a word association task which was roughly based on the semantic differential method [34]. Task was to list words that came to their mind when using Face Interface. Participants listed many different kinds of words. To the glasses it was linked words such as *eye glasses, sun glasses, gaze,* and *eye pointer.* About the technique that words such as *fast to absorb, handy, new, useful, fun, advanced, science fiction, future, modern, interesting, futuristic, challenge,* and *21st century* were mentioned. Some negative words were mentioned as well, such as *requires focusing, difficult, and troublesome.* Again, more positive than negative comments were mentioned.

5. Discussion

The aim of the layout selection experiment was to find out which of the three designed keyboard layouts would be the most promising one to be used with Face Interface and in the actual typing experiment. Because the statistical analyses did not reveal significant differences in the text entry rate (cpm) and MSD error rate between the three different keyboard layouts, it suggests that text entry was neither significantly faster nor significantly erroneous with any of the keyboard layouts. In general, avoiding small keys near the edges of the screen seems to have successfully compensated for the previously found problems in selecting objects mainly at the corners of the display as well as at the left and right edges of the display [14]. With the current keyboard layout designs that problem was overcome. Subjective ratings showed that participants preferred the design of Layout 2. This preference was supported by the results of KSPC. Thus, both subjective and objective data led us to choose the Layout 2 for the subsequent typing experiment.

The text entry experiment showed that the overall mean text input speeds with Face Interface and mouse were 20 cpm and 27 cpm, respectively. The ANOVA revealed that entering text with the mouse was significantly faster than entering text with Face Interface. The slower text entry speed of Face Interface can be explained with the fact that participants did not have any previous experience with Face Interface; they only had a practice of approximately 5 minutes prior to the experiment. With mouse, however, they had experience over 15 years on average. Thus, from this point of view the found difference in text entry speed is relatively small. In addition to the radical differences in earlier experiences in using these two interaction methods there can be other explaining factors. For example, there is evidence that during eye typing users, especially novices, tend to gaze at the results of typing which can slow down the typing speed [26, 42]. Also the randomization might have had an effect for this, because when eyes are used as both: input and observation method, it might cause slowness for typing because participant cannot look for the next character before she/he has typed the current one. On the other hand, when using mouse (i.e., hand) as an input method, then eyes are free for searching the next character while cursor is still on the previous character.

Further, Figure 10 shows minimum and maximum values for mouse and Face Interface for text entry speed for every participant. One interesting finding for Face Interface was that one participant actually had a maximum text entry speed value of 47.4 cpm which was even higher than that participant's maximum speed with mouse, that is, 43.3 cpm. On the other hand, it can be seen from the Figure 10 that the slowest values for Face Interface and mouse are on a similar level. In other studies where text entry with gaze-based solutions has been compared to mouse, the results have shown, similarly as in the current experiment, that the mouse has been faster in terms of speed [27, 28]. For GazeTalk, for example, the writing speed with mouse was reported to be approximately 7.5 wpm (for Danish text) and 15 cpm (for Japanese text) [28].

We note especially that the comparison between mouse and Face Interface must be done cautiously because Face Interface uses two different modalities that are not traditionally (in contrast to hands) used neither for controlling computers nor manipulating objects. First, eye, for example, is primarily a perceptual organ [43]. People move their eyes involuntarily towards new stimuli which may cause problems when using eye gaze as the pointing method. It is known that there are some problems that have an effect when gaze direction is used for pointing, for example, inaccuracy of the eye trackers. Second, even if a person thinks that his or her gaze is fixated on a target; his eyes are actually actively moving [44]. This movement is known as fixation jitter [45] and it can cause inaccuracy in eye tracking. Third, it is in fact a rather new invention to use facial muscle movements as the selection method [3, 11, 46]. Some problems may occur, for example, from the fact that some people may find voluntarily control of facial muscles to be difficult [47]. Thus, from the fact that there are some possible difficulties in both techniques, it could be assumed that an integrated use of voluntary gaze direction and facial muscle movements for interacting with computers can be challenging at first. For example, there may be a delay in selecting the object when the cursor is inside an object because the pointing and selection are operated with two different modalities. Of course with such little amount of practice as in the current study, the smooth combination of these two modalities to a fast interaction techniques is not possible. Based on the above discussion, it seems quite natural that error rate with Face Interface is much higher than error rate with mouse.

Even though this experiment was a different from a traditional text entry experiment in a sense that the aim was to compare two pointing and selection techniques, some comparative results to other techniques can be given. Because text entry rate in most of the other studies have been reported using wpm value [27, 28, 30, 48], converting values from cpm to wpm in the current study gives an impression of the writing speed as compared to other systems. Of course, converting the cpm to wpm might not be the most reliable in this case because participants wrote only one word at a time in the current experiment. However, the wpm values give the possibility to compare the results to other studies. Wpm values in the present study were for Face Interface 4 wpm and 5 wpm for the mouse. It is noteworthy to mention that, for example, first time users of Dasher wrote text with an average speed of 2.5 wpm after the first session [29]. In text entry studies with gaze gestures as the input method, a bit lower text entry speed has been achieved: approximately 2.3 wpm after the first session with EyeWrite [49]. Further, Porta and Turina [50] reported that their novice participants wrote one phrase that included 13 characters in 188.5 seconds which corresponds roughly to 4 cpm. For the GazeTalk [28], the grand mean text entry speed was 6.22 wpm for Danish text and 11.71 cpm for Japanese text. We note, again, that comparison to purely gaze based studies can be problematic because these do not require any other modality integration for functional user interface. In a different multimodal technique where the object was pointed by gaze and the selection was made utilizing signals from the brain, the text entry speed was found to be 9.1 cpm [51].

Error rate analysis using MSD revealed that participants made only few errors. This can be seen from the overall mean MSD error rate of 0.12 for Face Interface and 0.0 for the mouse. For the GazeTalk, the MSD error rate was 1.09 [28], and for the Dasher the MSD error rate was approximately 10. When interacting with on-screen keyboard using dwell time as the object selection method a MSD value of 1.28 has been reported [48]. The only possible comparison of the KSPC results is one with eye typing experiments. That is because KSPC as the measure is intended for such a text entry systems in which keys are pressed (i.e., keystrokes are created) which makes KSPC unsuitable for measuring the performance of, for example, for Dasher. The overall mean KSPC value for Face Interface was 1.1 and 1.0 for mouse. Majaranta et al. [48] reported the grand mean for KSPC of 1.09 in the first session within a longitudinal study which corresponds to this study because that session lasted approximately similar time period as the current experiment. Helmert et al. [31] reported KSPC values from 1.00 (dwell time of 700 ms) to 1.18 (dwell time of 350 ms) when one word at the time was written. The results of KSPC are very promising for Face Interface and they compare very well with other gaze based text entry techniques.

Quite naturally, the re-randomization of the letters after each written word had an effect to the text entry speed because participants had to find the correct characters time after time and the participants could not rely on their earlier experience about places of the keys as is the case, for example, in a QWERTY layout. However, the present aim was to study and compare two different pointing devices by specifically excluding the effects of letter placement. For this purpose, letter randomization was necessary. Even with this arrangement, the text entry speed in the current study compared well with other studies.

The ratings of the two techniques revealed that participants rated the use of mouse as more accurate, faster and easier than the use of Face Interface. In the ratings of general evaluation, efficiency and enjoyableness there were no statistically significant differences between the two techniques. In a way, this is a positive finding because it indicates that participants rated the use of the mouse and the prototype as equal with these three scales. Current ratings compare well with previous studies where similar techniques have been compared to mouse. For example, Surakka et al. [3] reported that participants rated the gaze combined with EMG technique as faster and less accurate and more difficult to

use than the computer mouse. Further, San Agustin et al. [2] found that their participants rated the gaze pointing combined with facial EMG as faster but less accurate to use than the mouse pointing. Thus, current ratings are similar to those reported earlier. Tuisku et al. [14] reported ratings that were on the same level as in current study. An interesting finding from the interviews was that even though the participants used the Face Interface prototype only for short period of time and were novices in using it, they were still able to name many possibilities in which Face Interface could possibly be used in future. Thus, it seems that they were able to see the potential of Face Interface.

The present results showed that entering text with the prototype is possible. This experiment revealed also possible designs for on-screen keyboard layout. Even though the results showed that mouse was faster in terms of text entry speed, the results were promising for future text entry with Face Interface. Present results also confirmed that smiling can be used as the selection technique with Face Interface which can offer more possibilities to use it in the future. That is, the user is able to choose the selection technique he/she would like to use from the three possible options (i.e., frowning, smiling, and raising the eyebrows). It is noteworthy to mention that for the people who the use of speech is not possible, interactive conversation is seen as tolerable when it achieves a minimum rate of 3 wpm [52]. Face Interface met these minimum requirements even with the randomized keyboard. To further improve the technique, next steps would be to decide the letter placement in the keyboard based on the used language's most common characters and to run a longitudinal study in order to see the actual text entry rate that can be achieved with Face Interface. Although the current results with the prototype were not superior to the mouse the results are encouraging for further research and development of face based technologies.

Acknowledgments

This research was funded by the Academy of Finland (project nos. 115997 and 116913) and the Finnish Doctoral Programme in User-Centered Information Technology (UCIT). The authors thank Dr. Pekka-Henrik Niemenlehto for the eye tracking and facial movement detection algorithms, Jarmo Verho for designing the electronics of the prototype, Dr. Oleg Špakov for his help in refining the signal processing software, and Dr. Scott MacKenzie for the use of his Java tools.

References

[1] C. A. Chin, A. Barreto, J. G. Cremades, and M. Adjouadi, "Integrated electromyogram and eye-gaze tracking cursor control system for computer users with motor disabilities," *Journal of Rehabilitation Research and Development*, vol. 45, no. 1, pp. 161–174, 2008.

[2] J. San Agustin, J. C. Mateo, J. P. Hansen, and A. Villanueva, "Evaluation of the potential of gaze input for game interaction," *PsychNology Journal*, vol. 7, no. 2, pp. 213–236, 2009.

[3] V. Surakka, M. Illi, and P. Isokoski, "Gazing and frowning as a new human-computer interaction technique," *ACM Transactions on Applied Perceptions*, vol. 1, no. 1, pp. 40–56, 2004.

[4] V. Surakka, P. Isokoski, M. Illi, and K. Salminen, "Is it better to gaze and frown or gaze and smile when controlling user interfaces?" in *Proceedings of the 11th International Conference on Human-Computer Interaction (HCI '05)*, CD-ROM, p. 7, July 2005.

[5] B. Ashtiani and I. S. MacKenzie, "BlinkWrite2: an improved text entry method using eye blinks," in *Proceedings of the ACM Symposium on Eye-Tracking Research and Applications (ETRA '10)*, pp. 339–346, March 2010.

[6] A. Sesin, M. Adjouadi, M. Cabrerizo, M. Ayala, and A. Barreto, "Adaptive eye-gaze tracking using neural-network-based user profiles to assist people with motor disability," *Journal of Rehabilitation Research and Development*, vol. 45, no. 6, pp. 801–818, 2008.

[7] H. Heikkilä and K. J. Räihä, "Simple gaze gestures and the closure of the eyes as an interaction technique," in *Proceedings of the Symposium on Eye Tracking Research and Applications (ETRA '12)*, pp. 147–154, March 2012.

[8] A. J. Fridlund, *Human Facial Expression: An Evolutionary View*, Academic Press, San Diego, Calif, USA, 1994.

[9] A. Królak and P. Strumiłło, "Eye-blink detection system for human-computer interaction," *Universal Access in the Information Society*, vol. 11, no. 4, pp. 409–219, 2012.

[10] P. M. Fitts, "The information capacity of the human motor system in controlling the amplitude of movement," *Journal of Experimental Psychology*, vol. 47, no. 6, pp. 381–391, 1954.

[11] V. Rantanen, P. H. Niemenlehto, J. Verho, and J. Lekkala, "Capacitive facial movement detection for human-computer interaction to click by frowning and lifting eyebrows," *Medical and Biological Engineering and Computing*, vol. 48, no. 1, pp. 39–47, 2010.

[12] V. Rantanen, T. Vanhala, O. Tuisku et al., "A wearable, wireless gaze tracker with integrated selection command source for human-computer interaction," *IEEE Transactions on Information Technology in BioMedicine*, vol. 15, no. 5, pp. 795–801, 2011.

[13] O. Tuisku, V. Surakka, Y. Gizatdinova et al., "Gazing and frowning to computers can be enjoyable," in *Proceedings of the 3rd International Conference on Knowledge and Systems Engineering (KSE '11)*, pp. 211–218, October 2011.

[14] O. Tuisku, V. Surakka, T. Vanhala, V. Rantanen, and J. Lekkala, "Wireless face interface: using voluntary gaze direction and facial muscle activations for human-computer interaction," *Interacting with Computers*, vol. 24, no. 1, pp. 1–9, 2012.

[15] I. S. MacKenzie, "Fitts' law as a research and design tool in human-computer interaction," *Human-Computer Interaction*, vol. 7, no. 1, pp. 91–139, 1992.

[16] S. A. Douglas and A. K. Mithal, "Effect of reducing homing time on the speed of a finger-controlled isometric pointing device," in *Proceedings of the SIGCHI Conference on Human Factors in Computing Systems (CHI '94)*, pp. 411–416, April 1994.

[17] C. Ware and H. H. Mikaelian, "An evaluation of an eye tracker as a device for computer input," in *Proceedings of the SIGCHI/GI Conference on Human Factors in Computing Systems and Graphics Interface (CHI '87)*, pp. 183–188, Ontario, Canada, April 1987.

[18] P. Majaranta and K. J. Räihä, "Twenty years of eye typing: systems and design issues," in *Proceedings of the Symposium on Eye Tracking Research and Applications (ETRA '02)*, pp. 15–22, New Orleans, La, USA, March 2002.

[19] F. E. Sandnes and A. Aubert, "Bimanual text entry using game controllers: relying on users' spatial familiarity with QWERTY," *Interacting with Computers*, vol. 19, no. 2, pp. 140–150, 2007.

[20] K. J. Räihä and S. Ovaska, "An exploratory study of eye typing fundamentals: dwell time, text entry rate, errors, and workload," in *Proceedings of the SIGCHI Conference on Human Factors in Computing Systems (CHI '12)*, pp. 3001–3010, May 2012.

[21] O. Špakov and P. Majaranta, "Scrollable keyboards for casual typing," *PsychNology Journal*, vol. 7, no. 2, pp. 159–173, 2009.

[22] X. Bi, B. A. Smith, and S. Zhai, "Quasi-Qwerty soft keyboard optimization," in *Proceedings of the 28th Annual CHI Conference on Human Factors in Computing Systems (CHI '10)*, pp. 283–286, April 2010.

[23] I. S. MacKenzie and S. X. Zhang, "Design and evaluation of a high-performance soft keyboard," in *Proceedings of the SIGCHI conference on Human Factors in Computing Systems (CHI '99)*, pp. 25–31, May 1999.

[24] D. Li, J. Babcock, and D. J. Parkhurst, "openEyes: a low-cost head-mounted eye-tracking solution," in *Proceedings of the Symposium on Eye Tracking Research and Applications (ETRA '06)*, pp. 95–100, San Diego, Calif, USA, March 2006.

[25] W. J. Ryan, A. T. Duchowski, E. A. Vincent, and D. Battisto, "Match-moving for area-based analysis of eye movements in natural tasks," in *Proceedings of the ACM Symposium on Eye-Tracking Research and Applications (ETRA '10)*, pp. 235–242, March 2010.

[26] H. Aoki, J. P. Hansen, and K. Itoh, "Learning to interact with a computer by gaze," *Behaviour and Information Technology*, vol. 27, no. 4, pp. 339–344, 2008.

[27] J. P. Hansen, A. S. Johansen, D. W. Hansen, K. Itoh, and S. Mashino, "Command without a click: dwell time typing by mouse and gaze selections," in *Human-Computer Interaction (INTERACT '03)*, M. Rauterberg, M. Menozzi, and J. Wesson, Eds., pp. 121–128, IOS Press, Amsterdam, The Netherlands, 2003.

[28] J. P. Hansen, K. Tørning, A. S. Johansen, K. Itoh, and H. Aoki, "Gaze typing compared with input by head and hand," in *Proceedings of the Symposium on Eye Tracking Research and Applications (ETRA '04)*, pp. 131–138, San Antonio, Tex, USA, March 2004.

[29] D. J. Ward and D. J. C. MacKay, "Artificial intelligence: fast hands-free writing by gaze direction," *Nature*, vol. 418, no. 6900, p. 838, 2002.

[30] O. Tuisku, P. Majaranta, P. Isokoski, and K. J. Räihä, "Now Dasher! Dash away!: longitudinal study of fast text entry by eye gaze," in *Proceedings of the Symposium on Eye Tracking Research and Applications (ETRA '08)*, pp. 19–26, March 2008.

[31] J. R. Helmert, S. Pannasch, and B. M. Velichkovsky, "Influences of dwell time and cursor control on the performance in gaze driven typing," *Journal of Eye Movement Research*, vol. 2, no. 4, pp. 1–8, 2008.

[32] P. Majaranta, I. S. MacKenzie, A. Aula, and K. J. Räihä, "Effects of feedback and dwell time on eye typing speed and accuracy," *Universal Access in the Information Society*, vol. 5, no. 2, pp. 199–208, 2006.

[33] D. A. Norman and D. Fisher, "Why alphabetic keyboards are not easy to use: keyboard layout doesn't much matter," *Human Factors*, vol. 24, no. 5, pp. 509–519, 1982.

[34] M. M. Bradley, "Measuring emotion: the self-assessment manikin and the semantic differential," *Journal of Behavior Therapy and Experimental Psychiatry*, vol. 25, no. 1, pp. 49–59, 1994.

[35] C. E. Osgood, "The nature and measurement of meaning," *Psychological Bulletin*, vol. 49, no. 3, pp. 197–237, 1952.

[36] R. Menzies, A. Waller, and H. Pain, "Peer interviews: an adapted methodology for contextual understanding in user-centred design," in *Proceedings of the 13th International ACM SIGAC-CESS Conference on Computers and Accessibility (ASSETS '11)*, pp. 273–274, Dundee, UK, October 2011.

[37] G. Bradski and A. Kaehler, *Learning Opencv: Computer Vision with the Opencv Library*, O'Reilly Media, Sebastopol, Calif, USA, 2008.

[38] D. Li, D. Winfield, and D. J. Parkhurst, "Starburst: a hybrid algorithm for video-based eye tracking combining feature-based and model-based approaches," in *Proceedings of the IEEE Computer Society Conference on Computer Vision and Pattern Recognition (CVPR '05)*, pp. 1–8, San Diego, Calif, USA, June 2005.

[39] V. Rantanen, J. Verho, J. Lekkala, O. Tuisku, V. Surakka, and T. Vanhala, "The effect of clicking by smiling on the accuracy of head-mounted gaze tracking," in *Proceedings of the Symposium on Eye Tracking Research and Applications (ETRA '12)*, pp. 345–348, March 2012.

[40] P. O. Kristensson and S. Zhai, "Relaxing stylus typing precision by geometric pattern matching," in *Proceedings of the 10th international conference on Intelligent user interfaces (IUI '05)*, pp. 151–158, San Diego, Calif, USA, January 2005.

[41] R. W. Soukoreff and I. S. MacKenzie, "Metrics for text entry research: an evaluation of MSD and KSPC, and a new unified error metric," in *Proceedings of the SIGCHI Conference on Human Factors in Computing Systems (CHI '03)*, pp. 113–120, April 2003.

[42] R. Bates, "Have patience with your eye mouse! Eye-gaze interaction with computers can work," in *Proceedings of the 1st Cambridge Workshop on Universal Access and Assistive Technology (CWUAAT '02)*, pp. 33–38, March 2002.

[43] S. Zhai, "What's in the eyes for attentive input," *Communications of the ACM*, vol. 46, no. 3, pp. 34–39, 2003.

[44] R. J. K. Jacob, "The use of eye movements in human-computer interaction techniques: what you look is what you get," *ACM Transactions on Information Systems*, vol. 9, no. 2, pp. 152–169, 1991.

[45] M. Ashmore, A. T. Duchowski, and G. Shoemaker, "Efficient eye pointing with a fisheye lens," in *Proceedings of Graphics Interface 2005 (GI '05)*, pp. 203–210, Ontario, Canada, May 2005.

[46] A. B. Barreto, S. D. Scargle, and M. Adjouadi, "A practical EMG-based human-computer interface for users with motor disabilities," *Journal of Rehabilitation Research and Development*, vol. 37, no. 1, pp. 53–64, 2000.

[47] R. W. Levenson, P. Ekman, and W. V. Friesen, "Voluntary facial action generates emotion-specific autonomic nervous system activity," *Psychophysiology*, vol. 27, no. 4, pp. 363–384, 1990.

[48] P. Majaranta, U. K. Ahola, and O. Špakov, "Fast gaze typing with an adjustable dwell time," in *Proceedings of the SIGCHI Conference on Human Factors in Computing Systems (CHI '09)*, pp. 357–360, Boston, Mass, USA, April 2009.

[49] J. O. Wobbrock, J. Rubinstein, M. W. Sawyer, and A. T. Duchowski, "Longitudinal evaluation of discrete consecutive gaze gestures for text entry," in *Proceedings of the Symposium on Eye Tracking Research and Applications (ETRA '08)*, pp. 11–18, Savannah, Ga, USA, March 2008.

[50] M. Porta and M. Turina, "Eye-S: a full-screen input modality for pure eye-based communication," in *Proceedings of the Symposium on Eye Tracking Research and Applications (ETRA '08)*, pp. 27–34, March 2008.

[51] X. Yong, M. Fatourechi, R. K. Ward, and G. E. Birch, "The design of point-and-click system by integrating a self-paced brain-computer interface with an eye-tracker," *IEEE Journal on Emerging and Selected Topics in Circuits and Systems*, vol. 1, no. 4, pp. 590–602, 2011.

[52] J. J. Darragh and I. H. Witten, *The Reactive Keyboard*, Cambridge University Press, New York, NY, USA, 1992.

7

RoboTable: An Infrastructure for Intuitive Interaction with Mobile Robots in a Mixed-Reality Environment

Haipeng Mi,[1] Aleksander Krzywinski,[2] Tomoki Fujita,[1] and Masanori Sugimoto[1]

[1] *Interaction Technology Laboratory, Department of Electrical Engineering and Information Systems, University of Tokyo, 7-3-1 Hongo, Bunkyo-ku, 113-8656 Tokyo, Japan*
[2] *The Interaction Research Group, Department of Information Science and Media Studies, University of Bergen, Fosswinckelsgate 6, 5020 Bergen, Norway*

Correspondence should be addressed to Haipeng Mi, mi@itl.t.u-tokyo.ac.jp

Academic Editor: Kiyoshi Kiyokawa

This paper presents the design, development, and testing of a tabletop interface called RoboTable, which is an infrastructure supporting intuitive interaction with both mobile robots and virtual components in a mixed-reality environment. With a flexible software toolkit and specifically developed robots, the platform enables various modes of interaction with mobile robots. Using this platform, prototype applications are developed for two different application domains: *RoboPong* investigates the efficiency of the RoboTable system in game applications, and *ExploreRobot* explores the possibility of using robots and intuitive interaction to enhance learning.

1. Introduction

In the past few years, much development has taken place in the research field of human-computer interaction. Several research approaches in this field, including tabletop interaction, tangible user interfaces (TUIs), augmented reality, and mixed-reality, show great promise for bringing new interaction styles to other related research domains. The research presented in this paper is an attempt to integrate several research approaches to create a mixed reality environment for novel human-robot interaction (HRI).

Because the horizontal surface of a table permits the placement of objects, and its large surface area enables spreading, piling, and organization of the items, digital tabletop user interfaces are becoming increasingly popular for supporting natural and intuitive interaction [1–3].

A TUI is a user interface in which a person interacts with digital information via the physical environment. It gives a physical form to digital information and computation, facilitating the direct manipulation of bits [4]. Such physical interactions are very natural and intuitive for human beings, because they enable two-handed input and can provide spatial and haptic feedback [5].

In this paper, we present RoboTable, an infrastructure that combines tabletop interaction with TUIs to support intuitive interaction with mobile robots. This framework can create a mixed-reality environment in which interaction with real robots and virtual objects can be combined seamlessly. This capability also extends the robot entity into the virtual world, enabling rich and complex HRIs to be supported in various applications.

Based on the RoboTable framework, we have developed two prototype applications for proof-of-concept purposes. *RoboPong* is a tabletop game in which a robot player also participates. This game supports touch input for virtual objects and graspable interaction with robots simultaneously. *ExploreRobot* is designed for educational purposes. It enables users to interact with the robot at a behavioral level, enabling the robot to be reconfigured easily for different tasks.

An important motivation for this research is to explore new possibilities for HRI in a tabletop mixed-reality environment. We believe that with these new interaction styles, the RoboTable system will enable us to build attractive games and playful educational applications, which will give instant and intuitive feedback to the user, further facilitating the entertainment or learning experience.

2. Related Work

In the past decade, several applications for HRI using mobile robots have been discussed in the literature. As an alternative solution to traditional HRI, TUIs have been developed in various forms. TUIs bridge the physical world and the digital world to enable users to manipulate information in a natural way [4]. Recent researchers are trying to develop HRI methods that are more intuitive, such as finger-touch control [6] and tangible-object control [7, 8].

Curlybot is an early example of enabling graspable manipulation for interaction with a mobile robot [9]. The curlybot robot has encoders for its motors by which robot movements corresponding to user manipulations can be recorded in the microcontroller. The recorded robot trajectory can be replayed after user definition.

Kato et al. developed a multitouch interface for controlling multiple robots [6]. This system utilizes ceiling-mounted cameras to track the mobile robots on the ground. A multitouch table enables users to control the robots by manipulating the corresponding image of each robot on the table.

Guo et al. discussed a manipulation method using TUIs [7, 8]. In this system, physical toys are used as indicators of robots on a table. Two multicamera systems are used to track the robot space and the toy-indicator space so that a mapping from the toy-indicator space to the robot space can be created. Users can manipulate toys on the table to move the corresponding remote robot to a desired position. A shortcoming of this system is that users and robots are insulated from each other, preventing the perception of physical feedback.

Other projects have investigated the intuitive control and programming of a mobile robot. Furthermore, other researchers have attempted to give users not only an intuitive control experience but also intuitive feedback during their interaction with mobile robots.

The Augmented Coliseum developed by Kojima et al. creates an environment in which a physical robot can be augmented by projection [10]. The robot has light sensors mounted on its top to enable tracking of a specifically designed light pattern projected onto the table. The robot will track and move to follow the projected image's translation and rotation. This configuration scheme realized robot control and its augmentation using only one projector. However, there was neither direct interaction between users and the robot nor between users and the environment.

IncreTable, developed by Leitner et al. [11] is another project utilizing projection-augmented robots. This system uses the same robots as those in the Augmented Coliseum project. Compared with the Augmented Coliseum project, IncreTable has improved user interaction. In this application, a special pen is used, with which the user can create virtual objects on the table. In addition, the system also enables interaction between physical and virtual objects. This system is an effective attempt at implementing a mixed-reality

environment on a tabletop platform. However, because of the limitations of the robots, graspable manipulation with the robots was not supported. Moreover, "placing" virtual objects with a pen cannot be considered intuitive.

Other recent projects have extended the capabilities of tabletop HRI applications. Robot Arena, developed by Calife et al. [12], is an augmented-reality platform for game development. This system utilizes camera tracking and Bluetooth (BT) communication for the robot to make the robot more flexible. This wireless communication enables users to control the robot remotely, and it can be extended to a multirobot system. Because the camera only tracks specifically designed color markers on the robot, and is not sensitive to hand manipulations, users cannot interact directly with the virtual world.

In reviewing these related projects, we found that no project creates a mixed-reality environment in which users can both directly interact with either real robots or virtual objects using familiar techniques and perceive all objects as cosituated in the same space. This consideration inspired and motivated us to develop the RoboTable system. This work tries to go beyond existing projects to explore a mixed-reality tabletop environment in which novel and intuitive HRI is enabled.

3. Robotable Implementation

3.1. Table. To achieve the research goal of creating a tabletop that supports both robot tracking and multitouch input, we implemented a combination of two different tracking techniques: frustrated total internal reflection (FTIR) [13] and diffused illumination (DI) [14].

Figure 1 shows the hardware setup for our table. A piece of 10 mm clear acrylic board is applied as the table surface. An infrared (IR) LED stripe is placed at the side of the acrylic board to generate the necessary light for FTIR. On top of this surface, we applied two thin layers of silicone-coated plastic film to form a compliant surface and a separate piece of tracing paper to act as a diffuser. Four IR illuminators fixed on the bottom of the baseplate create a light field inside the table for DI tracking. The combination of the two techniques, where DI helped the tracking of objects and FTIR enhanced finger-touch recognition, enables both tracking goals to be achieved.

A short-throw projector (Benq MP522T) is mounted underneath the surface. A piece of IR-block filter is applied to the projector lens to reduce hot spots introduced by the projector lamp. The projection area is 870 mm × 652 mm. A Firefly MV B/W camera (640 × 480 @ 60 fps) is mounted at the center of the baseplate with a piece of IR band-pass filter. In combination with particular tracking software, this table achieves a tracking resolution of 1.36 mm/pixel for both fingers and objects.

3.2. Robot. The definitions of "robot" range widely. For the RoboTable project, the robot is a simple mobile robot. Its microcontroller covers low-level motion control, whereas higher-level strategy and path planning take place in the remote console of the RoboTable system. Therefore, the

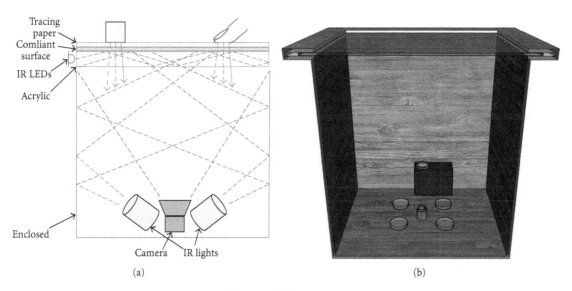

FIGURE 1: Tabletop setup.

robot used in this project can be classified as a nonautonomous mobile robot.

The robot is designed and developed using five design principles.

(1) It must have a small footprint because of the relatively small size of the table.

(2) It must be highly maneuverable.

(3) Its baseplate has to be as close to the table as possible because of the DI tracking.

(4) It must be able to communicate with the table system.

(5) It must be aesthetically pleasing and "touchable".

3.2.1. Actuation. The robot is a simple two-wheel design, with each wheel being actuated by an independent DC motor and gearbox unit to enable differential steering. With this arrangement, the robot can move forward or backward and turn with a zero-radius turning circle. The speed of the DC motor is controlled by the microcontroller via power width modulation (PWM).

3.2.2. Tracking. Each robot has a ReacTIVision [14] fiducial marker carved into the baseplate, creating a durable, high-contrast symbol that is easily tracked by the camera (Figure 2(a) left). The ReacTIVision fiducial markers are specifically designed and optimized for rapid and high-precision recognition of both position and direction in the tabletop system. The white dots in the fiducial marker have a minimum diameter of 5 mm, and the distance from the marker to the surface is only 0.5 mm. This design ensures stable tracking; the robot can move at high speed without tracking failure. The maximum speed for stable tracking is about 120 mm/sec.

3.2.3. Communication. We have chosen BT technology to connect the robot and the server in the RoboTable system,

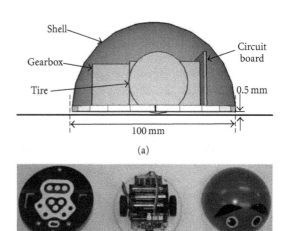

FIGURE 2: Robot.

which gives us a communication channel that has relatively low power consumption, readily available hardware, and software libraries and is easily able to accommodate several units simultaneously. However, most BT devices require manual setup before the connection can be established. For this project, a manual connection setup would significantly reduce the smoothness of the interaction because a robot unit may be introduced into the environment or be removed from the environment by users at any time. To solve this problem, we introduced an automatic connection-setup mechanism.

As shown in Figure 3, when a working robot is put on the surface, the system will recognize the fiducial marker of the robot and will look up the BT address of that particular robot. If the address is found, the system negotiates a connection with that address automatically. The connection will be established seamlessly within seconds of placing the robot on the surface.

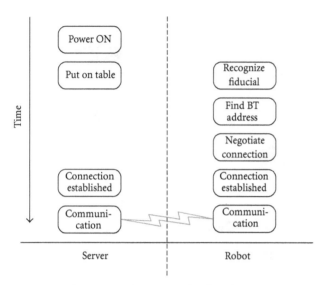

FIGURE 3: Robot connection flow chart.

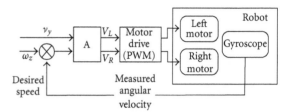

FIGURE 4: Motion control diagram.

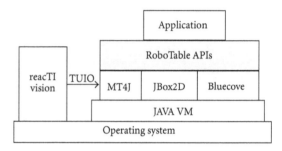

FIGURE 5: Software architecture.

3.2.4. Control. The robot uses a microcontroller (PIC16F886) as the main control unit, which receives commands from, and sends responses to, the server and drives each motor according to the received commands.

In addition, another important task of the microcontroller is to manage the differential steering. Because mechanical tolerances exist for each driving unit (DC motor, gearbox, wheel, and tire), there is always some imbalance between the wheels. To compensate for the deviation angle introduced by the imbalance in differential steering, a gyroscope sensor is also implemented to monitor the angular velocity of the robot in real time.

Figure 4 illustrates the feedback control diagram for the robot using a gyroscope sensor. v_y and ω_z are the desired robot speed and rotation parameters, respectively. A transformation matrix A transforms v_y and ω_z to left and right motor speeds V_L and V_R, which are then sent to the PWM drivers for the two motors. The actual rotation is observed by the gyroscope, and a control algorithm will correct the motion error.

3.2.5. Integration. All components of the robot sit on the baseplate, whose diameter is 100 mm (Figure 2(b) center). A hemispherical acrylic shell, which is painted and decorated, covers all components. The compact design fits snugly in a user's palm (Figure 2(b) right).

3.3. Software Implementation. All the RoboTable software components are developed in Java. We used several open-source tools in the project, developing specific drivers and application-programmer interfaces (APIs) for mixed-reality applications based on the RoboTable platform.

3.3.1. Software Architecture. The RoboTable API was implemented as a layer above the supporting layer, which comprised several libraries. These toolkits support event-handling and rendering functions, physical simulations and wireless communications. An independent tracking engine

delivers a stream of input events via a TUIO protocol. Figure 5 illustrates the software architecture of the developed infrastructure.

3.3.2. Tracking. The main tracking engine in our system was that used in the reacTIVision project. The reacTIVision engine [14] handles the segmentation, fiducial marker, touch recognition and tracking, and delivers a stream of TUIO-based data to a specific network address and port. Usually, the address is that of a local interface, but configurations where the workload is divided amongst several computers are easily implemented. Therefore, the TUIO stream provides simple add, update and remove events for both cursors (i.e., touches) and objects (i.e., tangibles with fiducial markers).

3.3.3. Physical Simulation. To accommodate mixed-reality applications, we must ensure that both the robots and the virtual objects on the screen behave in a way that is intuitive for users, being based on human experience of the real world. Otherwise, users will find it difficult to understand the interaction with the virtual objects on the table, and any advantage in usability leveraged by the familiarity of the user with everyday physical objects is lost. For the flat, horizontal surface of a table, it is most appropriate to simulate the interaction of bodies on a plane. Therefore, we used a 2D physics simulation framework provided by the JBox2D project [15]. (Simulating a third dimension normal to the surface is superfluous, justifying the limitation to two dimensions.) The chosen framework has powerful APIs for defining the properties of physical objects and their interaction with each other when set in motion, enabling us to create rapidly a world in which the objects on the screen collide and exert forces on each other.

3.3.4. Event Handling and Rendering. Another open-source framework, MultiTouch for Java (MT4J) [16], is included in the software toolkit for handling events, managing a canvas and rendering objects on a screen. MT4J is a powerful tool that handles all TUIO events, including both touches and objects. It also provides a rendering engine based on OpenGL technology that supports both 2D and 3D rendering. The MT4J framework has predefined many common gestures such as drag, rotate and zoom. By providing rich APIs, MT4J offers easy extension to different application areas.

3.3.5. Communications. We have chosen the Bluecove library [17] for BT communication to handle all the wireless communications between the robots and the RoboTable server.

3.3.6. The RoboTable API. For the RoboTable project, the mixed-reality application environment requires seamless management of both on-screen objects and physical robots. For example, an on-screen object will collide with another object if contact is made, whether on-screen or in the real world. In other words, both virtual objects and physical robots should have the same abstraction in the mixed-reality world. The RoboTable API provides such features to upper-layer application development, enabling a specific application with intuitive HRI to be developed easily via the RoboTable infrastructure.

4. Interaction

An important feature of the RoboTable system's interaction is that users can interact with both real and virtual objects in an intuitive way. Because the RoboTable system leverages the strong points of multitouch interfaces and TUIs, users can interact seamlessly with all objects involved in RoboTable applications in a mixed-reality environment.

4.1. Multitouch. The RoboTable system supports the most popular multitouch and gesture interactions. Users can manipulate on-screen objects simply, in ways they are familiar with. The multitouch interaction feature can be used in many tabletop applications.

4.2. Robot. The requirements for interaction with robots depend on the application. Interaction with robots in the RoboTable project falls mainly into two classes, namely, direct interaction and interaction at the behavioral level. These specialized HRIs enable the development of flexible game and learning-assistant applications involving mobile robots.

4.2.1. Direct Interaction. The robot used in the RoboTable system is, to some extent, a specific TUI. It has a physical form of input as an ordinary TUI that can be used as a physical token for manipulating virtual information. In addition, the robot also has the ability to transform responses from the virtual world back into the physical world. In RoboTable applications, the robot can be used as a normal TUI, enabling users to manipulate it via everyday actions such as pick up, move or put down. The robot will also respond to any change in the virtual environment (e.g., collision) by changing its physical properties such as position and movement accordingly.

4.2.2. Interaction at the Behavioral Level. The robots also have their own natural properties regarding specific behaviors. A robot with a certain behavior can be used in a variety of applications involving simulation tools, games and learning applications. However, in most of these applications, users expect the robot behavior to be changed easily. In other words, the robot behavior is like an attribution of this special object. Based on this consideration, we argue that if one can interact with the robot at the behavioral level, such as by changing the robot's behavior in a simple way, it can benefit several applications.

The robots used in the RoboTable project are capable of a certain level of autonomous action, and we introduce a behavior arbitration structure for them. The robot has a set of real sensors and actuators, and an additional range of virtual sensors (virtual actuators are also possible, such as those for controlling a virtual robot arm) that can report data about the virtual world in which the robot is cosituated. By being able to attach and detach various virtual sensors easily, the robot becomes reconfigurable. In addition, by having a simple robot behavior-definition feature, the reconfigurable robot can also be redefined (reprogrammed) with a different behavior.

5. Application Prototypes

As proof-of-concept tests for the platform, two application prototypes were developed to explore the characteristics of the RoboTable. The first, RoboPong, is a tabletop game that explores the basic interactions in a mixed-reality gaming environment. The second is ExploreRobot, a learning assistant application for school students and programming beginners. This application explores the features of interaction with robots at a behavioral level.

5.1. RoboPong. The goal of the development of the Robo-Pong game prototype was to explore basic interactions in a mixed-reality gaming environment.

The RoboPong game was developed from the classical arcade game of "Pong". The basic version of RoboPong enables two players to play together. Each player uses two fingers to create a paddle on the player's own side of the table, trying to place this paddle where the ball will hit it and bounce back to the opponent's side, hopefully scoring a point in the process.

Ball. The ball can be created simply by touching the center ring. Only one ball can be created at a time. Once created, the ball will move in a random direction at a certain speed. If the ball collides with the boundary or a paddle, it will rebound like an actual collision in a real environment.

Paddle. A paddle can be created if a player touches the player's own defense area with two fingers. The created paddle is a straight bar whose endpoints are the player's touch points. (The player can only create a paddle of up to 130 mm in length.) Only one paddle for each player can be created at a time. If a new paddle is created, the old paddle is removed immediately.

Score. If the ball reaches the baseline of a player, the player's opponent scores one point. A game will end with the winning player being the first to score five points.

The most important difference between RoboPong and classical Pong is the participation of the robot player. Various behaviors for the robot player were implemented, enabling the robot to influence the game in different ways. Figure 6 illustrates two game modes of RoboPong for which the robot is deployed differently.

Competitive Mode. In the competitive mode, a human player plays against a robot player. The robot carries a paddle and moves across the defense area to return the incoming ball. The robot will find the best defending position and automatically move to that position. In this mode, the human player competes with the robot player, aiming to achieve the higher score (Figure 6(a)).

Cooperative Mode. In the cooperative mode, two (human) players play with up to two robots. A robot joins one side as a member of that human player's team. The robot tries to chase the ball and return it to the opponent's side. The human player can pick up the robot and place it appropriately whenever necessary. In this mode, the robot effectively cooperates with the human player in playing the game (Figure 6(b)).

5.2. ExploreRobot. The goal of the development of the ExploreRobot application was to explore the features of interaction with robots at a behavioral level.

ExploreRobot was a learning assistant application targeting school students and programming beginners. The aim of this application was to help users understand the basic concepts of robot programming. A robot equipped with virtual radar is placed in a virtual maze. An acrylic plate is placed somewhere on the table to indicate the goal of the robot explorer.

The robot has virtual radar that can detect obstacles and the goal. The radar will report the approximate direction of a detected object as left, right, or front. A programming mechanism is introduced that involves radar detection and a simple behavior-definition method for users. As shown in Figure 7(a), the player can move the robot directly on the table to define a motion path. The recorded motion path can be assigned as a default behavior or a special behavior responding to a specific event.

Figure 7(b) illustrates how to assign a motion behavior to a specific event. As the robot is moved to a certain place involving particular radar events, the robot will enter the behavior-defining state and players can then assign the corresponding motion behavior to that specific event using the same method as described above.

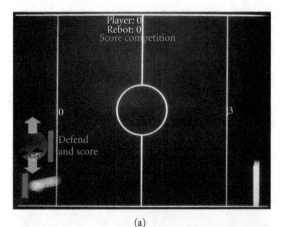

(a)

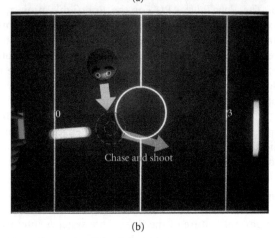

(b)

FIGURE 6: RoboPong game: competitive robot (a) and cooperative robot (b).

After defining the default behavior and response behavior for various cases, the robot-programming phase is completed, with all definitions being stored and organized automatically. When the player puts the robot into executing mode, the robot will start exploring the maze to find the goal, driven by the program created by the player. If the robot reaches the goal successfully, the player wins the game. Alternatively, the player can stop the execution and revise the robot's behavior by simply recalling the stored behaviors and redefining them.

Figure 8 is an example program for the simple maze-explorer robot. While no objects are detected, the default action will be executed repeatedly. If an event occurs that is caused by radar detection, the corresponding action will be executed immediately as an interrupt.

5.3. Exploratory Evaluation. As one of the research goal, RoboTable infrastructure is expected to improve users' experience by introducing real robots to create a mixed-reality environment. In order to better understand users' perception playing with real robots in mixed-reality applications compared to traditional graphical applications, we have carried out a preliminary evaluation experiment.

We have modified the RoboPong game as the test-bench which has two different setups. These two setups were almost

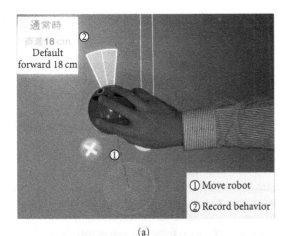

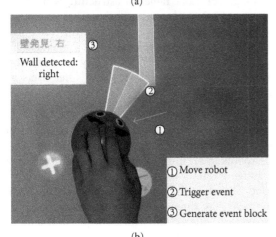

FIGURE 7: ExploreRobot: definition of motion path (a) and definition of event (b).

Default	Goal detected: left	Goal detected: right
Move 15 cm ↑ Rotate 2 deg →	Rotate 2 deg → Move 5 cm ↑	Rotate 2 deg ← Move 5 cm ↑

Wall detected: left	Wall detected: right	Wall detected: front
Rotate 5 deg →	Rotate 160 deg ←	Move 5 cm ↓ Rotate 30 deg →

FIGURE 8: A simple program for the maze explorer.

the same except the robot deployed in the game. Either a real robot or a virtual robot was deployed for each setup. In order to reduce effects caused by robot appearance and behavior, the virtual robot was presented with a photograph of the real robot and behaved exactly the same as the real robot so that the two robots look quite similar. In other words, one setup was a mixed-reality version of RoboPong game and the other setup was a traditional graphical version.

A number of participants were recruited to experience this game. Each participant was asked to play the game under two different setups. During the experiment, we have taken video record and memos of special dialogues or actions. After a video analysis and memo summary, we have found some interesting episodes from the evaluation experiment.

(1) *Episode 1.* Participant A was playing with a real robot, but could not defeat against the robot opponent. A heavily patted the robot with anger.

(2) *Episode 2.* Participant B was playing with a real robot, and got scored with the robot's help. B gently patted the robot with happiness.

(3) *Episode 3.* Participant C was playing with a real robot. C had a dialogue with the Experimenter (E):
(During the game)

> C: What's the name of this guy?
>
> E: It has no name yet.
>
> C: Tom? How about Tom?
>
> E: You gave a name to the robot?
>
> C: Yes! It's Tom!

(After the game)

> C: May I come to play again? With Tom!

It is a remarkable fact that these episodes were all observed when participants were playing with the real robot. We did not find any special episode in the case of playing with the virtual robot. Because the real robot is cosituated in the same space with players, it is possible for players to express their emotion by direct gestures such as push, pull, or pat. In addition, the dialogue happened in Episode 3 implies a fact that players may treat the real robot as an anthropomorphic co-player.

This result has an implication that mixed-reality games with real robot provide a higher social engagement to players compared to graphical games with virtual robot.

5.4. Analysis of Results. In terms of the goals set for this infrastructure, the results were satisfactory and promising, with respect to the techniques implemented in the system. The combination configuration of RoboTable provided stable tracking of both finger touches and objects simultaneously. Using the integrated calibration feature of ReacTIVision, the projection coordinates and the tracking coordinates coincided perfectly, enabling interaction with both virtual objects and the robot to be carried out seamlessly during the application. The robot's flexible maneuverability and rapid response enabled different levels of interaction. In addition, multiple robots worked together simultaneously and successfully. These basic tests of the configuration of the RoboTable infrastructure show great promise for supporting various applications that involve intuitive interaction with mobile robots in a mixed-reality environment.

The RoboPong prototype aimed to test direct interaction with mobile robots in games. As observed in the test, the robot interacts very well with the virtual world. It can interact not only with virtual objects (e.g., return the incoming ball), but can also respond to virtual environment changes (e.g., move according to the opponent's action). Interactions between virtual objects and the physical robot were successful. The impression that both robot and virtual objects were colocated in the same environment could be perceived.

The ExploreRobot prototype aimed to test interaction at a behavioral level. As observed in the test, a simple reconfigurable robot was achieved successfully. The redefinition method for robot-motion paths was simple and robust. In addition, virtual sensors can work very well with the real robot, and the addition of complexity to the behavior programming was tested successfully.

However, the two applications met problems in some special situations. RoboPong is a fast-paced game. The robot has only a few seconds to move to the desired position for defense against the opponent's action. However, the robot we implemented was not omnidirectional, having only the ability to move in a direction parallel to the wheels. In other words, to move to a desired position, the robot must first rotate to a specific direction and then move forward or backward. This maneuverability problem was sometimes the cause of the robot failing to defend against the incoming ball.

In a later prototype, the robot explorer met the problem of accumulated error. Here, the overall robot behavior can be decomposed into a sequence of motion actions, where each action is a user-defined motion path. However, with every execution of a motion action, a motion error is generated. Although a single error is not significant, repeated motions can generate a significant accumulated error, which can result in uncertain behavior by the robot. For example, if the robot is placed initially at exactly the same position with the same direction, and the program is executed several times, the final position of the robot will be variable. Although this problem was not serious in the ExploreRobot application, it could be a major problem for other applications with more stringent requirements.

Although some problems for robot control and maneuverability still exist, the RoboTable system has performed well overall. As one of the most important research issue, the result of exploratory evaluation implies that real robot and mixed-reality environment provide higher social engagement to users. The feature of integrating interactions with both real and virtual objects shows a great possibility of RoboTable infrastructure to develop several kinds of attractive and interactive applications.

6. Discussion

6.1. Interactions. Exploring interactions is the main objective of this work. In the RoboTable prototype applications, we uncovered some interesting issues concerning interaction.

Multitouch interaction extends traditional HRI to a mixed-reality environment. In aiming to manipulate virtual objects attached to the robot directly, the robot entity spreads to the virtual world. This enables the user to interact with the robot in new ways, such as moving the robot a little and then adjusting the parameters of the virtual components, or even

performing these actions in an arbitrary order, which enables the perception of manipulating a unified entity, rather than separate objects.

Another interesting issue is related to interaction at a behavioral level. RoboTable applications have the capability for users to reconfigure a robot directly as well as via its behavior. The simple interaction by which the user grasps and moves a robot to define a motion path as a segment of a behavior sequence ensures a direct and intuitive perception of a user wanting to reconfigure the robot. Even though this kind of "programming" is not precise, enabling only approximate definitions, we would argue that this intuitive programming method is suited to games and educational contexts because of its intuitiveness and tangibility.

Although the RoboTable infrastructure is only a combination of existing interaction techniques, we found new possibilities for HRI when we connected the real world and the virtual world, and enabled seamless interaction with all objects involved in the mixed-reality environment. We believe that the RoboTable system can offer users a new experience of HRI.

6.2. Application Domain. The RoboTable system creates a mixed-reality environment in which users can interact with mobile robots in an intuitive way. One main consideration is the range of application domains that can benefit from this kind of system. In general, the tabletop mixed-reality environment has three main strong points: a collaborative workspace, interaction with both physical and virtual objects, and reconfigurable robots.

The RoboTable system utilizes a tabletop interface, which offers the advantages of tabletop interaction such as face-to-face communication and a collaborative workspace. These advantages can benefit applications involving games, discussions and collaborative work and learning.

In addition, the mixed-reality environment created by the RoboTable system enables rich interaction with both virtual and real objects. By successfully implementing interactions between the real world and virtual world, all objects involved in RoboTable applications are perceived as colocated in the same environment. Interactions across the mixed-reality environment can be performed seamlessly.

Last but not least, the virtual components extend the capability of the robot by converting it into a reconfigurable robot. This feature widens the range of application domains for the RoboTable system.

With these advantages for the RoboTable system, we believe that the platform offers great benefits in the creation of applications for games, entertainment, and collaborative learning. Other possible application domains would include museum exhibitions and tactical simulation.

6.2.1. Games and Entertainment. The RoboTable platform is suited to the creation of a mixed-reality environment for face-to-face gaming. The physical robot as a game protagonist will enhance the attraction of the game, and the visual effects and virtual components greatly extend the boundaries of the physical gaming environment.

6.2.2. Collaborative Learning. As reported in some research articles [18], the TUI has benefits for some learning activities because of its physicality. In our experimental configuration of ExploreRobot, the intuitive interaction that helped users create a direct mapping between the program and the behavior of the robot showed great benefit for this specific learning activity. Moreover, collaborative learning can be implemented easily on the tabletop platform, further enhancing learning activities in some situations. In addition to programming-learning applications, the storytelling application domain [19] would be another possibility for collaborative learning.

6.3. Robot Maneuverability. Maneuverability is one of the most important characteristics of the mobile robot. The requirements for robot maneuverability depend on the application. Based on the experimental results for our prototype applications, two main issues related to robot maneuverability should be considered carefully.

The first issue concerns the robot architecture. In the RoboTable system, we implemented the robot using a simple two-wheel architecture, which only has maneuverability in two directions. Although a differential steering mechanism is implemented to realize zero-radius rotations, the additional rotation time will limit the robot's capability whenever the robot is expected to move rapidly to a desired position. A possible solution to this problem is to make the robot omnidirectional. However, this method will result in higher cost and greater complexity. Therefore, we consider that an omnidirectional robot should be used only if the application has stringent requirements for the timing of robot movements.

The second issue concerns robot control. Because we implemented the robot using only simple DC motors, the robot lacked a precise control capability. To improve the precision of the robot motion, there are two possible options. The first involves upgrading the motor systems to servomotors with a control unit, enabling the robot to move with a higher level of precision. The second option is to create a global observation and calibration unit from the software side. Because the RoboTable system can track the robot across the whole table-surface area, a prediction mechanism could be used to reduce the accumulated error of motion and calibrate the robot position dynamically. For most RoboTable applications, the latter solution is considered better because of its easy implementation and good performance. It is expected that it will be included in future developments of the system.

7. Conclusions

This work has two main achievements. First, we have created a complete framework that can create a mixed-reality environment involving mobile robots and that enables seamless interaction with both physical and virtual objects. The second contribution involves new possibilities for interaction styles.

To accommodate the goal of seamless interaction with different kinds of objects, we have developed the RoboTable framework by incorporating two approaches. First, we have successfully integrated existing interaction technologies to create an environment in which both robot tracking and finger-touch input could be used simultaneously and with a high degree of responsiveness. In this way, hand manipulation, such as touching and gesturing, for virtual objects is enabled, extending HRI from the real world to the virtual world. The extended robot entity, which now includes physical and virtual components, enables rich and complex interaction between the user and the robot. In addition, the physical simulation enables users to utilize their knowledge of the real world for interaction in the mixed-reality environment. The RoboTable system ensures that users perceive a unified world containing cosituated objects that interact in ways that fit the users' experience and common sense.

The framework provides three main interaction styles for users in the mixed-reality environment. The multitouch feature allows users to interact directly with virtual objects via touching and common gestures. In addition, interaction with the robot bridges the real world and the virtual world, with the robot responding not only to the user's direct physical interaction but also to interactions from the virtual world. Lastly, the robot has the capability of reconfiguration according to user requirements, where the behavior of the robot can be defined easily, using simple gestures.

For proof-of-concept purposes, we have developed two prototype applications. RoboPong is a simple game based on a classical arcade game. A human player uses touch to create a paddle, which can return an incoming ball in competition with an opponent. The robot is deployed in the game as a player with different behaviors. In competition mode, the robot can automatically move a virtual paddle to compete with a human player. In cooperation mode, the robot becomes a team member alongside one of the human players. The second application, ExploreRobot, is a learning-assistant application for school students and programming beginners. It provides simple sensors and programming mechanisms that enable users to redefine a robot's behavior, aiming to reach the goal in a virtual maze.

Robots have played an important role in education for many years, and their presence has proved stimulating for students [20]. The framework presented in this paper enables the creation of an intuitive and powerful interface that enables users to program robots easily for different tasks. Via programming and playful interaction with robots on a tabletop, students can learn concepts and principles in different disciplines such as mathematics and physics at different educational levels while also learning to think creatively, reason systematically, and work collaboratively.

The prototype applications demonstrate the possibility of developing interactive applications to support student learning, using the RoboTable framework. In addition, the advantages of the RoboTable system lead to prospects for several other application domains.

7.1. Future Work. The first task we will focus on is the improvement of global robot control. As discussed above, the current system has an accumulated error problem, which will affect applications that have stringent requirements for precise robot control. Compared with the hardware solution of upgrading the motors and control units inside the robot, the global tracking and calibration method is a more cost-effective solution. We will implement a predictor unit for the robot and a global control module that can correct the robot motion dynamically to enable its arrival at the required position.

Another promising direction for the RoboTable system is the investigation of its possible use in other serious application domains such as transportation simulation and urban planning. Because the robot provides a TUI in addition to physical forms of feedback, it is capable of representing a simulation target in some applications. The intuitive manipulation and physical representation of a simulation process might have benefits in some specific areas.

We will also consider another interesting direction of development for the RoboTable system, namely, implementing remote interaction between two tabletop systems. Because the robots can be treated as both input and output devices, they are capable of connecting two or more remote environments in which users can manipulate the robot as well as perceive physical outputs according to other users' manipulations. Remote interaction has great benefits for games and collaborative workspace applications.

Conducting serious user studies is a further objective, enabling the evaluation of different applications for different target users. Particularly for educational purposes, we hope to analyze the efficiency of the applications as teaching tools, and to collect user feedback that will help us improve the RoboTable system and applications further.

References

[1] E. Hornecker, "'I don't understand it either, but it is cool'— visitor interactions with a multi-touch table in a museum," in *Proceedings of the IEEE International Workshop on Horizontal Interactive Human Computer System (IEEE TABLETOP '08)*, pp. 113–120, Amsterdam, The Netherlands, October 2008.

[2] A. Mahmud, O. Mubin, J. R. Octavia et al., "Affective tabletop game: a new gaming experience for children," in *Proceedings of the 2nd IEEE International Workshop on Horizontal Interactive Human-Computer Systems (IEEE TABLETOP '07)*, pp. 44–51, Newport, RI, USA, October 2007.

[3] M. R. Morris, A. M. Piper, A. Cassanego, A. Huang, A. Paepcke, and T. Winograd, "Mediating group dynamics through tabletop interface design," *IEEE Computer Graphics and Applications*, vol. 26, no. 5, pp. 65–73, 2006.

[4] H. Ishii, "Tangible bits: beyond pixels," in *Proceedings of the 2nd International Conference on Tangible and Embedded Interaction (ACM TEI '08)*, pp. 15–25, Bonn, Germany, February 2008.

[5] D. Rosenfeld, M. Zawadzki, J. Sudol, and K. Perlin, "Physical objects as bidirectional user interface elements," *IEEE Computer Graphics and Applications*, vol. 24, no. 1, pp. 44–49, 2004.

[6] J. Kato, D. Sakamoto, M. Inami, and T. Igarashi, "Multi-touch interface for controlling multiple mobile robots," in *Proceedings of the 27th International Conference Extended Abstracts on Human Factors in Computing Systems (ACM CHI '09)*, pp. 3443–3448, Boston, Mass, USA, April 2009.

[7] C. Guo, J. E. Young, and E. Sharlin, "Touch and toys: new techniques for interaction with a remote group of robots,"

in *Proceedings of the 27th International Conference Extended Abstracts on Human Factors in Computing Systems (ACM CHI '09)*, pp. 491–500, Boston, Mass, USA, April 2009.

[8] C. Guo and E. Sharlin, "Utilizing physical objects and metaphors for human robot interaction," in *Proceedings of the Artificial Intelligence and the Simulation of Behaviour Convention (AISB '08)*, AISB Press, Aberdeen, UK, April 2008.

[9] P. Frei, V. Su, B. Mikhak, and H. Ishii, "Curlybot: designing a new class of computational toys," in *Proceedings of the Conference on Human Factors in Computing Systems 'The Future is Here' (ACM CHI '20)*, pp. 129–136, The Hague, The Netherlands, April 2000.

[10] M. Kojima, M. Sugimoto, A. Nakamura, M. Tomita, H. N II, and M. Inami, "Augmented coliseum: an augmented game environment with small vehicles," in *Proceedings of the 1st IEEE International Workshop on Horizontal Interactive Human-Computer Systems (IEEE TABLETOP '06)*, pp. 3–8, Adelaide, Australia, January 2006.

[11] J. Leitner, M. Haller, K. Yun, W. Woo, M. Sugimoto, and M. Inami, "IncreTable, a mixed reality tabletop game experience," in *Proceedings of the International Conference on Advances in Computer Entertainment Technology (ACM ACE '08)*, pp. 9–16, Yokohama, Japan, December 2008.

[12] D. Calife, J. L. Bernardes, and R. Tori, "Robot arena: an augmented reality platform for game development," *Computers in Entertainment*, vol. 7, no. 1, Article ID 11, 2009.

[13] J. Y. Han, "Low-cost multi-touch sensing through frustrated total internal reflection," in *Proceedings of the 18th Annual Symposium on User Interface Software and Technology (ACM UIST '05)*, pp. 115–118, Seattle, Wash, USA, 2005.

[14] M. Kaltenbrunner and R. Bencina, "ReacTIVision: a computer-vision framework for table-based tangible interaction," in *Proceedings of the 1st ACM International Conference on Tangible and Embedded Interaction (ACM TEI '07)*, pp. 69–74, Baton Rouge, La, USA, 2007.

[15] http://www.jbox2d.org.

[16] http://www.mt4j.org/mediawiki/index.php/Main_Page.

[17] http://bluecove.org.

[18] P. Marshall, "Do tangible interfaces enhance learning," in *Proceedings of the First International Conference on Tangible and Embedded Interaction (ACM TEI '07)*, pp. 163–170, Baton Rouge, La, USA, 2007.

[19] H. Mi, A. Krzywinski, and M. Sugimoto, "RoboStory: a tabletop mixed reality framework for children's role play storytelling," in *Proceedings of the 1st International Workshop on Interactive Storytelling for Children (ACM IDC '10)*, Association for Computing Machinery, Barcelona, Spain, June 2010.

[20] T. Fong, I. Nourbakhsh, and K. Dautenhahn, "A survey of socially interactive robots," *Robotics and Autonomous Systems*, vol. 42, no. 3-4, pp. 143–166, 2003.

8

Analysis of User Requirements in Interactive 3D Video Systems

Haiyue Yuan, Janko Ćalić, and Ahmet Kondoz

I-Lab, Multimedia Communications Research, Centre for Vision, Speech and Signal Processing, University of Surrey, Guildford Gu2 7XH, UK

Correspondence should be addressed to Janko Ćalić, j.calic@surrey.ac.uk

Academic Editor: Kiyoshi Kiyokawa

The recent development of three dimensional (3D) display technologies has resulted in a proliferation of 3D video production and broadcasting, attracting a lot of research into capture, compression and delivery of stereoscopic content. However, the predominant design practice of interactions with 3D video content has failed to address its differences and possibilities in comparison to the existing 2D video interactions. This paper presents a study of user requirements related to interaction with the stereoscopic 3D video. The study suggests that the change of view, zoom in/out, dynamic video browsing, and textual information are the most relevant interactions with stereoscopic 3D video. In addition, we identified a strong demand for object selection that resulted in a follow-up study of user preferences in 3D selection using virtual-hand and ray-casting metaphors. These results indicate that interaction modality affects users' decision of object selection in terms of chosen location in 3D, while user attitudes do not have significant impact. Furthermore, the ray-casting-based interaction modality using Wiimote can outperform the volume-based interaction modality using mouse and keyboard for object positioning accuracy.

1. Introduction

With the recent development of 3D stereoscopic display technology, 3D movies and 3D TV programmes are becoming a commonplace in our everyday lives. The launch of a number of broadcasted 3D channels, such as Sky 3D and BBC HD, TV viewers can immerse into 3D experience in their own living room. There has been a significant amount of ongoing related research into 3D content capture, production, and delivery. However, to the best of our knowledge, there has been very little research towards meaningful user interaction with real 3D video content. In terms of interaction design, there has been no evidence of differentiation between 2D and 3D video content. However, compared to the 2D video content, 3D video provides an additional viewing dimension and thus offers more immersive experience to the audience. Given this crucial characteristic of 3D video medium, surprisingly little attention has been dedicated towards developing an intuitive interactive technique for 3D video.

The aim of our research is to study user practices and propose technical solutions and design guidelines to develop intuitive interaction for 3D video content. In this paper, we follow the methodology outlined in our previous paper [1] by initially eliciting user requirements of stereoscopic 3D video interaction with an emphasis on potential interactive functionalities and interaction modalities, followed by a user preference study that investigates the impact of user attitudes, interaction modalities, depth profiles, and dominant eye on the selection task in 3D.

2. Related Work

There have been a number of studies that introduced advanced interactive 2D video user interfaces, facilitating intuitive interaction with video content. Two interactive video players, DRAGON (DRAGGable object navigation) [2] and DimP (direct manipulation player) [3], offer direct object manipulation of a video scene. Here, the user can browse the video by selecting and dragging an object in the scene instead of using the timeline slide. In addition, other features such as motion trajectories and annotations were used by Goldman [4], providing more categories for direct interaction with video content.

There has been a large body of research conducted on 3D interaction with computer generated (CG)/animated content. Bowman et al. [5] outline that 3D interaction consists of three common tasks: object manipulation, viewpoint manipulation, and application control. Object manipulation is usually related to tasks such as pointing, selecting, and rotating. Viewpoint manipulation refers to navigation in the virtual reality environment, as well as manipulating the zooming parameters, while the application control integrates the 2D control user interface with 3D environment to enhance the compatibility of 2D user interface. Thanks to the development of stereoscopic display technology, 3D video is able to offer an immersive experience to wide audience. However, compared with the plethora of research for 2D video interaction, there is very little research focusing on interacting with 3D video content. So far, many researchers have looked into the possible benefits of improving 3D interaction using stereoscopic technique especially in virtual reality and 3D user interface communities. Most of the research evaluate the stereo benefits for completing individual tasks such as selection or positioning. Research [6–10] reveals that stereoscopic viewing can help interaction in terms of improving user performance and depth perception. One of the motivations of our study is to see whether any of the benefits of stereoscopic viewing that have been demonstrated in interaction with 3D CG content would be advantageous for interaction with 3D video content.

A lot of research has been dedicated to develop intuitive interaction modalities for 3D stereoscopic CG content in virtual reality and 3D user interface communities. Park et al. [11] present an interactive 3D TV interface with an intelligent remote controller, which enables the user to change the viewpoint from the controller according to visual attention model. Similarly, Tamai et al. [12] introduce view control interface in 3D stereo environment using Wiimote. Ki and Kwon [13] developed a gaze-based interaction application, which is based on the calculation of degree of eye rotation and pupil centre distance to interact with 3D content. Furthermore, Steincke et al. [14] introduced the concept of interscopic interaction which means that the visualisation of 3D data is using stereoscopic techniques whereas the user interaction is performed via 2D graphical user interfaces. In their more recent work [15], they present an interscopic multitouch surfaces (iMUTS) application to support intuitive interaction with either 2D content and 3D content. In the same context of interscopic interaction, Valkov et al. [24] investigated user preferences of haptic interaction with 3D stereoscopic object on a 2D surface.

3. User Requirement Study

The aim is to elicit the user requirement and user preference for interacting with 3D stereoscopic TV in terms of interactive functionalities and interaction modalities. Interview is commonly used as a method to explore specific issue [17]

TABLE 1: Psychographic information.

Number	15
Age	24–30
Gender	Male: 12, female: 3
Occupation	Research students: 8, research staff: 4 Students: 2, employee: 1
3D experience	Extensively: 6, regularly: 3, rarely: 6

in user requirement analysis. Semistructured interview was implemented in this study to identify the requirements.

3.1. Participants. This study included a total number of 15 participants. 12 participants are male and 3 participants are female. Participants aged from 24 to 30 years old. 10 participants are from the same research centre and studying or working in 3D video-related research areas. Other 5 participants are nonexpert in 3D video technology. Each participant has previous experience of watching 3D video. Table 1 describes the psychographic information of all participants.

3.2. Procedure. The literature review and current practice of using 2D TV/video and 3D TV/video were used as the base to form the structure of the interview. It consists of four parts: (1) to gather background information for each participant; (2) to learn about the current usage of interactive service or applications for 2D video content; (3) to identify the user requirements for interactive functionalities; (4) to elicit the requirements for user interface to facilitate intuitive interactions. All the interviews were recorded using either audio recorder or video recorder, and transcribed entirely afterwards. The categorisation scheme was used to analyze the transcripts.

3.3. Results. Our results contain two main parts. One is requirement for interactive functionalities, another one is interaction modalities.

3.3.1. Interactive Functionality Requirements. During the interviews, we asked participants about what types of interactive functionalities for 2D video interaction can be applied to 3D video interaction. The discussion resulted in the common agreement that the general interactive functionalities for 2D video interaction such as "play," "pause," and "fast forward" can be applied for 3D video interaction. The analysis of transcripts focused on the interaction functionalities, which are tailored for 3D video content but not necessary for 2D video content.

Changing the Angle of View. One of the expected functionalities for the future 3D interactive video system was changing the angle of view. However, there was a differentiation of opinions between participants regarding the way of achieving this objective. One proposition was that the user can select an object or a region then manipulate it to change the viewpoint of the scene accordingly. Another proposition was to track viewer's head to change the angle of view. However based on the current technologies of 3D video production, it is more practical to implement this functionality using 3D multiview video rather than 3D stereoscopic video. The production of 3D multi-view video requires multiple cameras to capture the scene; therefore; it has the capability to render different views to the consumers. On the contrary, the production of 3D stereoscopic video content involves only single frontal parallel stereo camera so that there is limited source of captured scene to be rendered to the consumer. Speaking of content requirement, although movie and sports program have been extensively mentioned in this case, there are some interesting comments regarding this issue.

Participant 1: "Mostly action one, or in a time of goal, or nice shooting in baseball/basketball, I would like to change view in that time."

Participant 2: "For example, to watch live concert or live show, you can choose the position you want to watch thereby you have different angle of view."

Zoom In/Out. Being able to zoom in/out the 3D video content was one demanding requirement. It was expected to allow user to firstly select an object and then change the depth of the chosen object to make the illusion like pull the object close to audience, while keeping other objects in the scene at the original depth and original scale. The opposite recommendation was to zoom in the whole scene while all the objects in the scene should be scaled accordingly to keep the relative scale. There was no conclusive agreement of which way is more appropriate, it is a matter of user personalised choice. The possible solution might be providing compatible zoom in/out which can satisfy both requirements. The potential challenge of this issue in future work is to investigate the user preference of depth sensitivity, which can facilitate zoom in/out functionality and also improve user experience. The demanding video contents for this functionality were sports program, national geographical program, and documentary program were most in demand.

Textual Information. Textual information-based interaction allows the user to select an object in the scene to obtain corresponding information of the chosen object, which could be displayed in the format of text on the screen. The inspiration of having this interaction metaphor is related to the fact that the particular scene or object or event happening in the scene may not be the subject to what you are actually watching. If this happens, the response from the user is to search on the Internet or anywhere else. The potential challenge for the textual information-based interaction is to define where the text should be displayed and how the text is displayed in 3D without distraction. Participants would like to use this interaction to access information of the of interest object. For instance,

Participant 3: "Some program may contain some terminologies which I don't know them before,

so probably I have difficulties to understand this program, for instance I cannot understand the movie "Matrix" the first time I watched it."

The implication of this interaction can be used in documentary program, or getting knowledge of the footballer while watching a football game, or to obtain information of an actor/actress in a movie.

Dynamic Video Browsing. All the participants found it interesting when they were watching the demo video of direct manipulation video player [3, 4]. As a concept of select and drag an object in the scene to browse the video instead of timeline slide inspired by direct manipulation video player [3, 4], it can be adapted for 3D video content. The most interesting part for this interaction is to allow the user to browse the video in three dimensions. However, the concern was that the applicability mainly depends on the video content. It was not necessary to have this function for most of the programs, but for application like video analysis such as high-speed collision of objects, sports analysis, and surveillance analysis, where the observer or operator can test the exact moment of incidents happening to make a judge. For example, the operator can directly manipulate the football in the video reply to see whether the football crossed the line or not instead of dragging the timeline controller on the video player.

3.3.2. User Interface Requirements. The objective for this part is to find out the user preference of interaction modalities that can support 3D video interaction that proposed in previous stage. The dominant candidate was the hand gesture; however, the concern of using hand gesture was critical. It is mainly because (1) the hand gesture might lack of accuracy in the case of selecting an object; (2) deal; with the chaos caused by involuntary movement; (3) design; an effective system for multiple users; (4) implementing privacy control. Consider the above concerns, the alternatives were various such as small device with touch pad, virtual laser pointer, and digitalised glove. Although there was no conclusive result of user interface, the common agreement was that the user interface should merge the reality and virtual environment to offer immersive experience. The graphical representation of the derived user requirements is depicted in Figure 1.

Last but not least, it is not surprising to find that selection was frequently used as the first step for each interaction mentioned above. In the use case discussed during the interview, participants always firstly select the object in the video and then conduct different interaction with the video content. This is consistent with the findings from previous literatures, which indicate that selection is one of the essential building blocks of all interactive virtual environment systems. It is a process of identifying particular objects, which are the targets for the subsequent actions. The most significant characteristic of 3D video is the depth illusion caused by the disparity between left and right images. Unlike the ordinary selection task, to achieve accurate selection for 3D video content needs to acquire information

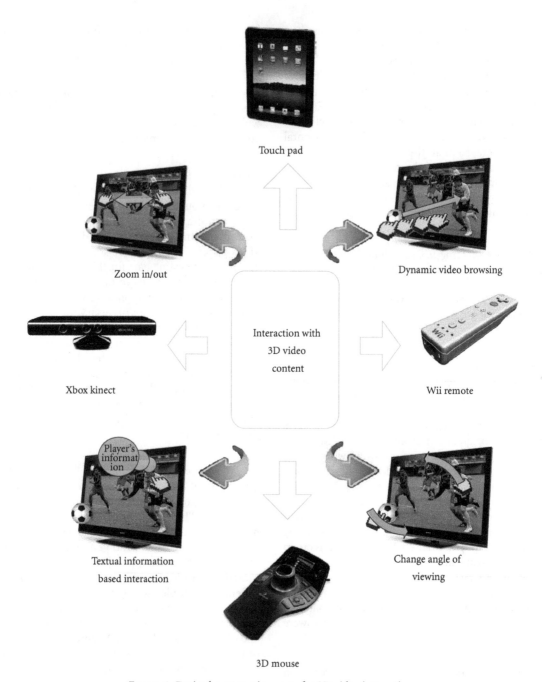

FIGURE 1: Derived user requirements for 3D video interaction.

of disparity, this makes selection in this case more complex and important.

4. User Preference of Object Selection in Stereoscopic 3D Virtual Environment

According to the findings from user requirement analysis, the conclusive agreement among all participants was that selection can be considered as the fundamental requirement for proposed 3D video interaction. Selection has been considered as one of the primary techniques for interactive applications especially in 3D virtual environment [18]. It

is a process of identifying particular objects, which are the targets for the subsequent actions. A large number of research has been looking into various techniques to support accurate and comfort selection. However, few has been focusing on studying user preference and user behavior of selection in virtual environment. In this part, we present a preference study from user's perspective, that investigate the impact of user attitudes, interaction modalities, depth profiles, and dominant eye on object selection in stereoscopic 3D environment.

Selection has been extensively addressed in previous literatures. Most of the selection techniques are variations of

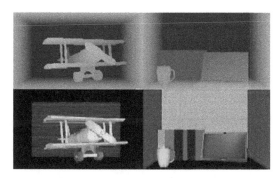

FIGURE 2: Two examples of the 3D scenes with their depth maps used in user preference study.

FIGURE 3: Experimental setup used in the user preference study with Wiimote.

TABLE 2: Psychographic information.

Number	15
Age	21–28
Gender	Male: 14, female: 1
Occupation	Research students: 13, research staff: 2
3D experience	Extensively: 8, regularly: 5, rarely: 2
Dominate eye	Left: 5, right: 10

the following two main classes: volume-based selection and ray-based selection [19–21]. Volume-based selection uses the virtual hand/cursor and cone selection to select an object, where requires intersection or collision detection between the virtual hand and the 3D object. As one of the variation of volume based selection, Go-Go interaction technique enables to extend user's arm length to select object at further distance [16]. Ray-based selection casts a virtual ray into the virtual world to select an object, which is hit by the virtual ray. The way of casting a virtual ray results in two main kinds of variations of ray-based selection. The ray cast from the hand is usually referred as ray-casting technique. The ray is cast from eye and passes through another point in the space that the user can control (e.g., the position of the tip of the finger, or a pointing device). This technique is usually referred to as image plane selection or occlusion selection.

We used both volume-based selection and ray-based selection techniques as the basis to develop two different interaction modalities respectively in this study in order to investigate their impact on the user preference of 3D selective position.

4.1. Experiment Design.
We conducted series of experiments to ask participants to finish the object selection task in 3D using two interaction modalities and two different user attitudes within twenty different depth profiles. The interaction modalities are designed based on the most frequently used selection techniques in 3D interaction. One is the implementation of volume-based selection using mouse and keyboard. Another one is based on ray-casting technique using Wiimote. The user attitudes refer to two different requirements for participants to complete the task: take time to select and select as soon as possible. Depth profile was used to simulate the different 3D scene (see Figure 2).

The reason we created different depth profile was twofold; one was attempting to find out the relationship between user preferred selective position in 3D and associated depth profile, another one was to simulate 3D scene. In order to build a controlled experimental environment, we used 3D stereoscopic CG (Computer Generated)/animated content in this study. Our intention was to learn user behaviour from this experiment and generate results of user preference of object selection in 3D, which can be transferable benefits for the 3D stereoscopic video interaction in our future work.

4.2. Participants.
There were 15 participants recruited for this experiment. Table 2 describes the psychographic information of all participants. They are all research students in the same research lab. Participants aged from 21 to 28, and contained 1 female and 14 males. All the participants have previous experience of watching 3D stereoscopic video and playing 3D game. Before conducting the experiments, we implemented a Dolman method known as hole-in-the-card to test each participant's dominant eye, 5 of them are left eye dominant, and 10 of them are right eye dominant. In addition, participants took a Randot stereoacuity test, and all of them had accepted stereo perception.

4.3. Apparatus.
The experiment was performed on a 46″ JVC stereoscopic display with passive polarization glasses (model number GD-463D10). The resolution of the display is 1920 × 1080 and the recommended viewing distance is 2 meters from the screen. The supported format for stereoscopic content is left and right side-by-side representation. We used mouse, keyboard, two Wiimotes with motion plus and a Wii sensor bar in the experiments. We produced and rendered the stereoscopic 3D content using OGRE (open source 3D graphics engine) [22] and use WiiYourself [23] to access Wiimote usage data. Figure 3 presents the setup during the experiment using Wiimote.

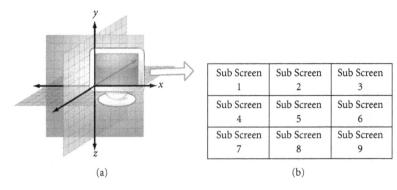

FIGURE 4: (a) Representation of coordinates system (b) Sub-screen distribution.

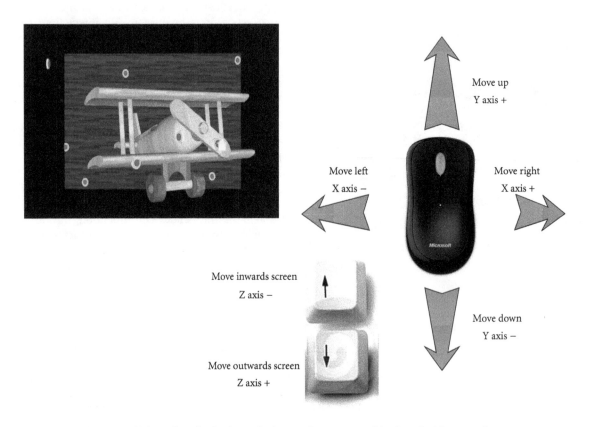

FIGURE 5: Volume-based selection techniques using mouse and keyboard with screenshot.

4.4. Procedure. A within-subjects design was used in which three factors were varied: user attitudes (take your time, as soon as possible), interaction modalities (mouse+keyboard, Wiimote), and depth profiles. As one of the dependent variables, task completion time was calculated from the moment that the object is selected to the moment that object is placed against the destination. Accuracy is another dependent variable, which measured the distance of placed object away from the destination. The smaller the distance is, the higher the accuracy is. The whole experiment is designed based on OGRE coordinates system (please see Figure 4(a)) and consists of two parts. We implemented the volume-based selection technique as a virtual cursor interaction modality in part 1 (please see Figure 5). Mouse is used to control 2-dimensional movement of the virtual cursor along x- and y-axis, and we use arrow key on the keyboard to move the virtual cursor inwards and outwards along z-axis. The selection is indicated by a mouse click, followed by a collision test activation. If the object is chosen successfully, the bonding box of the chosen object will be visible for the participant. In part 2, we implemented ray-based selection technique (please see Figure 6) to design an interaction modality of virtual laser pointer, which combined Wiimote, Wii motion plus, and Wii sensor bar. The combination of Wiimote and Wii sensor bar is used to locate the position of source of ray. The Wii motion plus is used to detect the degree of pitch and yaw of Wiimote which indicate the orientation of the source of the ray. The selection is executed

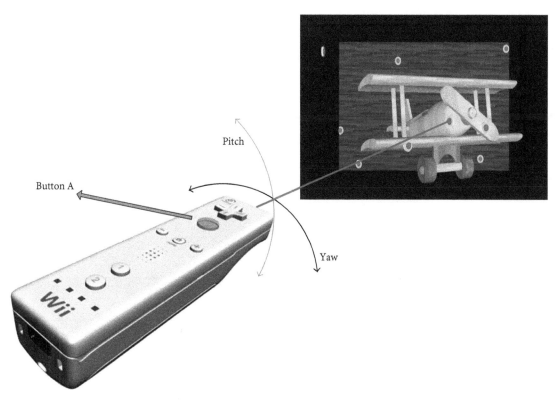

FIGURE 6: Ray-casting selection techniques using Wiimote with screenshot.

by pressing the button A, which emits a ray to the scene. Once the ray hits the object, the appearance of bounding box of the chosen object indicates effective selection.

There were 15 participants in total. We divided them into three groups, 5 participants each group. In order to cancel the learning effect, we apply counterbalancing to assign the order of task to each group. For groups 1 and 3, participants finish experiment part 1 and followed by conducting experiment part 2. For group 2, participants conduct experiment part 1 firstly and then finish experiment part 2.

Each part contained 2 sets. For the first set, each participant was asked to take time to choose one object which he/she liked the most and then put the selected object into the destination. For the second set, each participant was required to do the same task as quick as possible. For each set, [each participant needed to finish the selection task with 20 different depth profiles each trial for 3 trials.] The display was divided into 9 subscreens (please see Figure 4(b)). The purpose of introducing subscreens is to find out the popularity of each subregion on the display in terms of selection rate. For each trial, 1 object is allocated to a random position within its corresponding sub screens, so that 9 objects for 9 subscreens in total for participants to choose from. Each participant needs to choose only 1 object for each trial. At end of the experiment, we can obtain the status of how many times the object has been chosen from each sub screen, and thus to get the popularity of each subscreen. Overall each participant completed the task for $2 \times 2 \times 20 \times 3$

trials for the whole experiment. It took around 30 minutes to complete each part of the experiment and one hour for the whole experiment.

4.5. Experimental Results

4.5.1. User Attitude Impact. The participant was asked to choose the object in two different attitudes: one was to *take time* to choose the object which he/she liked the most and then put it into the destination, another attitude was to choose the object A.S.A.P (as soon as possible) and then put it into the destination. ANOVA (analysis of variance) was used to analyze the statistic difference between two attitudes regarding the task completed time and task completed accuracy, respectively. How far the placed object away from the selected destination was used to indicate the accuracy. The smaller the distance is, the higher the accuracy is. ANOVA showed a significant main effect ($F_{1,1783} = 101.7, P = 0.000$, see Table 3) of user attitude on the task completed time. It is not surprising that the participant spent about one more second on average to complete the task in Take Time attitude than in A.S.A.P attitude. For the accuracy, there was no significant difference between the two groups ($F_{1,1783} = 0.99, P = 0.319$), which indicated that the user attitude did not have significant impact on the accuracy of completing the task.

In addition, we investigated the impact of user attitude towards the matter of where the participant wants to select

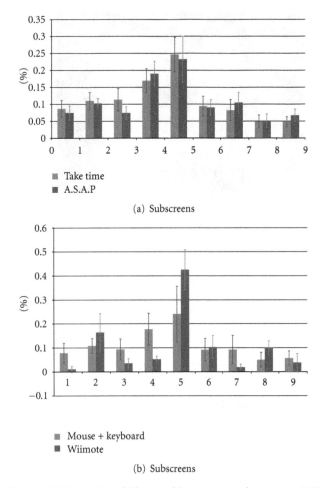

(a) Subscreens

(b) Subscreens

FIGURE 7: Percentage of chosen objects across subscreen at X-Y plane: (a) user attitudes; (b) interaction modalities.

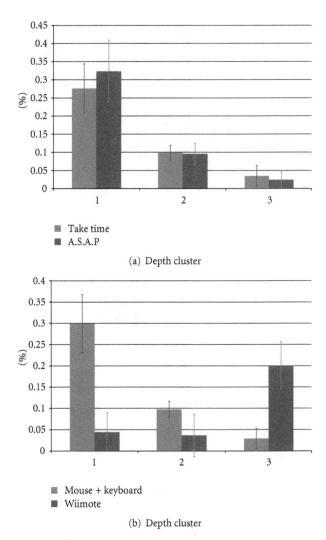

(a) Depth cluster

(b) Depth cluster

FIGURE 8: Percentage of chosen objects in the third dimension: (a) user attitudes; (b) interaction modalities.

TABLE 3: Impact of user attitudes on task completion time and accuracy.

Attitude	Task completed time	Accuracy
	Mean (std)	Mean (std)
Take time	3.73 s (3.00)	0.727 (1.862)
A.S.A.P	2.61 s (1.36)	0.645 (1.637)
ANOVA test	$F_{1,1784} = 101.7, P = 0.00$	$F_{1,1784} = 0.99, P = 0.319$

the object in X-Y plane and along z-axis respectively (please see Figure 4). The chosen rate of each sub screen was indicated by the percentage of chosen objects, which was the number of chosen objects divided by the total number of objects allocated in this subscreen. The corresponding distribution of object chosen percentage across sub screens is depicted in Figure 7(a).

Sub screen 4 and sub screen 5 had highest percentage for both user attitude scenarios. Sub screen 2, sub screen 6, and sub screen 7 had around 10 percent of chosen rate. In addition, we did a pairwise correlation test between the two groups. Significant correlation between the two groups ($r = 0.9483, P = 0.0001$) indicated that the user attitude did

not affect participant's choices of object selection in X-Y plane.

Furthermore, we took a look at the participant's preference of object selection along z-axis. We clustered the position of objects along z-axis into three categories: near, middle, and far. In OGRE units, 0 at z-axis indicates that the scene has 0 binocular disparity, which can be referred as screen level. Below 0 units refers to negative binocular disparity, which indicates that the scene is behind the screen. Above 0 units refers to positive binocular disparity, which indicates the scene is in front of the screen. The definition of "near," "middle," and "far" with equivalent OGRE units and disparity in pixels are shown in Table 4. We measured the percentage of chosen objects against all the objects that are in the same depth cluster (please see Figure 8(a)).

For both scenarios, participants preferred objects in front. The pairwise correlation test indicated the significant correlation between the two groups ($r = 0.9996, P = 0.0017$). Therefore, user attitude did not have effect on the participant's preference of object selection in third

TABLE 4: Clustering units.

	Near	Middle	Far
OGRE units (u)	$u \geq 2$	$-2 < u < 2$	$u \leq -2$
Disparity (d)	$d \geq 8$	$-10 < d < 8$	$d \leq -10$

TABLE 5: Impact of the interaction modality on the task completion time and its accuracy.

Modality	Task completed time Mean (std)	Accuracy Mean (std)
Mouse + keyboard	3.17 s (2.41)	0.69 (1.75)
Wiimote	3.22 s (2.22)	0.22 (0.61)
ANOVA test	$F_{1,1775} = 0.07, P = 0.79$	$F_{1,1775} = 17.61, P = 0.00$

TABLE 6: ANOVA test across depth profiles.

	Task completed time	Accuracy
Attitude	$F_{19,1784}$ (P)	$F_{19,1784}$ (P)
Take time	1.52 (0.08)	0.67 (0.849)
A.S.A.P	1.22 (0.2337)	0.7 (0.8198)
Modality	$F_{19,1775}$ (P)	$F_{19,1775}$ (P)
Mouse + keyboard	1.25 (0.2071)	0.71 (0.807)
Wiimote	0.89 (0.595)	0.82 (0.679)

TABLE 7: Correlation test for each depth profile.

DP	Attitude r (P)	Modalities r (P)	DP	Attitude r (P)	Modalities r (P)
1	**0.89 (0.00)**	**0.96 (0.00)**	11	**0.97 (0.00)**	0 (1.0)
2	**0.97 (0.00)**	**0.98 (0.00)**	12	**0.99 (0.00)**	0.10 (0.79)
3	**0.68 (0.04)**	−0.39 (0.29)	13	0.20 (0.61)	−0.59 (0.09)
4	**0.64 (0.06)**	0.48 (0.19)	14	**0.86 (0.00)**	**0.78 (0.01)**
5	0.44 (0.24)	−0.18 (0.64)	15	**0.74 (0.02)**	0.34 (0.37)
6	0.42 (0.26)	0 (1.00)	16	**0.96 (0.00)**	0.57 (0.11)
7	**0.96 (0.00)**	0.29 (0.45)	17	0.39 (0.30)	−0.20 (0.61)
8	0.46 (0.21)	0.58 (0.10)	18	0.57 (0.11)	**0.66 (0.05)**
9	**0.89 (0.00)**	**0.87 (0.00)**	19	**0.95 (0.00)**	**0.94 (0.00)**
10	**0.85 (0.00)**	0.32 (0.40)	20	**0.72 (0.03)**	0.14 (0.72)

DP stands for depth profile.

dimension. Above analysis was based on volume selection-based interaction modality using mouse and keyboard. Similar results have been found for ray-casting selection-based interaction modality using Wiimote.

4.5.2. Interaction Modality Impact. In this part, two interaction modalities were used to find out how do they affect participants' preference of 3D object selection. The dependent variable was task completed time and accuracy, respectively, the independent variable was interaction modality, which contain mouse+keyboard and Wiimote two categories. ANOVA indicated no significant difference ($F_{1,1775} = 0.07, P = 0.7891$, see Table 5) of task completed time between the two modalities.

For the accuracy analysis, significant difference ($F_{1,1775} = 17.61, P = 0.000$) between the two interaction modalities suggested that using Wiimote can offer higher accuracy of object positioning.

The comparison of object chosen rate in 2D between two interaction modalities across 9 sub screens is shown in Figure 7(b). The correlation analysis found correlation between two interaction modalities ($r = 0.7523, P = 0.01$) Although it was not highly correlated, sub screen 5 had the highest chosen rate for both scenarios and sub screen 2 and sub screen 6 had similar chosen rate.

The analysis of participant's preference of object selection in third dimension revealed that participant was more willing to choose further objects using Wiimote (see Figure 8(b)). No significant correlation have been found between two modalities in this case ($r = -0.664, P = 0.5373$). The reason of such bias of object selection in third dimension was because of the interaction techniques. The informal post experiment interview also backed up this result. It was easier to use laser pointer like metaphor to reach anywhere in the scene. The interaction modality had significant impact on the preference of object selection along Z-axis, and less impact on the preference of object selection in X-Y plane.

4.5.3. Depth Profile Impact. There were 20 different depth profiles in this study, we conducted ANOVA test across different groups (user attitude group and interaction modality group) to investigate the relationship between depth profiles in terms of task completed time and accuracy, respectively. The dependent variable was task completed time and accuracy, respectively, the independent variable was depth profile. As seen from Table 6, there was no significant difference within depth profiles between different user attitudes and between different interaction modalities.

In addition, we compared the correlation of object chosen rate each profile for 20 different depth profiles across different groups. For the majority of the depth profiles, participants had similar preference of object chosen rate across 9 sub screens no matter they take time to select the object or select the object as soon as possible. Only few significant correlation has been found for different interaction modalities. Numbers in bold in Table 7 indicate significant correlation between groups for each corresponding depth profile.

The results indicated that for different depth profiles, user attitudes had less impact than interaction modalities on the user preference of object selection. This is consistent with the previous findings from 4.5.1 and 4.5.2.

4.5.4. Dominant Eye Impact. One of the previous works by [24] was about touch interaction with 3D stereoscopic content. The major finding indicated that dominant eye can significantly influence participants' choice of where to interact with the 3D stereoscopic object. Inspired by their work, the aim is to look at the impact of dominant eye in our case of object selection.

The dependent variable was the relative horizontal distance between chosen object and centre of the screen,

TABLE 8: Dominant eye impact.

Distance	Coef	Std	t	P
Eye	0.586	0.14	4.19	0.000
Constant	−0.669	0.11	−6.17	0.000
$F = 17.52, P = 0.000$				

where minus distance indicated that the object is located at the left side of the centre and vice versa. The independent variable was dominant eye, where left eye dominant was indicated by dummy variable 0 and right eye dominant was indicated by dummy variable 1. Therefore, the hypothesis model is shown as below (1), where Y refers to distance, and X refers to eye dominance:

$$Yi = \alpha + \beta Xi + \epsilon i. \tag{1}$$

In order to test the difference between left dominant eye and right dominant eye, we have the null hypothesis (2) that there is no statistic difference of distance between participants with different dominant eye, and alternative hypothesis (3) as below:

$$H0 : \beta = 0; \tag{2}$$

$$Ha : \beta \neq 0. \tag{3}$$

A robust linear regression test has been implemented, and the results (i.e., $t = 4.17$, $P = 0.0000$, $F = 17.52$, $P = 0.0000$, please see Table 8) suggest that we cannot reject the null hypothesis, which indicate that there is a significant difference between dominant eyes:

$$Yi = -0.669 + 0.586 * Xi + \epsilon i. \tag{4}$$

Therefore as given in (4), if the participant is left eye dominant (i.e., eye = 0), the relative horizontal distance is −0.669. On the contrary, if the participant is right eye dominant (i.e., eye = 1), the relative horizontal distance is −0.083. The results indicated that participants with left dominant eye would choose the object more close to the left, hand side than the participants with right dominant eye.

4.6. Discussion. Selection is one of the essential building blocks of interaction in virtual environments. Large amount of work has focused on the selection techniques that facilitate accurate and comfortable object selection in interactive applications. However, little has been done to address the user preference of selective location in virtual environments as well as the impact from different parameters that influence users' choice of object selection. This work addresses these issues from the user's perspective to understand better their behaviour. We have looked into the impact of user attitudes, interaction modalities, depth profiles, and influence of the dominant eye on user's preferred location for selection in three dimensions.

Two tasks were studied: "take your time to select" and "select as soon as possible." These are two distinct user

attitudes towards the task. The expected results before conducting the user study was that the user would have different choices of locations for different attitudes. In addition, it was expected that different interaction modalities might increase the arbitrariness of the results. However, the experimental results revealed surprising findings that there were certain patterns of user preferences and user behaviours.

Regardless of the user attitudes and interaction modalities, participants have similar preference towards locations in the 2D domain, that is, the middle area of the screen is the hot spot for object selection, while the bottom right of the screen has lowest rate of selection.

When it comes to the location in the third dimension, the impact of user attitudes using the same interaction modality is not so significant. Nevertheless, different interaction modalities result in entirely contrasting user preferences of object selection in the third dimension. Using mouse and keyboard, participants prefer to select objects that are closer to the audience, while the chosen rate of object selection gradually decreases as the depth increases. On the contrary, using Wiimote ray-casting approach, the highest chosen rate of object selection is at the deeper end, while the lowest selection rate happens at the front. This is in accord with the characteristics of its underlying interaction techniques, where volume-based selection is more challenging when reaching the objects far from the participants, while the ray-casting selection provides more freedom of navigation in 3D. The investigation of various depth profiles in this study did not provide evidence that its impact would affect participants' preference of object selection in 3D. The analysis of dominant eye impact indicated that participants with left dominant eye would select the object more relatively close to the left of the display. These results can be applied in the design and production of stereoscopic 3D video interaction systems and gaming, enabling user centred approach and enhancing the user experience.

5. Conclusion and Future Work

This paper presents a set of user studies that focus on user requirements in 3D video interaction and the user preferences related to object selection in 3D. The results as well as design recommendations are listed below.

(i) Changing of the angle of view, textual information, zoom in/out, and dynamic video browsing are the interactive functionalities that can facilitate intuitive interaction with 3D video content. Object selection should be considered as the fundamental requirement in the design of the 3D video interaction.

(ii) Participants have consistent behaviour of object selection over different user attitudes while using the same interaction modality.

(iii) Participants have significantly different preferences related to object selection, especially in the third dimension while using different interaction modalities.

(iv) The choice of location for object selection in the third dimension significantly depends on interaction modality.

(v) The area around the centre of the screen has the highest rate of selection regardless of user attitudes, interaction modalities across depth profiles.

(vi) The virtual laser pointer based on ray-casting approach to selection using Wiimote can offer higher accuracy of object positioning when compared with the volume-based selection using the mouse and keyboard modality.

(vii) The participants with left dominant eye prefer selecting the objects relatively closer to the left side of the display.

In order to develop this research further, we will focus on two domains. One will investigate methodologies that will enable interactions with 3D video content proposed in this paper. The second one will conduct experiments to quantify user experience of different interaction modalities aimed at completing proposed interaction tasks as well as investigate the impact of depth to 3D video interaction. These studies will provide the understanding and guidelines of intuitive interaction with stereoscopic 3D video content from users perspective.

References

[1] H. Yuan, J. Ćalić, and A. Kondoz, "User requirements elicitation of stereoscopic 3d video interaction," in *Proceedings of the IEEE International Conference on Multimedia and Expo (ICME '12)*, 2012.

[2] T. Karrer, M. Weiss, E. Lee, and J. Borchers, "Dragon: a direct manipulation interface for frame-accurate in-scene video navigation," in *Proceedings of the twenty-sixth annual SIGCHI conference on CHI (CHI '08)*, pp. 247–250, ACM, New York, NY, USA, 2008.

[3] P. Dragicevic, G. Ramos, J. Bibliowicz et al., "Video browsing by direct manipulation," in *Proceedings of the 26th Annual SIGCHI Conference on CHI (CHI '08)*, pp. 237–246, ACM, New York, NY, USA, April 2008.

[4] D. B. Goldman, C. Gonterman, B. Curless, D. Salesin, and S. M. Seitz, "Video object annotation, navigation, and composition," in *Proceedings of the 21st ACM Symposium on User Interface Software and Technology (UIST '08)*, pp. 3–12, October 2008.

[5] D. A. Bowman, S. Coquillart, B. Froehlich et al., "3D user interfaces: new directions and perspectives," *IEEE Computer Graphics and Applications*, vol. 28, no. 6, pp. 20–36, 2008.

[6] S. Zhai, W. Buxton, and P. I. Milgram, "The Silk cursor: investigating transparency for 3D target acquisition," in *Proceedings of the Conference on Human Factors in Computing Systems (CHI '94)*, pp. 459–464, April 1994.

[7] J. Boritz and K. S. Booth, "Study of interactive 6 DOF docking in a computerized virtual environment," in *Proceedings of the IEEE Virtual Reality Annual International Symposium (VRAIS '98)*, pp. 139–146, March 1998.

[8] G. S. Hubona, P. N. Wheeler, G. W. Shirah, and M. Brandt, "The relative contributions of stereo, lighting, and background scenes in promoting 3d depth visualization," *ACM Transactions on Computer-Human Interaction*, vol. 6, pp. 214–242, 1999.

[9] M. Fujimoto and Y. Ishibashi, "The effect of stereoscopic viewing of a virtual space on a networked game using haptic media," in *Proceedings of the ACM SIGCHI International Conference on Advances in Computer Entertainment Technology (ACE '04)*, pp. 317–320, June 2005.

[10] R. J. Teather and W. Stuerzlinger, "Guidelines for 3D positioning techniques," in *Proceedings of the Conference on Future Play (Future Play '07)*, pp. 61–68, ACM, November 2007.

[11] M. C. Park, S. K. Kim, and J. Y. Son, "3D TV interface by an intelligent remote controller," in *Proceedings of the 1st International Conference on 3DTV (3DTV-CON '07)*, pp. 1–4, May 2007.

[12] M. Tamai, W. Wu, K. Nahrstedt, and K. Yasumoto, "A view control interface for 3D tele-immersive environments," in *Proceedings of the IEEE International Conference on Multimedia and Expo*, pp. 1101–1104, June 2008.

[13] J. Ki and Y. M. Kwon, "3D gaze estimation and interaction," in *Proceedings of the 3DTV-Conference: The True Vision—Capture, Transmission and Display of 3D Video (3DTV-CON '08)*, pp. 373–376, May 2008.

[14] F. Stenicke, T. Ropinski, G. Bruder, and K. Hinrichs, "Interscopic user interface concepts for fish tank virtual reality systems," in *Proceedings of the IEEE Virtual Reality Conference (VR '07)*, pp. 27–34, March 2007.

[15] J. Schöning, F. Steinicke, A. Krüger, uger, K. Hinrichs, and D. Valkov, "Bimanual interaction with interscopic multi-touch surfaces," in *Proceedings of the 12th IFIP TC 13 International Conference on Human-Computer Interaction: Part II (INTERACT '09)*, pp. 40–53, Springer, Berlin, Germany, 2009.

[16] I Poupyrev, M. Billinghurst, S. Weghorst, and T. Ichikawa, "The go-go interaction technique: nonlinear mapping for direct manipulation in vr," in *Proceedings of the 9th annual ACM symposium on UIST (UIST '96)*, pp. 79–80, ACM, New York, NY, USA, 1996.

[17] Y. Rogers, H. Sharp, and J. Preece, *Interaction Design: Beyond Human-Computer Interaction*, John Wiley & Sons, 2002.

[18] D. A. Bowman, E. Kruijff, J. J. LaViola, and I. Poupyrev, *3D User Interfaces: Theory and Practice*, Addison Wesley Longman, Redwood City, Calif, USA, 2004.

[19] A. Steed, "Towards a general model for selection in virtual environments," in *Proceedings of the IEEE Symposium on 3D User Interfaces (3DUI '06)*, pp. 103–110, March 2006.

[20] R. J. Teather and W. Stuerzlinger, "Pointing at 3D targets in a stereo head-tracked virtual environment," in *Proceedings of the IEEE Symposium on 3D User Interfaces (3DUI '11)*, pp. 87–94, March 2011.

[21] A. Douglas Bowman, *Interaction techniques for common tasks in immersive virtual environments: design, evaluation, and application [Ph.D. thesis]*, Atlanta, Ga, USA, 1999, AAI9953819.

[22] OGRE, http://www.ogre3d.org/.

[23] WiiYourself! Native C++Wiimote Library v1.15 RC3, http://wiiyourself.gl.tter.org/.

[24] D. Valkov, F. Steinicke, G. Bruder, and K. Hinrichs, "2D touching of 3D stereoscopic objects," in *Proceedings of the 29th Annual CHI Conference on Human Factors in Computing Systems (CHI '11)*, pp. 1353–1362, May 2011.

9

Usability Testing for Serious Games: Making Informed Design Decisions with User Data

Pablo Moreno-Ger,[1] **Javier Torrente,**[1] **Yichuan Grace Hsieh,**[2] **and William T. Lester**[2]

[1] *Facultad de Informática, Universidad Complutense de Madrid, 28040 Madrid, Spain*
[2] *Laboratory of Computer Science, Massachusetts General Hospital, Harvard Medical School, Boston, MA 02114, USA*

Correspondence should be addressed to Pablo Moreno-Ger, pablom@fdi.ucm.es

Academic Editor: Kiju Lee

Usability testing is a key step in the successful design of new technologies and tools, ensuring that heterogeneous populations will be able to interact easily with innovative applications. While usability testing methods of productivity tools (e.g., text editors, spreadsheets, or management tools) are varied, widely available, and valuable, analyzing the usability of games, especially educational "serious" games, presents unique usability challenges. Because games are fundamentally different than general productivity tools, "traditional" usability instruments valid for productivity applications may fall short when used for serious games. In this work we present a methodology especially designed to facilitate usability testing for serious games, taking into account the specific needs of such applications and resulting in a systematically produced list of suggested improvements from large amounts of recorded gameplay data. This methodology was applied to a case study for a medical educational game, MasterMed, intended to improve patients' medication knowledge. We present the results from this methodology applied to MasterMed and a summary of the central lessons learned that are likely useful for researchers who aim to tune and improve their own serious games before releasing them for the general public.

1. Introduction

As the complexity of new technologies increases, affecting wider portions of the population, usability testing is gaining even more relevance in the fields of human-computer interaction (HCI) and user interface (UI) design. Brilliant products run this risk of failing completely if end users cannot fully engage because of user interface failures. Consequently, product designers are increasingly focusing on usability testing during the prototype phase to identify design or implementation issues that might prevent users from successfully interacting with a final product.

Prototype usability testing is especially important when the system is to be used by a heterogeneous population or if this population includes individuals who are not accustomed to interacting with new technologies. In this sense, the field of serious games provides a good example where there should be special attention paid to usability issues.

Because educational serious games aim to engage players across meaningful learning activities, it is important to evaluate the dimensions of learning effectiveness, engagement, and the appropriateness of the design for a specific context and target audience [1]. Yet because serious games target broad audiences who may not play games regularly, usability issues alone can hinder the gameplay process negatively affecting the learning experience.

However, measuring the usability of such an interactive system is not always a straightforward process. Even though there are different heuristic instruments to measure usability with the help of experts [2]; these methods do not always identify all the pitfalls in a design [3]. Furthermore, usability is not an absolute concept per se but is instead relative in nature, dependent on both the task and the user. Consider the issue of complexity or usability across decades in age or across a spectrum of user educational backgrounds—what is usable for a young adult may not be usable for an octogenarian. It is situations like these where deep insight into how the users will interact with the system is required. A common approach is to allow users to interact with a prototype while developers and designers observe how the user tries to figure out how to use the system, taking notes of the stumbling points and design errors [4].

However, prototype evaluation for usability testing can be cumbersome and may fail to identify comprehensively all of the stumbling points in a design. When usability testing sessions are recorded with audio and/or video, it can be difficult to simultaneously process both recorded user feedback and onscreen activity in a systematic way that will assure that all pitfalls are identified. Thus usability testing using prototype evaluation can be a time-consuming and error-prone task that is dependent on subjective individual variability.

In addition, many of the principles used to evaluate the usability of general software may not be necessarily applicable to (serious) games [5]. Games are expected to challenge users, making them explore, try, fail, and reflect. This cycle, along with explicit mechanisms for immediate feedback and perception of progress, is a key ingredient in game design, necessary for fun and engagement [6]. So the very context that makes a game engaging and powerful as a learning tool may adversely affect the applicability of traditional usability guidelines for serious games.

For example, typical usability guidelines for productivity software indicate that it should be trivial for the user to acquire a high level of competency using the tool, and that hesitation or finding a user uncertain about how to perform a task is always considered as unfortunate events. A serious game connects the pathways of exploration and trial and error loops to help the player acquire new knowledge and skills in the process [7]. This makes it imperative to differentiate hesitations and errors due to a bad UI design from actual trial and errors derived from the exploratory nature of discovering gameplay elements, a nuance typically overlooked using traditional usability testing tools.

In this paper we present a methodology for usability testing for serious games, building on previous instruments and extending them to address the specific traits of educational serious games. The methodology contemplates a process in which the interactions are recorded and then processed by multiple reviewers to produce a set of annotations that can be used to identify required changes and separate UI issues, game design issues, and gameplay exploration as different types of events.

Most importantly, a main objective of this methodology is to provide a structured approach to the identification of design issues early in the process, rather than to provide an instrument to validate a product achieving a "usability score".

As a case study, this methodology was developed and employed to evaluate the usability of a serious game developed at the Massachusetts General Hospital's Laboratory of Computer Science. "MasterMed" is a game designed to help the patients understand more about their prescribed medications and the conditions for which they are intended to treat. The application of this methodology using an actual game has helped us to understand better the strengths and limitations of usability studies in general and of this methodology in particular. From this experience, we have been able to synthesize the lessons learned about the assessment methodology that can be useful for serious games creators to improve their own serious games before releasing them.

2. Usability Testing and Serious Games

Usability is defined in the ISO 9241-11 as "*the extent to which a product can be used by specified users to achieve specified goals with effectiveness, efficiency and satisfaction in a specified context of use*" [8]. This broad definition focuses on having products that allow the users to achieve goals and provides a base for measuring usability for different software products. However, digital games are a very specific type of software with unique requirements while serious games have the additional objective of knowledge discovery through exploratory learning. This presents unique usability challenges that are specific to serious games.

In this Section we provide an overview of the main techniques for usability testing in general, and then we focus on the specific challenges posed by serious games.

2.1. Usability Testing Methods and Instruments. Usability represents an important yet often overlooked factor that impacts the use of every software product. While usability is often the intended goal when developing a software package, engineers tend to design following engineering criteria, often resulting in products that seem obvious in their functioning for the developers, but not for general users, with correspondingly negative results [9].

There are a variety of methods typically used to assess for usability. As described by Macleod and Rengger [4], these methods can be broadly catalogued as (i) *expert methods*, in which experienced evaluators identify potential pitfalls and usability issues, (ii) *theoretical methods*, in which theoretical models of tools and user behaviors are compared to predict usability issues, and (iii) *user methods*, in which software prototypes are given to end users to interact.

Among user methods, two main approaches exist: observational analysis, in which a user interacts with the system while the developers observe, and survey-based methods, in which the user fills in evaluation questionnaires after interacting with the system. Such questionnaires may also be used when applying expert methods, and they are typically based on heuristic rules that can help identify potential issues [10].

There are a number of survey-based metrics and evaluation methodologies for usability testing. A method most commonly cited is the System Usability Scale (SUS) because it is simple and relatively straightforward to apply [11]. SUS focuses on administering a very quick Likert-type questionnaire to users right after their interaction with the system, producing a "usability score" for the system. Another popular and well-supported tool, the Software Usability Measurement Inventory (SUMI), provides detailed evaluations [12] by measuring usability across five different dimensions (efficiency, affect, helpfulness, control, and learnability). In turn, the Questionnaire for User Interaction Satisfaction (QUIS) [13] deals in terms more closely related with the technology (such as system capabilities, screen factors, and learning factors) with attention to demographics for selecting appropriate audiences. Finally, the ISO/IEC 9126 standard is probably the most comprehensive instrument, as described in detail in Jung and colleagues' work [14].

However, many of these metrics suffer from the same weakness in that they can yield disparate results when reapplied to the same software package [15]. In addition, it is very common for such questionnaires and methods to focus on producing a usability score for the system, rather than the identification and remediation of the specific usability issues. This focus on identifying remediation actions as well as the prioritization of the issues and the actions surprisingly is often missing in studies and applications [16].

When the objective is to identify specific issues that may prevent end users from interacting successfully with the system, the most accurate approaches are observational user methods [4], as they provide direct examples of how the end users will use (or struggle to use) the applications. However, observational analysis requires the availability of fully functioning prototypes and can involve large amounts of observational data that requires processing and analysis. The experts may analyze the interaction directly during the session or, more commonly, rely on video recordings of the sessions to study the interaction. This has also led to considerations on the importance of having more than one expert review each interaction session. As discussed by Boring et al. [16], a single reviewer watching an interaction session has a small likelihood of identifying the majority of usability issues. The likelihood of discovering usability issues may be increased by having more than one expert review each session [17]; but this increased detection comes at the expense of time and human resources during the reviewing process.

In summary, usability testing is a mature field, with multiple approaches and instruments that have been used in a variety of contexts. All the approaches are valid and useful, although they provide different types of outcomes. In particular, observational user methods seem to be the most relevant when the objective is to identify design issues that may interfere with the user's experience, which is the focus of this work. However, these methods present issues in terms of costs and the subjectivity of the data collected.

2.2. Measuring Usability in Serious Games. In the last ten years, digital game-based learning has grown from a small niche into a respected branch of technology-enhanced learning [18]. In addition, the next generation of educational technologies considers educational games (or serious games) as an instrument to be integrated in different formal and informal learning scenarios [19].

Different authors have discussed the great potential of serious games as learning tools. Games attract and maintain young students' limited attention spans and provide meaningful learning experiences for both children and adults [20], while offering engaging activities for deeper learning experiences [21].

However, as games gain acceptance as a valid educational resources, game design, UI development, and rigorous usability testing are increasingly necessary. And while there are diverse research initiatives looking at how to evaluate the learning effectiveness of these games (e.g., [1, 22, 23]), the usability of serious games has received less attention in the literature. Designing games for "regular" gamers is reasonably straightforward, because games have their own language, UI conventions and control schemes. However, serious games are increasingly accessed by broad audiences that include nongamers, resulting occasionally in bad experiences because the target audience "does not get games" [24].

Designing for broad audiences and ensuring that a thorough usability analysis is performed can alleviate these bad experiences. In this context, Eladhari and Ollila conducted a recent survey on prototype evaluation techniques for games [25], acknowledging that the use of *off-the-shelf* HCI instruments would be possible, but that the instruments should be adapted to the specific characteristics of games as reported in [26]. In this context, there are some existing research efforts in adapting Heuristic Evaluations (with experts looking for specific issues) to the specific elements of commercial videogames [27, 28]. However, usability metrics and instruments for observational methods are not always appropriate or reliable for games. Most usability metrics were designed for general productivity tools, and thus they focus on aspects such as productivity, efficacy, and number of errors. But games (both serious or purely entertainment) are completely different, focusing more on the process than on the results, on enjoyment than on productivity, and on providing variety than on providing consistency [5].

Games engage users by presenting actual challenges, which demand exploratory thinking, experimentation, and observing outcomes. Ideally, this engagement cycle intends to keep the users just one step beyond their level of skill for compelling gameplay whereas a game that can be easily mastered and played through without making mistakes results in a boring game [6]. Therefore, usability metrics that reflect perfect performance and no "mistakes" (appropriate for productivity applications) would not be appropriate for (fun) games [29].

A similar effect can be observed with metrics that evaluate frustration. Games should be designed to be "pleasantly frustrating experiences", challenging users beyond their skill, forcing users to fail, and therefore providing more satisfaction with victory [6]. In fact, the games that provide this pleasantly frustrating feeling are the games that are the most addicting and compelling. On the other hand, there are games that frustrate players because of poor UI design. In these cases, while the user is still unable to accomplish the game's objectives, failure is the result of bad UI or flawed game concepts. Usability metrics for serious games should distinguish in-game frustration from at-game frustration [30], as well as contemplating that "obstacles for accomplishment" may be desirable, while "obstacles for fun" are not [5].

Unfortunately, as game designers can acknowledge, there is no specific recipe for fun, and as teachers and educators can acknowledge, eliciting active learning is an elusive target. The usability and effectiveness of productivity tools can be measured in terms of production, throughput, efficacy, and efficiency. But other aspects such as learning impact, engagement, or fun are much more subjective and difficult to measure [31].

This subjectivity and elusiveness impacts formal usability testing protocols when applied to games. As White and colleagues found [32], when different experts evaluated the same game experiences (with the same test subjects), the results were greatly disparate, a problem that they attributed to the subjective perception of what made things "work" in a game.

In summary, evaluating the usability of games presents unique challenges and requires metrics and methodologies that aim to contemplate their variability and subjectivity of interacting with games, as well as their uniqueness as exploratory experiences that should be pleasantly frustrating.

3. General Methodology

As discussed in the previous section, gathering data to evaluate the usability of a serious game is an open-ended task with different possible approaches and several potential pitfalls. Therefore, there is a need for straightforward and reliable methods that help developers identify usability issues for their serious games before releasing them. In our specific case, we focus on facilitating an iterative analysis process based on observational methods, in which users play with early prototypes and researchers gather data with the objective of identifying and resolving design and UI issues that affect the usability of the games.

3.1. Requirements. From the discussion above it is possible to identify some initial requirements to perform usability testing of serious games.

(1) Test Users. First, it is necessary to have a set of test users to evaluate the prototype. These test users should ideally reflect the serous game's target audience in terms of age, gender, education, and any other demographic characteristics that might be unique or pertinent to the educational objective of the serious game. In terms of number of test users, according to Virzi [33], five users should be enough to detect 80% of the usability problems, with additional testers discovering a few additional problems. In turn, Nielsen and Landauer [34] suggested that, for a "medium" sized project, up to 16 test users would be worth some extra cost, but any additional test users would yield no new information. They also suggested that the maximum benefit/cost ratio would be achieved with four testers. We suggest selecting at least as many users that would span the range of your target audience, but not so many users that hinder the team performing the usability data analysis.

(2) Prototype Session Evaluators. Another important requirement is the consideration of the numbers of evaluators or raters to analyze the play session of each test user. Having multiple evaluators significantly increases the cost, making it tempting to use a single evaluator. However, while some analyses are performed with a single evaluator observing and reviewing a test user's play data, Kessner and colleagues suggested that it is necessary to have more than one evaluator to increase the reliability of the analysis, because different evaluators identified different issues [3]. This effect is even stronger when evaluating a game, because their high complexity results in evaluators interpreting different causes (and therefore possible solutions) for the problems [32]. Therefore, we suggest having more than one evaluator to analyze each play session and a process of conciliation to aggregate the results.

(3) Instrument for Serious Game Usability Evaluation. For an evaluator who is analyzing a play session and trying to identify issues and stumbling points, a structured method for annotating events with appropriate categories is a necessity [17]. Because serious games differ from traditional software packages in many ways, we suggest using an instrument that is dedicated to the evaluation of serious game usability. Section 3.2 below is dedicated to the development of a Serious Game Usability Evaluator (SeGUE).

(4) Data Recording Setup. Nuanced user interactions can often be subtle, nonverbal, fast paced, and unpredictable. A real-time annotation process can be burdensome, or perhaps even physically impossible if the user is interacting with the system rapidly. In addition, any simultaneous annotation process could be distracting to the user's game interactions and detract from the evaluative process. For these reasons, we recommend screen casting of the test play sessions along with audio and video recordings of the user with minimal, if any, coaching, from the evaluation staff. These recordings can be viewed and annotated later at an appropriate pace.

(5) "Ready-to-Play" Prototype. "Ready-to-Play" Prototype should be as close to the final product as possible for the test users to evaluate. The prototype should allow the test users to experience the interface as well as all intended functionalities so that the interactions could mimic the real play session, therefore, maximizing the benefits of conducting a usability test. When it is not feasible or cost effective to provide a full prototype, using an early incomplete prototype may fail to reflect the usability of the final product once it has been polished. White and colleagues [32] conducted their usability studies using a "vertical slice quality" approach, in which a specific portion of the game (a level) was developed to a level of quality and polish equivalent to the final version.

(6) Goal-Oriented Play-Session Script. Lastly, prior to the initiation of the study, a play-session script should be determined. The script for the evaluation session should be relatively brief and have clear objectives. The designers should prepare a script indicating which tasks the tester

is expected to perform. In the case of a serious game, this script should be driven by specific learning goals, as well as cover all the relevant gameplay elements within the design. There may be a need for more than one play session to be exposed to each user so that all the key game objectives could be included.

3.2. Development of the Serious Game Usability Evaluator (SeGUE). Evaluators who analyze a prototype play session will need a structured method to annotate events as they try to identify issues and stumbling points. This predefined set of event types is necessary to facilitate the annotation process as well as to provide structure for the posterior data analysis. This evaluation method should reflect the fact that the objective is to evaluate a serious game, rather than a productivity tool. As described in Section 2.2, serious games are distinct from other types of software in many ways. Importantly, serious games are useful educational resources because they engage the players on a path of knowledge discovery. This implies that the evaluation should focus on identifying not only those features representing a usability issue, but also the ones that really engage the user.

Since the objectives of evaluating a serious game not only focus on the prototype itself but also the process of interacting with the game and the user's experience, our research team developed a tool, the Serious Game Usability Evaluator (SeGUE), for the evaluation of serious game usability. The SeGUE was derived and refined using two randomly selected serious game evaluation sessions, in which a team comprising game programmers, educational game designers, and interaction experts watched and discussed videos of users interacting with an educational serious game. Two dimensions (system related and user related) of categories were created for annotation purposes. Within each dimension, several categories and terms were defined to annotate events.

Within the system-related dimension, there are six different event categories. Two event categories are related to the game design, including gameflow and functionality. Events of these categories are expected to require deep changes in the game, perhaps even the core gameplay design. Three event categories are related to the game interface and implementation, including content, layout/UI, and technical errors, where solutions are expected to be rather superficial and have less impact on the game. A nonapplicable category is also considered for events not directly related to the system, but still deemed relevant for improving the user experience.

In the user-related dimension, there are ten event categories across a spectrum of emotions: negative (frustrated, confused, annoyed, unable to continue), positive (learning, reflecting, satisfied/excited, pleasantly frustrated), or neutral (nonapplicable and suggestion/comment). For researchers' convenience an additional category named "other" was included in both dimensions for those events that were hard to categorize. Such events may be an indication that a new category is required due to specific traits of a specific game. More details about the categories and their meanings are presented in Tables 1 and 2.

3.3. Evaluation Process. We present here a step-by-step methodology to assess for usability events in serious games. Additionally we will show as a case study how we employed this methodology to assess for usability while accounting for the MasterMed game's specific learning objectives. According to the requirements described above, the methodology is organized in discrete stages, from the performance of the tests to the final preparation of a list of required changes. The stages of the methodology are as follows.

(1) Design of the Play Session. The evaluation session should be brief and have clear objectives. The designers should prepare a detailed script indicating which tasks the tester is expected to perform. This script should be driven by specific learning goals, as well as include all the relevant gameplay and UI elements within the design. There may be a need for more than one scripted play session to cover all the key objectives.

(2) Selection of the Testers. As noted above, invited testers' characteristics should closely represent the intended users and mimic the context for which the serious game is designed.

(3) Performance and Recording of the Play Sessions. The testers are given brief instructions about the context of the game and the learning objectives and prompted to play the game on their own, without any further directions or instructions. The testers are instructed to speak out loud while they play, voicing out their thoughts. During the play session, the evaluator does not provide any instructions unless the user is fatally stuck or unable to continue. Ideally, the session is recorded on video, simultaneously capturing both the screen and the user's verbal and nonverbal reactions.

(4) Application of the Instrument and Annotation of the Results. In this stage, the evaluators review the play sessions identifying and annotating all significant events. An event is a significant moment in the game where the user found an issue or reacted visibly to the game. Events are most commonly negative events, reflecting a usability problem, although remarkably positive user reactions should also be tagged, as they indicate game design aspects that are engaging the user and should be enforced. Each event is tagged according to the two dimensions proposed in the SeGUE annotation instrument (Section 3.2). Ideally each play session should be annotated by at least two evaluators separately.

(5) Reconciliation of the Results. Since multiple reviewers should annotate the videos independently, the annotations and classifications likely will end up being different. Therefore, it is necessary for all of the reviewers to confer for reconciliation of the results. There are several possibilities that result from initial discrepant event assessments: (1) an observed event may be equally recognized by multiple reviewers with identical tagging; (2) a single event might be interpreted and tagged differently by at least one reviewer;

TABLE 1: Event categories for the system dimension.

System-related event	
Functionality	An event is related to prototype's functionality when it is the result of the user activating a control item and it is related to one specific action.
Layout/UI	An event is related to layout/UI when the user makes a wrong assumption about what a control does, or when the user does not know how to do something (negative events). It is also a *layout/UI* positive event when a user appreciates the design (figures, attempts, colors, etc.) or having specific information displayed.
Gameflow	An event that is caused not by a single specific interaction, but as a consequence of the game sequences interactions and outputs and the specific gameplay design of the game.
Content	A content event is related to text blurbs and other forms of textual information provided by the game.
Technical error	A technical *error* event is related to a nonintentional glitch in the system that must be corrected.
Nonapplicable	When the event is not related to the system and/or not prompted by a system behavior.
Other	An event that is related to the system, but does not match any of the above (this suggests that a new category is needed).

TABLE 2: Event categories for the user dimension.

User-related event	
Learning	The user figures out how to perform an action that was unclear before (learn to play), or when the user is actively engaging in consuming content (learn content).
Reflecting	The user pauses or wonders what to do next. Unlike when the user is *confused* and does not know what to do, reflecting events indicate pause to create action plans within the game space.
Satisfied/excited	The user displays a remarkably positive reaction.
Pleasantly frustrated	The user expresses frustration in a positive manner. A pleasantly frustrating moment urges the user to try to overcome the obstacle again.
Frustrated	The user voices or displays negative feelings at not being able to complete the game or not knowing how to do something. A frustrating moment urges the player to stop playing.
Confused	The user does not know how to perform an action, misinterprets instructions, and/or does not know what he/she is supposed to do.
Annoyed	The user performs properly a task in the game (knows how to do it), but feels negatively about having to do it.
Unable to continue (fatal)	This is usually the consequence of one or more of the above, or of a fatal technical error. An event is related to when the user becomes definitely stuck and/or cannot continue without the help of the researcher. Such events are highlighted because the origin of these events must always be resolved.
Nonapplicable	An event is not related to the user (e.g., it is a remark by the researcher, or a glitch appeared but the user did not notice it).
Suggestion/comment	The user verbalizes a comment or a suggestion that is not related to a specific interaction or event.
Other	An event is related to the user, but does not match any of the above (this suggests that a new category is needed).

or (3) an event could be recognized and tagged by one observer and overlooked by another. In the latter two cases, it is important to have all the reviewers to verify and agree on the significance of the event and have subjective agreement on the proper tag. Most importantly, the objective of this task is not to increase the interrater reliability, but to study collaboratively the event in order to better understand its interpretation, causes, and potential remediation actions.

(6) Preparation of a Task List of Changes. Finally, the eventual product from this evaluation process should be a list of potential improvements for the game, with an indication of their importance in terms of how often the problem appeared and how severely it affected the user or interfered with the game's educational mission. For each observed negative event, a remediation action is proposed. Changes proposed should avoid interfering with the design and game-play elements that originate positive events to maintain engagement. Users' comments and suggestions may also be taken into account. Quite possibly, some of the encountered issues will occur across multiple users, and some events might occur multiple times for the same user during the same play session

(e.g., a user may fail repeatedly to activate the same control). For each action point there will be a frequency value (how many events were recorded that suggest this action point) and a spread value (how many users were affected by this issue).

Finally after reconciliation, the evaluation team should have an exhaustive list of potential changes. For each modification, the frequency, the spread, and a list of descriptions of when the event happened for each user all contribute to the estimating of importance and urgency for each action, as it may not be feasible to implement every single remediation action.

It must be noted that although a predefined set of tagging categories facilitate the annotation and reconciliation process, the work performed in stages 4 and 5 can be labor intensive and time consuming depending on the nature and quantity of the test user's verbal and non-verbal interactions with the prototype.

Finally, depending on the scope and budget of the project, it may be appropriate to iterate this process. This is especially important if the changes in the design were major, as these changes may have introduced further usability issues that had not been previously detected.

4. Case Study: Evaluating MasterMed

This SeGUE methodology, including the specific annotation categories, has been put to the test with a specific serious game (MasterMed) (see Figure 1), currently being developed at Massachusetts General Hospital's Laboratory or Computer Science. The goal of MasterMed is to educate patients about the medications they are taking by asking patients to match each medication with the condition it is intended to treat. The game will be made available to patients via an online patient portal, iHealthSpace (https://www.ihealthspace.org/portal/login/index.html), for patients who regularly take more than three medications. The target audience for this game is therefore a broad and somewhat older population that will be able to use computers, but not necessarily technically savvy. This makes it very important to conduct extensive usability studies with users similar to the target audience, to ensure that patients will be able to interact adequately with the game.

Performing an indepth evaluation of the MasterMed game helped us refine and improve the evaluation methodology, gaining insight into the importance of multiple reviewers, the effect of different user types in the evaluation, or how many users and reviewers are required. In addition, the experience helped improve the definitions of the categories in the SeGUE instrument.

In this section we describe this case study, including the study setup, the decisions made during the process, and the results gathered. From these results, we have extracted the key lessons learned on serious game usability testing, and those lessons are described in Section 5.

4.1. Case Study Setup

4.1.1. Design of the Play Session. The session followed a script, in which each participant was presented three increasingly difficult scenarios with a selection of medications and problems to be matched. The scenarios covered simple cases, where all the medicines were to be matched, and complex cases in which some medicines did not correspond with any of the displayed problems. In addition, we focused on common medication for chronic problems and included in the list potentially problematic medications and problems, including those with difficult or uncommon names. As a user progressed through the script, new UI elements were introduced sequentially across sessions. The total playing time was estimated to be around 30 minutes.

4.1.2. Selection of the Testers. Human subject approval was obtained from the Institutional Review Board of Partners Human Research Committee, Massachusetts General Hospital's parent institution. The usability testing used a convenience sampling method to recruit ten patient-like participants from the Laboratory of Computer Science, Massachusetts General Hospital. An invitation email message contained a brief description of the study, eligibility criteria, and contact information was sent out to all potential participants. Eligible participants were at least 18 years old and not working as medical providers (physicians or nurses). Based on a database query, our expected patient-gamer population should be balanced in terms of gender with roughly 54% of participants are female. Patient age ranges from 26 to 103 with a mean of 69.3 years (SD = 12.5) for men and a mean of 70.14 years (SD = 12.75) for women. We recruited five men and five women with their age ranged from mid-30 s to 60 s to evaluate the game.

4.1.3. Performance and Recording of the Play Sessions. Each participant was asked to interact with the game using a think-aloud technique during the session. The screen and participant's voice and face were recorded using screen/webcam capture software. The duration of the play sessions ranged between 40 and 90 minutes.

4.1.4. Application of the Instrument and Annotation of the Results. After conducting the sessions, a team of evaluators was gathered to annotate the videos identifying all potentially significant events. There were four researchers available, two from the medical team and two from the technical team. Five videos were randomly assigned to each researcher to review; thus two different researchers processed each video independently. In order to avoid any biasing factors due to the backgrounds of each researcher, the assignment was made so that each researcher was matched to each of the other three researchers at least once. The annotations used the matrix described in Section 3.2. Two more fields were added to include a user quote when available and comments describing the event in more detail.

4.1.5. Reconciliation of the Results. The reconciliation was performed in a meeting with all four researchers, where (i) each unique event was identified and agreed upon, (ii) each matched event classified differently was reconciled, and (iii) each matched event with the same tags was reviewed

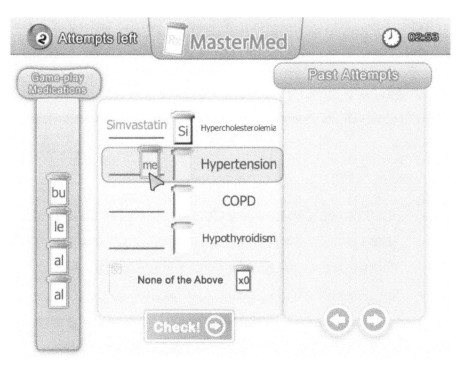

Figure 1: A screenshot of the MasterMed game, version 0.4.5: the user is dragging a medication to a condition.

for completeness. This process was crucial in determining the nature of overlooked events and facilitated the discussion on the possible causes for those events that had been tagged differently by the reviewers.

4.1.6. Preparation of a Task List of Changes. For each observed negative event, a remediation action was proposed and prioritized.

4.2. Case Study Results. The first artifact of the case study was a set of 10 video files resulting from the screen/webcam capture software. Since the evaluation method was experimental, two randomly selected videos were used for a first collaborative annotation process. This step helped refine and improve the tags described in Section 3.2. Therefore, the final evaluation was performed only on the eight remaining play sessions.

The average play session was around 30 minutes in length, although most users took between 40 and 60 minutes (and only one user as much as 90 minutes). A total of 290 events were logged. We summarize the events identified for each user (see Figure 2). A *unique* event is defined when the event was only tagged by one of the two researchers reviewing the video (and overlooked by the other). A *matched* event is defined when the event was tagged by both researchers and classified equally with the same tags and interpretation. Finally, a *reconciled* event is defined when the event was identified by two researchers, but tagged differently and then agreed upon during the reconciliation process.

In Figure 3, we summarize the number of appearances of each tag and the relative frequencies for each event type. The number of negative events (138) was much higher

than positive events (46). Also the number of interface and implementation events (179) is greater than events related to design (91).

Finally, in Table 3 we provide an excerpt of the action points that were derived from the analysis of the results. For each action, we also indicate the frequency (number of events that would be solved by this action) and the spread (number of users that encountered an event that would be solved by this action). Both numbers were used to determine the priority of each action.

4.3. Case Study Discussion. An interesting aspect for discussion is the variability of event statistics across users. Figure 2 is sorted according to the number of unique events, as this category requires special attention. Indeed, while a reconciled event indicates an event that was perceived different by each researcher, a unique event indicates that one of the researchers overlooked the event. In a scenario with only one reviewer per play session, such events may have gone unnoticed. The annotations for some users presented very high numbers of unique events. It is possible that this is related to the total number of events, affecting the subjective thresholds of the reviewers when the frequency of events is high. However, the results do not suggest that a correlation between the total number of events and the proportion of unique, matched, and reconciled events. For example, results from users with small total number of events vary, as user no. 2 presents 77.78% unique events while user no. 1 has only 30.77% unique events.

Regarding the tag statistics, the number of negative events in the user dimension is clearly predominant. This result may be considered normal, as evaluators are actively

TABLE 3: Excerpt of the prioritized action points list. It shows the type (D: design/I: interface), the frequency (number of occurrences), the spread (number of users affected), and the priority they were given according to these two numbers.

Priority	Action	Type	Freq.	Spread
1	Rearrange the tutorials (shortening and skipping)	D	28	8
2	Remove "none of the above" feature	D	23	8
3	Unify "close dialog" interactions	I	37	5
4	UI tweaking (color schemes, minor layout changes, etc.)	I	22	6
5	Review wording	I	13	6
6	Improve mouse clicking accuracy	I	11	4
7	Improve handout contents (remove unnecessary sections)	I	11	4

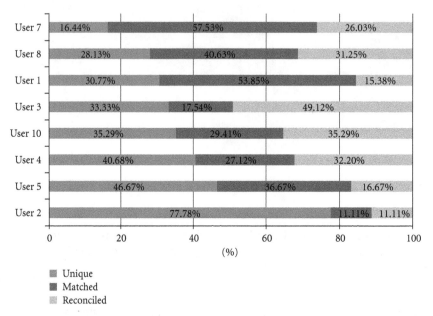

■ Unique
■ Matched
▨ Reconciled

FIGURE 2: Event statistics. Each bar shows the percentage of unique, matched and reconciled events for each individual user. The total number of events for each user is shown in parenthesis.

		Interface			Design		N/A	Total
		Content	Layout/UI	Technical error	Gameflow	Functionality		
Negative	Annoyed	12	3	4	12		1	32
	Confused	9	36	14	19	5	3	86
	Frustrated	1	3	5	3	2		14
	Unable to continue (fatal)	0	1	4		1		6
								138
Positive	Pleasantly frustrated	0			2			2
	Reflecting	1	3		2	3		9
	Satisfied/excited	1	2		9	7		19
	Learning	0	2		3	7	4	16
								46
Neutral	N/A	0		7			1	8
	Suggestion/comment	28	41	2	7	9	11	98
								106
Total		52	91	36	57	34	20	290
			179		91			

FIGURE 3: Tag statistics: the events are categorized on two dimensions: the source of the event (interface, design) and the reaction of the user.

looking for issues and pitfalls, while regular play working as intended may not be considered as an event. However, the identification of specific positive events was still helpful to identify specific game moments or interactions that really engaged the users in a visible way.

In the game element dimension, the number of events related to the design of the game was significantly less than the number of events related to the interface and implementation (91 versus 179). This data suggests that users were more satisfied with the flow and mechanics of the MasterMed game than with its look and feel. Nonetheless, this difference seems reasonable, as it is easier for users to identify pitfalls in superficial elements like the UI (e.g., font size is too small) then in the design (e.g., the pacing is not appropriate). The correlation between user and system dimensions is also interesting, as positive events are usually related to aspects of the game design. Since the gameplay design is the key element for engagement, this result may be considered an indication that the design was, in fact, successful.

The process to determine the remediation actions and a heuristic assessment of their importance deserves also some discussion. The prioritization of the list is not fully automatable. While the frequency was an important aspect to consider (an event that happened many times), so was the spread (an event that affected many users). These variables allowed researchers to limit the impact of having multiple occurrences of the same event for a single user. A specific example: the action "remove none of the above feature" was regarded as more important than "unify close dialog interactions" because it affected all users, even though the total number of occurrences was significantly lower (23 versus 37).

Other factors such as the cost of implementing a change or its potential return were not considered, but large projects with limited budget or time constraints may need to consider these aspects when prioritizing the remediation actions.

5. Lessons Learned

The result of the case study not only helped to identify improvement points, but also served as a test to improve and refine the SeGUE instrument for annotation. Some design decisions, taken on the base of the existing literature, were put to the test in a real study, which allowed us to draw important conclusions. And these conclusions are helpful for researchers using this methodology (or other variations) to evaluate and improve their own serious games. The main lessons learned are summarized below.

5.1. Multiple Evaluators. As discussed in Section 3.1, different studies have taken different stances when it comes to how many researchers should review and annotate each play session. The key aspect is to make sure that all usability issues are accounted for (or as many as possible).

The interrater reliability displayed by the results for our case study is, in fact, very low (Figure 2). Both matched and reconciled events were identified by both reviewers, but unique events were only registered by one of the reviewers.

For most users, the number of unique events is between 33% and 50%, giving a rough estimate of how many events may have been lost if only one reviewer had been focusing on one play session (user no. 2 has an unusually high number of unique events).

This result is consistent with the concerns expressed by White and colleagues [32] and confirms the importance of having multiple evaluators for each play session in order to maximize the identification of potential issues. While it might be very tempting for small-sized teams to use only one annotator per gameplay session to reduce costs, our experience shows that even after joint training the number of recorded unique events is high. Thus, multiple evaluators should be considered as a priority when planning for usability testing.

5.2. Importance of Think-Aloud Methods. Most observational methods do not explicitly require users to verbalize their thoughts as they navigate the software, as it is considered that the careful analysis of the recordings will suffice to identify usability issues, even with only one expert reviewing each recording.

However, the results from the case study indicate the importance of requesting (and reinforcing) users to think aloud while they play. For our case study MasterMed evaluation, there was a direct correlation between the number of unique events tagged and the amount of comments verbalized by users. While all users were instructed to verbalize their thoughts, not all users responded equally. On one extreme, user no. 7 was loquacious, providing a continuous stream of thoughts and comments. On the other extreme, user no. 2 was stoic, apparently uncomfortable expressing hesitations out loud, rarely speaking during the experiment, despite of being reminded by the researcher about the importance of commenting. This had a direct impact in the number of unique events (16.44% unique events registered for user no. 7 and 77.78% unique events for user no. 2), as it made it difficult for the researchers to distinguish between hesitations caused by a usability issue from actual pauses to think about the next move in the game.

5.3. Length of the Play Sessions. The length of the play sessions was estimated to be around 30 minutes, although the range was 40–90 minutes. During the play session, familiarity with the tool and its expected behaviors may improve, and this may mean that most usability issues would be detected in the first minutes of a play session. To get a better insight about this issue, we produced the event timestamp frequency histogram provided below in Figure 4. Most of the events were tagged during the first 13 minutes of the session (44.06%) after which the rate decreases, with only 24.95% of the events tagged in the following 13 minutes. Beyond this point, the rate slowed even further, even though new, more complex gameplay scenarios were being tested.

Users are also encouraged to verbalize their impressions and explain their reasoning when deciding the next move or interaction; but as the play session becomes longer, the users also grow tired. This suggests that play sessions

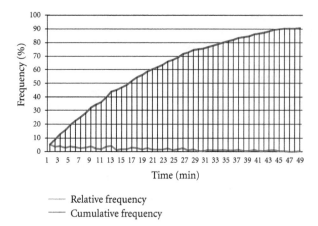

FIGURE 4: Frequency histogram of tagged events during MasterMed evaluation. Cumulative frequency graph shows that 40% of the events were tagged within the first 12 minutes.

should be kept short and focused. It should also be noted that researchers observing recorded play sessions thoroughly needed to stop, rewind, and rereview video footage frequently to tag the issues encountered, thereby requiring lengthy evaluation sessions. When more than 30 minutes are required to explore all the concepts, different sessions with breaks may be desirable.

5.4. Evaluator Profile.

5.4. Evaluator Profile. Even though the proposed methodology called for multiple experts evaluating each play session, we have found differences between the annotations depending on the researcher's profile. The foremost difference was between technical experts (developers) and field experts (clinicians).

Technical issues were one of the main sources of events that had to be reconciled (cases in which both researchers tagged the same event, but assigned different categories). Developers would spot subtle technical issues and tag them accordingly, while clinicians often attributed those events to usability problems related to the UI. This does not necessarily mean that an effort should be made to assign field experts and technicians to review each play session (although it may be desirable). However, it does reflect the importance of having experts from all sides participating in the reconciliation stage. In particular, the goal of the reconciliation stage is not necessarily to agree on the specific category of the event, but on its origin, impact on the user experience and significance; so that appropriate remediation actions can be pursued based on the data gathered.

5.5. Limitations. The methodology has a very specific objective: to facilitate the identification of design pitfalls in order to improve the usability of a serious game. As such, it does not deal with other very important dimensions of user assessment in serious games. In particular, it cannot be used to guarantee that the game will be effective in engaging the target audience or to assess the learning effectiveness of the final product. While the methodology takes care of identifying those elements that are especially engaging,

this is done in order to help the designers preserve the elements with good value when other design or UI issues are addressed. Before the final version of the game is released for the general public, further assessment of engagement and learning effectiveness should be conducted.

Another limitation that this methodology shares with typical observational methods (and in particular with think-aloud methods) is that the results are subjective and dependant on both the specific users and the subjective interpretations from the evaluators. The subjectivity of the process was highlighted in the case study in the number of events overlooked by at least one reviewer (number of *unique* events) and the discrepancies when annotating the perceived root cause of each event. While this subjectivity could be reduced by increasing the number of users and evaluators, this increases the cost of the evaluation process. This problem is further aggravated when the process is applied iteratively.

Small and medium sized development projects will need to carefully balance the number of users, evaluators, and iterations depending on their budget, although we consider that having more than one evaluator for each session is essential. Similarly, multiple iterations may be required if the changes performed affect the design or UI significantly, potentially generating new usability issues. In turn, bigger projects with enough budget may want to complement the observational methods by tracking physiological signals (e.g., eye tracking, electrocardiogram, brain activity) to gather additional insight into engagement. However, such advanced measurements fall beyond the scope of this work, which targets smaller game development projects with limited budgets.

6. Conclusions

The design of serious games for education is a complex task in which designers need to create products that engage the audience and provide an engaging learning experience, weaving gameplay features with educational materials. In addition, as with any software product targeting a broad audience, the usability of the resulting games is important. In this work we have discussed the unique challenges that appear when we try to evaluate the usability of a serious game before its distribution to a wide, nongamer audience. The key challenge is that typical usability testing methods focus on measurements that are not necessarily appropriate for games, focusing on aspects such as high productivity, efficacy, and efficiency as well as low variability, number of errors, and pauses. However, games contemplate reflection, exploration, variety and trial, and error activities.

While generic heuristic evaluative methods can be adapted to contemplate the specificities of games, observational instruments that generate metrics and scores are not directly applicable to serious games. In addition, observational data is by definition subjective, making it difficult to translate a handful of recorded play sessions into a prioritized list of required changes.

For these reasons, we have proposed a step-by-step methodology to evaluate the usability of serious games that focuses on obtaining a list of action points, rather than a single score that can be used to validate a specific game. Observational methods can be useful in determining design pitfalls but, as we have described in the paper, the process is subjective and sometimes cumbersome. The methodology provides a structured workflow to analyze observational data, process it with an instrument designed specifically for serious games, and derive a list of action points with indicators of the priority for each change, thus reducing the subjectivity of the evaluative process.

The Serious Games Usability Evaluator (SeGUE) instrument contemplates tagging events in the recorded play sessions according to two dimensions: the system and the user. Each observed event has an identifiable cause from a certain interaction or UI element and effect on the user (confusion, frustration, excitement, etc.). The categories for each dimension contemplate aspects specifically related to serious games, distinguishing, for example, between in-game frustration (a positive effect within the description of games as "pleasantly frustrating experiences") and at-game frustration (a negative event when the game interface, rather than the game design, becomes a barrier for achieving objectives).

The inclusion of positive events is relevant when studying the usability of serious games. These games need to engage users by both presenting challenges and variability and achieving a learning objective. The events in which the users are engaging intensively with the game (displaying excitement or pleasant frustration) are important parts of the game-flow, and the action points to improve usability should be designed such that they do not dilute the engagement.

The application of the SeGUE methodology in the MasterMed case study allowed us to draw some conclusions and summarize important lessons learned during the process, as summarized in Section 5. Among them, the experience provided answers to typically open questions regarding observational methods such as (a) the appropriate number of test subjects, (b) number of experts to review each play session, and (c) the importance of the think-aloud technique.

We expect the methodology, the SeGUE tagging instrument, and the summary of lessons learned to be useful for researchers who aim to improve the usability of their own serious games before releasing them. Small- and medium-sized projects can use this methodology to test the usability of their games, record data that is typically subjective and difficult to process, and then follow a structured methodology to process the data. The number of evaluation cycles, the specific designs, and the aspects of the games that need to be evaluated may vary across development projects. Therefore, these steps and the SeGUE instrument might be adapted and/or refined to incorporate any particular elements required by specific serious game developments.

Acknowledgments

This project was funded by the Partners Community Healthcare, Inc. System Improvement Grant program as well as the European Commission, through the 7th Framework Programme (project "GALA-Network of Excellence in Serious Games" -FP7-ICT-2009-5-258169) and the Lifelong Learning Programme (projects SEGAN-519332-LLP-1-2011-1-PT-KA3-KA3NW and CHERMUG 519023-LLP-1-2011-1-UK-KA3-KA3MP).

References

[1] S. de Freitas and M. Oliver, "How can exploratory learning with games and simulations within the curriculum be most effectively evaluated?" *Computers and Education*, vol. 46, no. 3, pp. 249–264, 2006.

[2] J. Nielsen, "Heuristic evaluation," in *Usability Inspection Methods*, J. Nielsen and R. L. Mack, Eds., vol. 17, pp. 25–62, John Wiley & Sons, 1994.

[3] M. Kessner, J. Wood, R. F. Dillon, and R. L. West, "On the reliability of usability testing," in *Proceedings of the Extended Abstracts on Human Factors in Computing Systems (CHI '01)*, p. 97, 2001.

[4] M. Macleod and R. Rengger, "The development of DRUM: a software tool for video-assisted usability evaluation," in *Proceedings of the 5th International Conference on Human-Computer Interaction (HCI '93)*, pp. 293–309, August 1993.

[5] R. J. Pagulayan, K. Keeker, D. Wixon, R. L. Romero, and T. Fuller, "User-centered design in games," in *Design*, J. A. Jacko and A. Sears, Eds., vol. 28, pp. 883–906, Lawrence Erlbaum Associates, 2003.

[6] R. Koster, *Theory of Fun for Game Design*, Paraglyph, Scottsdale, Ariz, USA, 2004.

[7] E. Ju and C. Wagner, "Personal computer adventure games: their structure, principles, and applicability for training," *Data Base for Advances in Information Systems*, vol. 28, no. 2, pp. 78–92, 1997.

[8] International Organization For Standardization, "ISO, 9241-11: guidance on usability," Ergonomic requirements for office work with visual display terminals, 1998, http://www.iso.org/iso/iso_catalogue/catalogue_tc/catalogue_detail.htm?csnumber=16883.

[9] A. R. Cooper, *The Inmates are Running the Asylum: Why High Tech Products Drive us Crazy and How to Restore the Sanity*, Macmillan Publishing, Indianapolis, Ind, USA, 1999.

[10] J. Nielsen and R. Molich, "Heuristic evaluation of user interfaces," in *Proceedings of the SIGCHI Conference on Human Factors in Computing Systems Empowering People (CHI '90)*, pp. 249–256, 1990.

[11] J. Brooke, "SUS: a 'quick and dirty' usability scale," in *Usability Evaluation in Industry*, P. W. Jordan, B. Thomas, B. A. Weerdmeester, and I. L. McClelland, Eds., pp. 189–194, Taylor & Francis, London, UK, 1996.

[12] J. Kirakowski and M. Corbett, "SUMI: the software usability measurement inventory," *British Journal of Educational Technology*, vol. 24, no. 3, pp. 210–212, 1993.

[13] B. D. Harper and K. L. Norman, "Improving user satisfaction: the questionnaire for user interaction satisfaction version 5.5," in *Proceedings of the 1st Annual Mid-Atlantic Human Factors Conference*, pp. 224–228, 1993.

[14] H. W. Jung, S. G. Kim, and C. S. Chung, "Measuring software product quality: a survey of ISO/IEC 9126," *IEEE Software*, vol. 21, no. 5, pp. 88–92, 2004.

[15] I. Wechsung and A. B. Naumann, "Evaluation methods for multimodal systems: a comparison of standardized usability questionnaires," in *Proceedings of the 4th IEEE tutorial and research workshop on Perception and Interactive Technologies for Speech-Based Systems: Perception in Multimodal Dialogue*

Systems (PIT '08), vol. 5078 of *Lecture Notes in Computer Science*, pp. 276–284, 2008.

[16] R. L. Boring, D. I. Gertman, J. C. Joe, and J. L. Marble, "Proof of concept for A human reliability analysis method for heuristic usability evaluation of software," in *Proceedings of the 49th Annual Meeting of the Human Factors and Ergonomics Society (HFES '05)*, pp. 676–680, Orlando, Fla, USA, September 2005.

[17] E. L. C. Law and E. T. Hvannberg, "Analysis of strategies for improving and estimating the effectiveness of heuristic evaluation," in *Proceedings of the 3rd Nordic Conference on Human-Computer Interaction (NordiCHI '04)*, pp. 241–250, Tampere, Finland, October 2004.

[18] P. Moreno-Ger, D. Burgos, and J. Torrente, "Digital games in elearning environments: current uses and emerging trends," *Simulation & Gaming*, vol. 40, no. 5, pp. 669–687, 2009.

[19] J. Kirriemuir and A. McFarlane, *Literature Review in Games and Learning*, NESTA Futurelab, Bristol, UK, 2004.

[20] R. Van Eck, "Digital game-based learning: it's not just the digital natives who are restless," *EDUCAUSE Review*, vol. 41, no. 2, pp. 16–30, 2006.

[21] J. P. Gee, *Good Videogames and Good Learning: Collected Essays on Video Games*, Peter Lang Publishing, New York, NY, USA, 2007.

[22] V. J. Shute, I. Masduki, and O. Donmez, "Conceptual framework for modeling, assessing, and supporting competencies within game environments," *Technology, Instruction, Cognition, and Learning*, vol. 8, no. 2, pp. 137–161, 2010.

[23] C. S. Loh, "Designing online games assessment as information trails," in *Games and Simulations in Online Learning: Research and Development Frameworks*, D. Gibson, C. Aldrich, and M. Prensky, Eds., pp. 323–348, Information Science Publishing, Hershey, Pa, USA, 2007.

[24] K. Squire, "Changing the game: what happens when video games enter the classroom," *Innovate*, vol. 1, no. 6, 2005.

[25] M. P. Eladhari and E. M. I. Ollila, "Design for research results: experimental prototyping and play testing," *Simulation & Gaming*, vol. 43, no. 3, pp. 391–412, 2012.

[26] E. Ollila, *Using Prototyping and Evaluation Methods in Iterative Design of Innovative Mobile Games*, Tampere University of Technology, Tampere, Finland, 2009.

[27] J. A. Garcia Marin, E. Lawrence, K. Felix Navarro, and C. Sax, "Heuristic Evaluation for Interactive Games within Elderly Users," in *Proceedings of the 3rd International Conference on eHealth, Telemedicine, and Social Medicine (eTELEMED '11)*, pp. 130–133, 2011.

[28] D. Pinelle and N. Wong, "Heuristic evaluation of games," in *Game Usability Advice from the Experts for Advancing the Player Experience*, K. Isbister and N. Schaffer, Eds., pp. 79–89, ACM Press, 2008.

[29] W. Ijsselsteijn, Y. De Kort, K. Poels, A. Jurgelionis, and F. Bellotti, "Characterising and measuring user experiences in digital games," in *Proceedings of the Avances in Computer Entertainment (ACE '07)*, June 2007.

[30] K. M. Gilleade and A. Dix, "Using frustration in the design of adaptive videogames," in *Proceedings of the ACM SIGCHI International Conference on Advances in Computer Entertainment Technology (ACE '04)*, pp. 228–232, Singapore, June 2005.

[31] G. Sim, S. MacFarlane, and J. Read, "All work and no play: measuring fun, usability, and learning in software for children," *Computers and Education*, vol. 46, no. 3, pp. 235–248, 2006.

[32] G. R. White, P. Mirza-Babaei, G. McAllister, and J. Good, "Weak inter-rater reliability in heuristic evaluation of video games," in *Proceedings of the 29th Annual CHI Conference on Human Factors in Computing Systems (CHI '11)*, pp. 1441–1446, May 2011.

[33] R. A. Virzi, "Refining the test phase of usability evaluation: how many subjects is enough?" *Human Factors*, vol. 34, no. 4, pp. 457–468, 1992.

[34] J. Nielsen and T. K. Landauer, "Mathematical model of the finding of usability problems," in *Proceedings of the Conference on Human Factors in Computing Systems (INTERACT '93) and (CHI '93)*, pp. 206–213, April 1993.

10

Interactive Language Learning through Speech-Enabled Virtual Scenarios

Hazel Morton, Nancie Gunson, and Mervyn Jack

Centre for Communication Interface Research, School of Engineering, University of Edinburgh, Edinburgh EH9 3JL, UK

Correspondence should be addressed to Hazel Morton, hazel.morton@ed.ac.uk

Academic Editor: M. Carmen Juan

This paper describes the evaluation of an educational game designed to give learners of foreign languages the opportunity to practice their spoken language skills. Within the speech interactive Computer-Assisted Language Learning (CALL) program, scenarios are presented in which learners interact with virtual characters in the target language using speech recognition technology. Two types of interactive scenarios with virtual characters are presented as part of the game: the one-to-one scenarios which take the form of practice question and answer scenarios where the learner interacts with one virtual character and the interactive scenario which is an immersive contextualised scenario where the learner interacts with two or more virtual characters within the scene to complete a (task-based) communicative goal. The study presented here compares learners' subjective attitudes towards the different scenarios. In addition, the study investigates the performance of the speech recognition component in this game. Forty-eight students of English as a Foreign Language (EFL) took part in the evaluation. Results indicate that learners' subjective ratings for the contextualised interactive scenario are higher than for the one-to-one, practice scenarios. In addition, recognition performance was better for these interactive scenarios.

1. Introduction

When learning a foreign language, opportunities for interaction in the target language can be limited. Unlike most other school subjects, language learning requires oral practice. A student studying a language in high school may receive only a few hours of language class per week and may have very limited one-on-one time with the teacher of the class. In the classroom situation, it may not be possible, due to time restrictions and resources, for the teacher to engage in a spoken dialogue with every student. However, it is necessary for language learning that the learner has an interlocutor with whom to interact.

It has been found that classroom exercises which are detached from real-life issues or activities fail to help the learner use the target language [1, 2]. Learning activities therefore focus less on the (correct) use of forms in a context-free learning environment in favour of using the language for a communicative purpose. Games are used in language learning to stimulate motivation and to create communicative opportunities for learners [3]. Interactivity and individual

action are fundamental properties of games and can be related to communicative approaches to language learning [4], where the focus is on communicating in the target language for meaning.

Simulation games are frequently used in language learning. Simulations offer learners the opportunities to be actively involved in the interactions in the target language. Simulations and role play follow an interactional view of language. The interactional perspective "sees language as a vehicle for the realization of interpersonal relations and for the performance of social transactions between individuals" [5, page 17]. Simulations offer the learner the opportunity for the development of their language in a given social context. Research has suggested that simulations can facilitate second language acquisition; learners acquire language when they are exposed to comprehensible input, and they are actively involved and have positive affect [6].

It has been suggested that language teaching should shift towards experiential learning where the learning occurs in contextualised or situational environments, and language forms are introduced during social activities [7]. Using simulations in a learning environment can offer students an opportunity for experiential learning, as they support "learning by doing" approaches [8]. In addition to exposure to comprehensible input, simulations can offer the learner the opportunity of expressing themselves in the target language within a relevant context. The interactions that learners make are part of the process of language learning and can have an effect on their language development. The use of simulations in an educational environment allows the learner to experience situations in which their decisions have real and immediate consequences.

The interaction hypothesis [9] states that conversational interaction between a learner and, for example, a native speaker can facilitate the learner's development as the learner can be involved in negotiated interaction which then gives them comprehensible input in the target language (L2). The approach described here builds on the interaction hypothesis to create situations in which a learner can engage in meaningful spoken interactions with the computer, and whose interactions can be negotiated in order that the learner can develop their oral language in the L2. In this game, learners can engage in negotiated interaction with the virtual agents. The agents act as the "audience" for the learner's oral language output. Learners' output in language learning is thought to be a necessary condition for language learning [10]. One of the key aspects in the design of the game was to consider the application as being one of the conversational participants in the L2 interaction. "It is useful to view multimedia design from the perspective of the input it can provide to learners, the output it allows them to produce, the interactions they are able to engage in, and the L2 tasks it supports" [11]. The virtual agents are able to offer feedback to the learner's utterances as well as continue the dialogue with the learner through a number of conversational turns within the defined context of the language lesson.

The language learning game described here creates contextualised scenarios which are simulations of real world situations in which learners can engage with virtual characters to practice their oral language skills. The game uses speech recognition, so the learner can interact with the system through speech in a simulated, and suitably constrained, environment; virtual agents and virtual worlds are used to depict a context in which the learner can engage in a conversational dialogue with the computer. Within this context, two different kinds of interaction are available between the learner and the virtual characters: the one-to-one scenarios and the interactive scenarios. The two scenario types differ in their pedagogical intent. The one-to-one scenarios allow the learner to interact with one virtual character in a series of question and answer turns, which represent a practice session of the key linguistic topics and forms for the given topic. The interactive scenario allows the learner an opportunity to interact with two or more virtual characters within a highly contextualised scene in order to accomplish a relevant task. In this study, we sought to investigate the one-to-one scenarios separately from the interactive scenario as the different contexts of interaction could influence the way in which the learner

chooses to interact with the system. Firstly, there may be differences in user attitudes and response types the learner makes as they progress through each of the scenarios in the "lesson." Secondly, there may be differences across these scores and the recognition performance between the scenario types.

Previous studies have been conducted using the program to investigate overall attitudes towards using the program for learners of Italian and Japanese [12], to investigate motivation [13], and to investigate help strategies [14]. The purpose of the study described in this paper is to investigate learner perceptions of and attitudes towards the speech interactive CALL game and how these attitudes change as the learner progresses through the game and for the different speech interactive scenarios. This paper first describes the various components of the speech interactive game and then provides details on the design. The experimental evaluation is then presented. Data are presented on learner attitudes towards interacting with the characters. In addition, learner response data on the utterances made while interacting with the characters are presented together with performance data on the speech recognition component of the different scenario types within the game.

2. Speech Interactive Language Learning

An important aspect of learning a foreign language is becoming comfortable and confident with speaking in the target language. However, for many learners of foreign languages; there are limited opportunities for practicing speaking in the target language. By using speech recognition technology, CALL programs can create more opportunities for learners to practice speaking in the target language and develop their oral language skills. Although a speech-enabled CALL program could not replace one-to-one interaction with a native speaker, it may be possible to offer a more realistic and beneficial simulation in a way that is absent from most CALL materials.

Virtual modelling can create animated characters with which users can interact, and virtual environments can be modelled in which the interaction takes place, which may increase the sense of immersion. Thus, immersive virtual scenarios can be entered by learners as places to practice their oral language skills in the target language.

2.1. Virtual Agents. Virtual agents endowed with speech recognition competency, otherwise known as embodied conversational agents, can introduce a social aspect to the interface. The term "embodied conversational agents" refers to humanlike or cartoon-like animated characters that often appear in computer interfaces [15]. The agents are endowed with conversational capabilities primarily through speech output generation (either synthesised or recorded speech), speech recognition software, and natural language processing. These agents are thought to "anthropomorphise" the interface by bringing lifelike qualities to the interaction: they can react to user's speech input and are capable of verbal and nonverbal output.

Virtual agents or animated agents are being increasingly used in computer user interfaces to offer a more personalised interaction between human and computer. Animated agents have also been used in pedagogical applications in which such pedagogical agents are defined as "lifelike characters that facilitate the learning process" [16]. Pedagogical agents have been used in a number of applications such as a 2D animated agent used to support students during medical problem solving activities in a web-based learning environment [17] and a 3D animated agent immersed in a simulated virtual world used as a teaching aid for engineering students [18]. Agents have also been used in a language training program for US soldiers [16, 19]. In this application, the agents reside in a highly contextualised 3D environment in which the interactions take place.

Early research in the use of animated agents in pedagogical applications has shown such agents to be effective when used in tutoring systems in which they can improve the learning experience by engaging students in effective conversations with their agent [20]. In addition, it has been shown that students who learn with an animated agent work harder to understand the lesson material than students who learn in a text-based environment [21].

The use of animated agents within the contextualised virtual world used in the CALL game described here offers the learner an opportunity for one-to-one conversation, designed to contribute to an enhanced learning experience. Animated pedagogical agents have been shown to "increase the computer's ability to engage and motivate students" [22]. In the context of CALL, it has been suggested that it may be important for learners to have an audience for their linguistic output so that the learners can "attempt to use the language to construct meanings for communication rather than solely for practice" [11]. In this way, animated pedagogical agents could serve as the cyber audience for language learners' output.

2.2. Virtual Worlds. Virtual reality has been defined as "an event or entity that is real in effect but not in fact [23]". In their use of virtual environments, users may experience *presence*, that is, the subjective sense of "being there" in the virtual world [24]. The underlying assumption is that if users experience such a sense of presence in a virtual environment, they will come to behave in the virtual environment in a way that is similar to the way they would behave in a similar environment in the real world. Indeed, Transfer appropriate processing asserts that memory is optimum in retrieval environments which closely match the environment in which the mental process was encoded [25]. Thus, if learners have the opportunity to practice skills in the virtual environment that are similar to skills needed in the real world task, the skills learned there are likely to carry over to similar situations in the real world. Virtual environments offer features that are superior to video presentations because of the sense of presence in the environment created through the manipulation of certain aspects of that environment and because of the interactivity they allow. The virtual worlds presented to the learner in the game reported here offer

a highly contextualised environment in which the learner can first observe the interactions between the virtual agents and then can enter the environment as an active dialogue participant.

2.3. Speech Recognition in CALL. The role of automated speech recognition technology in CALL programs has been explored for more than a decade, having been used for pronunciation practice in CALL programs [26–29] or to help learners with their fluency or conversation skills [16, 30–33]. Many CALL programs which utilise speech recognition technology for language learning are based on strategies where the learner selects their (spoken) response from a finite list offered by the CALL program itself. Such strategies have been used to effect in pronunciation training programs, although their utility is lower in the context of conversational programs. For programs designed to offer learners the opportunity to practice their conversational skills, providing a predefined list of utterances from which the learner can select their spoken response is limiting, as the learner is thereby restricted to use the utterances offered in the list rather than having the opportunity to formulate their own (even incorrect) utterances.

A challenge for speech interactive CALL is to create opportunities for learners to interact through speech with the program in a way that pushes them to develop their language skills by being able to formulate their own responses rather than choose from a preselected list. The CALL game described in this paper permits learners to respond openly, rather than selecting a response from a given list, by engaging in a spoken dialogue with the virtual characters, albeit within a defined lesson context.

3. Language Learning Game Design

The aim in the game is for learners to engage in a dialogue with the virtual characters within a defined context. The lesson content design used in this program adheres to a task-based approach in which the language is used to perform communicative tasks. Each individual lesson has an ultimate communicative goal (e.g., ordering food and drinks in a café), and each lesson focuses on the language required for this communicative goal. In the design of the lessons, the communicative goal of the lesson is defined and the necessary language to complete the goal of the lesson is then scripted into the scenarios.

Based on the interaction hypothesis [9], the virtual characters are designed to offer modifications of their input in cases where the learner appears to be having difficulties. Interaction provides learners with opportunities to receive comprehensible input and feedback [9, 34, 35]. Further, interaction allows learners to make changes to their own linguistic output [10, 36]. In the game, the learners are not told in advance what to say, nor are they given a finite list from which to choose their utterances; the speech recognition grammars are programmed with predicted responses for each individual stage of the dialogue, accounting for grammatical and some ungrammatical responses. This design poses a challenge for the speech recognition component with respect to how accurately the system is able to process the learners' responses.

Implicit feedback is preferable to corrective feedback for speech interactive CALL systems, as implicit feedback is likely to minimise potential problems resulting from imperfect speech recognition [37]. Feedback in the game is given implicitly in the form of recasts and reformulations. If the system detects that the learner has made an error in their utterance, the animated character recasts the learner's utterance. If the learner does not respond, the animated character repeats the question. If the system detects that the learner has given an answer that is not appropriate to the given stage, the system "rejects" this and the animated character reformulates the question, possibly offering a hint to the learner. These feedback strategies allow the dialogue with the learner to continue without explicit reference to a problem. This has the advantage of continuing the flow of the dialogue (and where necessary giving the learner another opportunity to respond, or implicitly correcting their response), and by being implicit in the feedback, this minimises attention to any potential errors made by the speech recognition component.

The program offers the learner three scenario types within each "lesson": observational, one-to-one, and interactive. Supplementary materials are also available to the learners to access if they require vocabulary, grammar files, a transcription of the observational dialogue, and cultural information.

3.1. The Observational Scenario. In order to provide the learner with the concepts required for the communicative goals of the lesson, the game contains an observational scenario which depicts a spoken dialogue between multiple characters within the defined context of the lesson. The key linguistic constructions relevant to the scene and which are useful for the learner in the subsequent scenarios are presented in the observational scenario.

The observational scenario contains a number of virtual characters situated within the virtual world (e.g., in a graphical representation of a "railway station" or "restaurant"). The virtual characters exhibit speech, gesture and facial animation, and manipulation of objects in the environment. They "speak" by means of prerecorded audio files. The virtual characters interact with each other in the target language, utilizing key linguistic structures appropriate for the given context. The learner observes this interaction and has control over the interaction in that they can pause, stop, and restart the dialogue and can access features to assist their understanding if required (e.g., vocabulary information or subtitles of the dialogue). The observational scenario presents the language relevant to the scene in a contextualised environment. The use of this observational scenario also gives the learner the opportunity to become accustomed to the virtual world in which they will become an active participant in the interactive scenarios, and it offers aural practice of the language within the contextualised environment.

3.2. The One-to-One Scenarios. Building on the exposure to the observational scenario, the one-to-one scenarios offer the learner the opportunity to practice key linguistic features by responding to questions on the related topic prior to their participation in the interactive scenario. In this way, they act as training scenarios for the learner before their ultimate immersion in the interactive scenario. The one-to-one scenarios involve one virtual character who asks the learner a series of questions relevant to the lesson topic. There is no movement around the scene, thus allowing the learner's focus to be on the virtual character and the questions asked. These short excerpts of dialogue are designed to ask the learner key questions related to the topic and feature a controlled degree of repetition in the questioning, as well as instructional support, mainly in the form of (implicit) feedback in the learner's responses.

When learners hear and comprehend language, the input is thought to be held briefly in their short-term memory and can be replaced with any forthcoming input unless the learner can focus their attention so that further mental processing can occur [38]. This further mental processing has been described as the process of going from input to intake [39]. Therefore, it is important in instruction to consider how to create opportunities for learners to be exposed to repeated occurrences of new language input, giving learners more opportunities to attend to the input they are exposed to, because the more the student pays attention to the input, the more the student is thought to learn [38]. Therefore, the shorter dialogue excerpts used here are designed to expose the learner to the structures of the language a number of times in order that they have more opportunities to pay attention to these structures.

In this research, participants completed two one-to-one scenarios: *About Train Times* and *Journey Details.* In the About Train Times scenario, the virtual character asks the learner some questions about the departure and arrival times of trains in Great Britain. To the side of the character on the screen is a timetable depicting the times. In the Journey Details scenario, the virtual character first asks where the learner would like to go. This dialogue stage is accompanied by a pop-up of a map of Great Britain, with 6 cities in each detailed. Following an appropriate response (i.e., the learner gives the name of a city, either in a one-word form, phrase, or full sentence response), the character then proceeds to ask about the departure and arrival times of the train to that city and the platform from which the train departs (again a timetable is displayed for these dialogue stages to the side of the virtual character). Following the completion of all four stages in the scenario, the character then summarises all the responses.

The one-to-one scenarios incorporate various levels of instructional support for the learner, both through spoken audio prompts from the virtual character and also in the form of text help menus within the scenes for cases where the learner is experiencing some difficulties. Additionally, the virtual tutor character offers implicit spoken feedback to the learner when the learner's utterance has been ungrammatical. As the one-to-one dialogue scenarios offer individualized practice of key linguistic features, they have to cater to individual learner preferences and abilities and have to be able to deal with a variety of response types from the learner, such as one-word, phrase, or full sentence responses. In cases where the response was not appropriate for the given dialogue stage, or the learner has not given a response, the system initiates the reformulation strategy, which in this case would first give the learner another opportunity to respond to the same question and subsequently give a hint to the learner if necessary.

For example,

> Virtual Character: *Where would you like to go?*
>
> Learner: (no response made)
>
> Virtual Character: *Where would you like to go?*
>
> Learner: *Um.*
>
> Virtual Character: *I would like to go to Oxford.*
> *Where would you like to go?*

In cases where the learner makes a response that is appropriate for the particular dialogue stage, but makes a grammatical error or responds with a one-word reply, the system initiates the recast strategy where the virtual character recasts the learner's response in a full sentence before moving on to the next dialogue stage. This provides additional input to the learner in the form of implicit feedback.

For example,

> Virtual Character: *Where would you like to go?*
>
> Learner: *I go to Oxford.*
>
> Virtual Character: *I see. You **would like to** go to Oxford.*

It should be noted that this full sentence recast approach is only implemented in the one-to-one training scenarios. The more immersive interactive scenario did not use a full sentence recast for cases where the learner did not produce a full sentence utterance.

3.3. The Interactive Scenario.

The interactive scenario provides the learner with the most immersive and true-to-life simulation of the given environment in which they can practice their spoken language skills. The learner's participation is necessary for the interaction between all dialogue participants (the learner and the virtual characters) in this scene to continue. In the interactive scenario, the most likely flow of possible interactions is scripted, and alternative paths are created, which allows a variety of inputs from the learner. The learner interacts through speech with the agents, but in contrast with the one-to-one scenarios, the agents respond appropriately through a number of conversational turns, which results in an appropriate dialogue relevant to the scene.

The camera viewpoint is from the learner perspective, as if through the learner's eyes, and hence a virtual representation (avatar) of the learner is not depicted. Instead, the viewpoint creates the impression that the learner is in the scene with the characters. The viewpoint also changes as the dialogue moves forward. As an example, the initial

FIGURE 1: Virtual characters in interactive scenario "At the Station."

viewpoint is from the front of the scene, as if walking into the railway station ticket office. The viewpoint then pans into the room towards the ticket agent with a slight up- and downward motion to indicate the learner walking to the ticket booth. Multiple interactions occur between the "friend" character and the "ticket seller" character with the learner and with each other. Addressing each other is made with gaze behaviours between the characters and the learner. The distance between the learner and the characters and the angles at which they are standing are such that it is obvious when the learner is being addressed and when the characters are in interaction with each other. This first-person perspective, which changes dynamically throughout the dialogue, was designed to create a sense of immersion for the learner.

Within this multiagent environment, it is apparent who is being addressed at any one time by the gaze of the virtual characters. The learner is directly addressed by the characters, and the characters are able to hand items within the scene to the implied body of the learner. In order to further stimulate immersion and participation, various items are used in the scene, relevant to the given context. When the learner orders the train tickets, a departure timetable board appears on the screen behind the ticket seller agent. Once the learner successfully orders their required tickets and relevant time of departure, the ticket seller character passes the tickets to the learner. This represents the feedback from a game perspective, whereas the virtual character's reformulations constitute feedback from a linguistic-instructional perspective.

Interacting in the interactive scenario allows learners to practice within the virtual setting the key transactional language necessary for train tickets in the target language. Figure 1 depicts the virtual characters in the interactive scenario.

The goal of the interactive scenario is to purchase tickets to the learner's preferred destination in the host country. The ticket seller asks the learner where they would like to go and subsequently takes them through a series of questions in order to sell the train ticket. The first question asked is an open question: *Hello, how can I help you?* This open question allows a number of responses in the grammar files: destination, number of tickets, and ticket type (single or return). Therefore more advanced learners can try out more complex responses, which contain more than one piece of information.

However, the system is also designed to accept any one of those pieces of information if that is what the learner supplies. If the learner is unable to respond to the open question, the dialogue moves into direct questioning which requires a simple yes or no response: *Would you like to buy tickets?* From here, the dialogue then directs the learner into a series of questions to determine their requested ticket purchase. The potential destinations from which the learner can choose are constrained to a total of six. These are depicted on the timetable screens above the ticket counter. Each destination has two corresponding departure times. Once the learner selects one of the given destinations, the ticket seller then asks which train they would like to take. The corresponding departure times grammar files are then selected in the code. In the cases where the learner has difficulty in selecting a departure time, a reformulation strategy is used where the ticket agent then offers the learner the choice of these two departure times. For example, if the learner selects "Oxford" as their destination but has not been able to select their preferred departure time, the ticket agent then asks: *At what time would you like to leave? At 11:15 or at 3:30?*

Once the learner has completed all questions relevant to the ticket purchase, the ticket seller hands the learner the required number of tickets.

3.4. Agent Animations. The agents are created in Virtual Reality Modelling Language (vrml) format with joints and body parts suitable for conversion to H-Anim 1.1 format, which allows the agents to be fully animated. Agent animations such as nods of acknowledgement and hand gestures were deemed important in creating the appearance of a realistic conversation with the agent. In the creation of a virtual agent, appropriate facial expression and gestures can be added to give a lifelike quality to the agent. These nonverbal behaviours are an important part in the perception of believability of the agent. Gestures can give an added dimension to the agents' speech. With gesture, the agent can indicate objects within their virtual context through deictic gestures, can refer to other agents in the scene or to the user of the application, and can draw users' attention to aspects of the virtual context. Facial animations can offer the user some insight into the agent's state; raised eyebrows can indicate surprise, a smile can indicate happiness, and a frown can indicate confusion. In this way, gestures and facial animation benefit the listener in that the listener can read into these non-verbal communications some information which is not expressed in the agent's speech. This is potentially useful for a language learner, as the learner may be able to interpret the agent's facial animations in instances of communicative difficulty; for example, if the

agent frowns when they have not understood what the user has said. The agent may also display some functional gestures within the scene. Additionally, the agent may display some listening animations when the user is speaking. The agents and animations used here were able to display the gestures and expressions required for each scene; however, they were somewhat rudimentary. For future applications, an off-the-shelf product is being considered (Complete Characters (http://www.rocketbox-libraries.com/) which should allow a more sophisticated look to our characters.

3.5. Speech Recognition Component. In creating the conversational dialogue, a semantic interpretation approach was adopted. In order to facilitate a spoken dialogue with the learner, the system must understand the semantic interpretation of the learner's utterance. This can be achieved by including task-relevant semantic information in the grammar used by the speech recognition component so that the outcome of the speech recognition process is not only a literal transcription of the utterance, but also an interpretation of its meaning. In this design, the semantic information is expressed within the grammar in the form of slot-value assignments, where the recognition of a particular word or phrase leads to the filling of a semantic slot with the information contained in that word or phrase. In addition, the game is designed to offer feedback to the learners on their responses. For this to occur, it must also be able to identify ungrammatical utterances that have been predicted and preprogrammed into the speech recognition files such that if the system detects that the learner has made an error in their utterance, the virtual character recasts the learner's utterance.

In the game, we used a commercially available speaker-independent recogniser (Nuance v8.0), not developed specifically for L2 learning. Therefore the recogniser's basic components, including its acoustic models and its language model, were not trained on nonnative speaker data. Given the state of the art of ASR applications for L2 learning, this approach might not seem evident. Using a speech recogniser that has been trained on non-native speaker data is seen as preferable in ASR-based CALL applications [40]. Much interest is focused on the area of speech recognition programs using non-native speaker models (e.g., [41, 42]). Acoustic models for language learning applications have been trained on L2 speech only [43] or L1 (first language) and L2 (target language) models used in parallel [44]. However, since our overall project aim was to create language games in a variety of L2 languages, equally with a variety of different L1 backgrounds, we used a commercially available recogniser that supports recognition engines for many different languages.

As described, the speech recogniser used in this game was trained primarily on native speaker models. In this recognition component, we were unable to change the acoustic models. However, we adapted the recogniser lexicon to include alternative pronunciations for each language pair, in consultation with language teachers. (It should be noted that this approach is somewhat limited in comparison

```
.Destination
[
DestinationOK
DestinationError
]
DestinationOK [
    (i [want (would like)] to go to Dest:d)
] {return($d)}
DestinationError [
    (?it's Dest:d)
    (to Dest:d)
    (?i go to Dest:d)
    (?i [want (would like)] ?to go Dest:d)
    (?i going ?to Dest:d)
]{<command recast> return($d)}
```

Figure 2: "At the station" recognition grammar extract.

to mixed acoustic models as only those phonemes present in the L2 acoustic models could be used in adaptation of possible L1 transfer errors.)

In addition, the recognition grammars (the language model) in the program were created specifically for non-native speaking learners using the lessons, including both grammatical and ungrammatical utterances constrained to each stage in the interaction; these recognition grammars were coded by hand by the authors. By using individual recognition grammars for each stage, the possible utterances at each given dialogue stage in a scenario are constrained, thus limiting the list from which the recogniser attempts to make a match. Figure 2 depicts a simplified sample grammar from the railway lesson for the dialogue stage "*Where would you like to go?*"

This example details the approach taken at every stage in the dialogue between the system (virtual character) and the learner. In this example, the top level grammar ("Destination") calls two sub-grammars: DestinationOK and DestinationError. DestinationOK contains a full sentence, grammatically correct response to the given question (such as "*I would like to go to Oxford*"). DestinationError contains accepted responses to the question, which may be incomplete sentences (such as "*Oxford*") or which may contain grammatical errors. Grammatical errors were accounted for in the grammar recognition files to reflect the kinds of errors that might be made by the learners. For example, grammatical errors included preposition omission and subject verb agreement. For example, "*I want to go Oxford*" is included in the recognition files, and is flagged as containing a preposition omission error. The recast command is triggered if the utterance is within the "error" category.

4. Evaluation of the Speech Interactive Scenarios

The experimental evaluation sought to investigate learner attitudes towards the different speech interactive scenarios

presented in the game and how these attitudes change as the learner progresses through the game and how they differ between the one-to-one practice scenarios and the immersive interactive scenario. In addition, investigation is made of the types of responses the learners make when interacting with the virtual characters in the scenarios and the accuracy with which the speech recognition component handled the learner responses.

4.1. Participants. A total of 48 students of English as a foreign language took part in the evaluation of the game; all the students recruited from the same junior high school in Beijing, China, and the evaluation took place on location at the school. In this evaluation, there were 22 males and 26 females. Participants were aged between 14 and 15 years at the time of the evaluation and had been studying English in school for an average of 6.8 years. All participants in this study came from the same junior high school in Beijing.

4.2. Experimental Procedure. Participants were first given a short tutorial on using the program (using the navigation and functionality controls, accessing the supplementary materials). Following this, the participants were asked to attempt various aspects of the "At the railway station" lesson. The participants were asked to watch the observational scenario, then try two of the one-to-one scenarios (here referenced as O-O1 and O-O2), and then try the interactive scenario (INT). The participants were informed that they could access other features in the program, for example, subtitles or vocabulary, as they wished. The researcher remained present during the program use. After each scenario, the participants were asked to complete an attitude questionnaire. During the interactions, the system automatically logged all the utterances made by the learners in their interactions for analysis of learners' response type and to investigate the recognition performance in this context.

4.3. User Attitude Questionnaires. User attitude questionnaires were administered after each scenario experienced in by the learners. The usability questionnaire was created in order to gather attitude data to each of the scenarios that the participants experienced. The questionnaires contained items which focused on affective issues, engagement issues, and issues relating to the interaction with respect to the dialogue itself and with respect to the content within the interaction. The attributes are presented in the following.

Affective issues:

(1) degree of control felt by the learner when talking with the character(s),

(2) degree of embarrassment when talking with the character(s),

(3) extent to which learner felt relaxed when talking with the character(s),

(4) extent to which learner felt stressed when talking with the character(s).

TABLE 1: Overall mean scores speech enabled scenarios.

Questionnaire Statement	"O-O1" (Mean = 5.03)	"O-O2" (Mean = 5.43)	Interactive (Mean = 5.58)
I felt in control when talking to the character.	4.50	4.90	5.08
I felt embarrassed when talking to the character.	4.31	5.25	5.52
I felt relaxed talking to the character.	4.52	5.58	5.58
I felt stressed talking to the character.	4.42	4.96	5.50
I enjoyed interacting with the character.	5.15	5.46	5.81
I prefer speaking English in class, rather than interacting with the character.	4.75	5.19	5.31
I would be happy to talk to the character again.	5.54	5.77	6.19
I felt that this interaction was useful for my learning of English.	6.33	6.33	6.31
I felt I always understood what the character said.	6.06	6.23	6.38
I felt I always knew how to respond to the character.	5.31	5.65	6.06
I felt that the character did not understand what I said.	4.49	5.27	5.25
I felt the character was difficult to understand.	5.58	5.84	5.90
I felt that the level of the language was difficult for me to understand.	5.81	6.08	6.13
I felt that this dialogue was too easy for me.	3.63	3.44	3.15

Engagement issues:

(5) extent of enjoyment of interacting with the character(s),

(6) preference for speaking target language in class,

(7) readiness to talk with the character(s) again,

(8) usefulness of interaction for learning language.

Interaction issues (conversational):

(9) extent of understanding what the character(s) said,

(10) extent of knowing how to respond,

(11) extent of being understood.

Interaction issues (content):

(12) extent of difficulty to understand content,

(13) extent of difficulty of language level,

(14) extent of difficulty of dialogue.

The questionnaire consisted of a series of short simple statements, each with a set of tick boxes on a Likert [45] seven-point scale labelled from "strongly agree" through "neutral" to "strongly disagree." The polarity of the statements is balanced to avoid the response acquiescence effect, where respondents may have a natural tendency to agree with proposals. The set of 14 statements was used in the questionnaire for the one-to-one and interactive scenarios. The questionnaire is a self-administered questionnaire and had been translated into Mandarin for students to complete themselves.

When analysing the results, responses to the questionnaire are first given a numerical value from 1 to 7; these values are then normalised for the polarity of the statements such that a "strongly agree" response to a positive statement is given a value of 7, whereas a "strongly agree" response to a negative statement is given a value of 1. After normalisation of the data, the overall attitude for each participant can be calculated as a mean of all of the scores on the items in the questionnaire. These values can then be used to calculate the overall attitude for all items in the questionnaire across all participants in the study. Additionally, mean scores for individual items in the questionnaire can be obtained for all participants.

5. Results

5.1. User Attitude Results. An overall mean score of 5.03 (on a 7-point scale) was obtained for the first one-to-one scenario "about train times," an overall mean score of 5.43 for the second one-to-one scenario "about journey details," and an overall mean score of 5.58 for the interactive scenario. Table 1 details the overall mean scores for the speech enabled scenarios.

It can be seen that attitude scores for the individual items increased across the three consecutive speech-enabled scenarios. Repeated measures analysis was conducted across the attitude data for the three speech-enabled scenarios. Comparing the O-O1 against O-O2, it was found that each of the affective issues scored significantly higher in the second scenario than in the first. Participants felt significantly more in control ($P = 0.033$); they felt highly significantly less embarrassed ($P = 0.000$); they felt highly significantly more relaxed ($P = 0.000$); and they felt significantly less stressed ($P = 0.011$). The affective issues are significantly better in the second one-to-one scenario. It appears that as the participants become more accustomed to the interaction there is a positive effect on their affective state.

Additionally, a preference for speaking the language in class, in comparison to speaking with the animated characters, was highly significantly less in the second scenario than in the first ($P = 0.000$), and the feeling that the

TABLE 2: Response type.

Interaction	Participants	Utterances	Answer only	Sentence	Verbal non answer
O-O1	48	341	64.5%	29.6%	5.9%
O-O2	48	316	64.9%	32.6%	2.5%
INT	48	452	79.8%	19.2%	0.9%

character did not understand them was highly significantly less in the second scenario than in the first ($P = 0.009$).

Comparing the O-O2 against the interactive scenario (the second one-to-one scenario was completed immediately prior to the interactive scenario) found significant differences amongst some individual items in the questionnaire. Participants felt highly significantly less stressed in the interactive scenario than in the second one-to-one scenario ($P = 0.002$); participants were highly significantly more happy to talk to the agents in the interactive scenario again ($P = 0.005$); participants were highly significantly more confident that they knew how to respond in the interactive scenario ($P = 0.009$).

The interactive scenario scored highly across all items in the questionnaire and significantly so in comparison to the one-to-one scenario for some items. Only one affective attribute (feeling stressed) was significantly higher between the interactive and the second one-to-one in comparison to all affective attributes in the earlier comparison. As learners progress through the scenarios, it would seem that their affective state becomes more positive, and therefore feelings of embarrassment and tension and stress subside. Significant results for feeling happy to talk with the characters again and feeling confident in knowing how to respond to the characters suggest an ease for the learners in their interactions with the agents in the immersive interactive scenarios.

5.2. Response Data. Participants' utterances when interacting with the system were recorded and later transcribed by hand (by human raters) for analysis of response type as well as recognition accuracy. The system also logged the recognition results at each stage of the dialogue.

Participants' utterances were categorised into three response types. As the interaction between characters and learner is a series of question and answer pairs, the shortest response type that facilitates the conversation is "answer only." This is often a one word answer (e.g., *two*) or a phrase response (e.g., *two tickets please*). The second response type employed is "sentence" which contains a main verb (e.g., *I would like to buy two tickets to Oxford*). The third response type is "verbal non answer." This final category constitutes responses where the learner has made an utterance (which triggers the recogniser) but does not answer the question. For example, mutterings, thinking aloud, verbal hesitations and nonlexical noises (e.g., coughs) are included in the "verbal non answer" category.

Table 2 details the response types for the participants in the evaluation. The response types are given for the individual dialogues within the lesson.

In each scenario, there was a preference for the learner to respond with an answer only response. However, this

TABLE 3: In-grammar and out-of-grammar user input.

Interaction	Utterances	IG	OOG
O-O1	341	47.2%	52.8%
O-O2	316	50.3%	49.7%
INT	452	72.1%	27.9%

percentage was much higher in the interactive scenario than in the one-to-one scenarios. Almost a third of responses in the one-to-one scenarios were full sentence responses; whereas, in the interactive scenario only fifth of responses were full sentences. The one-to-one scenarios, with their question and answer practice design, is more conducive to full sentence responses where the learner practices their grammatical constructions. In the interactive scenario, where the immersive nature suggests the learner is interacting in order to accomplish a goal, it is less intuitive to respond with a full sentence construction.

5.3. Speech Recognition Analysis. The accuracy of the speech recognition component is analysed by comparing the transcriptions of learner utterances with the output from the recogniser. The utterances are then grouped into in-grammar and out-of-grammar responses. In-grammar responses (IG) have been defined in the grammar recognition files (i.e., the system developer has predicted and programmed the exact word-for-word response). Out-of-grammar responses (OOG) are utterance strings which have not been included in the recognition grammar files.

Table 3 details the in-grammar and out-of-grammar responses for the participants in the evaluation.

For the two one-to-one scenarios, there was almost an even split between in-grammar and out-of-grammar utterances. That is, just over half of all utterances produced by the learners in the one-to-one scenarios were not predicted by the designers and written into the language model. Given that the recognition grammars were designed to incorporate a variety of responses, both grammatical and ungrammatical, constrained to each individual question in the dialogue, it is problematic that so many learner responses were out-of-grammar. Investigation of the responses made by the learners which were not included in the recognition grammars is made below (see out-of-grammar recognition analysis).

Looking at the interactive scenario compared with the one-to-one scenarios, it was found that far more utterances (72%) were in-grammar in the interactive scenario than the one-to-one scenarios. This may reflect the higher incidences of shorter (answer only) responses in the interactive scenarios, given the transactional nature of those scenarios. It does show, however, that learners made responses which fit into

TABLE 4: In-grammar recognition accuracy.

Interaction	IG utterances	Word for word	Semantic value	Misrec	Reject
O-O1	161	62.1%	71.4%	8.1%	20.5%
O-O2	159	67.3%	79.2%	3.1%	17.6%
INT	326	68.7%	81.0%	1.8%	17.2%

TABLE 5: Out-of-grammar recognition.

Interaction	OOG utterances	Correct reject	Recog semantic	Misrec semantic
O-O1	180	67.2%	16.7%	16.1%
O-O2	157	63.7%	26.1%	10.2%
INT	126	69.0%	26.2%	4.8%

the predicted language model more readily in the interactive scenario than in the less contextualised one-to-one scenarios.

6. In-Grammar Utterances

The speech recognition outputs for the IG utterances were analysed in terms of both word-for-word recognition and semantic value recognition. As the interaction in the dialogues follows a series of question and answer pairs, a semantic value is logged for each of the learner's utterances. As an example, the question from the program "What time does the train to Newcastle leave?" might elicit the answer "it leaves at six o'clock." In this response, the word-for-word recognition is the string "it leaves at six o'clock" which is one of the strings in the grammar; whereas, the semantic value is "six o'clock." If the program recognizes this utterance as "it leaves six o'clock", the word-for-word recognition is wrong but the semantic value is correct. Responses are also categorised where the semantic value is wrong, misrecognised [MisRec] or where the program rejects the utterance (in which case the reformulation strategy is employed giving the learner another opportunity to respond). Table 4 details the recognition accuracy for the in-grammar utterances.

Across the three scenarios, a similar pattern of word-for-word and semantic value accuracy was found. Accurate recognition of the semantic value allows the dialogue to continue effectively between the system and the learner; the system has "understood" the learner's response correctly. For example, in the data, to the question "Where would you like to go?" one participant answered "I want go Oxford." The system recognised this, incorrectly, as "I want to go Oxford." In this case, the system was able to respond to the participant's answer appropriately (by then asking questions relating to the departure time of the train to Oxford). The correct recognition of the semantic value is useful for the facilitation of the dialogue between the characters and the learner; however, it does not always indicate that the learner's errors have been identified.

A rather high rejection rate of IG utterances was found across the three scenarios. This is not ideal; however, given that the users of the system are non-native speakers of the target language (and of the recogniser's acoustic models), it is perhaps unsurprising. Technological limitations can be mitigated against in the design of the interactions. In this program, the effect of a system reject at any stage in the dialogues is that the character repeats or reformulates the initial question and the learner has another opportunity

to respond to the question. Although this does not hinder the dialogue between the system and the learner, it may contribute to participants' perceptions of the recognition performance of the application.

7. Out-of-Grammar Utterances

Investigation was made on the out-of-grammar utterances made by the participants. It is expected that out-of-grammar utterances should be rejected by the system, as the system is not programmed to "listen" for these utterances. However, although these utterances are out of grammar, the system may misrecognise some of these utterances for something within the recognition grammars. Analysis of the out-of-grammar utterances classifies the results into three categories: correct rejection of the utterance, recognition of the correct semantic value of the utterance or misrecognition of the semantic value of the utterance. For example, an utterance may contain a mid-utterance repetition, which would not be included in the recognition grammars. However, if the system then misrecognises this utterance for an utterance that is in the recognition grammars and the value of the recognition is accurate, then the system will proceed appropriately. Note that as with the semantic value recognition in the IG utterances, these correctly recognised semantic value utterances would not necessarily trigger the system to offer feedback to the learner in the form of recast. Again, they only indicate those utterances where the dialogue proceeds with the response that the participant intended. Table 5 details the category types for the out-of-grammar utterances across the two groups.

The majority of OOG utterances across all three scenarios were correctly rejected by the system. Such utterances include utterances in the participants' first language (thinking aloud), non-lexical responses, or hesitation noises as well as responses that are inappropriate to the question asked. With regards to these utterances, the system handles the responses by reformulating the question and giving the user another chance to respond. That is, even though the system designer has not predicted the response made here by the learner, by correctly rejecting the utterance, the system handles the response appropriately. A sizeable minority of OOG utterances were recognised with the correct semantic value. These utterances often include short disfluencies in the learner's utterance or self-repairs which entailed the utterance was OOG; however, the system recognised the utterance with the intended semantic value. An example of a self-repair in the data which resulted in the recognition of the correct semantic value is the response "*nine fifty in the aft- in the evening*" which was recognised as "*nine fifty in the evening.*" In these cases, the responses are technically out-of-grammar, however, the outcome of the recognition is an accurate response (as far as the user is aware). It is not possible to account for every possible user disfluency in the language models. Although the design of the recognition grammars incorporates user disfluency at the beginning of an utterance (e.g., "*eh nine*"), other disfluencies are not programmed into the recognition grammars.

Finally, the one-to-one scenarios produced a sizeable minority of utterances which were misrecognised with the wrong semantic value. The Interactive scenario only produced a very small percentage of such utterances. These are the most problematic as they are likely to cause confusion on the learner's part. Analysis of these OOG misrecognitions highlighted that there were some problems (which also occurred in the IG misrecognition results) with similar sounding time responses. For example, in the data there were multiple misrecognitions of "*thirteen*" for "*thirty,*" "*fourteen*" for "*forty*" and "*fifteen*" for "*fifty,*" and vice versa. Similar sounding responses can be avoided in the design of the dialogues by careful dialogue planning. However, in cases where it was felt that restricting the dialogue to exclude similar sounding expressions (which in the case of time expressions may not be appropriate), the CALL program designer could mitigate against such potential recognition errors by employing an additional confirmation stage where the virtual character seeks confirmation from the learner on their response (e.g., "*Did you say "ten o'clock"?*"). Such a strategy may mimic what would occur in a real-life situation if the coparticipant in the dialogue was unsure of what was said.

8. Discussion

The results of the evaluation indicate that speech interactive CALL systems are potentially very useful for language learners, despite misrecognitions by the speech recognition component. Analysis of the speech recognition component found in-grammar semantic value accuracy rates of up to 81% for the interactive scenario. However, word-for-word recognition performance was as low as 62% indicating that the recognition component is not robust enough to accurately determine exactly what the learner has said (within this open dialogue design). Regardless of recogniser inaccuracies, user attitude results indicate a high level of engagement and enjoyment with using the system. This is in accordance with research into the use of automatic speech recognition in CALL applications [32], which found that despite the limitations of the speech recogniser and the misrecognitions it generated, end users enjoy the interactions with the system and would prefer a speech interactive component to be included in the CALL application. This was also found in a previous evaluation of the software described here [12].

There are limitations to the open dialogue approach used in this program in the more difficult one-to-one scenarios. Contextualised help is provided in the immersive interactive scenario, which lends itself to more natural, shorter responses within the given context which is optimal for the speech recognition technology. The one-to-one scenarios are similar to traditional question and answer response type which are akin to the teacher in class asking a question that they know the answer to already. The interactive scenario is a more genuine question and answer where the responses lead to a communicative goal.

The design of the game, with open speech dialogue is optimal for the immersive contextualised interactive scenario. Users responded naturally in short answers which felt "right" and which was an easier challenge for the speech recognition technology. The interactive scenario design is a good fit for the technology and for the ways in which users interacted with the virtual characters.

Investigation of user responses in this study found that there was a tendency for shorter responses in the interactive scenarios in comparison with the one-to-one scenarios. With regards to coverage in the recognition grammars, participants in this study made responses which fit into the language model of the interactive scenario far more than in the one-to-one scenarios. In designs where the learner has to select a response from a finite list, the recognition grammar is fully constrained to those given responses. However, when there is no list from which the learner can choose their response, the recognition grammars must include a variety of possible responses, both grammatical and ungrammatical. Given the number of out-of-grammar responses was around the same as the in-grammar responses, it would appear that this approach is not usable. However, in the investigation of the out-of-grammar recognition results, we found that the majority of the responses were correctly rejected by the system (thus allowing another chance for the learner to respond), and a sizable minority of responses were recognised with the user's intended meaning.

On the whole, grammar coverage for the interactive scenario was measurably higher than in the one-to-one scenarios. That is, participants in this study produced responses which were included in the recognition grammars much more frequently in the interactive scenario than in the one-to-one scenarios. Therefore, it was easier to predict learner responses in the interactive scenario. In addition, participants tended to produce fewer hesitancies in their responses in the interactive scenario. Observation suggests this may be due to the fact that the physical context and visual cues in the interactive scenario served to make the meaning of the questions clearer, resulting in a higher proportion of in-grammar responses. Moreover, the situational context encourages the use of brief or one-word answers reducing the risk of an out-of-grammar response. For example, in response to the question "*How many tickets would you like?*" the reply "*Two please*" would be a natural response in conversation. To respond with a complete sentence such as "*I would like two tickets please*" in this case is more likely to appear unnatural.

It should be noted that each participant in the experiment experienced these scenarios in the same order. It was important to see if there was any effect on participants' attitudes towards interacting within the scenarios over time and more experience. As the Interactive scenario builds upon concepts and constructions which have been practised in the one-to-one scenarios, it might be expected that attitudes towards this scenario are more favourable than towards the one-to-one scenarios.

Allowing the learner to formulate their own responses to the animated agents' questions, rather than selecting from a predefined list, provides a facilitative environment for language learning. However, this poses a serious challenge for both the designer in terms of predicting learners' responses and the recogniser in having to match the response against a potentially lengthy recognition grammar.

The interactive scenario produced higher user attitude scores and better recognition, suggesting that this type of scenario is better suited to the technology limitations. It seems that interactive scenarios, where the communicative activity is highly contextualised, are more conducive to this type of open response dialogue design. While maximising the potential of ASR in speech interactive CALL, such interactive scenarios, or participatory dramas, also serve to motivate learners and reduce their inhibition [46].

The user response types show that learners were producing shorter responses in the interactive scenario and therefore potentially not pushing their linguistic capabilities in the target language in this context. The study shows an overall favourable attitude towards each of the scenarios and in particular the interactive scenario. The benefits to the one-to-one scenarios are the extended practice of the key linguistic forms and vocabulary for the given context. However, in future studies, an alternative approach restricting the variety of responses expected may be preferable without negatively impacting the learners' experience.

In this study, the focus was the learners' attitudes towards the scenarios, the responses they made, and the recognition performance. We did not investigate any effect of using the program on the learners' ability in the target language. Learners responded strongly that they felt the interactions were useful for their learning of English (6.3 on a 7-point scale), but no objective data was gathered in this area. Future experiments could include some pre- and post-testing of the key linguistic topics included within the lesson to ascertain any positive effects on learning.

9. Conclusion: Directions for Future Research with Scenario-Based CALL

Digital games for learning have the potential to offer an enhanced learning experience if designers consider the reasons why computer games are so engaging for learners. In a review of the literature, Mitchell and Savill-Smith [47] identified a number of reasons why computer games are so compelling for users. First, games are visually seductive in that they "use technology to represent reality or embody fantasy" [48]. They have an ultimate goal and motivate the learner via fun [49] and instant visual feedback [50]. Games provide a complete interactive playing environment [51]. Finally, the ambience information in the digital game creates

an immersive experience, sustaining the user's interest in the game [51].

Thus, engaging computer games offer an immersive fantasy or realistic world along with clearly defined achievable goals and instant and observable outcomes. Immediate and interactive feedback is a compelling quality of digital games [52]. A common element in digital games is where the game can "respond seamlessly to a player's input" and therefore offers "real-time game play that shifts and reacts dynamically to player decisions."

Designers of CALL games should look ahead at how commercial games could inspire the design of educational applications in order to make them more engaging and compelling for learners. Adaptation of the interaction or program could be tailored to suit the individual learner's needs. The game or activity must be seen as relevant and appropriate to the individual user. Activities which are designed to be fun and engaging can be found to be tedious and uninteresting by some users [53]. Commercial games are demographically targeted to specific users and styles, whereas resources may restrict such variety in learning games. Customisation of the game could allow the user some control to make changes to, for example, the skill level, speed of interaction, complexity of interaction, or time to respond, in order to make them suitable to the learner's own needs and wants.

Good computer games are "pleasingly frustrating" [50] which are mastered as they are played. Ideally, the game should be played without the need for consulting instructions external to the game. In immersive interactive environments especially, any halting of the game to deploy or exhibit instructions to the user could be detrimental to the immersive aspects of the game. If the system is nonintuitive, or if instructions are necessary for the game to proceed, the user has to quit their presence in the game in order to exit out to receive the instructions.

Taking the video games dimension a step further, learners could inhabit the virtual world as a "surrogate avatar," the virtual character the player is playing [50]. In this way, the learner must take on the mental states they believe the virtual character has in their decisions to achieve the goals of the game. Thus, the learner has the opportunity to experience "alternative identities" [54]. This type of virtual simulation can open up the space to fantasy and thus allow for a more compelling environment for future spoken CALL systems.

References

[1] A. Firth and J. Wagner, "On discourse, communication, and (some) fundamental concepts in SLA research," *The Modern Language Journal*, vol. 81, no. 3, pp. 285–300, 1997.

[2] L. van Lier, "From input to affordance: social-interactive learning from an ecological perspective," in *Sociocultural Theory and Second Language Learning*, J. P. Lantolf, Ed., pp. 245–259, Oxford University Press, Oxford, UK, 2000.

[3] M. Warschauer and D. Healey, "Computers and language learning: an overview," *Language Teaching*, vol. 31, pp. 57–71, 1998.

[4] B. H. Sørensen and B. Meyer, "Serious games in language learning and teaching—a theoretical perspective," in *Proceedings of the 3rd International Conference of the Digital Games Research Association*, pp. 559–566, Tokyo, Japan, 2007.

[5] J. C. Richards and T. S. Rogers, *Approaches and Methods in Language Teaching*, Cambridge University Press, Cambridge, UK, 1986.

[6] R. Scarcella and D. Crookall, "Simulation/gaming and language acquisition," in *Simulation, Gaming and Language Learning*, D. Crookall and R. L. Oxford, Eds., pp. 223–230, Newbury House, New York, NY, USA, 1990.

[7] L. van Lier, "An ecological-semiotic perspective on language and linguistics," in *Language Acquisition and Language Socialization: Ecological Perspectives*, C. Kramsch, Ed., pp. 140–164, Continuum, London, UK, 2002.

[8] K. Facer, "Computer games and learning," NESTA Futurlab Discussion Paper, pp. 1–11, 2005, http://www.nestafuturelab.org/research/discuss/02discuss01.htm.

[9] M. H. Long, "The role of the linguistic environment in second language acquisition," in *Handbook of Second Language Acquisition*, W. C. Ritchie and T. K. Bhatia, Eds., pp. 413–468, Academic Press, New York, NY, USA, 1996.

[10] M. Swain, "Three functions of output in second language learning," in *Principle and Practice in Applied Linguistics: Studies in Honour of H. G. Widdowson*, G. Cook and B. Seidlhofer, Eds., pp. 125–144, Oxford University Press, Oxford, UK, 1995.

[11] C. A. Chapelle, "Multimedia CALL: lessons to be learned from research on instructed SLA," *Language Learning & Technology*, vol. 2, no. 1, pp. 22–34, 1998.

[12] H. Morton, N. Davidson, and M. A. Jack, "Evaluation of a speech interactive CALL system," in *Handbook of Research on Computer-Enhanced Language Acquisition and Learning*, F. Zhang and B. Barber, Eds., 2008.

[13] H. Morton and M. Jack, "Speech interactive computer-assisted language learning: a cross-cultural evaluation," *Computer Assisted Language Learning*, vol. 23, no. 4, pp. 295–319, 2010.

[14] H. Morton, N. Gunson, and M. Jack, "Attitudes to subtitle duration and the effect on user responses in speech interactive foreign language learning," *Journal of Multimedia*, vol. 6, no. 5, pp. 436–446, 2011.

[15] J. Cassell, "Nudge, nudge, wink, wink: elements of face-to-face conversation for embodied conversational agents," in *Embodied Conversational Agents*, J. Cassell, J. Sullivan, S. Prevost, and E. Churchill, Eds., pp. 1–27, MIT Press, Cambridge, Mass, USA, 2000.

[16] W. L. Johnson, S. Choi, S. Marsella, N. Mote, S. Narayanan, and H. Vilhjálmsson, "Tactical language training system: supporting the rapid acquisition of foreign language and cultural skills," in *Proceedings of the InSTIL/ICALL Symposium on Computer Assisted Language Learning*, pp. 21–24, Venice, Italy, 2004.

[17] W. L. Johnson and E. Shaw, "Using agents to overcome difficulties in web-based courseware," in *Workshop on Intelligent Educational Systems on the World Wide Web (AI-ED '97)*, pp. 1–8, Kobe, Japan, 1997.

[18] W. L. Johnson, J. W. Rickel, and J. C. Lester, "Animated pedagogical agents: face-to-face interaction in interactive learning environments," *International Journal of Artificial Intelligence in Education*, vol. 11, pp. 47–78, 2000.

[19] W. L. Johnson and A. Valente, "Tactical language and culture training systems: Using artificial intelligence to teach foreign languages and cultures," in *Proceedings of the 23rd AAAI Conference on Artificial Intelligence and the 20th Innovative Applications of Artificial Intelligence Conference (AAAI '08/IAAI '08)*, pp. 1632–1639, Chicago, Ill, USA, July 2008.

[20] J. C. Lester, S. A. Converse, S. E. Kahler, S. T. Barlow, B. A. Stone, and R. S. Bhogal, "Animated pedagogical agents and problem-solving effectiveness: a large-scale empirical evaluation," in *Proceedings of the 8th World Conference on Artificial Intelligence in Education*, pp. 23–30, 1997.

[21] R. Moreno, R. E. Mayer, and J. C. Lester, "Life-like pedagogical agents in constructivist multimedia environments: Cognitive consequences of their interaction," in *Proceedings of World Conference on Educational Multimedia, Hypermedia and Telecommunications*, pp. 741–746, AACE Press, Charlottesville, VA, USA, 2000.

[22] W. L. Johnson, J. W. Rickel, and J. C. Lester, "Animated pedagogical agents: face-to-face interaction in interactive learning environments," *International Journal of Artificial Intelligence in Education*, vol. 11, pp. 47–78, 2000.

[23] M. Heim, *The Metaphysics of Virtual Reality*, Oxford University Press, Oxford, UK, 1994.

[24] M. Slater, M. Usoh, and A. Steed, "Depth of presence in virtual environments," *Presence, Teleoperators and Virtual Environments*, vol. 3, pp. 130–144, 1994.

[25] C. D. Morris, J. D. Bransford, and J. J. Franks, "Levels of processing versus transfer appropriate processing," *Journal of Verbal Learning and Verbal Behavior*, vol. 16, no. 5, pp. 519–533, 1977.

[26] W. Menzel, D. Herron, R. Morton, D. Pezzotta, P. Bonaventura, and P. Howarth, "Interactive pronunciation training," *ReCALL*, vol. 13, no. 1, pp. 67–78, 2001.

[27] J. Dalby and D. Kewley-Port, "Explicit pronunciation training using automatic speech recognition technology," *CALICO Journal*, vol. 16, no. 3, pp. 425–445, 1999.

[28] M. Eskenazi, "Using a computer in foreign language pronunciation training: what advantages?" *CALICO Journal*, vol. 16, no. 3, pp. 447–469, 1999.

[29] J. Murray, "Lessons learned from the Athena language learning project," in *Intelligent Language Tutors: Theory Shaping Technology*, V. Holland M, J. D. Kaplan, and M. R. Sams, Eds., pp. 243–256, Lawrence Erlbaum Associates, Mahwah, NJ, USA, 1995.

[30] J. Bernstein, A. Najmi, and F. Ehsani, "Subarashii: encounters in Japanese spoken language education," *CALICO Journal*, vol. 16, no. 3, pp. 361–384, 1999.

[31] W. G. Harless, M. A. Zier, and R. C. Duncan, "Virtual dialogues with native speakers: the evaluation of an interactive multimedia method," *CALICO Journal*, vol. 16, no. 3, pp. 313–337, 1999.

[32] M. Holland, J. D. Kaplan, and M. Sabol, "Preliminary tests of language learning in a speech-interactive graphics microworld," *CALICO Journal*, vol. 16, no. 3, pp. 339–359, 1999.

[33] H. Strik, F. Cornillie, J. Colpaert, J. van Doremalen, and C. Cucchiarini, "Developing a CALL system for practicing oral proficiency: how to design for speech technology, pedagogy and learners," in *Proceedings of the SlaTE-2009 Workshop*, Warwickshire, UK, 2009.

[34] T. Pica, "Research on negotiation: what does it reveal about second-language learning conditions, processes, and outcomes?" *Language Learning*, vol. 44, pp. 493–527, 1994.

[35] S. Gass, *Input, Interaction, and the Second Language Learner*, Lawrence Erlbaum Associates, Mahwah, NJ, USA, 1997.

[36] M. Swain, "Communicative competence: some roles of comprehensible input and comprehensible output in its development," in *Input in Second Language Acquisition*, S. Gass and

C. Madden, Eds., pp. 235–253, Newbury House Press, Rowley, Mass, USA, 1985.

[37] K. Wachowicz and B. Scott, "Software that listens: it's not a question of whether, it's a question of how," *CALICO Journal*, vol. 16, no. 3, pp. 253–276, 1999.

[38] C. Doughty and J. Williams, "Pedagogical choices in focus on form," in *Focus on Form in Classroom Second Language Acquisition*, C. Doughty and J. Williams, Eds., pp. 197–261, Cambridge University Press, Cambridge, UK, 1998.

[39] S. M. Gass, "Integrating research areas: a framework for second language studies," *Applied Linguistics*, vol. 9, no. 2, pp. 198–217, 1988.

[40] H. Strik, A. Neri, and C. Cucchiarini, "Speech technology for language tutoring," in *Proceedings of the Language and Speech Technology Conference (LangTech '08)*, pp. 73–76, Rome, Italy, 2008.

[41] J. Morgan and S. LaRocca, "Making a speech recognizer tolerate non-native speech through Gaussian mixture merging," in *Proceedings of InSTIL/ICALL Symposium on Computer Assisted Language Learning,*, pp. 213–216, Venice, Italy, 2004.

[42] N. Cylwik, A. Wagner, and G. Demenko, "The EURO-NOUNCE corpus of non-native polish for ASR-based pronunciation tutoring system," in *Proceedings of the SLATE Workshop on Speech and Language Technology in Education*, Warwickshire, UK, 2009.

[43] L. Neumeyer, H. Franco, M. Weintraub, and P. Price, "Automatic text-independent pronunciation scoring of foreign language student speech," in *Proceedings of the International Conference on Spoken Language Processing (ICSLP '96)*, pp. 1457–1460, October 1996.

[44] G. Kawai and K. Hirose, "A method for measuring the intelligibility and non-nativeness of phone quality in foreign language pronunciation training," in *Proceedings of the International Conference on Spoken Language Processing (ICSLP '98)*, pp. 1823–1826, Sydney, Australia, 1998.

[45] R. Likert, *A Technique for the Measurement of Attitudes*, Columbia University Press, New York, NY, USA, 1932.

[46] P. Hubbard, "Interactive participatory dramas for language learning," *Simulation and Gaming*, vol. 33, no. 2, pp. 210–216, 2002.

[47] A. Mitchell and C. Savill-Smith, "The use of computer and video games for learning. A review of the literature, Ultralab," 2004, http://gmedia.glos.ac.uk/docs/books/computergames4learning.pdf.

[48] Becta, "Computer games in education," Project Report, 2001.

[49] C. Bisson and J. Luckner, "Fun in learning: the pedagogical role of fun in adventure education," *Journal of Experimental Education*, vol. 19, no. 2, pp. 108–112, 1996.

[50] J. P. Gee, "Pleasure, learning, video, games and life: the projective stance," *E-Learning and Digital Media*, vol. 2, no. 3, pp. 21–223, 2005.

[51] M. Prensky, *Digital Game-Based Learning*, McGraw Hill, New York, NY, USA, 2001.

[52] K. Salen and E. Zimmerman, *Rules of Play: Game Design Fundamentals*, MIT Press, Cambridge, Mass, USA, 2004.

[53] S. Franciosi, "A comparison of computer game and language learning task design using flow theory," *CALL-EJ*, vol. 12, no. 1, pp. 1–25, 2011.

[54] R. Sandford and B. Williamson, *Games and Learning: A Handbook From Futurlab*, 2005, http://www2.futurelab.org.uk/resources/documents/handbooks/games_and_learning2.pdf.

11

Controlling Assistive Machines in Paralysis Using Brain Waves and Other Biosignals

Paulo Rogério de Almeida Ribeiro,[1,2,3] Fabricio Lima Brasil,[1,2,4]
Matthias Witkowski,[1,2] Farid Shiman,[1,2] Christian Cipriani,[5] Nicola Vitiello,[5]
Maria Chiara Carrozza,[5] and Surjo Raphael Soekadar[1,2]

[1] Institute of Medical Psychology and Behavioral Neurobiology and MEG Center, University of Tübingen, Silcherstraße 5,
72076 Tübingen, Germany
[2] Applied Neurotechnology Lab, Department of Psychiatry and Psychotherapy, University of Tübingen, Calwerstraße 14,
72076 Tübingen, Germany
[3] International Max Planck Research School for Neural Information Processing, Österbergstraße 3, 72074 Tübingen, Germany
[4] International Max Planck Research School for Neural & Behavioral Sciences, Österbergstraße 3, 72074 Tübingen, Germany
[5] The BioRobotics Institute, Scuola Superiore Sant'Anna, V.le R. Piaggio 34, 56025 Pontedera, Italy

Correspondence should be addressed to Surjo Raphael Soekadar; surjo.sockadar@uni-tuebingen.de

Academic Editor: Christoph Braun

The extent to which humans can interact with machines significantly enhanced through inclusion of speech, gestures, and eye movements. However, these communication channels depend on a functional motor system. As many people suffer from severe damage of the motor system resulting in paralysis and inability to communicate, the development of brain-machine interfaces (BMI) that translate electric or metabolic brain activity into control signals of external devices promises to overcome this dependence. People with complete paralysis can learn to use their brain waves to control prosthetic devices or exoskeletons. However, information transfer rates of currently available noninvasive BMI systems are still very limited and do not allow versatile control and interaction with assistive machines. Thus, using brain waves in combination with other biosignals might significantly enhance the ability of people with a compromised motor system to interact with assistive machines. Here, we give an overview of the current state of assistive, noninvasive BMI research and propose to integrate brain waves and other biosignals for improved control and applicability of assistive machines in paralysis. Beside introducing an example of such a system, potential future developments are being discussed.

1. Introduction

The way humans interact with computers has changed substantially in the last decades. While, for many years, the input from the human to the machine was mainly managed through keystrokes, then later through hand movements using a computer mouse, other potential input sources have been opened up allowing more intuitive and effortless control, for example, based on speech [1], gestures [2], or eye movements [3], all depending on a functional motor system.

As cardiovascular diseases increase and people live longer, an increasing number of people suffer from conditions that affect their capacity to communicate or limit their mobility [4], for example, due to stroke, neurodegenerative disorders, or hereditary myopathies. Motor disability can also result from traumatic injuries, affecting the central or peripheral nervous system or can be related to amputations of the upper or lower extremities. While these handicapped people would benefit the most from assistive machines, their capacity to interact with computers or machines is often severely impeded.

Among the most important causes of neurological disabilities resulting in permanent damage and reduction of motor functions or the ability to communicate are stroke, multiple sclerosis (MS), spinal cord injury (SCI), brachial plexus injury (BPI), and neurodegenerative diseases, such as amyotrophic lateral sclerosis (ALS) or dementia [4].

Stroke is the leading cause of long-term disability in adults and affects approximately 20 million people per year worldwide [5, 6]. Five millions remain severely handicapped and dependent on assistance in daily life [4]. Nearly 30% of all stroke patients are under the age of 65 [7]. Other diseases resulting in paralysis at such early age include MS, affecting more than 2.5 million people worldwide [8], or SCI with 12.1 to 57.8 cases per million [9, 10]. BPI, the disruption of the upper limb nerves leading to a flaccid paralysis of the arm, affects thousands of people every year [11]. Furthermore, every year there are approximately 2,000 new traumatic upper limb amputations in Europe [12].

While there is major progress in the development of assistive apparatuses built for instance to compensate for a lost or paralyzed limb for example, lightweight and versatile prostheses or exoskeletons [13–16], intuitive and reliable control of such devices is an enormous challenge.

Previous surveys on the use of artificial hands revealed that up to 50% of the amputees are not using their prosthetic hand regularly, mainly due to low functionality, poor cosmetic appearance, and low controllability [17].

Since early on, the use of electromyographic (EMG) signals for prosthetic control, for example, from the amputee's stump or contralateral chest muscles, was an important concept [18, 19]. However, its broader success is still limited due to many practical reasons that are valid for all assistive systems that depend on recording biosignals, primarily the effort and costs to provide good signal quality, a fast and effective calibration process, and, last but not least, the benefit of the system in the user's everyday life. Furthermore, increasing the signal-to-noise ratio or the specificity of such recordings by means of techniques such as the electric nerve stimulation [20] is possible but increases the overall system complexity [21]. Adding sensory qualities during utilization of prosthetic devices increasing the bidirectional interaction between users and the machine improves the functionality of assistive systems [22]. Here, however, the same limitation applies as to the motor domain that the majority of such systems depend on an intact peripheral sensory system.

Thus, the development and provision of assistive machines that are independent of the peripheral nervous system's integrity represent a promising and appealing perspective, particularly, if controlled intuitively and without requiring extensive training to gain reliable control.

2. Brain-Computer and Brain-Machine Interfaces: A General Overview

Since it was discovered that brain waves contain information about cognitive states [23, 24] and can be functionally specific [25, 26], the idea to use such signals for direct brain control of assistive machines became a major driving force for the development of the so-called brain-computer or brain-machine interfaces (BCI/BMI) [27]. Such interfaces allow direct translation of electric or metabolic brain activity into

TABLE 1: Categories of brain-computer and brain-machine interfaces.

Based on: **recording site of brain signals**	
Brain signal used	*Recording technique*
Invasive	
Single spike	Single cell recordings
Multiunit activity	Multiunit arrays (MUA)
Local field potentials (LFP)	Electrocorticogram (ECoG)
Noninvasive	
Electric brain potentials	Electroencephalography (EEG)
Neuromagnetic fields	Magnetoencephalography (MEG)
BOLD	Functional magnetic resonance imaging (fMRI)
Oxy/deoxyhemoglobin	Near-infrared spectroscopy (NIRS)
Based on: **mode of operation**	
Active	Asynchronous control
	Synchronous control
Reactive	N.A.
Passive	N.A.
Based on: **purpose**	
Assistive/biomimetic	Restorative/biofeedback
Used for restoration of	*Tested in the treatment of*
Communication	Stroke
Paralysis	Chronic pain
	Tinnitus
	Dementia
	Depression
	Schizophrenia

control signals of external devices or computers bypassing the peripheral nervous and muscular system.

As neural or metabolic brain activity can be recorded from sensors inside or outside the brain, BCI/BMI is categorized as invasive or noninvasive systems [28]. Other categorizations relate to the specific brain signal used for BCI/BMI control or the mode of operation (see Table 1).

Invasively recorded brain signals that were successfully used for BCI/BMI control include single-spike or multiunit activity and local field potentials (LFP) [29]. These signals are necessarily recorded from inside the skull, while electric or magnetic brain oscillations reflecting pattern formation of larger cell assemblies' activity [30] can also be recorded from outside the skull using electro- or magnetoencephalography (EEG/MEG). Each method offers access to specific unique properties of brain activity [31]. These noninvasive techniques allow, for example, detection and translation of slow cortical potentials (SCP), changes of sensorimotor rhythms (SMR), or event-related potentials (ERP), for example, the P300, translating them into control signals for external devices or computers. More recently, online interpretation of changes in metabolic brain activity [32, 33] was introduced for BCI/BMI application offering high spatial (in the range of mm), but low temporal, resolution (in the range of seconds). These systems use functional magnetic resonance imaging (fMRI) [32] or near-infrared spectroscopy (NIRS) [33, 34], both measuring changes in brain tissue's blood-oxygenation-level dependent (BOLD) signals.

In 1969, Fetz demonstrated that single neurons in precentral cortex can be operantly conditioned by delivery of food pellets [35]. Since then, operant conditioning of cortical activity was demonstrated in various paradigms [36], requiring, though, opening of the skull and insertion of electrodes into the brain with the risk of bleedings and infections [37, 38]. An intermediate, semiinvasive approach uses LFP recorded by epidural electrocorticography (ECoG) [29, 39]. LFP reflects neural activity of an area of up to $200\ \mu m^2$ comprising hundreds of thousands of neurons with numerous local recurrent connections and connections to more distant brain regions [40], while brain oscillations recorded noninvasively (e.g., using EEG or MEG) contain information of millions of neurons [41].

To control assistive devices or machines in paralysis, the following noninvasively recorded neurophysiologic signals were successfully used up to now: (1) slow cortical potentials (SCP) [42, 43], (2) sensorimotor rhythms (SMRs) and its harmonics [44, 45], and (3) event-related potentials (ERPs), for example, P300 [46].

The use of SCP in BCI/BMI applications goes back to Birbaumer and his coworker's work in the late 1970s showing that operant control of SCPs (slow direct-current shifts occurring event-related after 300 ms to several seconds) is possible while exhibiting strong and anatomically specific effects on behavior and cognition [47–49]. A tight correlation of central SCPs and blood-oxygen level-dependent (BOLD) signals in the anterior basal ganglia and premotor cortex was found [50] suggesting a critical role of the basal ganglia-thalamo-frontal network for operant control of SCP.

In contrast to SCPs, SMRs are recorded over the sensorimotor cortex usually at a frequency between 8 and 15 Hz. In analogy to the occipital alpha and visual processing [51], the SMR (or rolandic alpha) shows a clear functional specificity, disappearing during planned, actual, or imagined movements [52]. Accordingly, a close association with functional motor inhibition of thalamocortical loops was suggested [53]. Depending on the context, the SMR is also called μ-rhythm [54] or rolandic alpha and was extensively investigated by the Pfurtscheller group in Graz [55] and the Wolpaw group in Albany [56, 57].

Another well-established and tested BCI/BMI controller is the P300-based ERP-BCI introduced by Farwell and Donchin [58]. While SCP- and SMR-controls are learned through visual and auditory feedback often requiring multiple training sessions before reliable control is achieved, the P300-BCI needs no training at all. While, in the classical P300-ERP-BCI paradigm, the user focuses his attention to a visual stimulus, other sensory qualities such as tactile [59] or auditory stimuli [60, 61] were successfully implemented in ERP-BCI. Information rates of ERP-BCI can reach 20–30 bits/min: [62].

In terms of operation mode, active, passive, and reactive BCI/BMI applications can be distinguished [63]. While active

and reactive BCI/BMI require the user's full attention to generate voluntary and directed commands, passive BCI/BMI relates to the concept of cognitive monitoring introducing the assessment of the users' intentions, situational interpretations, and emotional states [64].

In active BCI/BMI applications, two forms of control can be distinguished: synchronous and asynchronous control [65]. In synchronous control, translation of brain activity follows a fixed sequence or cue. The user is required to be fully attentive, while in asynchronous or uncued control, a specific brain signal is used to detect the user's intention to engage in BCI/BMI control [65, 66].

3. Brain-Machine Interfaces in Neurorehabilitation of Paralysis

BMI used in neurorehabilitation follows two different strategies: while assistive or biomimetic BMI systems strive for continuous high-dimensional control of robotic devices or functional electric stimulation (FES) of paralyzed muscles to substitute for lost motor functions in a daily life environment [67–69], restorative or biofeedback BMI systems aim at normalizing of neurophysiologic activity that might facilitate motor recovery [70–74]. Insofar, restorative or biofeedback BMI can be considered as "training-tools" to induce use-dependent brain plasticity increasing the patient's capacity for motor learning [44, 75].

These two approaches derive from different research traditions and are not necessarily related to the invasiveness of the approach: in the early 80s of the last century, decoding of different movement directions from single neurons was successfully demonstrated [76]. Since then, reconstruction of complex movements from neuronal activity was pursued, using both invasive and noninvasive methods.

Firing patterns acquired through single cell recordings from the motor cortex [77] or parietal neuronal pools [78] in animals were remarkably successful for reconstruction of movement trajectories. Monkeys learned to control computer cursors towards moving targets on a screen activating neurons in motor, premotor, and parietal motor areas. It was shown that 32 cells were sufficient to move an artificial arm and perform skillful reaching movements enabling a monkey to feed himself [67]. Learned control of movements based on single cell activity was also shown using neurons outside the primary or secondary motor representations [79]. In 2006, successful implantation of densely packed microelectrode arrays in two quadriplegic human patients was demonstrated, enabling them to use LFP in order to move a computer cursor in several directions [68]. Most recently, a study using two 96-channel intracortical microelectrodes placed in the motor cortex of a 52-year-old woman with tetraplegia demonstrated robust seven-dimensional movements of a prosthetic limb [80].

In contrast to this work aiming at assistive appliance of invasive and noninvasive BMI technology, the development of restorative/biofeedback BMI systems is tightly associated with the development and successes of neurofeedback (NF) and its use to purposefully upregulate or downregulate brain activity—a quality that showed to have some beneficial effect in the treatment of various neurological and psychiatric disorders associated with neurophysiologic abnormalities [71]. In NF, subjects receive visual or auditory online feedback of their brain activity and are asked to voluntarily modify, for example, a particular type of brainwave. Successful modification becomes contingently rewarded. NF was successfully used in the treatment of epilepsy [81, 82], ADHD [83–85], chronic pain syndrome [86]. The rational to use this approach in the context of neurorehabilitation is based on data indicating that stroke patients with best motor recovery are the ones in whom ipsilesional cortical function is closer to that found in healthy controls [87]. A negative correlation between impairment and activation in ipsilesional M1 during hand motions has been documented [88]. Thus, a larger clinical study was performed at the University of Tübingen in Germany and the National Institute of Neurological Disorders and Stroke (NINDS, NIH) in USA with over 30 chronic stroke patients testing the hypothesis that augmentation of ipsilesional brain activity would improve motor recovery [89, 90]. In this study, all participating patients suffered from complete hand paralysis and were unable, for example, to grasp. The study showed that one month of daily ipsilesional BMI training combined with goal-directed physiotherapy resulted in significant motor improvements, while random BMI-feedback did not. Further analysis of neurophysiological parameters indicated that motor evoked potentials (MEP) from the ipsilesional hemisphere reflecting the integrity of the corticospinal tract could predict motor recovery of the trained patients [91]. Currently, further improvements of this training paradigm, for example, related to the feedback or specificity and effectiveness of training [44], for example, using electric brain stimulation to enhance neuroplasticity [92], are being tested.

4. Noninvasive Assistive Brain-Machine Interfaces in Paralysis

Both invasive and noninvasive BCI and BMI found their way into assistive systems, for example, allowing communication in locked-in patients [42] or restoration of movement in patients with paralysis [28, 93]. The Graz group was the first to use volitional SMR modulation for control of electric stimulation of a quadriplegic patient's paralyzed hand [69, 94]. While the patient imagined a movement, the associated modulation of SMR was translated into functional electric stimulation (FES) of his upper limb muscles resulting in grasping motions. After this proof-of-concept study, numerous publications addressed the different aspects that are important to allow intuitive and seamless control of biomimetic devices [20] or FES [95] in a daily life environment [96]. While many challenges were successfully mastered in the last years, three major aspects were not satisfyingly solved yet: (1) intuitive, asynchronous BCI/BMI control, (2) 100% reliability, and (3) unambiguous superiority (in terms of information transfer rate, ITR, and necessary preparation effort) over the use of other biosignals (e.g., related to speech, gestures, or eye movements).

These aspects do not apply to BCI use for communication in complete paralysis, for example, complete locked-in-state

(CLIS) in ALS, as no asynchronous mode is necessary, reliability is secondary, and no other biosignals are available anymore [97].

A system that is unreliable in daily does not only limit its practicality, but limits its practicality, but would be also associated with ethical difficulties [98, 99]. While there are good arguments suggesting that invasive BCI/BMI can provide a higher ITR [100], it is still unclear how much meaningful information, for example, for reconstruction of hand movements, can be extracted from noninvasively recorded brain signals [101]. Recently, work by Contreras-Vidal's group at the University of Houston suggested that slow-frequency EEG (oscillations with a frequency of up to 4 Hz) might provide as much information as invasive recordings [102, 103], for example, for reconstruction of three-dimensional hand movements [103]. Currently, implementation of this approach in closed-loop paradigms is being pursued. Nevertheless, it is conceivable that the only viable solution to satisfyingly solve those three aspects will be the inclusion of other biosignals into a system merging different biosignal sources to detect user's intentions and integrating this information into the current context of the user to further increase intuitive control and assure reliability of the system. Such systems that merge brain control with other biosignals were recently summarized under the term "brain-neural computer interaction" (BNCI) systems receiving notable funding through the 7th Framework Program for Research and Technological Development (FP7) of the European Union.

Particularly promising in this context is integrating eye movements using electrooculography (EOG) or eye tracking into prosthetic control. At the University of Tübingen, a first prototype system was conceptualized that allows asynchronous BCI/BMI control while solving the reliability issue by using eye tracking, EOG, and computer vision-based object recognition. A computer equipped with a 3D camera recognizes objects placed on a table. The system detects when the user fixates any of the objects recognized as graspable, for example, a cup or ball. Once an object is fixated with the eyes, the BCI/BMI mode switches on, detecting whether the user wants to grasp the object. A robotic hand or exoskeleton (both developed by the BioRobotics Institute, Scuola Superiore Sant'Anna, Pisa, Italy) performs the grasping motion (Figure 1). The motion becomes interrupted if the user does not fixate the object anymore as measured by eye tracking and EOG (see Figure 2). This assures that no action of the system depends exclusively on brain wave control that might be susceptible to inaccuracies. Such system, integrating perceptual and contextual computing developed in the field of human-computer interaction (HCI) research into BCI applications, promises to overcome many limitations of brain control alone, mainly the reliability issue, likewise broadening the repertoire of modern HCI research to infer user state and intention from brain activity.

As trauma or stroke can affect motor and body functions very differently in each individual, proper and fast calibration for inclusion into seamless BNCI control is often impeded. Thus, inclusion of eye movements is the most promising biosignal in this context so far. Particularly as visual interaction plays a key role when planning, executing, and

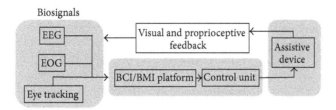

FIGURE 1: Organization of the University of Tübingen' prototype system controlling assistive devices using brain waves and eye movements.

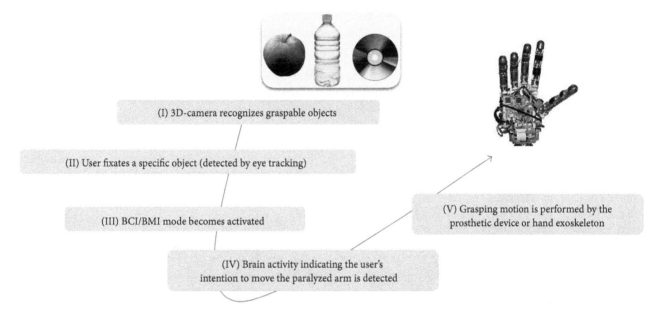

FIGURE 2: Illustration of the processing chain for performing grasping motions of an assistive system using brain waves and eye movements. The grasping motion stops once the user does not fixate the object with his eyes anymore.

adapting motor control. Beside electric biosignals such as EOG and EMG, other measures that can be used for BNCI control include magnetic, mechanic, optic, acoustic, chemical, and thermal biosignals. These biosignals, however, are more susceptible for artifacts and exhibit larger variability depending on the environmental conditions. Future research, however, might find novel ways to advantageously include such biosignals into BNCI control and application.

The organisms' behavior measurable in these various biosignals reflects conscious and unconscious processes that can be inferred and purposefully used for BNCI control. In case of eye movement control, changing fixation of an object can point to inattention, distraction, or volitional (conscious) act to interrupt unwanted output of the BNCI for example.

Practicality of such approach is limited when, for instance, eyesight or eyeball control is impaired due to a disease or trauma. This can be the case in multiple sclerosis, traumatic brain injury, stroke, or neurodegenerative disorders such as ALS. ALS may lead to CLIS, where classical semantic conditioning might be the only way to sustain a communication channel [104] while inclusion or use of other biosignals seemed not particularly helpful [94]. Also, inclusion of other biosignals often increases preparation time for placing and calibrating the required biosensors further

limiting practicality. This is particularly relevant when the system requires handicapped persons to place and handle the sensors in a home environment. Nevertheless, these technical limitations might dissolve in the course of near-future research and development.

An important conceptual advantage of including other biosignals into BCI control relates to the improved reliability, which not only increases usability in daily life, but also the degree of self-efficacy, a dimension that should not be underestimated in acceptance of such technology, but also in the context of restorative/biofeedback BCI training for example. Here, the fact that a patient experiences full control of a completely paralyzed limb might facilitate overcoming "learned nonuse" and motivate the user to engage in behavioral physiotherapy [105].

5. Conclusion

BCI/BMI systems promise to enhance applicability of assistive technology in humans with a compromised or damaged motor system. While information transfer rates of noninvasive BCI/BMI are sufficient for communication, for example, in locked-in-state, versatile control of prosthetic devices using brain waves will require major research and development efforts to provide intuitive, asynchronous control sufficiently reliable in daily life environments. Many reasons suggest that using the combination of brain waves with other biosignals might entail many attractive solutions to control assistive, noninvasive technology even after severe damage of the central or peripheral nervous system.

Authors' Contribution

Paulo Rogério de Almeida Ribeiro and Fabricio Lima Brasil contributed equally to this work.

Acknowledgments

This work was supported by the EU Project WAY FP7-ICT-2011-288551, the Italian Project AMULOS (Industria 2015, MI01 00319), the Regional Project EARLYREHAB (Regione Toscana, Health Regional Research Programme 2009), the German Federal Ministry of Education and Research (BMBF, 01GQ0831, and 16SV5840), and the Deutsche Forschungsgemeinschaft (DFG SO932-2), Open Access Publishing Fund of the University of Tübingen, as well as CNPq/DAAD (National Council for Scientific and Technological Development—Brazil; German Academic Exchange Service—Germany) scholarships.

References

[1] S. Furui, "50 years of progress in speech and speaker recognition research," *ECTI Transactions on Computer and Information Technology*, vol. 1, no. 2, p. 64, 2005.

[2] H. S. Yoon, J. Soh, Y. J. Bae, and H. Seung Yang, "Hand gesture recognition using combined features of location, angle and velocity," *Pattern Recognition*, vol. 34, no. 7, pp. 1491–1501, 2001.

[3] M. R. Ahsan, M. I. Ibrahimy, and O. O. Khalifa, "EMG signal classification for human computer interaction: a review," *European Journal of Scientific Research*, vol. 33, no. 3, pp. 480–501, 2009.

[4] W. H. O., *World report on disability*: World Health Organization, 2011.

[5] N. S. Ward and L. G. Cohen, "Mechanisms underlying recovery of motor function after stroke," *Archives of Neurology*, vol. 61, no. 12, pp. 1844–1848, 2004.

[6] S. MacMahon, "Introduction: the global burden of stroke," in *Clinician's Manual on Blood Pressure and Stroke Prevention*, J. Chalmers, Ed., pp. 1–6, Science Press, London, UK, 2002.

[7] N. I. O. N. Disorders and Stroke, *Stroke: hope through research*, National Institute of Neurological Disorders and Stroke, National Institutes of Health, 1999.

[8] T. C. Frohman, D. L. O'Donoghue, and D. Northrop, *A Practical Primer: Multiple Sclerosis for the Physician Assistant*, Southwestern Medical Center, Dallas, Tex, USA, 2011.

[9] F. W. A. Van Asbeck, M. W. M. Post, and R. F. Pangalila, "An epidemiological description of spinal cord injuries in The Netherlands in 1994," *Spinal Cord*, vol. 38, no. 7, pp. 420–424, 2000.

[10] F. Martins, F. Freitas, L. Martins, J. F. Dartigues, and M. Barat, "Spinal cord injuries—epidemiology in Portugal's central region," *Spinal Cord*, vol. 36, no. 8, pp. 574–578, 1998.

[11] W. Pondaag, M. J. A. Malessy, J. G. Van Dijk, and R. T. W. M. Thomeer, "Natural history of obstetric brachial plexus palsy: a systematic review," *Developmental Medicine & Child Neurology*, vol. 46, no. 2, pp. 138–144, 2004.

[12] S. Banzi, E. Mainardi, and A. Davalli, "Analisi delle strategie di controllo per protesi di arto superior in pazienti con amputazioni transomerali o disarticolati di spalla," in *Biosys, ANIPLA*, pp. 290–300, 2005.

[13] J. L. Pons, "Rehabilitation exoskeletal robotics. The promise of an emerging field," *IEEE Engineering in Medicine and Biology Magazine*, vol. 29, no. 3, pp. 57–63, 2010.

[14] N. Vitiello, T. Lenzo, S. Roccella et al., "NEUROExos: a powered elbow exoskeleton for physical rehabilitation," *IEEE Transactions on Robotics*, vol. 29, no. 1, pp. 220–235, 2013.

[15] A. Chiri, N. Vitiello, F. Giovacchini, S. Roccella, F. Vecchi, and M. C. Carrozza, "Mechatronic design and characterization of the index finger module of a hand exoskeleton for post-stroke rehabilitation," *IEEE/ASME Transactions on Mechatronics*, vol. 17, no. 5, pp. 884–894, 2012.

[16] J. Iqbal, N. G. Tsagarakis, A. E. Fiorilla, and D. G. Caldwell, "A portable rehabilitation device for the hand," in *Proceedings of the 32nd Annual International Conference of the IEEE Engineering in Medicine and Biology Society (EMBC '10)*, pp. 3694–3697, September 2010.

[17] D. J. Atkins, D. C. Y. Heard, and W. H. Donovan, "Epidemiologic overview of individuals with upper-limb loss and their reported research priorities," *Journal of Prosthetics and Orthotics*, vol. 8, no. 1, pp. 2–11, 1996.

[18] B. Peerdeman, D. Boere, H. Witteveen et al., "Myoelectric forearm prostheses: state of the art from a user-centered perspective," *Journal of Rehabilitation Research and Development*, vol. 48, no. 6, pp. 719–737, 2011.

[19] M. Zecca, S. Micera, M. C. Carrozza, and P. Dario, "Control of multifunctional prosthetic hands by processing the electromyographic signal," *Critical Reviews in Biomedical Engineering*, vol. 30, no. 4-6, pp. 459–485, 2002.

[20] R. Rupp and H. J. Gerner, "Neuroprosthetics of the upper extremity—clinical application in spinal cord injury and challenges for the future," in *Operative Neuromodulation*, vol. 97 of *Acta Neurochirurgica Supplements*, pp. 419–426, 2007.

[21] A. Fougner, O. Stavdahl, P. J. Kyberd, Y. G. Losier, and P. A. Parker, "Control of upper limb prostheses: terminology and proportional myoelectric control—a review," *IEEE Transactions on Neural Systems and Rehabilitation Engineering*, vol. 20, no. 5, pp. 663–677, 2012.

[22] D. J. Weber, R. Friesen, and L. E. Miller, "Interfacing the somatosensory system to restore touch and proprioception: essential considerations," *Journal of Motor Behavior*, vol. 44, no. 6, pp. 403–418, 2012.

[23] W. J. Ray and H. W. Cole, "EEG alpha activity reflects attentional demands, and beta activity reflects emotional and cognitive processes," *Science*, vol. 228, no. 4700, pp. 750–752, 1985.

[24] W. Klimesch, "EEG alpha and theta oscillations reflect cognitive and memory performance: a review and analysis," *Brain Research Reviews*, vol. 29, no. 2-3, pp. 169–195, 1999.

[25] G. E. Chatrian, M. C. Petersen, and J. A. Lazarte, "The blocking of the rolandic wicket rhythm and some central changes related to movement," *Electroencephalography and Clinical Neurophysiology*, vol. 11, no. 3, pp. 497–510, 1959.

[26] E. G. Walsh, "'Visual attention' and the alpha-rhythm," *The Journal of Physiology*, vol. 120, no. 1-2, pp. 155–159, 1953.

[27] J. R. Wolpaw, N. Birbaumer, D. J. McFarland, G. Pfurtscheller, and T. M. Vaughan, "Brain-computer interfaces for communication and control," *Clinical Neurophysiology*, vol. 113, no. 6, pp. 767–791, 2002.

[28] N. Birbaumer, "Breaking the silence: brain-computer interfaces (BCI) for communication and motor control," *Psychophysiology*, vol. 43, no. 6, pp. 517–532, 2006.

[29] G. Schalk and E. C. Leuthardt, "Brain-computer interfaces using electrocorticographic signals," *IEEE Reviews in Biomedical Engineering*, vol. 4, pp. 140–154, 2011.

[30] F. Lopes da Silva, "Neural mechanisms underlying brain waves: from neural membranes to networks," *Electroencephalography and Clinical Neurophysiology*, vol. 79, no. 2, pp. 81–93, 1991.

[31] J. Malmivuo, "Comparison of the properties of EEG and MEG in detecting the electric activity of the brain," *Brain Topography*, vol. 25, no. 1, pp. 1–19, 2012.

[32] N. Weiskopf, R. Veit, M. Erb et al., "Physiological self-regulation of regional brain activity using real-time functional magnetic resonance imaging (fMRI): methodology and exemplary data," *NeuroImage*, vol. 19, no. 3, pp. 577–586, 2003.

[33] R. Sitaram, H. Zhang, C. Guan et al., "Temporal classification of multichannel near-infrared spectroscopy signals of motor imagery for developing a brain-computer interface," *NeuroImage*, vol. 34, no. 4, pp. 1416–1427, 2007.

[34] T. Nagaoka, K. Sakatani, T. Awano et al., "Development of a new rehabilitation system based on a brain-computer interface using near-infrared spectroscopy," in *Oxygen Transport to Tissue XXXI*, vol. 662 of *Advances in Experimental Medicine and Biology*, pp. 497–503, 2010.

[35] E. E. Fetz, "Operant conditioning of cortical unit activity," *Science*, vol. 163, no. 3870, pp. 955–958, 1969.

[36] E. E. Fetz, "Volitional control of neural activity: implications for brain-computer interfaces," *The Journal of Physiology*, vol. 579, no. 3, pp. 571–579, 2007.

[37] E. Behrens, J. Schramm, J. Zentner, and R. König, "Surgical and neurological complications in a series of 708 epilepsy surgery procedures," *Neurosurgery*, vol. 41, no. 1, pp. 1–10, 1997.

[38] A. M. Korinek, J. L. Golmard, A. Elcheick et al., "Risk factors for neurosurgical site infections after craniotomy: a critical reappraisal of antibiotic prophylaxis on 4578 patients," *British Journal of Neurosurgery*, vol. 19, no. 2, pp. 155–162, 2005.

[39] D. Moran, "Evolution of brain-computer interface: action potentials, local field potentials and electrocorticograms," *Current Opinion in Neurobiology*, vol. 20, no. 6, pp. 741–745, 2010.

[40] J. Linke, S. H. Witt, A. V. King et al., "Genome-wide supported risk variant for bipolar disorder alters anatomical connectivity in the human brain," *NeuroImage*, vol. 59, no. 4, pp. 3288–3296, 2012.

[41] D. Turner, P. Patil, and M. Nicolelis, "Conceptual and technical approaches to human neural ensemble recordings," in *Methods for Neural Ensemble Recordings*, M. A. L. Nicolelis, Ed., Boca Raton, Fla, USA, 2nd edition, 2008.

[42] N. Birbaumer, N. Ghanayim, T. Hinterberger et al., "A spelling device for the paralysed," *Nature*, vol. 398, no. 6725, pp. 297–298, 1999.

[43] T. Elbert, B. Rockstroh, W. Lutzenberger, and N. Birbaumer, "Biofeedback of slow cortical potentials. I," *Electroencephalography and Clinical Neurophysiology*, vol. 48, no. 3, pp. 293–301, 1980.

[44] S. R. Soekadar, M. Witkowski, J. Mellinger, A. Ramos, N. Birbaumer, and L. G. Cohen, "ERD-based online brain-machine interfaces (BMI) in the context of neurorehabilitation: optimizing BMI learning and performance," *IEEE Transactions on Neural Systems and Rehabilitation Engineering*, vol. 19, no. 5, pp. 542–549, 2011.

[45] C. Neuper, G. R. Müller-Putz, R. Scherer, and G. Pfurtscheller, "Motor imagery and EEG-based control of spelling devices and neuroprostheses," *Progress in Brain Research*, vol. 159, pp. 393–409, 2006.

[46] G. R. Müller-Putz and G. Pfurtscheller, "Control of an electrical prosthesis with an SSVEP-based BCI," *IEEE Transactions on Biomedical Engineering*, vol. 55, no. 1, pp. 361–364, 2008.

[47] N. Birbaumer, T. Elbert, A. G. M. Canavan, and B. Rockstroh, "Slow potentials of the cerebral cortex and behavior," *Physiological Reviews*, vol. 70, no. 1, pp. 1–41, 1990.

[48] N. Birbaumer, L. E. Roberts, W. Lutzenberger, B. Rockstroh, and T. Elbert, "Area-specific self-regulation of slow cortical potentials on the sagittal midline and its effects on behavior," *Electroencephalography and Clinical Neurophysiology*, vol. 84, no. 4, pp. 353–361, 1992.

[49] N. Birbaumer, H. Flor, W. Lutzenberger, and T. Elbert, "Chaos and order in the human brain," *Electroencephalography and Clinical Neurophysiology*, vol. 44, pp. 450–459, 1995.

[50] T. Hinterberger, R. Veit, B. Wilhelm, N. Weiskopf, J. J. Vatine, and N. Birbaumer, "Neuronal mechanisms underlying control of a brain—computer interface," *European Journal of Neuroscience*, vol. 21, no. 11, pp. 3169–3181, 2005.

[51] P. Eberlin and D. Yager, "Alpha blocking during visual afterimages," *Electroencephalography and Clinical Neurophysiology*, vol. 25, no. 1, pp. 23–28, 1968.

[52] R. C. Howe and M. B. Sterman, "Cortical-subcortical EEG correlates of suppressed motor behavior during sleep and waking in the cat," *Electroencephalography and Clinical Neurophysiology*, vol. 32, no. 6, pp. 681–695, 1972.

[53] C. Neuper and G. Pfurtscheller, "Event-related dynamics of cortical rhythms: frequency-specific features and functional correlates," *International Journal of Psychophysiology*, vol. 43, no. 1, pp. 41–58, 2001.

[54] H. Gastaut, "Electrocorticographic study of the reactivity of rolandic rhythm," *Revue Neurologique*, vol. 87, no. 2, pp. 176–182, 1952.

[55] G. Pfurtscheller, C. Neuper, and N. Birbaumer, "Human brain-computer interface (BCI)," in *Motor Cortex in Voluntary Movements. A Distributed System for Distributed Functions*, pp. 367–401, 2005.

[56] J. R. Wolpaw and D. J. McFarland, "Control of a two-dimensional movement signal by a noninvasive brain-computer interface in humans," *Proceedings of the National Academy of Sciences of the United States of America*, vol. 101, no. 51, pp. 17849–17854, 2004.

[57] J. R. Wolpaw, "Brain-computer interfaces as new brain output pathways," *The Journal of Physiology*, vol. 579, no. 3, pp. 613–619, 2007.

[58] L. A. Farwell and E. Donchin, "Talking off the top of your head: toward a mental prosthesis utilizing event-related brain potentials," *Electroencephalography and Clinical Neurophysiology*, vol. 70, no. 6, pp. 510–523, 1988.

[59] A. Chatterjee, V. Aggarwal, A. Ramos, S. Acharya, and N. V. Thakor, "A brain-computer interface with vibrotactile biofeedback for haptic information," *Journal of NeuroEngineering and Rehabilitation*, vol. 4, article 40, 2007.

[60] I. Käthner, C. A. Ruf, E. Pasqualotto, C. Braun, N. Birbaumer, and S. Halder, "A portable auditory P300 brain-computer interface with directional cues," *Clinical Neurophysiology*, vol. 124, no. 2, pp. 327–338, 2012.

[61] M. Schreuder, B. Blankertz, and M. Tangermann, "A new auditory multi-class brain-computer interface paradigm: spatial hearing as an informative cue," *PLoS ONE*, vol. 5, no. 4, Article ID e9813, 2010.

[62] A. Lenhardt, M. Kaper, and H. J. Ritter, "An adaptive P300-based online brain-computer interface," *IEEE Transactions on Neural Systems and Rehabilitation Engineering*, vol. 16, no. 2, pp. 121–130, 2008.

[63] T. O. Zander and C. Kothe, "Towards passive brain-computer interfaces: applying brain-computer interface technology to human-machine systems in general," *Journal of Neural Engineering*, vol. 8, no. 2, Article ID 025005, 2011.

[64] T. Zander and S. Jatzev, "Context-aware brain-computer interfaces: exploring the information space of user, technical system and environment," *Journal of Neural Engineering*, vol. 9, no. 1, Article ID 016003, 2012.

[65] G. R. Müller-Putz, R. Scherer, G. Pfurtscheller, and R. Rupp, "Brain-computer interfaces for control of neuroprostheses: from synchronous to asynchronous mode of operation," *Biomedizinische Technik*, vol. 51, no. 2, pp. 57–63, 2006.

[66] S. G. Mason and G. E. Birch, "A brain-controlled switch for asynchronous control applications," *IEEE Transactions on Biomedical Engineering*, vol. 47, no. 10, pp. 1297–1307, 2000.

[67] M. Velliste, S. Perel, M. C. Spalding, A. S. Whitford, and A. B. Schwartz, "Cortical control of a prosthetic arm for self-feeding," *Nature*, vol. 453, no. 7198, pp. 1098–1101, 2008.

[68] L. R. Hochberg, M. D. Serruya, G. M. Friehs et al., "Neuronal ensemble control of prosthetic devices by a human with tetraplegia," *Nature*, vol. 442, no. 7099, pp. 164–171, 2006.

[69] G. Pfurtscheller, C. Guger, G. Müller, G. Krausz, and C. Neuper, "Brain oscillations control hand orthosis in a tetraplegic," *Neuroscience Letters*, vol. 292, no. 3, pp. 211–214, 2000.

[70] N. Birbaumer and L. G. Cohen, "Brain-computer interfaces: communication and restoration of movement in paralysis," *The Journal of Physiology*, vol. 579, no. 3, pp. 621–636, 2007.

[71] N. Birbaumer, A. Ramos Murguialday, C. Weber, and P. Montoya, "Neurofeedback and brain-computer interface: clinical applications," *International Review of Neurobiology*, vol. 86, pp. 107–117, 2009.

[72] J. J. Daly and J. R. Wolpaw, "Brain-computer interfaces in neurological rehabilitation," *The Lancet Neurology*, vol. 7, no. 11, pp. 1032–1043, 2008.

[73] D. Broetz, C. Braun, C. Weber, S. R. Soekadar, A. Caria, and N. Birbaumer, "Combination of brain-computer interface training and goal-directed physical therapy in chronic stroke: a case report," *Neurorehabilitation and Neural Repair*, vol. 24, no. 7, pp. 674–679, 2010.

[74] A. Caria, C. Weber, D. Brötz et al., "Chronic stroke recovery after combined BCI training and physiotherapy: a case report," *Psychophysiology*, vol. 48, no. 4, pp. 578–582, 2010.

[75] W. Wang, J. L. Collinger, M. A. Perez et al., "Neural interface technology for rehabilitation: exploiting and promoting neuroplasticity," *Physical Medicine and Rehabilitation Clinics of North America*, vol. 21, no. 1, pp. 157–178, 2010.

[76] A. P. Georgopoulos, A. B. Schwartz, and R. E. Kettner, "Neuronal population coding on movement direction," *Science*, vol. 233, no. 4771, pp. 1416–1419, 1986.

[77] M. A. L. Nicolelis, D. Dimitrov, J. M. Carmena et al., "Chronic, multisite, multielectrode recordings in macaque monkeys," *Proceedings of the National Academy of Sciences of the United States of America*, vol. 100, no. 19, pp. 11041–11046, 2003.

[78] H. Scherberger, M. R. Jarvis, and R. A. Andersen, "Cortical local field potential encodes movement intentions in the posterior parietal cortex," *Neuron*, vol. 46, no. 2, pp. 347–354, 2005.

[79] D. M. Taylor, S. I. H. Tillery, and A. B. Schwartz, "Direct cortical control of 3D neuroprosthetic devices," *Science*, vol. 296, no. 5574, pp. 1829–1832, 2002.

[80] M. Velliste, A. McMorland, E. Diril, S. Clanton, and A. Schwartz, "State-space control of prosthetic hand shape," in *Proceedings of the Annual International Conference of the IEEE Engineering in Medicine and Biology Society (EMBC '12)*, pp. 964–967, 2012.

[81] A. R. Seifert and J. F. Lubar, "Reduction of epileptic seizures through EEG biofeedback training," *Biological Psychology*, vol. 3, no. 3, pp. 157–184, 1975.

[82] B. Kotchoubey, U. Strehl, C. Uhlmann et al., "Modification of slow cortical potentials in patients with refractory epilepsy: a controlled outcome study," *Epilepsia*, vol. 42, no. 3, pp. 406–416, 2001.

[83] N. Birbaumer, T. Elbert, B. Rockstroh, and W. Lutzenberger, "Biofeedback of slow cortical potentials in attentional disorders," in *Cerebral Psychophysiology: Studies in Event-Related Potentials*, pp. 440–442, 1986.

[84] U. Strehl, U. Leins, G. Goth, C. Klinger, T. Hinterberger, and N. Birbaumer, "Self-regulation of slow cortical potentials: a new treatment for children with attention-deficit/hyperactivity disorder," *Pediatrics*, vol. 118, no. 5, pp. e1530–e1540, 2006.

[85] T. Fuchs, N. Birbaumer, W. Lutzenberger, J. H. Gruzelier, and J. Kaiser, "Neurofeedback treatment for attention-deficit/hyperactivity disorder in children: a comparison with methylphenidate," *Applied Psychophysiology and Biofeedback*, vol. 28, no. 1, pp. 1–12, 2003.

[86] M. Lotze, W. Grodd, N. Birbaumer, M. Erb, E. Huse, and H. Flor, "Does use of a myoelectric prosthesis prevent cortical reorganization and phantom limb pain?" *Nature Neuroscience*, vol. 2, no. 6, pp. 501–502, 1999.

[87] T. Platz, I. H. Kim, U. Engel, A. Kieselbach, and K. H. Mauritz, "Brain activation pattern as assessed with multi-modal EEG analysis predict motor recovery among stroke patients with mild arm paresis who receive the Arm Ability Training," *Restorative Neurology and Neuroscience*, vol. 20, no. 1-2, pp. 21–35, 2002.

[88] C. Calautti, M. Naccarato, P. S. Jones et al., "The relationship between motor deficit and hemisphere activation balance after stroke: a 3T fMRI study," *NeuroImage*, vol. 34, no. 1, pp. 322–331, 2007.

[89] E. Buch, C. Weber, L. G. Cohen et al., "Think to move: a neuromagnetic brain-computer interface (BCI) system for chronic stroke," *Stroke*, vol. 39, no. 3, pp. 910–917, 2008.

[90] A. Ramos-Murguialday, D. Broetz, M. Rea et al., "Brain-machine-interface in chronic stroke rehabilitation: a controlled study," *Annals of Neurology*, 2013.

[91] F. Brasil, M. R. Curado, M. Witkowski et al., "MEP predicts motor recovery in chronic stroke patients undergoing 4-weeks of daily physical therapy," in *Human Brain Mapping Annual Meeting*, Beijing, China, 2012, 33WTh.

[92] J. M. Carmena and L. G. Cohen, "Brain-machine interfaces and transcranial stimulation: future implications for directing

functional movement and improving function after spinal injury in humans," in *Spinal Cord Injuries E-Book*, vol. 109 of *Handbook of Clinical Neurology*, chapter 27, pp. 435–444, 2012.

[93] C. R. Hema, M. Paulraj, S. Yaacob, A. H. Adom, and R. Nagarajan, "Asynchronous brain machine interface-based control of a wheelchair," in *Software Tools and Algorithms for Biological Systems*, pp. 565–572, 2011.

[94] G. Pfurtscheller, G. R. Müller, J. Pfurtscheller, H. J. Gerner, and R. Rupp, "'Thought'—control of functional electrical stimulation to restore hand grasp in a patient with tetraplegia," *Neuroscience Letters*, vol. 351, no. 1, pp. 33–36, 2003.

[95] A. H. Do, P. T. Wang, A. Abiri, C. King, and Z. Nenadic, "Brain-computer interface controlled functional electrical stimulation system for ankle movement," *Journal of NeuroEngineering and Rehabilitation*, vol. 8, no. 1, article 49, 2011.

[96] M. Tavella, R. Leeb, R. Rupp, and J. D. R. Millán, "Towards natural non-invasive hand neuroprostheses for daily living," in *Proceedings of the 32nd Annual International Conference of the IEEE Engineering in Medicine and Biology Society (EMBC '10)*, pp. 126–129, September 2010.

[97] A. R. Murguialday, J. Hill, M. Bensch et al., "Transition from the locked in to the completely locked-in state: a physiological analysis," *Clinical Neurophysiology*, vol. 122, no. 5, pp. 925–933, 2011.

[98] J. Clausen, "Ethische Aspekte von Gehirn-Computer-Schnittstellen in motorischen Neuroprothesen," *International Review of Information Ethics*, vol. 5, pp. 25–32, 2006.

[99] J. Clausen, "Man, machine and in between," *Nature*, vol. 457, no. 7233, pp. 1080–1081, 2009.

[100] J. L. Collinger, B. Wodlinger, J. E. Downey et al., "High-performance neuroprosthetic control by an individual with tetraplegia," *The Lancet*, vol. 381, no. 9866, pp. 557–564, 2013.

[101] S. T. Grafton and C. M. Tipper, "Decoding intention: a neuroergonomic perspective," *NeuroImage*, vol. 59, no. 1, pp. 14–24, 2012.

[102] A. Presacco, L. W. Forrester, and J. L. Contreras-Vidal, "Decoding intra-limb and inter-limb kinematics during treadmill walking from scalp electroencephalographic (EEG) signals," *IEEE Transactions on Neural Systems and Rehabilitation Engineering*, vol. 20, no. 2, pp. 212–219, 2012.

[103] T. J. Bradberry, R. J. Gentili, and J. L. Contreras-Vidal, "Reconstructing three-dimensional hand movements from noninvasive electroencephalographic signals," *The Journal of Neuroscience*, vol. 30, no. 9, pp. 3432–3437, 2010.

[104] N. Birbaumer, G. Gallegos-Ayala, M. Wildgruber, S. Silvoni, and S. R. Soekadar, "Direct brain control and communication in paralysis," *Brain Topography*. In press.

[105] S. R. Soekadar and N. Birbaumer, "Improving the efficacy of ipsilesional brain-computer interface training in neurorehabilitation of chronic stroke," in *Brain-Computer Interface Research: A State-of-the-Art Summary*, C. Guger, B. Allison, and G. Edlinger, Eds., Springer, 2013.

12

Does Humanity Matter? Analyzing the Importance of Social Cues and Perceived Agency of a Computer System for the Emergence of Social Reactions during Human-Computer Interaction

Jana Appel,[1] Astrid von der Pütten,[1] Nicole C. Krämer,[1] and Jonathan Gratch[2]

[1] Department of Social Psychology: Media and Communication, University of Duisburg-Essen, Forsthausweg 2,
47057 Duisburg, Germany
[2] Institute for Creative Technologies, University of Southern California, 12015 Waterfront Drive Playa Vista, Los Angeles,
CA 90094-2536, USA

Correspondence should be addressed to Astrid von der Pütten, astrid.von-der-puetten@uni-due.de

Academic Editor: Kiyoshi Kiyokawa

Empirical studies have repeatedly shown that autonomous artificial entities elicit social behavior on the part of the human interlocutor. Various theoretical approaches have tried to explain this phenomenon. The agency assumption states that the social influence of human interaction partners (represented by avatars) will always be higher than the influence of artificial entities (represented by embodied conversational agents). Conversely, the Ethopoeia concept predicts that automatic social reactions are triggered by situations as soon as they include social cues. Both theories have been challenged in a 2 × 2 between subjects design with two levels of agency (low: agent, high: avatar) and two interfaces with different degrees of social cues (low: textchat, high: virtual human). The results show that participants in the virtual human condition reported a stronger sense of mutual awareness, imputed more positive characteristics, and allocated more attention to the virtual human than participants in the text chat conditions. Only one result supports the agency assumption; participants who believed to interact with a human reported a stronger feeling of social presence than participants who believed to interact with an artificial entity. It is discussed to what extent these results support the social cue assumption made in the Ethopoeia approach.

1. Introduction

Since the computer found its way into private households, new standards for usability were necessary. Handling the computer had to become more easy and intuitive. Designing the computer to be and act more human-like seemed to be a good solution to improve human-computer interaction. This approach seems to have an impact on the way people interact with computers. Early psychological studies show that human-like interaction styles of computer interfaces had a greater impact on individuals' self-appraisals than machine-like interaction styles [1]. Subsequently, Nass and colleagues [2, 3] proved that people show similar social behavior during human-computer interaction (HCI) by systematically adapting studies from the field of human-human interaction (HHI) to HCI. In their CASA studies (computers are social actors) they could replicate many findings

from HHI, for example, that people show polite behavior towards computers [4, 5], use gender stereotypes for judging computers with female or male voices [6, 7], or reported a feeling of team spirit after being grouped in the same team with a specific computer [8]. Technological progress facilitates the development of computer interfaces with even more social cues like for instance virtual characters which are utilized in a variety of applications, for example, in games, application programs, or in the Internet. Many terms are in use to describe these characters: interface agent, embodied conversational agent, virtual assistant, autonomous agent, or avatar. The major difference with regard to the terms avatar and agent lies within the control of the virtual character. Bailenson and Blascovich [9] define an avatar as "a perceptible digital representation whose behaviors reflect those executed, typically in real time, by a specific human being," and an agent as "a perceptible digital representation whose behaviors reflect a computational algorithm designed to accomplish a specific goal or set of goals" [9, page 64].

Empirical results show that both types of representation can elicit social reactions on the side of the user, but opinions differ about the extent to which agents and avatars are able to elicit these social reactions. According to Blascovich et al. [10] the (perceived) agency of a virtual representation is crucial. While an avatar will always elicit social reactions because the user knows that the interaction partner is human whereas an agent will not do so unless it shows sufficiently realistic behavior. Indeed previous research found differing social influence regarding agency (e.g., [11–13]). Besides these two factors (agency and behavioral realism of the interactant) Blascovich et al.'s model of social influence in virtual environments also proposes that the social influence may be enhanced by the self-relevance of the interaction. Moreover, it is important to consider which behavioral-response system is targeted within an experimentation. When a virtual character shots a gun and produces a very loud sound, participants will most likely respond equally fearful, regardless whether they believe their counterpart is controlled by a human or an algorithm. If participants solved a cooperative task together with a virtual character, they might be more influenced by a positive feedback coming from the human-controlled avatar compared to the agent.

However, besides agency the number of social cues provided by the system is widely considered to be of great importance for the question whether people react socially. Recent studies about the impact of anthropomorphic virtual humans indicate that increasing the number of social cues leads to even stronger social reactions on the part of the user [13–20].

Although both approaches are very popular and well investigated, there were little attempts to systematically test both approaches against each other. In a previous study challenging both approaches, von der Pütten et al. [14] compared the importance of agency and behavioral realism of a virtual character and found the extent of displayed social behavior to be of greater importance than the participants' knowledge about the virtual agent being introduced as an avatar or an agent. Although it is astonishing that the rather subtle variation of social cues in this study (virtual character with and without head nodding) had more impact than the knowledge of whether one interacted with a fellow human or a machine, it cannot be concluded that it is first and foremost social cues instead of agency that result in social reactions on the part of the user, because a multitude of social cues were present in all conditions, since in all conditions a human-like virtual agent was employed. The present study addresses this shortcoming by comparing the impact of agency on the one hand and a more explicit variation of social cues on the other hand. While agency is again varied by means of the instruction the participants are given, the number of social cues is varied by applying either a virtual figure (presented as either agent or avatar) or a text tool (presented as either textchat with a fellow human or as computer interface). In the following we give a detailed overview about previous work on this topic from which we derived our hypotheses.

2. Theoretical Background

As mentioned previously, there is empirical evidence that already conventional computers (using, e.g., command lines or graphical interfaces) elicit social behavior. The same is true for virtual characters in general, regardless whether they are avatars or agents. But opinions differ about which factor, agency, or number of human features/social cues are most crucial and in explaining how and why these social reactions happen.

2.1. The Effect of Social Cues. Nass and colleagues [3, 15] emphasize that people automatically treat artificial entities like real humans. They established the Ethopoeia term to describe these immediate automatic and unconscious reactions due to seemingly social characteristics of a computer. These basic social cues like speech, interactivity, or the filling of social roles [15] trigger social scripts and expectations, and humans cannot be prevented from reacting in social ways when they are confronted with social cues. This is seen as resulting from our evolutionary heritage; the human brain evolved in a time where only humans showed human social behavior. For instance, the usage of language was a definite sign of humanness, which made further cognitive efforts to assign an object into human or nonhuman category needless. The processing of situations and their social cues ensues mindless. Mindlessness [21–23] can be best understood as the failure to draw novel distinctions as no active information processing takes place. People adapt social scripts from human-human interaction (HHI) and use them in human-computer interaction (HCI), even though this behavior seems inappropriate. Indeed, Nass and colleagues have shown in numerous studies that mechanisms known from human-human communication also apply in HCI; people show politeness and cooperation towards computers and apply gender stereotypes and other rules of person perception [4–8]. Several of these computer as social actor studies were replicated with virtual agents (who besides speech, interactivity, and the fulfillment of social roles also often have a human-like appearance and show nonverbal behavior). For instance, Rossen et al. [24] showed that people apply ethnic stereotypes to agents. Caucasian medical students with a prejudice against Afro-Americans were found to show more empathetic verbal and nonverbal behavior towards an agent with a light skin tone than to an agent with a dark skin tone. The results from the politeness study [5] were replicated in an experiment with the virtual agent MAX [25]. Participants evaluated MAX more positively when it itself asked for their judgment compared to an evaluation via paper-and-pencil questionnaire.

Moreover, studies utilizing a large variety of virtual agents demonstrate that virtual humans draw attention just as real humans do [26], person perception was shown to be like that of real humans [27], cooperation and trust is fostered [28, 29], tasks are facilitated or inhibited by "social" presence of a virtual agent [30], and socially desirable behavior is triggered [29]. Several studies that compare plain text interfaces to virtual characters suggest that indeed the human-like appearance of the virtual agents is one factor that increases social reactions towards the artificial entity. Sproull et al. [29] showed that participants preferred to interact and spend more time with a talking face compared to the interaction with a text interface. They referred to the mindless paradigm from Nass and colleagues [6] as explanation, why an obviously artificial talking face evoked stronger reactions than the text interface. This finding was affirmed by Krämer et al. [31] who found that participants who had the choice between a documentary about the life of Albert Einstein, a James Bond movie, or the daily TV listings were more likely to choose the socially desirable documentary when they were asked by an anthropomorphic interface agent compared to participants asked by a mere text-based or speech-based interface.

2.2. The Effects of Agency.

Besides the social cues of a system, the second factor which is extensively discussed and considered to greatly influence the elicitation of social reactions is agency. Several researchers state that the perceived agency matters and impacts the elicitation of social reactions. Also, several studies present results that favor the importance of agency. For instance, Guadagno et al. [13] examined the effects of agency and behavioral realism on persuasion and found some supporting results for the importance of agency. Besides other results, participants in the avatar group experienced more social presence than subjects in the agent group. Hoyt et al. [12] demonstrated classic effects of social inhibition when participants were asked to perform a novel task. Task performance was inhibited when participants performed in front of two avatars, whereas performance was not inhibited in front of two agents or when performing the task alone. Conversely, they did not find effects of social facilitation when participants performed well-trained tasks in front of the avatars compared to performing alone or in the presence of agents. Also, other studies give evidence for the importance of agency but also do not yield consistent results; Aharoni and Fridlund [32] investigated the influence of the factor agency. Participants in their study interacted with a standard computer with prerecorded speech output. Participants believed that they were either interacting with a human interviewer or an artificial intelligent computer. The experimenters reported that participants used more silence fillers and smiled more while interacting with the human interviewer compared to the computer. However, the evaluation of the interviewer as well as the subjective emotional state of the participants was not affected by the factor agency. Surprisingly, also Nass and colleagues present results that show the influence of agency and are therefore not in line with their assumptions. In a study that analyzed the influence of humor on task performance [11], the perceived agency of the interaction partner and the level of humor (humor or no humor) were varied. Participants either believed to interact with a computer system or a human via text chat. The answers either contained humorous parts or no humor at all. The results were partially inconsistent with the assumptions drawn from the CASA paradigm. People in the HCI condition showed social reactions towards the computer, but those in the mocked CMC condition were even stronger than those in the HCI condition. Confronted with these inconsistent results, Nass and colleagues searched for explanations: "In sum, although many results supported the SRCT [social responses to communication technologies] model, other findings point to a limitation in SRCT theory: HCI and CMC are not identical. In other words, the equating of HCI and human-human interaction (as proposed by [3]) is called into question here. Specifically, there is evidence for a conception of socialness as a continuum rather than a dichotomy" [11, page 423]. However, in a study about the in-group out-group phenomenon based on ethnicity Nass and colleagues were able to demonstrate results that affirmed their hypotheses [33]. Participants thought to either interact with an agent or with an avatar, whose skin color also was varied. There was no evidence for a significant difference due to the perceived agency. In line with the hypothesis, people evaluated the virtual character better, that seemed to have the same ethnicity. With a few exceptions (see [11]), the "human" conditions in these experiments have *not* elicited stronger social responses than the "computer" conditions." [15, page 99]. Finally, Nowak and Biocca [34] found no effect of agency in a study about the influence of agency and anthropomorphism. Participants believed that they were interacting either with an agent or an avatar. Additionally, the degree of anthropomorphism was varied from no picture (control group), abstract eyes and mouth, (low anthropomorphism) to a realistic picture of a virtual character (high anthropomorphism). Agency showed no effects on the perceived degree of copresence or social presence, but participants reported increased social presence when confronted with a high anthropomorphic picture compared to a low anthropomorphic picture.

As neither the results from Blascovich and colleagues [12, 13] nor those from Nass and colleagues [11, 33] could clarify the role of the agency for the development of social reactions on the part of the user, a recent study [14] evaluated whether participants' belief in interacting with either an avatar or an agent leads to different social effects. Von der Pütten and colleagues [14] used a design with two levels of agency (agent or avatar) and two levels of behavioral realism (showing feedback behavior versus showing no behavior). It could be found that the belief of interacting with either an avatar or an agent barely resulted in differences with regard to the evaluation of the virtual character or behavioral reactions, whereas higher behavioral realism affected both. It seems that behavioral realism plays an important role in human-agent interaction. Von der Pütten et al. see these results in line with the Ethopoeia concept: "The assumption that the more computers present characteristics that are associated with humans, the more likely they are to elicit social behavior [15, page 97] is confirmed in our experiment" [14, page 1647]. However, as noted above, the study does not allow for conclusions on the effects of social cues in general but only on the effects of the variation of a specific social cue, namely the presence of nonverbal feedback behavior. It has not yet been tested in comparison, what effects will be yielded by an agency manipulation if on the other hand the number of social cues (in terms of text-based interaction versus communication with a virtual character) is varied.

Does Humanity Matter? Analyzing the Importance of Social Cues and Perceived Agency of a Computer System for the
Emergence of Social Reactions during Human-Computer Interaction

119

3. Hypotheses

(H1) The social effects will be higher in the conditions with a presented virtual character as interaction partner (high number of social cues) than in the conditions with a presented text-based interface as interaction partner (low number of social cues). (The effect of social cues).

(H2) The social effects will be higher in the conditions with an assumed avatar as interaction partner (high agency) than in the conditions with an assumed agent as interaction partner (low agency). (The effect of agency).

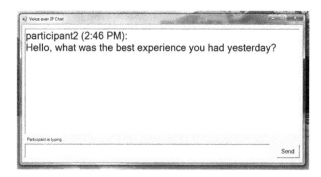

FIGURE 1: Mocked messenger interface for the high agency condition.

3.1. Experimental Design. To test our hypotheses, we used a 2 × 2 between subjects design with two levels of agency (*low: agent, high: avatar*) and two interfaces with different numbers of social cues (*low: textchat, high: virtual human*). Participants were randomly assigned to the conditions. Gender was distributed equally across conditions. During the interaction, the participants were asked three personal questions of increasing intimacy by the virtual character or by the textchat.

3.1.1. Factor Agency. For the factor agency, we varied the instruction given to the participants by the experimenter. Although, in fact, all of the questions asked by either the virtual character or the text chat were initiated manually by the experimenter in the room next door, half of them were led to believe that they interacted with a real person in another room (who was either mediated through the avatar or the chat system), and half of them were instructed that they interacted with a computer (which was either displayed as an agent or a text chat).

The agency was varied by giving different instructions to the participants. In the conditions with low agency (agent-condition), the participants were told that the interaction partner is a computer which uses an artificial intelligence program to talk to them.

In the conditions with high agency (avatar-condition), the participants were told that their interaction partner would be another participant in a room next door. Depending on the number of social cues, the instructions differed. When communicating with the virtual character, they were told that participant 2, the listener, would see a live video image of them and that they would see the avatar, whose movements copy the movements of Participant 2. If participant 2 moves his/her head or nods, the avatar would do the same at the same time. Because the virtual character did not provide any facial expressions, they were told that the avatar was not able to copy the facial expressions of participant 2. The instructions differed slightly when communicating with the text-based interface. Participants in the chat condition were led to believe that participant 2 posts questions through an instant messenger system. They were also told that participant 2 would see a live video image of them so that they would be able to use speech.

3.1.2. Factor Social Cues. The number of social cues of the system was varied by either using a virtual character or a text based interface. The virtual character possesses multiple human cues (such as a female voice, a human appearance, and the use of nonverbal feedback), while the only human cue of the text-based interface is the use of written language. The utilized systems will now be explained in detail.

3.1.3. Text-Based Interface. The text-based interface was applied because of its small number of social cues. In order to guarantee believability it was necessary to create two slightly different interfaces. In the condition with high agency, the participant had to be convinced of the existence of participant 2. Therefore we edited the appearance of the chat interface in order to make it more look like a real instant messenger system (Figure 1).

A text gadget with a send button was created, similar to those known from real text messenger systems. This text gadget was never used by the participants because they were asked to only answer verbally. Its only purpose was to simulate a fully functional messenger system. Second, a time delay was deployed before the appearance of the next question on the screen. This delay simulated the time necessary for the other person to type the next question. Additionally, during that 15–30 sec delay the status message "participant is typing..." was displayed. This should give the participant a feeling of real-time conversation. In the low agency condition a plain text window was used (Figure 2).

3.1.4. Virtual Character. For the condition with the virtual character we used the Rapport Agent, which was developed by Gratch et al. [16] at the Institute for Creative Technologies. The agent displays listening behaviors that correspond to the verbal and nonverbal behavior of a human speaker. The Rapport Agent has been evaluated in several studies [16–18] and has proven to be capable of creating the experience of rapport comparable with face-to-face conditions in certain contexts (e.g., storytelling, interview). To produce listening behaviors, the Rapport Agent first collects and analyzes the features from the speaker's voice and upper-body movements via microphone and a Videre Design Small Vision System stereo camera, which was placed in front of the participants to capture their movements. Watson, an

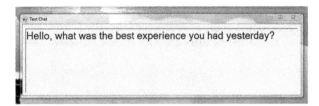

FIGURE 2: Plain text window for the low agency condition.

FIGURE 3: Female rapport agent.

image-based tracking library developed by Morency et al. [35], uses images captured by the stereo camera to track the participant's head position and orientation. Acoustic features are derived from properties of the pitch and intensity of the speech signal using a signal processing package, LAUN, developed by Grath et al. [16]. The Rapport Agent displays behaviors that show that the animated character is "alive" (eye blinking, breathing) and listening behaviors such as posture shifts and head nods are automatically triggered by the system corresponding to participants' verbal and nonverbal behavior. A female virtual character was used for this experiment (Figure 3).

3.1.5. Setting. All participants were asked to tell three short stories about their daily life. The whole conversation was fixed to five sentences. They appeared either as text on the text-based interfaces or were verbally asked by the virtual character. Therefore, five sentences were prerecorded with a female voice. All participants received the same questions. The following five sentences were used.

(i) Okay, I'm ready.

(ii) What was the most special experience for you yesterday?

(iii) Which of your characteristics are you most proud of?

(iv) What has been the biggest disappointment in your life?

(v) Thank you. You're done.

3.2. Dependent Variables. As dependent variables, we assessed the participants' emotional state (PANAS) after the interaction, the person perception of the virtual character, the self-reported experience of social presence, and self-reported rapport. Besides these self-report measures, we also measured the following objective variables: the total number of words the participants used during the interaction and the percentage of pause fillers and interrupted words. We also carried out a qualitative analysis of the degree of self-disclosure. In the following, all measurements will be described in detail.

3.2.1. Quantitative Measurements. In the present study, we used the Positive And Negative Affect Scale [36] consisting of 20 items (e.g., strong, guilty, active, ashamed, etc.), which are rated on a 5-point Likert scale from "very slightly or not at all" to "extremely." The factorial analysis for the Positive And Negative Affect Scale resulted in three factors. The first factor, *Positive High-Dominance*, explains 32,53% of the variance (Cronbach's Alpha = .931). The second factor, *Negative High-Dominance*, explains 25,01% of the variance (Cronbach's Alpha = .876). The third factor, *Negative Low-Dominance*, explains 6,69% of the variance (Cronbach's Alpha = .759).

For the person perception (of the agent), we used a semantic differential with 27 bipolar pairs of adjectives (e.g., friendly-unfriendly, tense-relaxed), which are rated on a 7-point scale. The factor analysis for the person perception of the virtual character resulted in three factors. The first factor, *Negative Low-Dominance*, explains 39,14% of the variance (Cronbach's Alpha = .912). The second factor, *Negative High-Dominance*, explains 8,63% of the variance (Cronbach's Alpha = .839). The third factor, *Positive High-Dominance*, explains 6,69% of the variance (Cronbach's Alpha = .770).

Social presence [37] was measured by two scales: the social presence scale [19] with five items (e.g., "I perceive that I am in the presence of another person in the room with me") and the Networked Minds Questionnaire (NMQ; [38–40]). We concentrated on the following five aspects of the NMQ: empathy (with 4 items), mutual awareness (with 2 items), attention allocation (with 4 items), mutual understanding (with 3 items), and behavioral interdependence (with 4 items). All items from both scales were rated on a 7-point Likert scale.

To measure perceived rapport, we used a scale that had been developed for previous studies with the Rapport Agent. This scale contains ten items from the rapport construct by Tickle-Degnen [41], which were already in use in an experiment on the effects of nonverbal signal delay in telepsychiatry (see [42]). 19 ad hoc items were added, which proved to measure rapport in several studies [16–18]. The resulting 29 items were measured on an 8-point Likert scale. Because of the text chat conditions, another version of the Rapport Scale had to be prepared. Five items target the perceived embodiment of the interaction partner (e.g., "I watched the listener as I told the story"). These items had to be excluded in the text-based conditions because of the lack of embodiment. Therefore, the chat version of the Rapport Scale includes 24 items. Both versions of the Rapport Scale were used for a combined factor analysis.

TABLE 1: Main effect for agency on the social presence scale.

	Human-human interaction		Human-computer interaction				
	μ	SD	μ	SD	F	η^2	P
Social presence scale	4.182	1.392	3.236	1.396	10.870	.112	.001

The factor analysis for the self-reported rapport revealed four factors. The first factor, *Feelings and Self-Efficiency*, explains 37,3% of the variance (Cronbach's alpha = .926), the second factor, *Rapport and Connection*, 11,73% (Cronbach's alpha = .954), the third, *Attention Allocation*, 6,78% (Cronbach's alpha = .648%), and the fourth factor, *Embodiment*, explains 5,72% of the variance (Cronbach's alpha = .538).

3.2.2. Verbal Behavior. In addition, we analyzed the participants' verbal behavior. We counted the total amount of words, the amount of pause-fillers ("erm," "hm"), and the amount of broken words (e.g., "I was in the bib… library"). From the latter two, we calculated the percentage of speech disfluencies in relation to the total amount of words.

3.2.3. Qualitative Measurements. We conducted a qualitative analysis of the participants' answers to the questions asked by the virtual character. The first question ("What was the most special experience you had yesterday?") was excluded from the analysis because of too much variance due to the weekday on which they participated. When participants took part in the experiment on a Monday, they had more possibilities to report about their activities (i.e., on Sunday) than people who took part on a Thursday.

For the second question ("Which of your characteristics are you most proud of?"), we counted the number of characteristics the participants revealed. For the third question ("What has been the biggest disappointment in your life?"), we used a categorical coding scheme [43] with three categories: (1) no answer: the subject gives no answer or uses excuses to avoid an answer (e.g., "-um-… I don't know. I th+ I don't think I've had anything horrible happen to me yet. I'm lucky"); (2) low-intimacy answer: the disappointment (or unfulfilled wish) has not sustainably affected the private or business life of the subject (e.g., "I'd like to be wealthy so I think that's my biggest disappointment" or "-um- Not finishing tasks that I start or not following through with things I want to follow through with"); (3) high-intimacy answers: the disappointment (or unfulfilled wish) has sustainably affected the private or business life of the subject (e.g., "-The biggest disappointment in my life. -um- I would say probably the fact that -um- I never remarried -um- after being divorced for many years and -um- I'm starting now to feel a little disappointed about that fact that I didn't find another mate for myself"). The coding was processed by two coders. The interrater reliability showed substantial agreement (Cohen's Kappa = .810).

4. Procedure

Upon arrival, the participants were asked to read and sign informed consent forms. After completing a web-based questionnaire [44] about their background including demographic data and the questionnaires of the explanatory variables, participants received a short introduction about the equipment and were given the instructions regarding their interaction partner and the task of the experiment (see above). Then, participants took a seat in front of a 30" screen, which displayed the interaction partner (virtual character or text chat). They were equipped with a headset with microphone. In order to assess the participants' verbal and nonverbal behavior, the whole session was videotaped. The camera was directed towards the participants and situated directly under the screen with the Rapport Agent in combination with the stereovision camera. Participants were instructed to wait until the systems starts, indicating readiness by a ping sound. They were asked three questions by the Rapport Agent with increasing intimacy. After the interaction, the participants completed the second web-based questionnaire. They were fully debriefed, given $20, and thanked for their participation.

5. Participants

Ninety persons (49 females and 41 males) participated in the study. The mean age was 36.26 (SD = 12.26), ranging from 19 to 62 years. Participants were recruited via http://www.craigslist.com/ from the general Los Angeles area and were compensated $20 for one hour of their participation.

6. Results

We calculated MANOVAS with the two independent variables agency and number of social cues and the dependent variables: three PANAS factors, three person perception factors, four rapport factors, the social presence scale, the constructs empathy, attention allocation, mutual awareness, mutual understanding and behavioral interdependence from the NMQ, the total amount of words, the percentage of speech disfluencies, and the number of revealed characteristics.

We identified only one main effect for agency. A significant main effect on the dependent variable Social Presence Scale emerged by varying the perceived agency (Table 1). The feeling of social presence was more intense after communicating with the "other subject" via avatar or Textchat (F(1;90) = 10.870; P = .001; partial eta^2 = .112) than after communicating with the computer.

On the other hand, several effects of the number of social cues emerged. Subjects in the virtual character conditions (high number of social cues) had a stronger feeling of social presence (factor Mutual Awareness, see Table 2) (F(1;90) =

TABLE 2: Main effect for social cues on the factor mutual awareness.

	Virtual character		Chat				
	μ	SD	μ	SD	F	η^2	P
Mutual awareness	2.728	1.223	3.693	1.095	15.207	.150	.000

TABLE 3: Main effect for social cues on the factor negative high-dominance.

	Virtual character		Chat				
	μ	SD	μ	SD	F	η^2	P
Negative high-dominance	−.217	.970	.226	.991	4.516	.050	.036

TABLE 4: Main effect for social cues on the factor attention allocation.

	Virtual character		Chat				
	μ	SD	μ	SD	F	η^2	P
Attention allocation	−.248	1.071	.302	.882	6.943	.075	.010

15.207; P = .000; partial eta^2 = .150) than subjects in the text conditions (low number of social cues).

Also, a main effect for social cues with regard to the factor Negative High-Dominance of the Person Perception Scale emerged. Subjects in the virtual character conditions (high number of social cues) described the interlocutor less negative (F(1;90) = 15.207; P = .000; partial eta^2 = .150, see Table 3) than subjects in the text-conditions (low number of social cues). A further significant main effect of social cues emerged on the dependent variable attention allocation (Table 4) of the Rapport Scale. Subjects in the virtual character conditions (high number of social cues) reported to pay more attention to the interaction partner (F(1;90) = 6.943; P = .010; partial eta^2 = .075) than subjects in the text-conditions (low number of social cues). Low means are associated with paying more attention to the interaction partner. There were no effects with regard to the total amount of words, self-disclosure of information (number of characteristics), or percentage of speech disfluencies in relation to the total amount of words. Also, Chi-square tests did not reveal any effect with regard to the categories of question three. We also found no interaction effects of the factors agency and number of social cues.

7. Discussion

The main goal of this research was to empirically test which factors account for the emergence of social behavior in human-computer interaction. Two competing explanations were tested against each other: the agency and the number of social cues approach. To test the factor agency, we varied the factor agency by instructing the participants that they would either communicate with an artificial intelligence program or another real participant in the room next door. The other factor, number of social cues, was varied by using either a text-based interface (low number of social cues) or an animated character (high number of social cues). We used a wide range of dependent variables including quantitative and qualitative behavioral data, scales previously used within

the paradigm, and standardized psychological measures used for face-to-face interactions.

With regard to the agency assumption which basically states that there will be a difference between the assumed interaction with a computer or a human being—in the direction of real humans as interlocutor evoking stronger social reactions than computers—the results of this study do not provide a strong support for agency. Only one main effect for agency was found for the feeling of social presence which was more intense after communicating with the "other subject" via avatar or textchat than after communicating with the computer. However, this effect could also be a result of the wording of the Social Presence Scale, which explicitly asks for the presence of a real living person (e.g., "the person appears to be sentient (conscious and alive) to me") and therefore provoked stronger reactions when participants were told that they interacted with a real person. Further studies investigating the agency assumption should use a revised version asking, for example, the interaction partner. Moreover, other measure should be considered like participants' nonverbal behavior or psychophysiology. Besides this main effect, none of the other 19 dependent factors showed effects for agency. According to the social model of influence in virtual environments, it is especially surprising that we had no effects concerning the qualitative analysis of the verbal answers, since the interview situation was at least medium self-relevant, because participants were asked very personal and intimate questions. Moreover, answers to intimate questions can be regarded as a measure within a rather high-level behavioral-response system which should more easily lead to differences between the two agency conditions according to the model. Therefore, the hypothesis that *social effects will be higher in the conditions with an assumed avatar as interaction partner (high agency) than in the conditions with an assumed agent as interaction partner (low agency)* has to be rejected.

In contrast to the agency factor, we found several results supporting the assumption that the number of social cues displayed influences the strength of social reactions. For three

Does Humanity Matter? Analyzing the Importance of Social Cues and Perceived Agency of a Computer System for the
Emergence of Social Reactions during Human-Computer Interaction

123

dependent variables main effects emerged which indicate that a human-like virtual character (high number of social cues) triggers stronger social reactions than a plain text-based interface (low number of social cues). Subjects in the virtual character conditions described the interlocutor less negative and had a stronger feeling of mutual awareness and reciprocal attention allocation than subjects in the text conditions. However, due to the relative small number of main effects for the independent variable social cues (three of in total twenty dependent variables) there is only partial support for hypothesis 1 which claimed stronger effects in those conditions with a higher number of social cues. Based on the results of von der Pütten et al. [14] and the results of the current study the assumption that "the more computers present characteristics that are associated with humans, the more likely they are to elicit social behavior" [15, page 97] seems to be reasonable.

8. Limitations

Although the amount of social cues can be regarded as a continuous variable, we used only two levels of social cues and treated it as a dichotomy variable for the purpose of our study. Future research should address this shortcoming by comparing more levels of social cues. Moreover, the two conditions differed not only in the amount of social cues but also in the modality, and this could have caused the differences in the attention participants paid to the system. Participants in the chat group were presented the questions as written text which stayed on screen until they finished giving their answer, while the participants in the virtual character condition were presented the questions as prerecorded sentences delivered by the virtual character. Thus it is possible that in the latter condition participants had to be more attentive to the character, because otherwise they would miss the question. In addition, unlike the chat window the virtual character presents continuous feedback by showing nonverbal responses to the participant's verbal input. This also might bias the attention allocation in favor for the condition with the virtual character. This problem can be solved when providing continuous feedback for the chat condition as well by, for instance, showing the well-known rotating sandglass with the text "verbal input is being processed" or a red light indicating that recording and transmission of the signal is on air. As mentioned above, the Social Presence Scale probably was not adequate to use, because participants were biased by the wording of the scale. Future studies should also focus on the analysis of nonverbal behavior or psychophysiological measures which have been proven to be indicators of social presence (e.g., [19, 20]).

9. Conclusion

In sum, the results of the present study do not provide strong support for the assumption of the model of social influence in virtual environments [10] which claims general dissimilar social impact of agents and avatars due to their agency. The cognitive-mediated knowledge about the interlocutor's nature did not have a strong impact on the participants' experience and behavior. The Ethopoeia concept by Nass and colleagues seems to be a better approach to explain the emergence of social reactions towards computers. Although not for all dependent variables, it could be shown that a high number of social cues provokes stronger social reactions on the part of the user. It has to be noted that this design did only consist of two levels of social cues, namely, high (humanoid appearance) and low (text) number of social cues. Additional studies should concentrate on systematically and gradually varying the level of social cues to analyze the relations in greater detail. This will provide a deeper insight into whether social reactions gradually become stronger along with a gradual increase of social cues. For example, it is still unclear whether single features, like the human appearance, the human voice, or the combination of all, triggered the social reactions. More research is needed to gain answers to these questions.

Acknowledgment

This research was supported by the National Scientific Foundation under grant # IIS-0916858 and the U.S. Army Research, Development, and Engineering Command. The content does not necessarily reflect the position or the policy of the U.S. Government, and no official endorsement should be inferred. This work was partially supported by a scholarship of the German Academic Exchange Service.

References

[1] L. Quintanar, C. Crowell, J. Pryor, and J. Adampoulos, "Human computer interaction: a preliminary social psychological analysis," *Behaviour Research Methods & Instrumentation*, vol. 14, no. 2, pp. 210–220, 1982.

[2] C. Nass, E. Tauber, and H. Reeder, "Anthropomorphism, agency and ethopoeia: computers as social actors," in *Proceeding of the International Conference Companion on Human Factors in Computing Systems (CHI '93)*, pp. 111–112, 1993.

[3] B. Reeves and C. I. Nass, *The Media Equation: How People Treat Computers, Television, and New Media Like Real People and Places*, Cambridge University Press, New York, NY, USA, 1996.

[4] C. Nass, J. Steuer, and E. R. Tauber, "Computer are social actors," in *Proceedings of the Conference on Human Factors in Computing Systems (CHI '94)*, pp. 72–78, ACM Press, New York, NY, USA, April 1994.

[5] C. Nass, Y. Moon, and P. Carney, "Are people polite to computers? Responses to computer-based interviewing systems," *Journal of Applied Social Psychology*, vol. 29, no. 5, pp. 1093–1110, 1999.

[6] C. Nass, Y. Moon, and N. Green, "Are machines gender neutral? Gender-stereotypic responses to computers with voices," *Journal of Applied Social Psychology*, vol. 27, no. 10, pp. 864–876, 1997.

[7] C. Nass, J. Steuer, L. Henriksen, and D. C. Dryer, "Machines, social attributions, and ethopoeia: performance assessments of computers subsequent to "self-" or "other-" evaluations," *International Journal of Human-Computer Studies*, vol. 40, no. 3, pp. 543–559, 1994.

[8] C. Nass, B. J. Fogg, and Y. Moon, "Can computers be teammates?" *International Journal of Human-Computer Studies*, vol. 45, no. 6, pp. 669–678, 1996.

[9] J. N. Bailenson and J. Blascovich, "Avatars," in *Encyclopedia of Human-Computer Interaction*, pp. 64–68, Berkshire Publishing Group, 2004.

[10] J. Blascovich, J. Loomis, A. C. Beall, K. R. Swinth, C. L. Hoyt, and J. N. Bailenson, "Immersive virtual environment technology as a methodological tool for social psychology," *Psychological Inquiry*, vol. 13, no. 2, pp. 103–124, 2002.

[11] J. Morkes, H. K. Kernal, and C. Nass, "Effects of humor in task-oriented human-computer interaction and computer-mediated communication: a direct test of SRCT theory," *Human-Computer Interaction*, vol. 14, no. 4, pp. 395–435, 1999.

[12] C. L. Hoyt, J. Blascovich, and K. R. Swinth, "Social inhibition in immersive virtual environments," *Presence*, vol. 12, no. 2, pp. 183–195, 2003.

[13] R. E. Guadagno, J. Blascovich, J. N. Bailenson, and C. McCall, "Virtual humans and persuasion: the effects of agency and behavioral realism," *Media Psychology*, vol. 10, no. 1, pp. 1–22, 2007.

[14] A. von der Pütten, N. C. Krämer, J. Gratch, and S.-H. Kang, "'It doesn't matter what you are!' explaining social effects of agents and avatars," *Computers in Human Behaviour*, vol. 26, no. 6, pp. 1641–1650, 2010.

[15] C. Nass and Y. Moon, "Machines and mindlessness: social responses to computers," *Journal of Social Issues*, vol. 56, no. 1, pp. 81–103, 2000.

[16] J. Gratch, A. Okhmatovskaia, F. Lamothe, S. Marsella, M. Morales, R. J. van der Werf et al., "Virtual rapport," in *Proceedings of the 6th International Conference on Intelligent Virtual Agents*, Springer, Marina Del Rey, Calif, USA, 2006.

[17] J. Gratch, N. Wang, J. Gerten, E. Fast, and R. Duffy, "Creating rapport with virtual agents," in *Proceedings of the 7th International Conference on Intelligent Virtual Agents (IVA '07)*, C. Pelachaud, J.-C. Martin, E. André, G. Chollet, K. Karpouzis, and D. Pelé, Eds., LNAI 4722, pp. 125–138, Springer, Paris, France, 2007.

[18] J. Gratch, N. Wang, A. Okhmatovskaia, F. Lamothe, M. Morales, and L.-P. Morency, "Can virtual humans be more engaging than real ones?" in *Proceedings of the 12th International Conference on Human-Computer Interaction: Intelligent Multimodal Interaction Environments, Part III (HCII '07)*, J. Jacko, Ed., LNCS 4552, pp. 286–297, Springer, Beijing, China, 2007.

[19] J. N. Bailenson, J. Blascovich, A. C. Beall, and J. M. Loomis, "Equilibrium theory revisited: mutual gaze and personal space in virtual environments," *Presence*, vol. 10, no. 6, pp. 583–598, 2001.

[20] J. N. Bailenson, J. Blascovich, A. C. Beall, and J. M. Loomis, "Interpersonal distance in immersive virtual environments," *Personality and Social Psychology Bulletin*, vol. 29, no. 7, pp. 819–833, 2003.

[21] E. J. Langer, "Matters of mind: mindfulness/mindlessness in perspective," *Consciousness and Cognition*, vol. 1, no. 3, pp. 289–305, 1992.

[22] E. J. Langer, *Mindfulness*, Addison-Wesley, Reading, Mass, USA, 1989.

[23] E. J. Langer and M. Moldoveanu, "The construct of mindfulness," *Journal of Social Issues*, vol. 56, no. 1, pp. 1–9, 2000.

[24] B. Rossen, K. Johnson, A. Deladisma, S. Lind, and B. Lok, "Virtual humans elicit skin-tone bias consistent with real-world skin-tone biases," in *Proceedings of the 8th International Conference on Intelligent Virtual Agents (IVA '08)*, H. Prendinger, J. Lester, and M. Ishizuka, Eds., LNAI 5208, pp. 237–244, Springer, Tokyo, Japan, 2008.

[25] L. Hoffmann, N. C. Krämer, A. Lam-chi, and S. Kopp, "Media equation revisited: do users show polite reactions towards an embodied agent?" in *Proceeding of 9th International Conference on Intelligent Virtual Agents (IVA '09)*, Z. Ruttkay et al., Ed., LNAI 5773, pp. 159–165, Springer, Amsterdam, Netherlands, 2009.

[26] D. M. Dehn and S. van Mulken, "The impact of animated interface agents: a review of empirical research," *International Journal of Human-Computer Studies*, vol. 52, no. 1, pp. 1–22, 2000.

[27] G. Bente, N. C. Krämer, A. Petersen, and J. P. de Ruiter, "Computer animated movement and person perception: methodological advances in nonverbal behavior research," *Journal of Nonverbal Behavior*, vol. 25, no. 3, pp. 151–166, 2001.

[28] S. Parise, S. B. Kiesler, L. Sproull, and K. Waters, "Cooperating with life-like interface agents," *Computers in Human Behavior*, vol. 15, no. 2, pp. 123–142, 1999.

[29] L. Sproull, M. Subramani, S. Kiesler, J. H. Walker, and K. Waters, "When the interface is a face," *Human-Computer Interaction*, vol. 11, no. 2, pp. 97–124, 1996.

[30] R. Rickenberg and B. Reeves, "The effects of animated characters on anxiety, task performance, and evaluations of user interfaces," in *Proceedings of the SIGCHI Conference on Human Factors in Computing Systems (CHI '00)*, pp. 49–56, April 2000.

[31] N. C. Krämer, G. Bente, and J. Piesk, "The ghost in the machine. The influence of Embodied Conversational Agents on user expectations and user behaviour in a TV/VCR application," in *Proceedings of the International Workshop on Mobile Computing, Assistance, Mobility, Applications (IMC '03)*, G. Bieber and T. Kirste, Eds., pp. 121–128, Rostock, Germany.

[32] E. Aharoni and A. J. Fridlund, "Social reactions toward people vs. computers: how mere lables shape interactions," *Computers in Human Behavior*, vol. 23, no. 5, pp. 2175–2189, 2007.

[33] C. Nass, K. Isbister, and E.-J. Lee, "Truth is beauty: researching embodied conversational agents," in *Embodied Conversational Agents*, J. Cassell, J. Sullivan, S. Prevost, and E. Churchill, Eds., pp. 374–401, The MIT Press, Cambridge, Mass, USA, 2000.

[34] K. Nowak and F. Biocca, "The influence of agency and the virtual body on presence, social presence and copresence in a computer mediated interaction," in *Proceedings of the 3rd International Presence Workshop*, Philadelphia, Pa, USA, 2001.

[35] L. P. Morency, C. Sidner, and T. Darrell, "Towards context-based visual feedback Recognition for Embodied Agents," in *Proceedings of the Symposium on Conversational Informatics for Supporting Social Intelligence and Interaction*, pp. 69–72, AISB, Hatfield, UK, 2005.

[36] D. Watson, A. Tellegen, and L. A. Clark, "Development and validation of brief measures of positive and negative affect: the PANAS scales," *Journal of Personality and Social Psychology*, vol. 54, no. 6, pp. 1063–1070, 1988.

[37] J. Short, E. Williams, and B. Christie, *The Social Psychology of Telecommunications*, John Wiley & Sons, London, UK, 1976.

[38] F. Biocca and C. Harms, "Defining and measuring social presence: contribution to the net-worked minds theory and measure," in *Proceedings of the 5th International Workshop on Presence*, F. R. Gouveia and F. Biocca, Eds., pp. 7–36, 2002.

[39] F. Biocca, C. Harms, and J. K. Burgoon, "Toward a more robust theory and measure of social presence: review and suggested criteria," *Presence*, vol. 12, no. 5, pp. 456–480, 2003.

Does Humanity Matter? Analyzing the Importance of Social Cues and Perceived Agency of a Computer System for the Emergence of Social Reactions during Human-Computer Interaction

125

[40] F. Biocca, C. Harms, and J. Gregg, "The networked minds measure of social presence: pilot test of the factor structure and concurrent validity," in *Proceedings of the 4th Annual International Workshop on Presence*, Philadelphia, Pa, USA, May 2001.

[41] L. Tickle-Degnen and R. Rosenthal, "The nature of rapport and its nonverbal correlates," *Psychological Inquiry*, vol. 1, no. 4, pp. 285–293, 1990.

[42] T. R. Manning, E. T. Goetz, and R. L. Street, "Signal delay effects on rapport in telepsychiatry," *Cyberpsychology and Behavior*, vol. 3, no. 2, pp. 119–127, 2000.

[43] P. Mayring, *Einführung in die Qualitative Sozialforschung. Eine Anleitung zu qualitativem Denken*, Psychologie Verlags Union, Weinheim, Germany, 3rd edition, 1996.

[44] D. Leiner, "ofb.msd-media.de," 2009, http://ofb.msd-media.de/.

:

13

Testing Two Tools for Multimodal Navigation

Mats Liljedahl,[1] **Stefan Lindberg,**[1] **Katarina Delsing,**[1] **Mikko Polojärvi,**[2] **Timo Saloranta,**[2] **and Ismo Alakärppä**[3]

[1] *The Interactive Institute, Acusticum 4, 941 28 Piteå, Sweden*
[2] *University of Oulu, PL 8000, Oulun Yliopisto, 90014 Oulu, Finland*
[3] *University of Lapland, P.O. Box 122, 96101 Rovaniemi, Finland*

Correspondence should be addressed to Mats Liljedahl, mats.liljedahl@tii.se

Academic Editor: Kiyoshi Kiyokawa

The latest smartphones with GPS, electronic compasses, directional audio, touch screens, and so forth, hold a potential for location-based services that are easier to use and that let users focus on their activities and the environment around them. Rather than interpreting maps, users can search for information by pointing in a direction and database queries can be created from GPS location and compass data. Users can also get guidance to locations through point and sweep gestures, spatial sound, and simple graphics. This paper describes two studies testing two applications with multimodal user interfaces for navigation and information retrieval. The applications allow users to search for information and get navigation support using combinations of point and sweep gestures, nonspeech audio, graphics, and text. Tests show that users appreciated both applications for their ease of use and for allowing users to interact directly with the surrounding environment.

1. Introduction

Visual maps have a number of advantages as a tool for navigation, for example, overview and high information density. Over the last years, new technologies have radically broadened how and in what contexts visual maps can be used and displayed. This development has spawned a plethora of new tools for navigation. Many of these are based on graphics, are meant for the eye, and use traditional map metaphors. The Google Maps application included in, for example, iPhone and Android smartphones is one example. However, visual maps are usually abstract representations of the physical world and must be interpreted in order to be of use. Interpreting a map and relating it to the current surroundings is a relatively demanding task [1]. Moreover, maps often require the users' full visual attention, disrupt other activities, and may weaken the users' perception of the surroundings. All in all, maps are in many ways demanding tools for navigation.

One major challenge for developers of navigation services based on smartphones is handling the inaccuracy of sensor data, especially GPS location data. The location provided by GPS in urban environments is often very inaccurate from pedestrians' perspective. Furthermore, the accuracy is heavily influenced by nearby buildings as well as other factors such as the positions of the satellites and weather.

This paper addresses the problems described above. The problem with current navigation tools' demands on users' attentional and cognitive resources was addressed using multimodal user interfaces built on a mix of audio, pointing gestures, graphics, and text. The aim was to study to what extent such interfaces could reduce the demands put on the users compared to more traditional navigation tools. To test the idea, two multimodal interfaces were developed. The main inputs to both applications are the device's GPS location and the direction in which the user is pointing the device. Both interfaces generate sound to indicate directions to targets and also present simple graphics and small amounts of text. The interfaces are built on the users' natural ability to locate sound sources and to follow a pointing arrow on the device screen and can to large degrees be used eyes-free.

This study was inspired and guided by four concepts and aims: minimal attention user interfaces, eyes-free interaction, decreased cognitive loads on the users, and aesthetics of interaction. The study is also inspired by and based on a number of previous research efforts from several disciplines, including computer games, electronic navigation, and ubiquitous computing.

2. Background

Modes like auditive or haptic senses have been used for navigation applications in many studies. Examples include Tsukada and Yasymua [2], Frey [3], Amemiya et al. [4], Spath et al. [5], Loomis et al. [6], Kramer et al. [7], and Evett et al. [8]. But, as is often the case, the visual modality has drawn most attention when researching new interfaces for navigation. Also, as pointed out by McGookin et al. [9], work done on auditory navigation has primarily been geared towards people with visual impairments. There have been, though, a number of efforts developing auditory systems for navigation for sighted. *AudioGPS* by Holland et al. [10] is early work with spatial, nonspeech audio to convey information about the direction and distance to a target. *GpsTunes* by Strachan et al. [11] and *Ontrack* [12] by Jones et al. used spatially modified music to convey the same information. *Ontrack* plays music to lead the user towards a target destination; the music's spatial balance and volume indicate the directions the user should choose. A majority of test subjects were able to successfully navigate both a virtual and the physical world using the nonspeech audio provided by the system. *Ontrack* links to our own previous work on audio-based navigation in a virtual environment. *Beowulf* [13] showed that a soundscape together with a low-resolution graphic map is enough to present an entertaining and suitably challenging computer game. In *Audio Bubbles*, McGookin et al. [9] used audio to inform tourists about nearby points of interest. The users of the system can attend to or ignore the audio information. The aim of the Audio Bubbles is to promote a serendipitous or "stumble upon" type of navigation that is more targeted to exploration and experience than efficiency. The bearing-based navigation used in this study holds the potential to work in a similar way.

HaptiMap has produced a number of results related to the design, implementation, and evaluation of maps and location services that are more accessible through the use of several senses such as touch, hearing, and vision. See, for example, [14, 15]. Suitable angle sizes for pointing gestures were studied in [16]. *SoundCrumbs* [17] uses an interesting navigation method where a trail of virtual "crumbs" is laid out and the application helps a user to follow this trail via vibrotactile cues. The method can be described as based on bearings to a sequence of relatively close targets. The *PointNav* [18] prototype allows a user to both scan for points of interest (POIs) and to get guidance to selected POIs using a combination of pointing gestures, vibrotactile cues, and speech.

The works referred to above have all been successful in using multimodal interfaces to guide users to selected locations. The study described in this article continues this work and adds insights into the attentional and cognitive resources needed when using this approach on navigation.

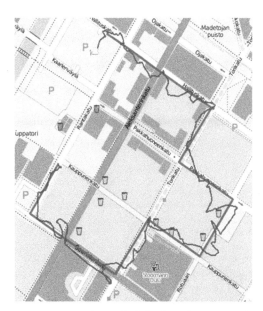

FIGURE 1: Route actually walked (red) and corresponding GPS locations logged (blue).

Smartphone devices cannot supply as high accuracy in location and direction data as car navigators can. Decreased accuracy makes it troublesome to apply the turn-by-turn type of navigation used in car navigators to smartphone-based navigation applications for pedestrians. Another challenge is, as Pielot and Bol [19] point out, that pedestrians use navigation services in significantly different contexts compared to car drivers. Thus, it is important to find alternative navigation solutions for pedestrians. In a prestudy to the work reported here, one researcher walked a route in a city centre while logging GPS locations. When the logged data was compared to the route actually walked it was obvious that the logged locations often differed 30 metres or more from the actual locations. The map in Figure 1 shows the difference between the route actually walked (the thin red line) and the corresponding GPS locations logged (blue line).

Djajadiningrat et al. [20] argue that good interaction design should respect all of man's skills: cognitive, perceptual-motor, and emotional skills. This leads to interaction design where also what the user perceives with her senses and what she can do with her body become important in the design process. Hekkert [21] divides experience into three levels: aesthetic level, understanding level, and emotional level and sees aesthetics as "pleasure of the senses." It can generally be argued that aesthetics is a vital part of any user experience and is essential in developing useful, easy to use, and attractive products. The work reported here has strived to embody these ideas in the applications developed. The bearing-based guide function puts the users' cognitive and perceptual-motor skills at play in an attempt to overcome problems with fluctuating accuracy in GPS localization. But we also strongly believe that, at the same time, this promotes a qualitatively different experience compared to turn-by-turn navigation along the lines of "serendipitous navigation."

(a)   (b)

FIGURE 2: (a): Map showing one of the routes. (b): Placement of one of the letter signs.

3. Two Studies

Two studies were made. The first compared navigation using a paper map to navigation using a multimodal application. Two aspects of navigation were compared: the user's ability two follow a route and her awareness of the surroundings while navigating. The second study looked at users' reactions to using a multimodal application to find and to navigate to locations in a city environment. Two prototypic mobile applications were developed as tools for the studies. Both applications had multimodal user interfaces built on point and sweep gestures, spatial and nonspatial sounds, and text and simplistic graphics.

3.1. The First Study: The Audio Guide. The first study focused on providing answers to the following research questions and testing the corresponding hypotheses.

- Q1: Do the users show and experience any difference in awareness and mental presence in the surroundings when using the multimodal application compared to using a map?

- H1: Users will be more aware of and mentally present in the surroundings when using the multimodal application compared to using the map.

- Q2: Do the test subjects perceive any difference in how mentally and physically demanding a navigation task is using the multimodal application compared to using a traditional map?

- H2: The users will experience the multimodal application as less demanding mentally and physically compared to a traditional map.

The users' task was to navigate a predefined route by foot while at the same time looking for small signs with letters along the route. One-half of the route was navigated using a map and the other half using a multimodal application; the Audio Guide. The users were told to write down the letters in the order they found them along the route. Each route had seven or eight size A5 signs, each with a single black lowercase letter on white background. The letters did not form any intelligible word. Each sign was placed in a clearly visible location within 1–10 meters from the road. Each route was roughly 2 km long along roads, sidewalks, or bikeways and featuring 8-9 straight turns (Figure 2).

After an introduction based on a PowerPoint presentation the users were randomly given one of the navigation tools and asked to navigate the route alone. The multimodal application rendered sounds on top of environmental sounds, via loose-fitting headphones. Halfway through the route, the test leader met the users and gave them a questionnaire related to the navigation tool used. The users filled out the questionnaire and were asked to navigate the rest of the route using the other navigational tool. The questionnaire was based on the NASA Task Load Index (TLX) [22]. Since the test at hand did not put any timely constraints on the users, the question about temporal demands in the original NASA TLX was replaced by the question "How attentive were you while performing the task?". The question about frustration in the original NASA TLX was rephrased "How irritated were you while you performed the task?".

To complement the NASA TLX, the test users also rated three statements on six-level Lickert scales from "Do not agree at all" to "Completely agree." Each statement concerning the multimodal application (Application) had a counterpart for the map (Map). The statements were as follows.

(1) *Application:* The Audio Guide was a good aid to find the way even if I did not look at it all the time, but, for example, kept it in my pocket.

   Map: The map was a good aid to find the way even if I did not look at it all the time, but, for example, kept it in my pocket.

(2) *Application:* To search for the correct way using the application's sound pointer was a powerful tool for navigation.

   Map: To search for the correct way by looking at the map and orienting it to the surroundings was a powerful tool for navigation.

(3) *Application:* I found it difficult to understand and use the Audio Guide.

   Map: I found it difficult to understand and use the map.

The test was conducted in the same way in three cities: in Oulu and Rovaniemi in Finland and in Piteå in Sweden. A total of 28 test users were recruited to the study. The test users' average age was 30 years, youngest 20, oldest 42, and median 27 years old. 14 were male and 14 female. Test users were students and staff at the universities in the three cities and volunteered to the test. The tests were performed in October and November 2010. Weather and daylight conditions differed between the tests. The tests in Oulu and Piteå were done in good weather conditions, in daylight, with no precipitation, and temperature above freezing. In Rovaniemi, half of the participants did the test in daylight and no precipitation and half in dusk and snowfall, temperature somewhat below zero.

3.1.1. Multimodal Application Used in the First Study.

The Audio Guide application guided users along predefined routes using turn-by-turn navigation. The application had two distinct modes, follow and seek. Both modes primarily gave the user information via directional, nonverbal audio in stereo headphones.

In follow mode, users walked along the route waiting for instructions to turn left or right. The application tracked the user's location using the device's GPS system. The data supplied by the operating system was used without filtering or other manipulation. When the user was less than 30 meters from a waypoint, the application first played a notification sound alerting the user about the next instruction. When the user got closer than 20 meters from the waypoint, the application played an action sound indicating that the user should change course by turning left or right. All instructions provided by the application were short (0.3–3.2 s), nonverbal sound effects. The turn left and right signals were panned towards left and right ear, respectively.

Seek mode allowed users to detect the next waypoint from a distance. The application calculated direction and distance to the next waypoint using data from the mobile phone's GPS and compass sensors. Therefore, in seek mode the orientation of the phone affected the instructions. The direction to the waypoint was conveyed to the user through a graphical arrow on the device screen and a sound in the user's headphones. The left-right panning of the sound was continuously updated to point towards the waypoint and the user experienced the sound as coming from the waypoint. When the user pointed the device to the right of the waypoint, the sound was stronger in the user's left ear and vice versa. The distance to the waypoint was shown as text on the device screen.

The follow mode was intended as the default mode to be used without holding the mobile device in the hand and possible to use even when riding a bicycle. The seek mode was intended to be used if the user became uncertain about the direction to the next waypoint. The user was free to switch between the two modes at any time.

The application used in the test was implemented as a Java MIDP 2.0 [23] application and tested on Nokia E55 and 6210 Navigator running Symbian S60 3rd edition.

3.2. Results from the First Study

3.2.1. Quantitative Results from the First Study.

The test did not proceed completely without problems. Of the 28 test users, a total of six did not complete the test according to

TABLE 1: Results for finding letter signs.

Found signs	App (%)	Map (%)	Stddev app	Stddev map	P (2-tailed)
Average all cities	89	84	11.2	14.8	0.2983
Piteå	93	79	9.3	13.8	0.0316
Oulu	81	90	15.3	9.4	0.4237
Rovaniemi	90	85	5.1	20.0	0.9362

the given instructions. In this study our focus was not on detecting or correcting the misuse of the navigation tools, therefore the results from these six test users are not included in the statistical analysis presented next. However, these cases are discussed in more detail later.

Table 1 shows the average percentage of letter signs found in correct order when using the multimodal application (App) and the map (Map), respectively. P values are calculated using the Mann-Whitney U test. Overall, the test subjects were able to find most of the letter signs along the routes.

The results from the three cities vary. This can be explained by several factors. In Piteå, all users managed to follow their route and weather and daylight conditions were good. The result from this test shows a statistically significant difference ($P = 0.03$) in the percentage of signs found when navigating using the application (93%) compared to using the map (79%). The same difference is not significant in the results from the tests in Oulu and Rovaniemi.

Table 2 shows the NASA TLX results from the study. NASA TLX values can be interpreted in a straightforward fashion, for example, "1" indicates the smallest "Mental demand." The results indicate that the users did not consider the task especially demanding either mentally or physically, regardless whether they used the map or the application. In the results from the tests in Oulu and Rovaniemi, the users did not consider either of the navigational tools requiring much effort. There was significant difference in the results from Piteå, where the users considered using the map demanding noticeably more effort (mean 2.5) than using the application (mean 1.7). This is a statistically significant difference on a 5% level ($P = 0.05$). For the total result in effort needed, the difference between using the application and the map shows a P value of 0.1. Significance was calculated using the Mann-Whitney test. Given the cases where the user completed the task according to the instructions, neither of the navigation tools was reported as significantly irritating. Finally, there was no significant difference in the reported awareness of the surrounding world.

When comparing results from the three extra statements concerning the application to the corresponding results concerning the map, statement 2 shows significant difference. For this statement for the application, the mean value = 4.9 and standard deviation (stddev) = 0.95. For the corresponding statement for the map, the mean value equals 4.0 and stddev = 1.4. The Mann-Whitney U test revealed that the difference was significant ($U = 161$, $z = 2.26$, $P = 0.02$, two-tailed).

TABLE 2: NASA TLX results from study 1. Means from answers on scale 1–6.

Parameter	Application				Map			
	Total	Piteå	Oulu	Rov	Total	Piteå	Oulu	Rov
Mental demand	2.2	2.3	1.8	1.8	2.2	2.6	1.7	2.2
Physical demand	1.4	1.4	1.2	1.7	1.6	1.5	1.3	2.0
Performance	5.1	5.2	5.0	5.0	4.9	4.8	4.8	5.2
Effort	1.4	1.7	1.2	1.7	2.0	2.5	1.3	1.8
Irritation	1.4	1.3	1.7	1.2	1.6	1.8	1.2	1.8
Attentiveness	4.7	4.6	4.5	5.2	4.6	4.2	5.0	4.8

3.2.2. Qualitative Results from the First Study. In order to find qualities and dimensions of the multimodal application missed or overlooked by the research team, oral feedback was collected from the test subjects on all three test sites. Strengths and weaknesses of the concept were discussed and the test subjects were asked to convey their experiences for the trial period.

Over all, the applications user interface was perceived as intuitive and easy to understand and the application's sound design was generally appreciated. Some users perceived the action sounds, panning from the centre to the left and right ear, respectively, as less clear than if the panning was omitted and the sound played in only one ear. Several comments related to poor integration between sound and graphics in the application—what is heard should also have a graphical counterpart.

It was stated that the map attracted and captivated the users' eyes more than necessary for the navigation task at hand. The application on the other hand was said not to demand the users full attention more than just before turns at waypoints. When using the map, some users reported frequent feelings of uncertainty about their current position and the correct route. As a contrast, the users reported that they felt great confidence in the application showing the way in a trustworthy manner.

Due to varying accuracy in GPS positioning, action sounds were reported to play very early or very late at some waypoints, causing confusion. A weakness in the design was said to be that the users did not get any confirmation that they turned in the right direction at waypoints. Another related weakness was said to be that the application just played the action sound once.

It was commented that maps give overview but the application does not. Being able to provide the users with, for example, a sense of distance left to the next waypoint would be a useful enhancement. Three participants stated that given the choice between the application and a traditional map when in a foreign city, they would choose the application.

3.3. The Second Study: PING! Leveraging from the experiences acquired from the first study, the second study focused on test users' experiences of and attitudes towards two aspects of pedestrian city navigation. The first aspect studied was the use of a multimodal search function for finding information about points of interest. The second aspect was to study if a multimodal bearing-based guide

function could help overcoming problems with varying GPS location accuracy that make turn-by-turn navigation troublesome for smartphone users. The research questions and corresponding hypotheses for the second study were as follows.

Q3: Can an interface based on a combination of point and sweep gestures, audio feedback and text be used to effectively find information about nearby points of interest?

H3: Users will be able to effectively find information about nearby points of interest using a search method based on a combination of point and sweep gestures, audio feedback, and text.

Q4: Can users effectively navigate to specified locations in a city using a guide function that is based on a combination of virtual, spatial sound sources, and a graphical arrow to indicate directions to targets and text to indicate distance?

H4: A majority of users can effectively navigate to specified locations in a city using a guide function that is based on a combination of virtual, spatial sound sources, and a graphical arrow to indicate directions to targets and text to indicate distance.

Q5: Can the interfaces described in Q3 and Q4 be effectively and successfully used despite varying accuracy in GPS location and compass directional data?

H5: Dividing the responsibility for finding the way to the target between the user and the application will help the user cope with varying accuracy in GPS positioning and electronic compass data.

The find and guide functions were implemented in a smartphone application designed for pedestrians. Both functions were based on point and sweep gestures for input and sound and simple graphics for output. The users' task was to use the find function to find directions to three target locations in the city. Then they should use the guide function to navigate there. In contrast to the first study, the approach was to let the users explore and choose the way to the target themselves, providing only information about distance and direction to targets.

The second study was conducted in August 2011 in Oulu with 24 users. The age range was 14 to 50 years, 15 users were female and 9 male. Each of the four test sessions lasted for three hours and followed the same structure. 22 of the test

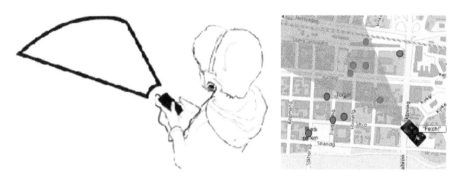

FIGURE 3: The Fetch function retrieved information about POIs in a 30-degree sector in front of the device.

users were sent out two-by-two, forming 11 pairs. Two test users were sent out alone. Each pair of users had one smartphone and two headphones connected to the phone using a headphone output split adapter. Each group also had paper and pen to take notes on details from the target location to show that the correct location had been reached.

The structure of the test was the following. First 20 minutes introduction and instructions indoors followed by 10 minutes instructions and application demonstration outdoors. After this, the test users were sent out for 90 minutes for the actual test. After this the test users were brought back indoors where they filled out a questionnaire. The first part of this was the same version of the NASA Task Load Index used in the first study. One question was added: "How much did the application hinder your awareness of the world around you." The second part of the questionnaire had six statements relating to complementary aspects of the navigation experience. The users graded their answers on six grade Lickert scales ranging from "totally disagree" to "totally agree." In order to reveal aspects and qualities of the test not captured by the questionnaire all test subjects also took part in focus-group interviews.

3.3.1. Multimodal Application Used in the Second Study.
The application used in the test had a database with points of interest (POI). Each database item held information about GPS location, street address, a photo, and some extra information about opening hours, and so forth.

The find function used point and sweep gestures as input and a combination of nonspeech sound, graphic icons, and text as output and was used in three steps. When using the find function, the user slowly swept the device back and forth (i.e. left to right and back). When the device was pointing towards a POI in the database the application played a short sound. The sound changed depending on the distance to the POI. The idea was to give users information about the density of POIs and distances to these in different directions. The next search step was called Fetch. The user pointed the device in some interesting direction and pressed the Fetch button. The application searched the database for POIs located in a sector with an angle -15 to $+15$ degrees from the device's current direction and up to a maximum distance of 2 km (Figure 3). Angles were selected based on the work by Magnusson et al. in [16].

POIs found by the Fetch function were presented in a scrollable list with name and distance from the user's current location. If the user wanted more detailed information about an item, she tapped the item in the list and the application switched to the item detail view. From this view, the user could get guidance from the current location to the item's location by tapping the "Guide me" button. In the guide view, the direction and distance to the target were presented. Based on this information the user herself decided the actual route to the target. The aim was to divide the responsibility for finding the way to the target more equally between the application and the user compared to turn-by-turn navigation.

The guide function conveyed information about distance and direction to targets using directional audio in headphones, following the ideas of Robinson et al. [24]. As the user moved and turned, a sound moved in the users stereo image such that the sound seemed to come from the target. The more to the left of the target the user pointed the device, the more to the right ear the sound moved and vice versa. The sound was low-pass filtered as a function of distance to the target. Distance was also shown as a number on screen and direction was shown using a graphical arrow pointing towards the target.

The application was implemented on the Android platform and tests were done using Samsung Galaxy S2 devices.

3.4. Results from the Second Study

3.4.1. Quantitative Results from Second Study.
All test users managed to find and walk to all the three target locations. Figure 4 shows the results from the NASA TLX. The graph does not show any high mental or physical loads on the users. Also, the users reported thinking they succeeded well in navigating the city using the application. They were not overly irritated while doing the task and the application did not hinder their awareness of the surroundings to any great extent while using it.

There are some differences in the results from the teenagers compared to the results from the adults. The teenagers reported succeeding somewhat better than the adults. A Mann-Whitney U test shows that the difference is statistically significant ($P = 0.02$). There are no significant differences for the other measures.

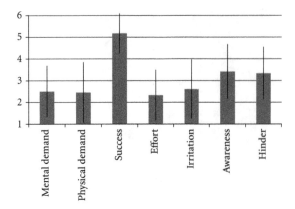

FIGURE 4: NASA Task Load Index. Average of all users.

Figure 5 shows results from the six complementary statements in the questionnaire as the percentage of users in strong agreement with the statements (1 or 2 on the Lickert scales), in strong disagreement with the statements (5 or 6 on the Lickert scales), or showing a weak opinion (3 or 4 on the Lickert scales).

3.4.2. Second Study Focus-Group Interviews. All participants took part in focus-group interviews. The results are summarized below.

General Usefulness. Overall, the application was perceived as easy to use and to find the targets using the application's find and guide functions. It was noted that having information in sound leaves the eyes free for exploration. The guide function, showing only the direction towards the target, leaves the users free to choose their own way. This, in turn, was said to have benefits.

Comparison to Maps and Car Navigators. When using maps, users stated that they are often unsure if they interpret the map correctly in relation to the environment. Several users appreciated the application for its ability to know where you are and to show you the direction in the physical environment. Several of the teenagers referred to car navigators as annoying.

Sound Feedback. The audio feedback from the application received mixed opinions. Some users reported they did not actively listen to the sound feedback at all, instead using the onscreen graphic and textual information to search for and navigate to targets. Other users appreciated the ability to use the application "eyes-free," just listening to the audio feedback. The guide function's spatial audio and the ability to determine the number of POIs in some given direction by sweeping were found useful by these users. The ability to visually observe the surroundings while using the application was a good feature mentioned by several users.

Some users asked for greater diversity between the different sounds in order to more easily discriminate between them and their different meanings. At some occasions, the

sound from the application was drowned by background noise from traffic or machines. To some users the application did not convey enough information through audio about direction (left/right) or distance to target. Using speech to give the information "turn left" and "turn right" was suggested as a solution.

Balance between Sound, Graphics, and Text. Overall, the users reported having relied to the graphical and textual information on the screen more frequently than to the information conveyed by the sound feedback. The sound feedback was useful to get information about direction to target, but in order to get an idea about distance to the target, the users still had to rely primarily on the onscreen text information. The users also reported relying on the onscreen information when the sound from the application was drowned by background noise.

4. Discussion

4.1. The First Study. The tests could not verify the hypothesis that a multimodal application would let the users be more aware of and mentally present in the surroundings compared to a traditional map (H1). The results from the three test sites differ somewhat. The tests in Sweden were performed with the least disturbances from weather and other conditions. The results from these favourable conditions show a significant difference in number of letter signs found using the multimodal application compared to using the map. Tested under less favourable conditions this difference is not significant. The difference in overview the map gave compared to what the application gave probably affected the results. Some users were for example so familiar with the surroundings that a short glance at the map to check where to turn next was enough for walking several hundred meters without worrying about getting lost.

The tests could not fully verify the hypothesis that a multimodal application would put a lower mental and physical load on the users compared to a traditional map (H2). The NASA Task Load Index does not show any significant differences in the mental or physical demands the two navigation tools put on the users. However, users reported that the overall effort needed to perform the task was significantly lower using the application compared to using the map.

It can be concluded that navigation based on primarily turn-by-turn-based instructions similar to car navigators is not sufficient in pedestrian settings. The primary cause for this is the inaccuracy of the GPS sensor, even 30 meter errors are common. Often this leads to situations where turning signals come too early or too late in relation to the turning point. This is a significant problem. If the signal comes too soon, the user may end up choosing the wrong turn. If too late, the user may get confused over whether she should return to the previous intersection or continue to the next. There are also many intersections where simple 90-degree turn signals are not sufficient to signify which direction the users should go. Another conclusion is that during the first minutes of using a new application, learning the application

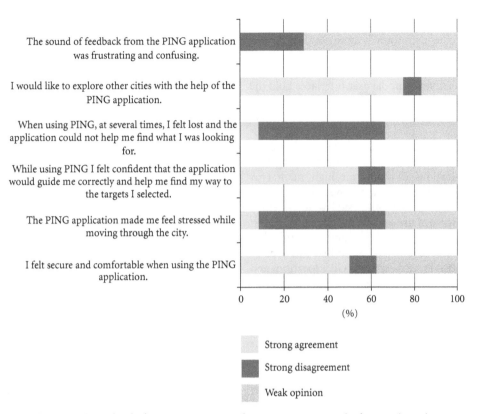

FIGURE 5: Users level of agreements to complementary statements in the questionnaire.

might absorb some users. This might in turn pose security risks to these users.

4.2. The Second Study. The results from the second study indicate that the hypothesis holds true that the users are able to find information about nearby points of interest using a search method based on point and sweep gestures, audio feedback, and text information (H3). The results also indicate that the hypothesis holds true that a majority of users will be able to find routes and navigate to selected points of interest with the help of a guide function showing (only) the direction and distance to the selected POI using a combination of spatial audio, a graphic, onscreen pointer, and text (H4).

The turn-by-turn navigation used in the first study imposed high demands on GPS-location accuracy and required the users to stick to major roads. The target bearing-based navigation method used in the second study was designed to overcome this problem by dividing the responsibility for finding the way more equally between the user and the device. Despite large documented variances in GPS position accuracy, all users managed to successfully use the target-bearing guide to navigate to the targets. This suggests that the hypothesis holds true that dividing the responsibility for finding the way to the target between the user and the application helps the user cope with varying accuracy in GPS positioning and electronic compass data (H5).

The results from the NASA Task Load Index suggest that using the application did not put heavy mental or physical loads on the users. The users reported that they thought they succeeded well in navigating the city using the application and they were not overly irritated while doing so. These results indicate that the application did not hinder the users' awareness of the surroundings to any greater extent. The same is true for how aware of the surrounding world the users were while doing the task. Informal statements from the test users indicate that for many of them, the test situation was their first encounter with bearing-based navigation, for some also with smartphones and touch screens. This suggests that learning curve effects are parameters affecting the results. Being occupied with learning a new user interface and interpreting auditory and graphic feedback from it may have influenced the awareness of the surroundings and how much the test users perceived the application to hinder this awareness. Together the results give further support for hypotheses H3, H4, and H5.

4.3. Overall Discussion. Two prototype applications for navigation and information retrieval were developed. These applications did not rely on maps presented on graphical user interfaces but were instead based on users' innate abilities to use point and sweep gestures to indicate directions and to use directional hearing to locate sound sources. The graphical user interface presented general information about points of interests, distances to them, and directions to selected POIs. Point and sweep gestures made by the user and spatial audio were in the main roles in these user interfaces.

The applications were evaluated in two studies. Based on the results from these it can be argued that applications for navigation featuring multimodal user interfaces hold the potential to help users find the way, while at the same time leaving them more free to experience and explore the surrounding environment compared to navigation using traditional maps. The studies show several similarities. The users perceived themselves as successful in fulfilling the navigation tasks and the applications did not put high mental or physical loads on the users. Both quantitative and qualitative data indicate that both applications tested were generally appreciated for their ease of use and overall efficiency.

The application tested in the first study used turn-by-turn navigation. In the study it was found that this type of navigation is sensitive to variances in GPS location and compass-direction accuracy. The target-bearing based navigation used in the second study divides the responsibility for the navigation task more equally between the user and the device. The user is free to explore the city; the application helps the user to stay on a route towards the target, without distracting the exploration too much. The second study revealed that this type of navigation is less sensitive to varying accuracy in GPS location and compass-direction data. That is, the bearing-based application is more robust than the turn-by-turn application, because there are no waypoints requiring accurate calculations from the application and swift reactions from the user. Moreover, single errors have only a momentary effect as calculations are always based on the latest sensor values. A user does not need to react to instructions exactly at waypoints, but to check periodically the direction and distance to the target and decide the route in the environment herself based on this information. Finally, since there is no predefined, correct route there is no need to check whether the user is on that route and correct her if not.

For some users, sound feedback can be hard to interpret and to make use of. The application used in the second study did some integration between sound and graphics/text, so when a sound was played some onscreen information changed at the same time. Integrating several modalities might produce good user experiences for larger user groups and facilitate learning the application.

Several of the adult users expressed that they found the turn-by-turn navigation used in car navigators better and more efficient than the target bearing-based navigation used in the second study. This preference towards turn-by-turn navigation might simply be because of their greater and more long-time experience with this type of devices. Despite the inherent technical problems in implementing turn-by-turn navigation in pedestrian settings with GPS technology, turn-by-turn navigation may still prove a useful mix with other navigation methods. This observation is supported by the first study, where the majority of the testers were still able to navigate the given route with primarily turn-by-turn audio instructions. Moreover, some waypoints might be necessary when a large obstacle like a river or a railway station requires a detour. On the other hand, guidance based on target bearing was successful and all test users navigated successfully to all given target locations. This guidance style can be seen as a very promising approach to cope with GPS inaccuracies.

The implemented applications also serve as examples how good user experiences do not require the state of the art technology like displays with the best resolutions and largest sizes, but instead careful design of multimodal, natural user interfaces can provide good results.

Acknowledgments

The II City project was funded by EU Interreg IV A North, the County Administrative Board of Norrbotten (Länsstyrelsen i Norrbotten), Sweden, the Regional Council of Lapland (Lapin Liitto), Finland, and The Interactive Institute, Sweden. Jukka Riekki, Mikko Pyykkönen, and Jari Koliseva at University of Oulu, Elisa Jaakkola at University of Lapland, and Nigel Papworth at The Interactive Institute, Sonic Studio are all acknowledged for their participation to the development work and contribution to this paper.

References

[1] A. M. MacEachren, *How Maps Work: Representation, Visualization, and Design*, The Guilford Press, 1995.

[2] K. Tsukada and M. Yasymua, "ActiveBelt: belt-type wearable tactile display for directional navigation," in *Proceedings of the 6th International Conference on Ubiquitous Computing (Ubicomp '04)*, pp. 384–399, Springer, 2004.

[3] M. Frey, "CabBoots: Shoes with integrated guidance system," in *Proceedings of the 1st International Conference on Tangible and Embedded Interaction*, pp. 245–246, ACM, February 2007.

[4] T. Amemiya, H. Ando, and T. Maeda, "Lead-me interface for a pulling sensation from hand-held devices," *Transactions on Applied Perception*, vol. 5, no. 3, article 15, pp. 1–17, 2008.

[5] D. Spath, M. Peissner, L. Hagenmeyer, and B. Ringbauer, "New approaches to intuitive auditory user interfaces," in *Proceedings of the Conference on Human Interface: Part I (HCII '07)*, M. J. Smith and G. Salvendy, Eds., vol. 4557 of *Lecture Notes in Computer Science*, pp. 975–984, 2007.

[6] J. M. Loomis, J. R. Marston, R. G. Golledge, and R. L. Klatzky, "Personal guidance system for people with visual impairment: a comparison of spatial displays for route guidance," *Journal of Visual Impairment and Blindness*, vol. 99, no. 4, pp. 219–232, 2005.

[7] R. Kramer, M. Modsching, and K. Ten Hagen, "Development and evaluation of a context-driven, mobile tourist guide," *International Journal of Pervasive Computing and Communications*, vol. 3, no. 4, pp. 378–399, 2007.

[8] L. Evett, S. Battersby, A. Ridley, and D. Brown, "An interface to virtual environments for people who are blind using Wii technology—mental models and navigation," *Journal of Assistive Technologies*, vol. 3, no. 2, pp. 26–34, 2009.

[9] D. McGookin, S. Brewster, and P. Priego, "Audio bubbles: employing non-speech audio to support tourist wayfinding," in *Proceedings of the 4th International Conference on Haptic and Audio Interaction Design (HAID '09)*, pp. 41–50, Springer, 2009.

[10] S. Holland, D. R. Morse, and H. Gedenryd, "AudioGPS: spatial audio navigation with a minimal attention interface," *Personal Ubiquitous Computing*, vol. 6, no. 4, pp. 253–259, 2002.

[11] S. Strachan, P. Eslambolchilar, and R. Murray-Smith, "Gps-Tunes—controlling navigation via audio feedback," in *Proceedings of the 7th International Conference on Human Computer Interaction with Mobile Devices and Services (MobileHCI '05)*, pp. 275–278, ACM, September 2005.

[12] M. Jones, S. Jones, G. Bradley, N. Warren, D. Bainbridge, and G. Holmes, "Ontrack: dynamically adapting music playback to support navigation," in *Personal and Ubiquitous Computing*, vol. 12, pp. 513–525, Springer, 2008.

[13] M. Liljedahl, N. Papworth, and S. Lindberg, "Beowulf: an audio mostly game," in *Proceedings of the 4th International Conference on Advances in Computer Entertainment Technology (ACE '07)*, pp. 200–203, June 2007.

[14] D. McGookin, C. Magnusson, M. Anastassova, W. Heuten, A. Rentería, and S. Boll, *Proceedings from Workshop on Multimodal Location Based Techniques for Extreme Navigation*, Helsinki, Finland, 2010.

[15] M. Anastassova, C. Magnusson, M. Pielot, G. Randall, and G. B. Claassen, "Using audio and haptics for delivering spatial information via mobile devices," in *Proceedings of the 12th International Conference on Human-Computer Interaction with Mobile Devices and Services (Mobile HCI'10)*, pp. 525–526, ACM, September 2010.

[16] C. Magnusson, K. Rassmus-Gröhn, and D. Szymczak, "Angle sizes for pointing gestures," in *Proceedings of the Workshop on Multimodal Location Based Techniques for Extreme Navigation*, Helsinki, Finland, 2010.

[17] C. Magnusson, B. Breidegard, and K. Rassmus Gröhn, "Soundcrumbs—hansel and gretel in the 21st century," in *Proceedings of the 4th international workshop on Haptic and Audio Interaction Design (HAID '09)*, 2009.

[18] C. Magnusson, M. Molina, K. Rassmus-Gröhn, and D. Szymczak, "Pointing for non-visual orientation and navigation," in *Proceedings of the 6th Nordic Conference on Human-Computer Interaction: Extending Boundaries (NordiCHI '10)*, pp. 735–738, ACM, October 2010.

[19] M. Pielot and S. Bol, "In fifty meters turn left": why turn-by-turn Instructions fail pedestrians," in *Proceedings of the Workshop Using Audio and Haptics for Delivering Spatial Information via Mobile Devices (MobileCHI '10)*, Lisbon, Portugal, 2010.

[20] T. Djajadiningrat, S. Wensveen, J. Frens, and K. Overbeeke, "Tangible products: redressing the balance between appearance and action," in *Personal and Ubiquitous Computing 8*, pp. 294–309, Springer, London, UK, 2004.

[21] P. Hekkert, "Design aesthetics: principles of pleasure in design," *Psychology Science*, vol. 48, no. 2, pp. 157–172, 2006.

[22] S. G. Hart and L. E. Staveland, "Development of nasa-tlx (task load index): results of empirical and theoretical research," in *Human Mental Workload*, pp. 139–183, 1988.

[23] Java MIDP 2.0, http://jcp.org/aboutJava/communityprocess/final/jsr118/index.html.

[24] S. Robinson, M. Jones, P. Eslambolchilar, R. Murray-Smith, and M. Lindborg, "I did it my way": moving away from the tyranny of turn-by-turn pedestrian navigation," in *Proceedings of the 12th International Conference on Human-Computer Interaction with Mobile Devices and Services (Mobile HCI '10)*, pp. 341–344, ACM, September 2010.

14

A Game-Based Virtualized Reality Approach for Simultaneous Rehabilitation of Motor Skill and Confidence

Alasdair G. Thin

School of Life Sciences, Heriot-Watt University, Edinburgh EH14 4AS, UK

Correspondence should be addressed to Alasdair G. Thin, a.g.thin@hw.ac.uk

Academic Editor: Francesco Bellotti

Virtualized reality games offer highly interactive and engaging user experience and therefore game-based approaches (GBVR) may have significant potential to enhance clinical rehabilitation practice as traditional therapeutic exercises are often repetitive and boring, reducing patient compliance. The aim of this study was to investigate if a rehabilitation training programme using GBVR could simultaneously improve both motor skill (MS) and confidence (CON), as they are both important determinants of daily living and physical and social functioning. The study was performed using a nondominant hand motor deficit model in nonambidextrous healthy young adults, whereby dominant and nondominant arms acted as control and intervention conditions, respectively. GBVR training was performed using a commercially available tennis-based game. CON and MS were assessed by having each subject perform a comparable real-world motor task (RWMT) before and after training. Baseline CON and MS for performing the RWMT were significantly lower for the nondominant hand and improved after GBVR training, whereas there were no changes in the dominant (control) arm. These results demonstrate that by using a GBVR approach to address a MS deficit in a real-world task, improvements in both MS and CON can be facilitated and such approaches may help increase patient compliance.

1. Introduction

Functional impairment of human motor function can arise due to a number of different causes including a variety of disease processes, physical trauma, and aging. The best treatment outcomes are seen when rehabilitation exercises are instituted early and in an intensive and repetitive manner in order to promote neural plasticity and muscle hypertrophy [1]. Given the often long and arduous nature of treatment programs requiring many thousands of exercise repetitions over many months, if not years, it is hardly surprising that patients commonly complain that the therapeutic exercises are repetitive and boring and this leads to poor compliance with the prescribed exercises and results in suboptimal optimal treatment outcomes. Not only is this scenario likely to impact on a patient's quality of life, but also it may ultimately result in a loss of their ability to live independently and necessitate long-term provision of care. Treatment programs are also very often resource intensive in terms of the time a physical therapist needs to devote to an individual patient and also the time spent traveling in connection with treatment. A range of technology-based solutions are therefore currently being actively investigated in terms of their potential for improving the efficiency and effectiveness of rehabilitation programs and to also increase the independence of patients and empower them to take control of their own treatment [2].

Virtual rehabilitation has been defined as "the combination of computers, special interfaces, and simulation exercises used to train patients in an engaging and motivating way." [3]. A range of different systems developed so far include remote monitoring of therapeutic exercises enhanced by virtual reality (VR) [4, 5], finger strengthening and hand-eye coordination exercises and games using VR combined with a haptic glove [6, 7]. For the purposes of this paper the term "Game-based Virtualized Reality" (GBVR) is considered to include all forms of games that involve players physically interacting with virtual objects that only exist as a digital representation on a screen.

The potential for game-based approaches in rehabilitation practice to provide a more engaging and motivating experience and that large numbers of game-based rehabilitation scenarios could be developed to provide greater realism and to correspond more closely to a wide range of everyday activities is now being more fully recognised [8–12]. Furthermore, there is now a growing evidence base to support their use in a variety of different rehabilitation applications including mobility and aerobic fitness [13–15], post-stroke rehabilitation of hand-arm function [16–18], balance [14, 19–21], pain distraction while undergoing treatment/therapy [22], and treatment of amblyopia ("lazy eye") [23].

There is a long standing call to have rehabilitation programs focus simultaneously on improving both physical motor skill and confidence (i.e., self-efficacy) [24] as the importance of a person's perception of their ability has long been recognized as an important determinant of physical performance [25]. Video games are a highly interactive and engaging form of entertainment [26] and incorporate clear goals, immediate feedback and rich visual and aural information [27]. It would therefore seem plausible that GBVR training could rise to this challenge and go a long way to meeting these dual treatment goals. This study was therefore undertaken to investigate if a rehabilitation training programme using a GBVR approach could simultaneously improve both motor skill and confidence. In order provide a stable and reliable experimental setting for both this study and future basic research into the development and refinement of GBVR, a nondominant hand motor deficit model was devised and will be described in subsequent sections.

2. Materials and Methods

2.1. Design. In order to be able to attribute any increase in motor skill and/or confidence to the GBVR rehabilitation training, a nondominant hand motor skill deficit model was conceived whereby each subject acted as their own control with their dominant and nondominant arms act as the control and intervention conditions, respectively.

2.2. Subjects. Nonambidextrous, young adults with no reported health issues were recruited from the student population at Heriot-Watt University. Potential subjects were asked if they had experience of playing racket sports and any reporting regular recreational participation or any competitive matches were excluded. The study was subject to local ethical committee approval and all subjects gave written, informed consent and underwent health screening. A total of 20 subjects were recruited although three subjects withdrew at various stages from the study. The 17 subjects (8 male) who completed the study ranged in age from 18 to 21 years with a mean (±SD) height 1.74 ± 0.09 m, weight 71.2 ± 10.4 kg, and a body mass index of 23.5 ± 2.6 kg/m^2. The study comprised a total of six sessions comprising an initial familiarisation session and then five sessions on consecutive days (Monday through to Friday). In order to minimise any effect of bias on the results, the subjects were unaware of the potential rehabilitation applications of the outcome of the study. Furthermore, the subjects were not given any feedback on their performance by the experimenters.

2.3. Familiarisation Session. In the familiarisation session subjects' height and weight were measured using a portable stadiometer (model 225, Seca Ltd, Birmingham, UK), and weighing scales (model 770, Seca Ltd) respectively. Subjects then completed the Edinburgh Handedness Inventory [28] which comprises a series of questions relating to hand preferences (left or right) for a range of everyday activities. Scoring of the inventory gives a Laterality Quotient (LQ) ranging from -100 for total left-hand dominance to $+100$ for total right-hand dominance. The LQ obtained for each individual subject was used to designate his or her dominant and nondominant arms. Subjects were then shown a short video clip illustrating how the tennis real-world motor task (RWMT) skill assessment would be conducted. Finally, the subjects performed a basic target shooting game on the game console used in the study (Wii Play, Nintendo of Europe GmbH, Grossostheim, Germany) using the hand-held motion sensitive controller in a point-and-shoot manner.

2.4. Baseline Assessment Session. The RWMT skill assessment session took place in indoors on a squash court in order to ensure consistent conditions. The RWMT involved using a tennis racket (Slazenger Smash 2", Dunlop Slazenger Int. Ltd, Shirebrook, UK) to strike a tennis ball served by a machine (Tennis Twist, Sports Tutor Inc., Burbank, US) over the net and to try and hit a 1.4 m^2 target on the back wall of the squash court. The tennis RWMT assessment set-up is illustrated in Figure 1. The tennis balls were served to the subjects in a consistent arc trajectory by the serving machine with an interval of 5 seconds between balls. The subjects then had to strike the ball back over the net and aim so as to hit the square target marked out on the back wall. As layed out in Figure 1, with the subject having right-hand dominance, dominant forearm, and nondominant backhand strokes were performed in this configuration. For the other two strokes (nondominant forearm and dominant backhand), the serving machine and the subject were placed at the opposite mirror positions on the court.

Self-efficacy is the term used to refer to task-specific confidence (i.e., the conviction that the behaviour required to achieve a particular outcome can be performed successfully) [25]. Prior to commencement of the RWMT skill assessment, the self-efficacy ratings of the subjects were assessed using a questionnaire designed using published guidelines [29]. Subjects were asked to indicate the number of shots on target they thought they would be able to achieve for each of the four separate tennis strokes.

Subjects had a practice run through the four different stokes (forehand and backhand for both dominant and nondominant arms) comprising 10 trials of each stroke with a short break between strokes allow for adjusting of the position of the tennis serving machine. Performance of RWMT was then assessed with a further 10 trials in turn for each of four strokes with an observer recording the position of each ball that struck the back wall of the squash court and whether or not it was on target.

2.5. Game-Based Virtualized Reality Training Sessions. During three days following the baseline RWMT assessment, subjects undertook three separate GBVR training sessions each of 30 minutes duration. The sessions involved working progressively through the training drills that formed part of the tennis game (Wii Sports, Nintendo of Europe GmbH, Grossostheim, Germany) and which involved developing the ability to play shots in different directions towards fixed and moving targets and also periods of match play using equally both dominant and nondominant arms. Screen shots of the drills and match play are shown in Figure 2. In order to mimic as closely as possible the RWMT, a commercially available imitation tennis racket (Play On, Toys R Us, Gateshead, UK) was attached to the motion sensitive hand-held controller used to control the game and mass was added by means of a solid plastic cylinder machine to fit inside the shaft to make the weights of the two rackets equivalent (Figure 3).

2.6. Post-Training Assessment Session. The post-training RWMT assessment session occurred the day after the last GBVR training session and was an exact repeat of the baseline assessment session.

2.7. Statistical Analysis. All data are reported as mean ± standard error of the mean (SEM) with the exception of the demographic data (±SD). The impact of the GBVR training on self-efficacy ratings and RWMT skill performance (number of shots on target) was assessed using Wilcoxon Signed Rank tests (SPSS 14.0 for Windows, SPSS Inc., Surrey, UK) due to the nonparametric nature of the data with Holm's sequential Bonferroni adjustment for multiple comparisons. Congruence between actual subjects' self rating of their ability and their actual number of shots on target was assessed using the method described by Cervone [30] and the confidence interval of the estimate determined by using Bootstrapping.

3. Results

Sixteen of the subjects reported right-hand dominance and the other remaining subject left-hand dominance. The magnitude of the LQs ranged from 50 to 100 and indicated that all subjects had a clear hand preference and that none could be classed as ambidextrous. Prior to the baseline RWMT skill assessment, the subjects' confidence in their ability to hit the target (self-efficacy ratings) was significantly lower for both nondominant arm forehand and backhand strokes versus the dominant arm (control) strokes (Table 1). As expected, there was a deficit in motor skill performance of both nondominant arm strokes (Table 1). After the GBVR training there were significant increases in the self-efficacy ratings for both nondominant arm strokes (Table 1). With regard to motor performance, there was a significant improvement in the nondominant arm backhand stroke performance

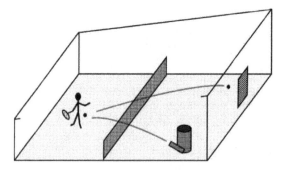

FIGURE 1: Illustration of the set-up of the tennis RWMT assessment performed indoors in a squash court. The tennis serving machine is denoted by the cylinder plus arm shape.

(Table 1) while the improvement in nondominant forehand stroke just failed to reach statistical significance ($P = 0.06$). In contrast there were no changes in the dominant arm strokes. Congruence between self-efficacy ratings estimates and actual performance was consistent across all conditions and the grand mean across all subjects and strokes was 81% and out-with the 95% confidence interval for random chance alone.

4. Discussion

The key findings of this study were that a performance deficit in a real-world motor task (RWMT) improved in response to a game-based virtualized reality (GBVR) training programme that closely mimicked the RWMT. Furthermore, the improvement was manifest as concomitant increases in both motor skill and self-efficacy (i.e., increased confidence in ability to perform the task).

As the subjects completed the self-efficacy ratings prior to the RWMT performance assessments, the post-training ratings given by the subjects (Table 1) predicted a differential improvement in their nondominant strokes compared with no change in the performance of their dominant hand strokes. The most likely explanation for the subjects' change in their perception of their ability to perform the nondominant strokes were due to an improvement as a result of the GBVR training. While care was taken by the experimenters not to give any explicit feedback during training, the subjects would have seen the consequences of their actions in displayed on the screen and through the game scoring mechanisms. Given that the baseline RWMT assessment comprised a total of only 20 shots of each stroke (10 familiarisation and 10 assessment), it seems unlikely that the baseline assessment session could have provided an adequate training stimulus to explain the observed effects. However, were the RWMT to be used for training, it is likely that performance improvements similar to those in the current study would be observed.

The experimental model designed for this study was based on the fact that in non-ambidextrous subjects, the nondominant arm has less well developed motor skill than that of the dominant arm, which by definition has much better developed motor skill due its preferential use in daily

FIGURE 2: Screen shots from the GBVR training drills and match play.

FIGURE 3: Conventional tennis racket for the tennis RWMT assessment and the tennis game controller.

life and therefore has much less potential for improvement in motor performance. In contrast, the relative under-use of subjects' nondominant arms (again by definition) means that they have a lower baseline level of motor skill and therefore much greater scope for improvement in response to training.

There is a growing interest in the use of GBVR approaches to rehabilitation practice [8–10] and in particular its potential for reducing the need for patient travel and reaching out to rural communities [2, 19]. However, the focus of attention has predominantly been on developing new forms of treatment modalities with a view to improving physical outcomes. The results of this study indicate that there is also the potential for significant positive psychological outcomes. The game used in this study provided the subjects with a number of different forms of feedback on their performance. When the user makes "contact" with the virtual tennis ball, a sound is played through a small speaker in the handheld controller. In addition, the trajectory of the ball in the on screen game play reflects the angle, speed, and timing at which the virtual ball is "struck". The game play environment also provides additional visual (in terms of game score) and aural (cheers of spectators) feedback on performance. The impact of the GBVR training was such that the relative deficit in the RWMT performance in the subjects' nondominant arms was rehabilitated closer to that of the corresponding dominant arm stroke. Furthermore, it would appear that the subjects were able to sense this motor skill improvement as a result of the GBVR training and that it was reflected in an increase in the self-efficacy ratings for the nondominant arm strokes prior to the post-training RWMT skill assessment. Thus, while the GBVR training did not fully replicate the sensation of striking a physical ball, nor did it directly replicate the geometry of the tennis RWMT, it did provide a training stimulus that was adequate enough to elicit an effect.

As described in the Introduction, rehabilitation treatment programs are usually long and arduous and therefore supporting and sustaining patient motivation is a major challenge. Game-based approaches are of particular interest in this regard due to the motivational appeal of video games [26]. Developing GBVR approaches to rehabilitation therefore require a degree of trade-off to be made, whereby the training stimulus may not quite match the real world equivalent, but that this is more than compensated for by appropriately designed selections of games that promote and maintain patient motivation and long-term adherence to a treatment program by providing immediate feedback on performance, in-game achievements and rewards, and a sense of accomplishment as they progress through the game. Also, there is evidence to indicate that both the challenge and the immersive potential offered by games controlled by body movement can result in a greater flow experience compared to traditional forms of exercise [31].

In order for GBVR approaches to be incorporated into routine clinical rehabilitation practice, it will require the development of game systems that are fit for purpose [19]. They will need to have sufficient fidelity in their detection of motion that the can keep the patient within the desired movement envelope. The physical exercises that the game play requires will need to correspond the prescribed therapeutic exercises and scenarios and will also need to be capable of providing sufficient stimulus to promote the desired restoration of function. There is also a requirement for the therapist to be able to tailor the game to match the precise rehabilitation requirements of each individual patient and to be able to regularly monitor a patient's progress and have the ability to adjust the specific game demands over time [8]. The game will also need to appeal to patient and be capable of sustaining their interest. However, not only is there a scope for a wide range of genres of games to appeal to different users, but more fundamentally, if appropriately programmed, a game could adapt and respond to any improvements in a given user's performance. This would help ensure that the game presents a challenge at an appropriate level for each individual and as the rehabilitation treatment program progressed, the game scenarios would become increasingly demanding. Other features which could be incorporated into games for rehabilitation include offering helpful tips and coaching, rewarding, and praising the user when they make progress, monitoring game use time, and providing some form of progress chart. It is not necessary and indeed may not be

TABLE 1: Baseline and post-training self-efficacy ratings and motor task performance.

| Real-world motor task | Baseline | | Post-training change | |
Tennis stroke	Self-efficacy rating	Motor task performance	Self-efficacy rating	Motor task performance
Dominant forearm	7.2 ± 0.4	7.1 ± 0.6	$+0.1 \pm 0.4$	$+0.4 \pm 0.6$
Dominant backhand	5.4 ± 0.5	6.4 ± 0.6	$+0.4 \pm 0.4$	$+0.8 \pm 0.5$
Nondominant forearm	$4.1 \pm 0.3^*$	$4.7 \pm 0.5^*$	$+1.2 \pm 0.4^\dagger$	$+1.2 \pm 0.6^\ddagger$
Nondominant backhand	$3.4 \pm 0.3^*$	$4.1 \pm 0.4^*$	$+1.2 \pm 0.3^\dagger$	$+1.7 \pm 0.5^\dagger$

Baseline data are shown as mean $\pm$ SEM shots on target. Post-training data are shown as mean change (delta values) $\pm$ SEM shots on target. *indicates significantly lower baseline for nondominant stroke compared to corresponding stroke for dominant arm ($P < 0.05$). †indicates significant increase for nondominant stroke post-training ($P < 0.05$). ‡indicates increase for nondominant stroke post-training just failed to reach statistical significance ($P = 0.06$).

desirable that these functions are performed by a virtual representation of a human, but rather they can be subtlety incorporated into the game play experience [32].

4.1. Clinical Rehabilitation Impact. GBVR approaches to rehabilitation have the potential to facilitate simultaneous improvements in motor skill and confidence and may also help increase patient compliance. The availability of low-cost motion sensors and increasingly sophisticated games development tools means significant progress is to be expected in this field over the next few years. The nondominant hand motor deficit model outlined in this study is intended as far as possible to mimic the impact of trauma or disease process on arm motor function, whereby the reduced motor performance in the nondominant arm mimics the functional loss due to trauma or disease process and which therefore is in need of rehabilitation as part of the treatment programme. However, the model does not incorporate the complex nature of different clinical scenarios nor does it reflect the fact that even with specific conditions there is significant variability between patients. While this might potentially be seen as a limitation, there are in fact significant advantages to having a stable and reliable experimental setting in order to undertake basic research into the development and refinement of GBVR approaches including hardware, software, game design, clinical interfaces, and data logging [19]. Furthermore, the convenience of being able to use healthy human subjects and having each subject act as there own control will further reduce potential sources of variability and therefore make experimental testing even more efficient.

With regard to clinical interfaces, it is an essential requirement that therapists are able to precisely control the parameters of the rehabilitation exercises (e.g., specific movements, range of motion, number of repetitions, and frequency of exercise) and also get detailed information via data logging and summary reports on patient performance in order to track rehabilitation progress and adjust their programme when required. It should be noted that existing commercial off-the-shelf interactive games (including the game used in this study) have little or no functionality in this regard. Once solutions that address these issues are developed, it will then be a much more realistic proposition to transition to clinical settings in order to tailor approaches to specific clinical needs and to undertake comprehensive clinical evaluations. Finally, there are also a number of

infrastructure issues that will need to be addressed before routine clinical adoption of GBVR rehabilitation is possible including accessibility issues [33], licensing and reimbursement [10], and issues of resource allocation and treatment policies [11].

5. Conclusion

GBVR training has significant potential in the development of rehabilitation practice. However, significant hardware and software design issues still need to be addressed and the nondominant hand motor deficit model described in this study provides useful paradigm for conducting basic research and development. The results of this study indicate that improvements in confidence, which is an important determinant of treatment outcome in terms of daily living and physical and social functioning, should be added to the list of potential benefits of GBVR training in rehabilitation practice.

Conflict of Interests

The author declares that there are no conflict of interests associated with this work.

Acknowledgments

Liam Baird and Graham McCraw who undertook data collection and Annemarie Crozier who provided technical support. This work has been funded in part by the EU under the FP7, in the Games and Learning Alliance (GALA—http://www.galanoe.eu) Network of Excellence, Grant Agreement no. 258169.

References

[1] S. H. Jang, S. H. You, Y. H. Kwon, M. Hallett, M. Y. Lee, and S. H. Ahn, "Cortical reorganization associated lower extremity motor recovery as evidenced by functional MRI and diffusion tensor tractography in a stroke patient," *Restorative Neurology and Neuroscience*, vol. 23, no. 5-6, pp. 325–329, 2005.

[2] T. G. Russell, "Physical rehabilitation using telemedicine," *Journal of Telemedicine and Telecare*, vol. 13, no. 5, pp. 217–220, 2007.

[3] G. C. Burdea, P. L. T. Weiss, and D. Thalmann, "Guest editorial special theme on virtual rehabilitation," *IEEE Transactions on*

Neural Systems and Rehabilitation Engineering, vol. 15, no. 1, p. 1, 2007.

[4] J. E. Deutsch, J. A. Lewis, and G. Burdea, "Technical and patient performance using a virtual reality-integrated telerehabilitation system: preliminary finding," *IEEE Transactions on Neural Systems and Rehabilitation Engineering*, vol. 15, no. 1, pp. 30–35, 2007.

[5] M. K. Holden, T. A. Dyar, and L. Dayan-Cimadoro, "Telerehabilitation using a virtual environment improves upper extremity function in patients with stroke," *IEEE Transactions on Neural Systems and Rehabilitation Engineering*, vol. 15, no. 1, pp. 36–42, 2007.

[6] A. Heuser, H. Kourtev, S. Winter et al., "Telerehabilitation using the Rutgers Master II glove following carpal tunnel release surgery: proof-of-concept," *IEEE Transactions on Neural Systems and Rehabilitation Engineering*, vol. 15, no. 1, pp. 43–49, 2007.

[7] V. G. Popescu, G. C. Burdea, M. Bouzit, and V. R. Hentz, "A virtual-reality-based telerehabilitation system with force feedback," *IEEE Transactions on Information Technology in Biomedicine*, vol. 4, no. 1, pp. 45–51, 2000.

[8] B. Lange, S. M. Flynn, and A. A. Rizzo, "Game-based telerehabilitation," *European Journal of Physical and Rehabilitation Medicine*, vol. 45, no. 1, pp. 143–151, 2009.

[9] H. Sveistrup, "Motor rehabilitation using virtual reality," *Journal of NeuroEngineering and Rehabilitation*, vol. 1, no. 1, article 10, 2004.

[10] D. Theodoros and T. Russell, "Telerehabilitation: current perspectives," *Studies in Health Technology and Informatics*, vol. 131, pp. 191–209, 2008.

[11] D. Kairy, P. Lehoux, C. Vincent, and M. Visintin, "A systematic review of clinical outcomes, clinical process, healthcare utilization and costs associated with telerehabilitation," *Disability and Rehabilitation*, vol. 31, no. 6, pp. 427–447, 2009.

[12] A. Rizzo and G. J. Kim, "A SWOT analysis of the field of virtual reality rehabilitation and therapy," *Presence*, vol. 14, no. 2, pp. 119–146, 2005.

[13] H. L. Hurkmans, G. M. Ribbers, M. F. Streur-Kranenburg, H. J. Stam, and R. J. van den Berg-Emons, "Energy expenditure in chronic stroke patients playing Wii Sports: a pilot study," *Journal of NeuroEngineering and Rehabilitation*, vol. 8, article 38, 2011.

[14] M. Brien and H. Sveistrup, "An intensive virtual reality program improves functional balance and mobility of adolescents with cerebral palsy," *Pediatric Physical Therapy*, vol. 23, no. 3, pp. 258–266, 2011.

[15] C. Bryanton, J. Bossé, M. Brien, J. McLean, A. McCormick, and H. Sveistrup, "Feasibility, motivation, and selective motor control: virtual reality compared to conventional home exercise in children with cerebral palsy," *Cyberpsychology and Behavior*, vol. 9, no. 2, pp. 123–128, 2006.

[16] A. S. Merians, E. Tunik, G. G. Fluet, Q. Qiu, and S. V. Adamovich, "Innovative approaches to the rehabilitation of upper extremity hemiparesis using virtual environments," *European Journal of Physical and Rehabilitation Medicine*, vol. 45, no. 1, pp. 123–133, 2009.

[17] G. Saposnik and M. Levin, "Virtual reality in stroke rehabilitation: a meta-analysis and implications for clinicians," *Stroke*, vol. 42, no. 5, pp. 1380–1386, 2011.

[18] L. Zollo, E. Gallotta, E. Guglielmelli, and S. Sterzi, "Robotic technologies and rehabilitation: new tools for upper-limb therapy and assessment in chronic stroke," *European Journal of Physical and Rehabilitation Medicine*, vol. 47, no. 2, pp. 223–236, 2011.

[19] B. Lange, S. Flynn, R. Proffitt, C. Y. Chang, and A. S. Rizzo, "Development of an interactive game-based rehabilitation tool for dynamic balance training," *Topics in Stroke Rehabilitation*, vol. 17, no. 5, pp. 345–352, 2010.

[20] T. Szturm, A. L. Betker, Z. Moussavi, A. Desai, and V. Goodman, "Effects of an interactive computer game exercise regimen on balance impairment in frail community-dwelling older adults: a randomized controlled trial," *Physical Therapy*, vol. 91, no. 10, pp. 1449–1462, 2011.

[21] M. Thornthon, S. Marshall, J. McComas, H. Finestone, A. McCormick, and H. Sveistrup, "Benefits of activity and virtual reality based balance exercise programmes for adults with traumatic brain injury: perceptions of participants and their caregivers," *Brain Injury*, vol. 19, no. 12, pp. 989–1000, 2005.

[22] G. J. Carrougher, H. G. Hoffman, D. Nakamura et al., "The effect of virtual reality on pain and range of motion in adults with burn injuries," *Journal of Burn Care and Research*, vol. 30, no. 5, pp. 785–791, 2009.

[23] P. Waddingham, R. Eastgate, and S. Cobb, "Design and development of a virtual-reality based system for improving vision in children with amblyopia," *Studies in Computational Intelligence*, vol. 337, pp. 229–252, 2011.

[24] M. E. Tinetti, C. F. Mendes de Leon, J. T. Doucette, and D. I. Baker, "Fear of falling and fall-related efficacy in relationship to functioning among community-living elders," *Journals of Gerontology*, vol. 49, no. 3, pp. M140–M147, 1994.

[25] A. Bandura, N. E. Adams, and J. Beyer, "Cognitive processes mediating behavioral change," *Journal of Personality and Social Psychology*, vol. 35, no. 3, pp. 125–139, 1977.

[26] R. M. Ryan, C. S. Rigby, and A. Przybylski, "The motivational pull of video games: a self-determination theory approach," *Motivation and Emotion*, vol. 30, no. 4, pp. 347–363, 2006.

[27] J. L. Sherry, "Flow and media enjoyment," *Communication Theory*, vol. 14, no. 4, pp. 328–347, 2004.

[28] R. C. Oldfield, "The assessment and analysis of handedness: the Edinburgh inventory," *Neuropsychologia*, vol. 9, no. 1, pp. 97–113, 1971.

[29] D. L. Feltz and M. A. Chase, "The measurement of self-efficacy and confidence in sport," in *Advances in Sport and Exercise Psychology Measurement*, J. L. Duda, Ed., pp. 65–80, Fitness Information Technology, Morgantown, WVa, USA, 1998.

[30] D. Cervone, "Randomization tests to determine significance levels for microanalytic congruences between self-efficacy and behavior," *Cognitive Therapy and Research*, vol. 9, no. 4, pp. 357–365, 1985.

[31] A. G. Thin, L. Hansen, and D. McEachen, "Flow experience and mood states while playing body movement-controlled video games," *Games and Culture*, vol. 6, no. 5, pp. 414–428, 2011.

[32] I. Bogost, *Persuasive Games: The Expressive Power of Videogames*, The MIT Press, Cambridge, Mass, USA, 2007.

[33] D. M. Brennan and L. M. Barker, "Human factors in the development and implementation of telerehabilitation systems," *Journal of Telemedicine and Telecare*, vol. 14, no. 2, pp. 55–58, 2008.

15

A Review of Hybrid Brain-Computer Interface Systems

Setare Amiri, Reza Fazel-Rezai, and Vahid Asadpour

Biomedical Signal and Image Processing Laboratory, Department of Electrical Engineering, University of North Dakota, Grand Forks, ND, USA

Correspondence should be addressed to Reza Fazel-Rezai; Reza.Fazel-Rezai@engr.und.edu

Academic Editor: Dimitrios Pantazis

Increasing number of research activities and different types of studies in brain-computer interface (BCI) systems show potential in this young research area. Research teams have studied features of different data acquisition techniques, brain activity patterns, feature extraction techniques, methods of classifications, and many other aspects of a BCI system. However, conventional BCIs have not become totally applicable, due to the lack of high accuracy, reliability, low information transfer rate, and user acceptability. A new approach to create a more reliable BCI that takes advantage of each system is to combine two or more BCI systems with different brain activity patterns or different input signal sources. This type of BCI, called hybrid BCI, may reduce disadvantages of each conventional BCI system. In addition, hybrid BCIs may create more applications and possibly increase the accuracy and the information transfer rate. However, the type of BCIs and their combinations should be considered carefully. In this paper, after introducing several types of BCIs and their combinations, we review and discuss hybrid BCIs, different possibilities to combine them, and their advantages and disadvantages.

1. Introduction

A brain-computer interface (BCI) system can provide a communication method to convey brain messages independent from the brain's normal output pathway [1]. Brain activity can be monitored using different approaches such as standard scalp-recording electroencephalogram (EEG), magnetoencephalogram (MEG), functional magnetic resonance imaging (fMRI), electrocorticogram (ECoG), and near infrared spectroscopy (NIRS) [1–4]. However, EEG signals are considered as the input in most BCI systems. In this case, BCI systems are categorized based on the brain activity patterns such as event-related desynchronization/synchronization (ERD/ERS), steady-state visual evoked potentials (SSVEPs), P300 component of event related potentials (ERPs), and slow cortical potentials (SCPs) [5–16]. Each BCI type has its own shortcoming and disadvantages. To utilize the advantages of different types of BCIs, different approaches are combined, called hybrid BCIs [15, 16]. In a hybrid BCI, two types of BCI systems can be combined. It is also possible to combine one BCI system with another system which is not BCI-based, for example, combining a BCI system

with an electromyogram (EMG)-based system. However, one can debate if this type of system should be defined as hybrid BCI. In the rest of this paper, we assume that if an EEG BCI system is combined with another physiological signal (e.g., EMG) based system, a hybrid BCI system will be constructed.

Although different BCI methods can be combined, it should be noted that not all combinations of different brain imaging methods are feasible and possible. One of the limiting factors is the technology. For example, although MEG is a very high resolution brain imaging technique, it is not practical to use it when subjects need to move around. In addition, different techniques and their combinations should be utilized based on the application that the hybrid BCI is going to be used for. The main purpose of combining different systems to form a "hybrid" BCI is to improve accuracy, reduce errors, and overcome disadvantages of each conventional BCI system. Different types of hybrid BCI systems can be defined according to the types of systems which are combined, how systems are joined, and what types of inputs are considered. In non-hybrid BCIs, based on the property of EEG signals used as the input of BCI system, four major EEG-based BCIs are considered: SSVEP, P300, SCP, and ERD/ERS.

Evoked response in EEG signals to repetitive visual stimulations is called SSVEP. In a SSVEP BCI paradigm, specific frequencies are allocated to the repetitive stimuli. For SSVEP detection, the frequency spectrum of the EEG is computed. Around the frequency of the repetition of stimulus in which the subject focuses, there will be peak on the frequency spectrum. By detecting this frequency, an intention of the subject can be detected. This can be translated to a control signal for a BCI system. There are some issues about SSVEP BCIs, one is gaze dependence [9, 17]. Another issue is that in some users, the flickering stimulus is annoying and produces fatigue. Using higher frequencies for the flickering stimuli reduces the annoyance, but on the other hand, it is harder to detect the SSVEP. SSVEP BCIs have some advantages such as no significant training requirement and high information transfer rate [6, 18, 19].

In P300-based BCIs, intention of the subjects is measured using the P300 component of the brain evoked response [20]. After stimulus onset, positive and negative deflections occur in the EEG. These deflections are called event-related potential (ERP) components. Depending on the latency of these deflections, they are grouped as "exogenous components" and "endogenous components" [10]. The exogenous components occur until about 150 msec after the eliciting stimulus. The endogenous components have longer latency. The largest positive deflection that occurs between 250 to 750 msec after the stimulus onset is called "P300". The P300 component is the most used ERP component in BCI systems. The paradigm that elicits P300 is called the "oddball paradigm" [21]. In an oddball paradigm, events that elicit the P300 fall into two classes in which one of the classes is less frequent. Inter-stimulus interval time and the frequency of the oddball stimulus are among the parameters that determine the amplitude of the P300 component. The first BCI P300-based system was introduced by Farwell and Donchin for spelling characters in 1988 [13].

Slow negative voltage shifts that occur in the EEG recorded over sensorimotor cortex, while actual or imagined movement happens [9] are called SCP. SCP-based BCI consists of series of trials [22]. Early SCP BCIs were especially slow, since in each trial only one selection was possible and the time needed for each selection was at least 10 sec. The temporal efficiency was improved by Kübler et al. to 4 sec [23]. Shortening the time process further was not possible because users were uncomfortable with the shortened trial time. Over the past decade studies about the SCP approach have been limited because of several SCP BCI problems, which reduce the applicability of this type of BCI. Among others, SCP BCIs have three main problems: poor multidimensional control, high probability of error, and long-term training.

Rhythmic activity of EEG in terms of event-related desynchronization/synchronization (ERD/ERS) has been used as one of the sources in BCI [1]. Motor imagery is one way to induce changes in ERD/ERS and has been used in many BCI systems [24]. During motor imagery of movements, ERD occurs predominantly over the contralateral brain motor area and, therefore, can be used as a signal for a BCI system. ERD/ERS BCIs have been used in different applications such as achieving two-dimensional cursor control.

2. Hybrid BCI Systems

In recent years, there has been more attention to hybrid BCI systems. Based on Scopus search engine [25] and keyword (("Brain-Computer Interface" or "BCI") and "Hybrid"), the number of journal papers found before 2010 was only three. This number was 6 and 10 for 2010 and 2011, respectively. This shows increased attention to hybrid BCIs in the recent years.

In general, in a hybrid BCI, two systems can be combined sequentially or simultaneously [26]. In a simultaneous hybrid BCI, both systems are processed in parallel. Input signals used in simultaneous hybrid BCIs can be two different brain signals, one brain signal, or one brain signal and another input. In sequential hybrid BCIs, the output of one system is used as the input of the other system. This approach is mostly used when the first system task is to indicate that the user does not intend to communicate or as a "brain switch" [26].

3. Review of Different Hybrid BCIs

The combinations of the BCI types and a summary of important features of different hybrid BCIs which are discussed and reviewed in this paper are shown in Table 1.

3.1. SSVEP-Motor Imagery Hybrid BCI. In order to acquire better understanding about a hybrid based on SSVEP and motor imagery BCI, short summaries of approaches are mentioned as follows. In [15], the proposed hybrid was evaluated during the task and was applied under three conditions: ERD BCI, SSVEP BCI, and ERD-SSVEP BCI. During the ERD BCI task, two arrows appeared on the screen. When the left arrow appeared, subjects were instructed to imagine opening and closing their left hand. For the right arrow, subjects imagined opening and closing the corresponding hand. In the SSVEP task, subjects were instructed to gaze at either left (8 Hz) or right (13 Hz) LED depending on which cue appeared. In the hybrid task, when the left arrow was showed, subjects were imagining the left hand opening and closing while gazing at the left LED simultaneously. The task was similar for the right arrow. Results show the average accuracy of 74.8% for ERD, 76.9% for SSVEP, and 81.0% for hybrid. The number of illiterate subjects, who achieved less than 70% accuracy [38], reduced to zero from five using the hybrid approach.

A hybrid SSVEP/ERD BCI was introduced in [16] for orthosis control application. The SSVEP-based BCI was utilized for opening the orthosis at the activating stage, and an ERS-based BCI was used as a switch to deactivate the LEDs that were mounted on the orthosis for SSVEP evocation in the resting stage. The SSVEP-based stage entails four steps for opening and closing the orthosis completely. Frequencies 8 and 13 Hz LEDs were used for the opening and closing tasks, respectively. During training sessions, subjects were instructed to close the brain switch. Then, they were instructed to open and close the orthosis by gazing at the LEDs mounted on the orthosis. In the next stage, the SSVEP-based BCI was turned off by opening the brain switch. This switch was kept open during the resting period. At the end of the resting period, the brain switch was closed, and SSVEP task was repeated. After this experiment, subjects undertook

TABLE 1: A comparison of several different BCI hybrid systems.

Paper #	Hybrid type	System organization	Improvement	Number of subjects	Classification
[15]	ERD, SSVEP	Simultaneous	Accuracy significantly improved compared to ERD and slightly better than SSVEP	14	LDA
[16]	ERD, SSVEP	Sequential	False positive rate was reduced	6	FLDA
[27]	ERD, SSVEP	Sequential	Application of BCI for FES triggering was improved	3	Filters and thresholds
[28]	ERD, SSVEP	Simultaneous	Feedbacks were added to the work done in [15]	12	LDA
[29]	P300, SSVEP	Sequential	Improved ITR	10	FLDA and BLDA
[30]	P300, SSVEP	Sequential	New application (smart home)	3	LDA
[31]	P300, ERD	Sequential	Improvement in application (wheelchair control)	2	Frequency analysis
[32]	P300, ERD	Sequential	Expand control functions in virtual environment	4	SVM and FLDA
[33]	P300, ERD	Simultaneous	Increase reliability	4	Fisher's discriminant analysis
[34]	ERD, NIRS	Simultaneous	Improvement in classification accuracy and performance	14	LDA
[35]	EEG, EMG	Simultaneous	Improvement in performance	12	Frequency analysis and Gaussian classifier
[36]	ERD, EOG	Simultaneous	Improvement in classification accuracy, reduction in number of electrodes and training time	3	Frequency analysis
[37]	ERD, EOG	Sequential	Improvement in performance	7	LDA

the SSVEP-based BCI task alone and the LEDs were flickering during the resting period. For SSVEP detection, the power density spectrum was used. For the activity period, the true positive rate and false positive rate were measured and for resting period, the false positive rate. It was shown that false positive rate was reduced by more than 50% when hybrid BCI was utilized.

SSVEP and ERD were combined in [27] to make a two-stage hybrid BCI system for triggering a Functional Electrical Stimulation (FES) system. In the first stage, SSVEP was presented for object selection. For evoking SSVEP, three LEDs with 15, 17 and 19 Hz frequencies were considered. The EEG was acquired from O1, O2, and Oz channels while considering Cz as a reference. The object selection task represented three basic grasps: palmar, lateral and precision grasp. For the analysis, Oz channel was chosen as the SSVEP activity in this channel was more noticeable compared to other channels. For SSVEP detection, Butterworth's band pass filters were used to separate frequency bands and a threshold for each subject was fixed manually. After selecting one of the three grasp options based on SSVEP, the next task was reaching movement in which ERD-based BCI was used. EEG signals for this task were recorded from the C3 channel. The Cz channel was used as the reference point. The signal was filtered utilizing Butterworth's band pass filters. The detection algorithm was based on the real-time mu and beta band-power estimation. The signal was compared with the manual adjusted threshold and a drop under the threshold was considered as a movement command. 98.1% accuracy was achieved in the SSVEP stage. Using mu and beta bands, 100% and 98.1% accuracy were achieved, respectively. This study showed that the presented hybrid BCI can be

considered as one of the appropriate combinations for FES triggering application.

In general, hybrid BCIs are more complex and depending on the types of the BCIs, the difficulty may be increased and user acceptability may be decreased. The user acceptability can be measured based on a questionnaire from the subjects. In [28], subjects found the hybrid BCI slightly more difficult than non-hybrid BCIs. In [28], ERD and SSVEP were combined for a simultaneous hybrid task. Bipolar channels C3, Cz, C4, O1, and O2 were utilized for EEG recording. After training sessions, in the online run for SSVEP task, a cue pointed to the top LED, which was flickering with 8 Hz and then pointed to the bottom 13 Hz LED. Subjects received a real-time feedback from a rectangular appearing on the screen. During the ERD task, a cue pointed to the top of the screen and subjects imagined the opening and closing of both hands. When the cue pointed to the bottom of screen, subjects were instructed to imagine moving both feet. In the hybrid condition, both tasks were done simultaneously. The data from the training sessions was used for setting up the LDA classifier. The cross-validation classification accuracy was calculated for both online and the training sessions. In the training sessions, mean classification accuracy was 79.9%, 98.1%, and 96.5% for ERD, SSVEP, and hybrid condition, respectively. The analysis of the online performance showed that the mean classification accuracy was 76.9%, 94%, and 95.6% for ERD, SSVEP, and hybrid condition. For the same conditions maximum ITR was 3.2, 6.1, and 6.3 bits per min. In another analysis, the ERD and SSVEP features were classified separately in the hybrid BCI which showed that subjects were not doing only one of the tasks. Based on a questionnaire, two subjects indicated that hybrid BCI was much more difficult and their performance declined compared to the SSVEP condition. Four subjects indicated that there was not any difference in difficulty of the hybrid condition compared to two other conditions and their performance stayed the same or improved in the hybrid condition. Overall from the questionnaire, the hybrid condition was moderately more difficult. Comparing the results of this experience with the previous one [15], improvement was seen in the ERD results as the performance of the task had been changed (right hand versus left hand movement imagination in the previous study and both hand versus both feet movement imagination in this study). Other results, such as the lower accuracy in ERD condition and the higher performance in SSVEP condition, were consistent. The accuracy in the hybrid BCI is not significantly different from the SSVEP condition. By changing the classification or the combinations of the features, improvement in results may appear. However, the reliability of the system is improved as the SSVEP BCI is added to the conventional ERD BCI system. For subjects with low performance with ERD, or in the case of fatigue, the SSVEP BCI is appropriate option.

3.2. P300-SSVEP Hybrid BCI. P300 and SSVEP BCI were introduced as hybrids in an asynchronous BCI system in [29]. It seems the P300 and SSVEP combination worked well as the stimuli for evoking both patterns, which can be shown on one screen simultaneously. The P300 paradigm considered in this study is a 6 × 6 speller matrix based on the original P300 row/column paradigm introduced by Farwell and Donchin [13]. Only one frequency is allocated for the SSVEP paradigm. The background color was flashed with a frequency slightly less than 18 Hz. The background color change facilitates the SSVEP detection. During the classification, P300 and SSVEP signals were separated by a band pass filter. The SSVEP was utilized as a control state (CS) detection. When the user was gazing at the screen, the SSVEP was detected and it was assumed that the user intended to send a command. The system detected the P300 target selection and CS simultaneously.

For SSVEP detection, the mean power spectral density (PSD) in the narrow band near the desired frequency and the PSD in the wider range near the desired frequency were utilized in an objective function. These values were subtracted from each other and divided over the PSD value from the wide band and the function value was compared to a specified threshold. During the data acquisition, the channels for acquiring EEG signals were not fixed for all subjects. For P300 classification, Bayesian linear discriminant analysis (BLDA) or Fischer's linear discriminant analysis (FLDA) were utilized [39, 40]. The experiment was presented as an offline and online test. Ten subjects participated in the experiment. In the offline test, forty characters were presented for detection, which were divided into four groups. For better evaluation, SSVEP was presented only to two groups out of four groups. In CS, subjects were instructed to count the number of times they distinguished the highlighted character. In the non-control state (NCS), subjects were instructed to do a mental task like multiplication of two numbers and relax with closed eyes. For four out of five subjects, the accuracy

was improved insignificantly during the presence of SSVEP and P300 detection was not determinate. Between the ten character's detection, there was a break of a certain time, which was due to the subject pressing a keyboard button. When the NCS time was almost finished, an auditory cue alerted subjects. For P300 an average classification accuracy of 96.5% and control state detection accuracy of 88% with the information transfer rate (ITR) of 20 bits/min were achieved during the offline test. The online test was presented under a semi synchronous condition. The experiment consisted of blocks with five rounds, for detecting each character. SSVEP detection for at least three out of five runs showed the control state detection by the subject, and P300 was detected during the control state. If the control state was not detected, the "=" character would be shown on the screen. The break time and the auditory alert were the same as the offline test. An average control state detection accuracy of 88.15%, a classification accuracy of 94.44%, and an ITR of 19.05 bits/min were achieved during the online test.

P300 and SSVEP combination was also introduced to control smart home environments in [30]. P300-based BCI was used for controlling the virtual smart home environment and SSVEP was implemented as a toggle switch for the P300 BCI operation. Results from this experiment show that P300 is suitable for discrete control commands and SSVEP is suitable for continuous control signals. The hybrid BCI achieved high accuracy and reliability in all subjects.

3.3. P300-Motor Imagery Hybrid BCI. Another possible combination for a hybrid BCI is P300 and motor imagery (MI)-based BCI [31–33]. The basic concept in this type of hybrid is based on the features of P300 and ERD/ERS in control applications. P300 is a reliable BCI type for selecting one item out of several items and can be used for discrete control commands. On the other hand, due to the low degree of freedom presented by MI-based BCI, this type of BCI is more efficient for continuous control commands. These two types of BCIs can be joined to present more complicated control commands in one task.

In [31], for controlling a wheelchair in a home environment, several approaches using different BCI techniques were introduced. The wheelchair control commands were divided into three steps.

Step 1 (Destination Selection). In this task, the user should select the destination of the wheelchair motion by selecting one of the items among a list of destinations. To implement this control command, an accurate and reliable interface is needed and false acceptance rates should be as low as possible. For this task, a P300 BCI presented at a screen was utilized. The experiments on healthy subjects showed a response time of about 20 seconds, the false acceptance rate 2.5% and the error less than 3%. The results showed that P300 was an appropriate option for the interface. But there are a couple of points to be considered: First, all subjects were healthy. For users with severe disability, the accuracy of the results may differ. Second, there is concern about the applicability of the interface, if it is proper for daily use. A more applicable situation should be considered for evaluating this approach.

Step 2 (*Navigation*). An autonomous motion control was introduced for this step. The destination was selected and the wheelchair started its motion toward the destination following virtual guiding paths. A proximity sensor was considered for stopping the wheelchair facing obstacles.

Step 3 (*Stopping Command*). For this control command, the interface needs to be fast, reliable and have a low false acceptance rate. Two approaches for a stopping command were presented. The first approach was the fast P300, in which, on the screen, there is only one item "The Stop" and the task is the detection of user's intention. Experimental results showed reduction in response time. However, increase in false acceptance makes this approach inapplicable. The second approach was to use a mu-beta BCI. The position of a cursor was considered for presenting the visual feedback for the mu-beta BCI system and the control of the cursor was based on an arm movement imagination. Results showed approximately the same response time as the fast P300 approach, but for false acceptance, a rate of zero was achieved. Since the low false acceptance rate and fast response are the most important needs for this type of BCI, it seems that mu-beta BCI is a more reliable system for this application.

In [32], different states and control commands needed for operating the system were controlled in a virtual environment. P300/MI hybrid BCI was used for operating the system. Two sequential states covered the areas of the virtual environment, navigation, and device control state. The interface strategy is explained as follows. For navigation, MI BCI was used with the continuous control commands limited number of commands. By imagination of left and right hand movement, control commands were issued. The position in the virtual environment was updated by each control command.

In the device control state, the commands were discrete. By considering features of control commands and paradigms, an interface was developed. For this paradigm, the P300 oddball paradigm was considered. When the area coverage changed to the device control state, the MI command detection stopped and the controller switched to system state. The system state then switched to device control state automatically. The P300 BCI presented the control panel to subjects. A switch for navigation happened by the selection of the "quit" command using the P300 oddball paradigm. If the "quit" was not detected after 6 commands, the controller would switch to the system state automatically.

Experiments were performed by four subjects. To evaluate the hybrid approach, the experiment was also implemented for P300 and MI BCIs separately. 22 testing runs were considered in three blocks: (1) A block for hybrid control testing, (2) A block for MI-based navigation, and (3) A block for P300-based device control. Three tasks with a combination of navigation and device control commands were considered for evaluating the hybrid control strategy. In block presenting MI-based navigation, the tasks were the same, with the difference that in the device control state areas, the device control panels were not evoked. In the third block, navigation was not available and two of the tasks were tested

for P300 BCI evaluation. The online accuracy was used for comparing different approaches. Comparing the P300 task in the hybrid BCI and the single P300 BCI showed little reduction in the accuracy of the hybrid strategy. The accuracy for two of the subjects reduced in MI part of the hybrid BCI compared to the single MI BCI. However, by utilizing the hybrid BCI, more complicated tasks can be accomplished in a virtual environment.

In [33], P300 and ERD were introduced to be components of the hybrid BCI in robotic control decision applications. Parallel and asynchronous classifications were introduced. The system task was to detect the intended pattern. Classification accuracy was evaluated during the experiment, which was considered for presenting the hybrid. Sixty trials were presented to four subjects: thirty trials for P300 presentation and thirty trials for MI. During the second thirty trials, the P300 stimuli were also presented but the subjects were not supposed to pay any attention to the stimuli.

3.4. EEG (MI-Based)-NIRS Hybrid BCI. A type of hybrid BCI that uses EEG and NIRS [41] was introduced by [34]. Coyle et al. [4] introduced an approach of utilizing NIRS as an optical BCI. In [34], EEG and NIRS measurements were utilized simultaneously for ERD-based BCIs. In this study, the experiment consisted of 2 blocks of motor execution and 2 blocks of motor imagery. For all blocks, both EEG and NIRS were measured simultaneously. The increase in concentration of oxygenated hemoglobins (HbO) and decrease in concentration of deoxygenated hemoglobins (HbR) were measured using NIRS. The global peak cross-validation accuracy for each subject was considered for evaluation of the hybrid BCI. The mean classification accuracies of HbO, HbR, and EEG for executed movement tasks were 71.1%, 73.3%, and 90.8%. For motor imagery tasks they were 71.7%, 65.0%, and 78.2%. The mean classification accuracies of EEG/HbO, EEG/HbR, and EEG/HbO/HbR for executed movement tasks were 92.6%, 93.2%, and 87.4%, and for motor imagery tasks were 83.2%, 80.6%, and 83.1%, respectively. It was shown that the combination of EEG and NIRS improved the classification accuracy in both MI and executed movement tasks. However, the information transfer rate may decrease. This type of hybrid BCI may enhance the performance of subjects who are not able to use EEG-based BCI properly.

3.5. SSVEP-NIRS Hybrid BCI. The NIRS-based BCI was used as a brain switch for a SSVEP BCI system [26]. The objective was to open and close an orthosis. One subject with four runs performed an experiment. A 60 sec break was considered between two runs. For starting a command, the optical BCI was utilized as a switch for SSVEP BCI starting point. By using a switch, false positives were detected during the first two runs, but in the third run, the performance was improved and only one false positive occurred. In the last run, the performance was perfect with 100% accuracy.

3.6. EEG-EMG Hybrid BCI. EEG and EMG were fused to devise a hybrid BCI in [35]. EEG signals were recorded through 16 channels. EMG activities were recorded from four channels over the flexor and extensor of the right and the left forearms. Two classifiers were used for EEG and EMG and the probabilities from these classifiers were used for controlling the BCI feedback. In the first approach of this experiment, a switch with weights equally balanced between the two classifiers was implemented between the input channels as the fusion of EEG and EMG. In the second approach, the Bayesian fusion method was utilized. Two conditions were considered for EEG and EMG separately and four conditions for the fusion of EEG and EMG depending on the increase of muscular fatigue. The accuracy for EEG activity alone was 73% and for EMG activity alone was 87%. It was improved 91% in the hybrid BCI, in the first approach, the accuracy was 90% for 10% attenuation due to the fatigue, 85% for 50% attenuation, and 73% for 90% attenuation. Results had the same trend in the second approach with smaller standard deviation (SD). The accuracy was 92% for 50% attenuation, and 60.4% for 90% attenuation. In the third condition, the accuracy achieved was less than the accuracy in EEG BCI and this is because of the assumption of fixed value sources in the Bayesian fusion technique calculations. Utilizing multimodal fusion techniques led to enhancement in performance reliability.

3.7. EEG-EOG Hybrid BCI. Since the majority of people with disabilities can have control on their eye movement, the electrooculogram (EOG) signals could be an appropriate option as input signals for BCI system. EEG and EOG combination was introduced to make a hybrid BCI [36]. In this study, EOG and EEG signals were taken from two channels and were utilized simultaneously. The technique in generating control commands based on EEG/EOG hybrid BCI is explained as follows.

The "turn left" and "turn right" control commands were derived from EOG signals based on the right/left eye gazing pattern. Subjects performed maximum right and left eye gazing, and the positive and negative potential were recorded, respectively. 75% of the recorded amplitudes were considered as the threshold for detecting the right and left eye movements. If the amplitude recorded from the right eye during the trials was greater than the threshold related to the right eye, the "turn right" command was detected. For the "turn left" control command detection, the absolute value of the negative potential recorded from the left eye should be greater than the related threshold. If both values were less than the related threshold values, the "no action" control command was detected. Classification accuracy of 100% was achieved for "turn left" and "turn right" control commands. Average accuracy of 95% was achieved for "no action" control command. The "forward", "no action", and "completely stop" control commands were detected from EEG. The parameter used for deriving the control commands from the EEG was PSD in the alpha and beta band. A threshold was considered for comparison to the maximum PSD detected from the alpha and beta band. Three subjects in three trials and 50 control commands in each trial performed experiments. At the beginning of the test, software calibration was performed by the subjects. The maximum PSD in alpha band was

recorded from the subjects with closed eyes and 75% of the PSD from the calibration was considered as threshold. For the "completely stop" command, the subjects were instructed to close their eyes to increase the alpha activity. Then, the maximum PSD in the alpha band was compared to a threshold. If the maximum PSD was greater than the threshold, the "completely stop" command was issued. For the "forward" control command, the subjects were instructed to think about moving forward. If the maximum PSD recorded in the beta band was greater than the maximum PSD recorded in the alpha band, the "forward" control was issued. The "no action" control command was issued if the maximum PSD in the beta band was less than the maximum PSD in the alpha band and both were less than the threshold. The average classification accuracy over the whole trials was 100% for "completely stop" and 87% for "forward" control commands. The "no action" control command was common in both EEG and EOG control command detection parts and the average classification accuracy of 95% was related to the both parts of the task. The interface implementation and the feedback were presented by employing the test on a toy truck. In addition to high classification accuracy, small number of electrodes and short training time showed the advantage of introduced hybrid.

In another approach [37], a self-paced BCI system was combined with an eye-tracker system to establish a self-paced hybrid BCI [26]. In this system, for cursor control, an eye tracker was utilized by detecting the user's eye gaze. A BCI was utilized for clicking on a selected item on computer screen. Subjects were instructed to first gaze at an intended letter on the screen to select it, then for click on the selected letter, hand extension movement was needed. EEG was recorded from the cortex area with 15 electrodes. For EOG, two pairs of electrodes were used. In addition, four pairs of electrodes were used for recording facial muscle activities, from which the facial muscle artefacts can be detected. PSD of 30 combinations of bipolar EEG channels was computed based on Fast Fourier Transform (FFT). For feature selection, stepwise LDA was considered [42]. Then, the features were classified with LDA and adaptive LDA and for more improvement moving average.

For removing EOG and EMG artefacts from the EEG signal, an algorithm was proposed in [43], which showed improvement in the performance of the introduced self-paced hybrid BCI [37]. Stationary wavelet transform and an adaptive threshold mechanism were used in the proposed algorithm. Results were evaluated based on two types of data; real EEG signals with simulated artefacts (semi-simulated EEG signals) and real EEG signals. In semi-simulated EEG signals, signal distortion was decreased and in real EEG signals, the true positive rate was increased using the proposed algorithm.

4. Conclusion

To overcome limitations and disadvantages of conventional BCIs, different BCI systems or BCI and non-BCI systems can be combined to form a "hybrid BCI". In this paper, different methods of establishing a hybrid BCI system were discussed and compared. Hybrid BCIs have been used for different applications such as 2D control of a cursor, target selection, and virtual environment.

There are several advantages of sequential combination when one of the BCIs is used as a switch or different BCIs are used for different tasks sequentially. When combined sequentially, complicated tasks can be distributed to several stages in series. For each stage, a specific BCI can be used. An example of this approach is a virtual environment application [30]. Based on the required type of control commands, different BCI systems can be implemented. In [16], one BCI (ERD) was used as a switch for another BCI (SSVEP) and the false positive rate was decreased for this sequential hybrid BCI. However, the main advantage of the simultaneous combination is that in general the accuracy can be improved if the BCIs are combined appropriately for all subjects. With adaptive pattern recognition algorithms, a hybrid system can adapt to subjects based on their performance. In addition, classification methods can use more BCI outputs. Hybrid BCIs combining different systems simultaneously may be more complicated than a single BCI and more difficult to be accepted by all users. Therefore, the paradigm design of a hybrid BCI plays a very important role in the overall performance of the system. Similarly, when a BCI system is combined with a non-BCI, which is not based on EEG signals, the system performance can be improved. In general, in a hybrid BCI, the complexity of the system paradigm is increased compared to a non-hybrid BCI. Therefore, the use of hybrid systems might be more complicated from the user's point of view. Thus, in designing a hybrid system paradigm, the complexity and user acceptability are important performance criteria to be considered carefully. Another consideration for the user acceptability is the number of channels used in a hybrid BCI system.

In conclusion, although hybrid BCIs have shown great improvements in several performance criteria such as accuracy and information transfer rate, complexity of the system, and user acceptability should be reported as important performance criteria of hybrid BCI systems. With the current trend in introducing hybrid BCIs, we will soon see more than two BCI systems combined sequentially or simultaneously. It is also possible to combined BCIs in a combined sequentially/simultaneously approach. This will create a network of BCIs which cannot be distinguished as sequential or simultaneous any more. For example, for tasks with heavy object selections, SSVEP can be used for one stage and P300 for another stage. After the object selection, ERD/ERS BCI would be presented for continuous control tasks for other commands.

References

[1] J. R. Wolpaw, N. Birbaumer, D. J. McFarland, G. Pfurtscheller, and T. M. Vaughan, "Brain-computer interfaces for communication and control," *Clinical Neurophysiology*, vol. 113, no. 6, pp. 767–791, 2002.

[2] N. Weiskopf, R. Veit, M. Erb et al., "Physiological self-regulation of regional brain activity using real-time functional magnetic resonance imaging (fMRI): methodology and exemplary data," *NeuroImage*, vol. 19, no. 3, pp. 577–586, 2003.

[3] S. Waldert, H. Preissl, E. Demandt et al., "Hand movement direction decoded from MEG and EEG," *Journal of Neuroscience*, vol. 28, no. 4, pp. 1000–1008, 2008.

[4] S. Coyle, T. Ward, C. Markham, and G. McDarby, "On the suitability of near-infrared (NIR) systems for next-generation brain-computer interfaces," *Physiological Measurement*, vol. 25, no. 4, pp. 815–822, 2004.

[5] N. Birbaumer, N. Ghanayim, T. Hinterberger et al., "A spelling device for the paralysed," *Nature*, vol. 398, no. 6725, pp. 297–298, 1999.

[6] E. E. Sutter, "The brain response interface: communication through visually-induced electrical brain responses," *Journal of Microcomputer Applications*, vol. 15, no. 1, pp. 31–45, 1992.

[7] J. J. Vidal, "Toward direct brain-computer communication," *Annual Review of Biophysics and Bioengineering*, vol. 2, pp. 157–180, 1973.

[8] J. J. Vidal, "Real-time detection of brain events in EEG," *Proceedings of the IEEE*, vol. 65, no. 5, pp. 633–641, 1977.

[9] B. Allison, J. Faller, and C. H. Neuper, "BCIs that use steady-state visual evoked potentials or slow cortical potentials," in *Brain-Computer Interfaces: Principles and Practice*, Wolpaw and E. W. Wolpaw, Eds., Oxford University Press, 2012.

[10] E. Sellers, Y. Arbel, and E. Donchin, "BCIs that uses P300 event-related potentials," in *Brain-Computer Interfaces: Principles and Practice*, J. Wolpaw and E. W. Wolpaw, Eds., Oxford University Press, 2012.

[11] J. Kalcher, D. Flotzinger, C. Neuper, S. Gölly, and G. Pfurtscheller, "Graz brain-computer interface II: towards communication between humans and computers based on online classification of three different EEG patterns," *Medical and Biological Engineering and Computing*, vol. 34, no. 5, pp. 382–388, 1996.

[12] B. Z. Allison, E. W. Wolpaw, and J. R. Wolpaw, "Brain-computer interface systems: progress and prospects," *Expert Review of Medical Devices*, vol. 4, no. 4, pp. 463–474, 2007.

[13] L. A. Farwell and E. Donchin, "Talking off the top of your head: toward a mental prosthesis utilizing event-related brain potentials," *Electroencephalography and Clinical Neurophysiology*, vol. 70, no. 6, pp. 510–523, 1988.

[14] C. Brunner, B. Z. Allison, D. J. Krusienski et al., "Improved signal processing approaches in an offline simulation of a hybrid brain-computer interface," *Journal of Neuroscience Methods*, vol. 188, no. 1, pp. 165–173, 2010.

[15] B. Z. Allison, C. Brunner, V. Kaiser, G. R. Müller-Putz, C. Neuper, and G. Pfurtscheller, "Toward a hybrid brain-computer interface based on imagined movement and visual attention," *Journal of Neural Engineering*, vol. 7, no. 2, Article ID 026007, 2010.

[16] G. Pfurtscheller, T. Solis-Escalante, R. Ortner, P. Linortner, and G. R. Muller-Putz, "Self-paced operation of an SSVEP-based orthosis with and without an imagery-based "brain switch": a feasibility study towards a hybrid BCI," *IEEE Transactions on Neural Systems and Rehabilitation Engineering*, vol. 18, no. 4, pp. 409–414, 2010.

[17] B. Allison, T. Luth, D. Valbuena, A. Teymourian, I. Volosyak, and A. Graser, "BCI demographics: How many (and what kind of) people can use a SSVEP BCI?" *IEEE Transactions on Neural Systems and Rehabilitation Engineering*, vol. 18, no. 2, pp. 107–116, 2010.

[18] E. E. Sutter, "The visual evoked response as a communication channel," in *Proceedings of the Symposium on Biosensors*, pp. 95–100, 1984.

[19] Y. Wang, Y. T. Wang, and T. P. Jung, "Visual stimulus design for high-rate SSVEP BCI," *Electronics Letters*, vol. 46, no. 15, pp. 1057–1058, 2010.

[20] R. Fazel-Rezai, B. Z. Allison, C. Guger, E. W. Sellers, S. C. Kleih, and A. Kübler, "P300 brain computer interface: current challenges and emerging trends," *Frontiers in Neuroengineering*, vol. 5, 2012.

[21] E. Donchin and M. G. Coles, "Is the P300 component a manifestation of context updating?" *Behavioral and Brain Functions*, vol. 11, pp. 357–374, 1998.

[22] W. Lutzenberger, T. Elbert, B. Rockstroh, and N. Birbaumer, "The effects of self-regulation of slow control potentials on performance in a signal detection task," *International Journal of Neuroscience*, vol. 9, no. 3, pp. 175–183, 1979.

[23] A. Kübler, B. Kotchoubey, T. Hinterberger et al., "The thought translation device: a neurophysiological approach to communication in total motor paralysis," *Experimental Brain Research*, vol. 124, no. 2, pp. 223–232, 1999.

[24] G. Pfurtscheller and F. H. Lopes Da Silva, "Event-related EEG/MEG synchronization and desynchronization: basic principles," *Clinical Neurophysiology*, vol. 110, no. 11, pp. 1842–1857, 1999.

[25] http://www.scopus.com/home.url.

[26] G. Pfurtscheller, B. Z. Allison, C. Brunner et al., "The hybrid BCI," *Frontiers in Neuroscience*, vol. 4, 2010.

[27] A. Savic, U. Kisic, and M. Popovic, "Toward a hybrid BCI for grasp rehabilitation," in *Proceedings of the 5th European Conference of the International Federation for Medical and Biological Engineering Proceedings*, pp. 806–809, 2012.

[28] C. Brunner, B. Z. Allison, C. Altstätter, and C. Neuper, "A comparison of three brain-computer interfaces based on event-related desynchronization, steady state visual evoked potentials, or a hybrid approach using both signals," *Journal of Neural Engineering*, vol. 8, no. 2, Article ID 025010, 2011.

[29] R. C. Panicker, S. Puthusserypady, and Y. Sun, "An asynchronous P300 BCI with SSVEP-based control state detection," *IEEE Transactions on Biomedical Engineering*, vol. 58, no. 6, pp. 1781–1788, 2011.

[30] G. Edlinger, C. Holzner, and C. Guger, "A hybrid brain-computer interface for smart home control," in *Proceedings of the 14th international conference on Human-Computer Interaction. Interaction Techniques and Environments*, pp. 417–426, 2011.

[31] B. Rebsamen, E. Burdet, Q. Zeng et al., "Hybrid P300 and Mu-Beta brain computer interface to operate a brain controlled wheelchair," in *Proceedings of the 2nd International Convention on Rehabilitation Engineering and Assistive Technology*, pp. 51–55, 2008.

[32] Y. Su, Y. Qi, J. X. Luo et al., "A hybrid brain-computer interface control strategy in a virtual environment," *Journal of Zhejiang University*, vol. 12, no. 5, pp. 351–361, 2011.

[33] H. Riechmann, N. Hachmeister, H. Ritter, and A. Finke, "Asynchronous, parallel on-line classification of P300 and ERD for an efficient hybrid BCI," in *Proceedings of the 5th International IEEE/EMBS Conference on Neural Engineering (NER '11)*, pp. 412–415, May 2011.

[34] S. Fazli, J. Mehnert, J. Steinbrink et al., "Enhanced performance by a hybrid NIRS-EEG brain computer interface," *Neuroimage*, vol. 59, pp. 519–529, 2011.

[35] R. Leeb, H. Sagha, R. Chavarriaga, and J. D. R. Millán, "A hybrid brain-computer interface based on the fusion of electroencephalographic and electromyographic activities," *Journal of Neural Engineering*, vol. 8, no. 2, Article ID 025011, 2011.

[36] Y. Punsawad, Y. Wongsawat, and M. Parnichkun, "Hybrid EEG-EOG brain-computer interface system for practical machine control," in *Proceedings of the IEEE Engineering in Medicine and Biology Society Conference (EMBC '10)*, pp. 1360–1363, 2010.

[37] X. Yong, M. Fatourechi, R. K. Ward, and G. E. Birch, "The design of a point-and-click system by integrating a self-paced brain-computer interface with an eye-tracker," *IEEE Journal on Emerging and Selected Topics in Circuits and Systems*, vol. 1, no. 4, pp. 590–602, 2011.

[38] A. Kubler and K. R. Muller, "An introduction to brain-computer interfacing," in *Toward Brain-Computer Interfacing*, G. Dornhedge, J. R. Millan, T. Hinterberger, D. J. McFarland, and K. R. Muller, Eds., pp. 1–25, MIT Press, Cambridge, Mass, USA, 2007.

[39] D. J. Krusienski, E. W. Sellers, F. Cabestaing et al., "A comparison of classification techniques for the P300 Speller," *Journal of Neural Engineering*, vol. 3, no. 4, article 299, 2006.

[40] U. Hoffmann, J. M. Vesin, T. Ebrahimi, and K. Diserens, "An efficient P300-based brain-computer interface for disabled subjects," *Journal of Neuroscience Methods*, vol. 167, no. 1, pp. 115–125, 2008.

[41] T. Tsubone, T. Muroga, and Y. Wada, "Application to robot control using brain function measurement by near-infrared spectroscopy," in *Proceedings of the 29th IEEE Engineering in Medicine and Biology Society (EMBC '07)*, pp. 5342–5345, August 2007.

[42] P. A. Lachenbruch and M. Goldstein, "Discriminant analysis," *Biometrics*, vol. 35, no. 1, pp. 69–85, 1979.

[43] X. Yong, M. Fatourechi, R. K. Ward, and G. E. Birch, "Automatic artefact removal in a self-paced hybrid brain-computer interface system," *Journal of NeuroEngineering and Rehabilitation*, vol. 9, article 50, 2012.

16

Designing Interactive Applications to Support Novel Activities

Hyowon Lee,[1] **Nazlena Mohamad Ali,**[2] **and Lynda Hardman**[3]

[1] *Singapore University of Technology and Design, 20 Dover Drive, Singapore 138682*
[2] *Institute of Visual Informatics (IVI), Universiti Kebangsaan Malaysia, 43600 Bangi, Selangor, Malaysia*
[3] *Centrum Wiskunde & Informatica (CWI) and University of Amsterdam, Science Park 123, 1098 XG Amsterdam, The Netherlands*

Correspondence should be addressed to Hyowon Lee; hlee@sutd.edu.sg

Academic Editor: Kerstin S. Eklundh

R&D in media-related technologies including multimedia, information retrieval, computer vision, and the semantic web is experimenting on a variety of computational tools that, if sufficiently matured, could support many novel activities that are not practiced today. Interactive technology demonstration systems produced typically at the end of their projects show great potential for taking advantage of technological possibilities. These demo systems or "demonstrators" are, even if crude or farfetched, a significant manifestation of the technologists' visions in transforming emerging technologies into novel usage scenarios and applications. In this paper, we reflect on design processes and crucial design decisions made while designing some successful, web-based interactive demonstrators developed by the authors. We identify methodological issues in applying today's requirement-driven usability engineering method to designing this type of novel applications and solicit a clearer distinction between designing mainstream applications and designing novel applications. More solution-oriented approaches leveraging design thinking are required, and more pragmatic evaluation criteria is needed that assess the role of the system in exploiting the technological possibilities to provoke further brainstorming and discussion. Such an approach will support a more efficient channelling of the technology-to-application transformation which are becoming increasingly crucial in today's context of rich technological possibilities.

1. Introduction

Technological advancements are at an unprecedented pace. Supported by ever-increasing computing power, storage capacity, network infrastructure, and scalability and further fuelled by the general public's awareness of technology and their increasing willingness to try new services and the consequent marketing opportunities, many technology research laboratories around the world are fiercely investigating and experimenting on technological possibilities as never before. Multimedia, computer vision, information retrieval, artificial intelligence, and language technology are some examples of computational technology fields that are leading this advancement boom, promising a high-impact outcome that will shape the way we interact with technology as well as how we interact with each other in the coming years.

In dominantly technically focused projects that have long been developed in these fields, the end of a project often sees a "demonstrator" or "demo system" that showcases possible end-user interactivity with the developed piece of technology. For example, the VideOlympics [1] is an annual event in the multimedia research community to showcase and promote various outcomes of video retrieval research, where the researchers bring to the event their interactive systems and demonstrators that incorporate cutting-edge video retrieval techniques and algorithms. These demonstrators highlight interactivity in which an end user might engage to search, browse, and be entertained by video content in ways that have not been tried before. The technological possibilities witnessed in this event are extremely intriguing and inspirational, although often they display low-quality interaction design and poor usability due to the reasons that will be addressed later in this paper.

Exemplified by these technology demonstration systems are *novel applications*—applications that are new and have no existing user base or usage practice today. Opposed to these are the mainstream or *conventional applications*—applications that support existing practices with existing groups of users, for example, word processing software, library management systems, museum kiosks, and online travel websites. Most of the software industry today is naturally geared towards developing conventional applications to support their current customers' needs.

Very successful in incrementally refining the details of user-interfaces, the *user centred design* approach that focuses on fully understanding and documenting the target users and their work practices into detailed requirements before designing the system is one of the most significant contributions of the human-computer interaction (HCI) discipline with its provision of methods, tools, and procedures to today's software industry. This requirements-driven design methodology works well when developing mainstream applications because it aims to make the system fit as closely as possible to their target users' practices and contexts.

Conversely, applications created in technology research labs as demonstrators and exploratory proof-of-concept prototypes have quite a different purpose to their creation. Novel applications are developed to demonstrate technological possibilities and how they might manifest in user interactivity, help inspire the research community, foster brainstorming and discussion exploring more possibilities from the demonstration, and ground and guide future research directions to more feasible scenarios. Though this type of novel application development effort is an important investment for the future, little understanding of designing for these purposes exists today. With the conventional wisdom of understanding end users and their contexts in the mainstream application development as amply emphasised by HCI and practiced in the industry today, many technology research groups try to adopt user-centred and requirements-driven design methods to guide the development of their demonstrator systems. However, they tend to result in wasted resources due to (i) insufficient information sources from the beginning, notably the absence of user base, and the lack of usage practice and (ii) insufficient know-how and the lack of methodological support for converting the project's technological agenda into effective end-user features.

Given the immense potential of these demonstration systems in shedding light on how the technological advancements could shape our future interactivity with technology, a proper facilitation of suitable tools and methods in place to guide the design process for these novel systems becomes a significant issue.

This paper presents a reflective analysis on some recently completed technology projects. Based on the decade-long, first-hand experience in designing novel demonstrators and applications that incorporate various emerging technological tools, the reflections in this paper focus on how some of the crucial design decisions were made and how they steered the design process, especially in shaping the unidentified user needs and trying to satisfy them. The contributions of this paper are:

(i) to highlight the existence of the on-going work in designing novel applications in technology-related R&D laboratories and to emphasise the significance

of this line of applications in helping shape people's interactivity with technologies in the near future;

(ii) to inform the current situation which many technology R&D communities are facing where the usability engineering approach in the requirements-centred tradition of HCI design methodology they take does not effectively support designing novel applications;

(iii) to characterise the design process and evaluation criteria suitable for this line of applications by reflecting on past projects that resulted in successful novel application development.

Through these contributions, we hope that the activity of designing technology demonstrators will gain the attention that they deserve, a suitable design methodology will be instrumented for technology R&D sectors, and eventually, the pace of innovation in these sectors in turning the emerging technological advancements into feasible and usable application scenarios will accelerate.

2. Designing Novel Application: Three Examples

Within the past 12 years, the authors of this paper have designed over 50 novel interactive systems incorporating some of the advanced and emerging computational technologies, 33 of which resulted in concrete and complete user-interaction strategies, 21 of them were formally user-tested, and 8 of them were deployed and used by people over time. In this section, three examples from them were chosen to illustrate the ways in which novel systems are designed. The examples chosen represent the novel technology systems with 3 quite different degrees of novelty in terms of supporting what people do or do not do today and how much these are expected to change the way people engage in the activities in the near future, that is, from a less novel (shifting the sequence of tasks that people used to do) to a somewhat novel (adding an additional task to enhance the value of what people used to do) to a highly novel (supporting a completely new activity that people have not done before). The chosen examples in this section are on purpose limited to the applications on the same interaction platform, that is, web-based desktop PC applications, in order to reduce the possible discussion points on the affordances of different interaction modalities (and the design decisions to be made for these), so as to help focus on the comparative design decisions made for the respective examples. Through these examples, characteristics of novel application design projects will be highlighted and how their design process differs from a more conventional design process.

2.1. "My Friends' Faces"—Exploiting Face Recognition. This project aimed to develop an application that leverages *automatic face detection* and *recognition* techniques, which have been popular topics in computer vision for many years. Face detection typically uses a combination of visual features (e.g., colour, shape, and texture) and a classifier trained on example faces in photos to determine the existence of a face in a new photo. Face recognition then uses the face detection output to calculate the visual similarity between the detected faces to establish whether two faces belong to the same person. If one detected face had been initially labelled with a person's name, then all other detected faces with the similarity level above a certain threshold can be labelled with the same name. Such techniques can, if accurately performed, considerably reduce the user's manual annotation burden when the number of photos to deal with is large.

The ideation of the application started with the usage context of personal photo management, but it particularly focused on exploiting the face detection and recognition techniques to highlight their power and to show how such techniques might be used to provide new ways of photo consumption that have not been featured before.

One obvious strategy that arose early in the design process was to plug in the face detection and recognition techniques at the back end of any typical personal photo management service such as Flickr or Picasa. When a user visits the website and browses photos as normal, she notices that the photos have already been annotated or tagged with people's names. In this case, the face detection and recognition techniques are there simply to *automate* the manual annotation task without requiring any major interaction shift or change in design on the front end. Many automatic media indexing tools currently being researched and developed have the potential to be used in this way, as they try to automate what human users or indexers had to do conventionally.

Given our focus on emphasising incorporated techniques and providing a feature that had not been tried before, we reexamined the overall idea of a conventional, Flickr-like photo browsing interaction that typically starts with a user selecting a group of photos organised by events, date, and time and then selecting a photo in an event to view an enlarged photo. This led us to the assumption that the need for browsing their photos stems from people's desire to see their friends or family members captured in various situations, and the photos themselves are merely a means of doing it.

We changed the interaction sequence as follows: a user first browses a "face index," which is a list of thumbnail-size faces (face icons) of people who regularly appear in the user's collection (see the left side of Figure 1). The face icons in this list are fully automatically selected and cropped by the system from various photos in the user's collection. Beside each face icon, the name of that person and the frequency of that person's appearance in the collection are indicated. The face index is initially sorted by appearance frequency in the user's collection. Selecting a face icon will retrieve all photos and events that contain that particular person in increasing order of the number of people present in the photos. Figure 1 shows that the user selected "Georgina" in the face index and clicked the "Go" button at the bottom. The result is a panel of photos in the middle of the screen, starting with 1-person photos of Georgina, before proceeding to 2-person photos including Georgina and so on. When the user clicks on any of the retrieved photos, an enlarged version of the photo with its detailed information will appear similar to other conventional personal photo management services.

The interaction difference between this and other conventional photoware might seem subtle, but the novelty of

FIGURE 1: Primary photo access point is the "face index" as fully automatically prepared by the system.

this interaction is the automatically prepared face index and appearance frequency *as the primary access point* and *starting point of interaction*.

The user interface has undergone a dozen refinement iterations with informal testing, a cognitive walkthrough, discussions, and brainstorming throughout the design process, with overall layout and sequencing, individual features and the look and feel modified and refined accordingly. At the end of this project, a formal user evaluation was conducted with 4 test users to identify usability problems and ascertain overall opinions and comments on the application [2]. Among many useful findings, the face index was overall perceived as only "slightly useful," partly due to some missing faces and incorrectly annotated names. When the main premise of the application (i.e., face detection and recognition) does not perform perfectly, the user interface that exploits that feature will reveal such an inaccuracy and the trust of the system by the users decreases immediately. In addition, having used popular photo services such as Flickr and Picasa for many years, our test users naturally wanted interaction styles similar to those.

The application was considered a state-of-the-art system in terms of demonstrating the face recognition technology that revised the conventional photoware interaction to take advantage of the technology and served as a prop in brainstorming for new projects.

2.2. "Mo Músaem Fíorúil" (My Virtual Museum)—Exploiting Object Matching. Identifying objects in images and videos and then comparing the visual characteristics among the identified objects are on-going research topics in the field of multimedia. The seed idea for this application was to exploit an object matching algorithm called the scale-invariant feature transform (SIFT) [3], which uses multiple visual keypoints around the outlines of objects in two images and can determine whether they belong to the same object, even when the two objects show different angles and scales. Before a series of brainstorming sessions and discussions commenced, we had a vague notion of a museum usage scenario where

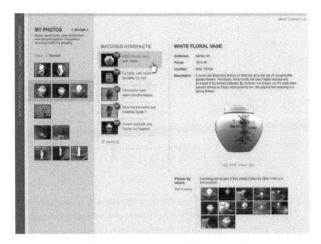

FIGURE 2: User's photos are automatically grouped by unique artefacts and then matched to authoritative photos with the relevant information presented.

FIGURE 3: Reviewing the day's highlights and viewing the past events similar to a particular event from today.

a user visits a museum and takes many photos of museum artefacts and wants to find detailed information about the artefacts after returning home. We developed this notion into a detailed interaction sequence for this application.

We incorporated the SIFT technique's capability in two sequential ways during the user interaction: (1) the system automatically groups the users' photos by unique artefacts, and (2) it matches each group of photos to an authoritative artefact photo from the museum. In the designed scenario, the user comes home and uploads all the photos to the web-based application, whereupon the uploaded photos are presented in groups of unique artefacts. In Figure 2, a total of 11 photos uploaded are shown automatically grouped into 5 rows (on the left column), with each row representing a unique artefact.

The accuracy of the automatic grouping by unique artefacts depends on the performance of the SIFT technique. If the technique did not perform correctly, the user can manually move a misplaced photo from one group into another simply by drag-and-drop action, whereupon the back-end SIFT technique will recalculate and improve the performance for the next stage of interaction in real time.

The user can then select a group, and the most similar artefact candidates from the museum's archive are presented (5 items with circular green icons in the middle column in Figure 2). Here again, the technique's accuracy becomes a design issue: if the SIFT performance was 100% accurate, the stage of presenting the top 5 candidates would have been unnecessary and selecting one group of photos could immediately show the details of that unique artefact matched from the museum's database. Selecting one candidate of the matched artefacts will then present detailed information about that particular artefact (right side of Figure 2). Blighe et al. [4] present more details on this application.

There is no tool today that supports an interaction feature such as this, though there are many museum visitors who take photos of museum artefacts. Potential users, if interviewed, would not have expected or expressed such a feature because it was a purely technological possibility that facilitated such

an application scenario. The design process was more geared towards properly incorporating the SIFT technique in the user interactivity given its imperfect performance, rather than incorporating users' known behaviours and needs.

Though born of technical inspiration with no substantial end-user engagement, the application has become a valuable demonstrator within the multimedia research community as well as more application-focused field such as human-computer interaction that effectively highlighted a technical possibility resulting in a novel usage scenario.

2.3. "My Visual Diary"—Exploiting Event Detection from Lifelog Photos. Visual and continuous lifelogging is an active research area today, but no member of the general public has actually practised a lifelogging activity in any significant way. Using a passive photo capture device such as SenseCam or Vicon Revue (Vicon Revue, Memories for Life, http://viconrevue.com/), our day-to-day activities can be visually recorded on a continuous and long-term basis. Amounting to 2,000–3,000 photos a day (approximately 1 million photos a year, if captured every day), these devices pose a considerable challenge for accessing the captured photos in an easy and meaningful way.

A conventional way to access them would be if, each day, the lifelog user could review that day's photos by quickly slide showing all of the photos temporally, which typically takes 10–30 minutes depending on the speed of the slide show.

Content-based image indexing techniques can automatically group a day's photos by distinctive "events" that happened throughout the day, pick the most representative photos from each event, and determine which events were more important than others that day. While experimenting with various technical possibilities for automatically indexing and structuring months and years of SenseCam photos collected by some of our group members, a visual summarisation idea emerged.

In Figure 3, the main part of the screen presents 19 photos, each representing a major event that happened that day, as automatically chosen by the system. The photo size is proportional to the importance of that event, as calculated by the system by looking at all of the events within the past week and comparing the uniqueness of each event [5]. Using a packing algorithm to display images in a more condensed way [6], the system composes an intriguing comic book-style layout, visually emphasising the outcome of event importance calculation.

For any event presented, clicking on "Find Similar" button retrieves a group of past events that are visually similar to the selected event (in Figure 3, the retrieved similar events are presented on the right side, all of which show the user chatting with a colleague in a lab environment).

As the concept of lifelogging and visual reviewing of one's day after continuous photo capture becomes more widespread and capture devices become cheaper, smaller, and more convenient to carry, people will start experimenting and engaging in such an activity in the near future. This application was created for that time, and it will be at that time when the application could be deployed and user-tested and its features and be refined to better fit to what people at that time will need and want. The application has served as an excellent brainstorming tool to obtain feedback, engage in further discussions, and guide future agendas for content-based indexing research, and the variations derived from this application have been developed for more specific target user groups, including a simplified touch-sensitive version for elderly users [7].

3. Discussion

The previously applications introduced have a number of design aspects in common.

(i) Their usage scenario and interactivity is novel in that the tasks that the applications support are not something people practice today.

(ii) Their design decisions were driven by the aim of exploiting particular technological tools rather than fitting the technology to specific user needs.

(iii) They were developed with a strong design discipline approach rather than a usability engineering approach when establishing solutions.

(iv) They are valuable for demonstrating technical possibilities and provoking further discussions on how they might be applied to create novel activities.

These points will be discussed in more detail below.

3.1. Underlying Needs and Novelty. A novel application implies that there is a *novel activity* that the application can support or the type of activity that is new to people today. The intention of coming up with a novel application, then, is to invent a tool to create a new activity that people can start engaging in to benefit their lives in some way. For example, the activity of tweeting had not existed until the tool Twitter was created, and subsequently people started using it, and the value of using it became apparent. The activities of online video sharing and voting, blogging, social networking,

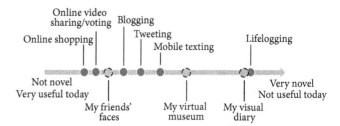

FIGURE 4: Novelty spectrum with example novel activities.

mobile texting, internet shopping, or even TV watching are among the many examples of innovative systems or services that created novel activities (rather than supporting existing activities) at the time of their invention.

At the early stage of the development of the three novel applications in Section 2, establishing clear user needs was problematic because the premise of the projects was to exploit an emerging computational tool in a way that has not been used before. However, there were different degrees in which this problem of lacking the understanding of user needs affected the design process. In the case of My Friends' Faces, once the role the back-end computational tool to be exploited (face detection and recognition) had been mapped to the novel feature of the iconised face index as the interaction starting point, the rest of the design process proceeded in a relatively straightforward manner. In the case of My Visual Diary, however, the uncertainty of user needs and operating the project under that uncertainty strongly influenced the design and evaluation throughout the project, making the undertone of the project quite different from My Friends' Faces. For example, in analysing the user evaluation of My Friends' Faces, it was possible to solicit the test users' views and opinions on the novel feature in comparison to their prior experiences of using other more conventional photo management services because, even with the novel face index mechanism as the default interaction starting point, they were more or less agreeing on the overall purpose and the value of the system under testing; it was not the case for My Visual Diary.

There are different degrees of novelty in the novel applications. Blogging, for example, was a novel activity when it first started, but one might argue that people's inherent need for expressing themselves had existed and manifested in the forms of writing letters and keeping diaries, until the timely online tool came out and satisfied our needs more conveniently and with bigger impact (by being able to reach a wider audience); tweeting activities may be traced to the need for staying connected with people, hitherto satisfied with shorter blog entries or mobile texting, or face-to-face small talk; online video sharing may be traced back to physically posting a parcel of video tapes or CDs that contain family videos; lifelogging activities may be comparable to an extreme case of proactive photo-taking or obsessive note taking during special events. Depending on how novel the need supported by the invented application is compared to any known or existing need, we can draw a spectrum of novelty. Figure 4 depicts some novel activities invented in approximately the last decade and located on the novelty spectrum by the degree of novelty at the time of invention (for they have now become mainstream activities and are thus not considered novel anymore).

For example, online shopping is a less novel activity because the need for shopping had been well known before any online shopping service was invented. Mobile texting is more novel than blogging because the need for instant messaging had not been explicitly known beforehand, while the need for diary keeping had been known.

Also plotted in this spectrum are the three example applications from the previous section. In the case of My Friends' Faces, though the overall activity of online photo browsing and sharing is not novel today, the way the application invites the user to browse the list of faces (instead of a group of photos) as the starting point of interaction is the novel aspect of this application afforded by the fully automatic face detection and recognition techniques. More novel than this is a museum visitor being able to browse his/her photos to gain detailed information about the artefacts. While people do visit museums and take photos of artefacts today, the need for uploading them to a system to organise them by unique artefacts and learn more details was unknown and most likely nonexistent. My Visual Diary, for visual lifelog users, is much more novel, as the need for lifelogging and reviewing one's day is not a familiar concept as a "need" by the general public today.

In some cases, especially those on the left side of the spectrum in Figure 4, we may be able to create novel activities by observing people's existing activities and identifying the inherent needs of those activities before trying to link those needs with recent or emerging technical possibilities. Here, *proxy activities* and *proxy users* could be used to identify useful information as the basis for inventing more novel activities and tools to support them (e.g., studying active photo bloggers to inform the design of a novel photoware system). Conversely, for those activities that are more novel (those on the right side of the spectrum), *observation of people's existing activities is likely to have less benefit* because what is to be created can greatly differ from what people need and practise today. In this sense, those activities on the left side of the novelty spectrum tend to have a greater chance of benefiting from user studies (including interviews and observing people's behaviour) than those activities on the right side, when creating new applications to support them.

The tension between creating novel products and conventional ones has certainly been a reality in industry and a topic of interest in academia, witnessed from the early most advanced yet acceptable (MAYA) principle by the well-known industrial designer Raymond Loewy (Raymond Loewy, The Father of Industrial Design, http://www.raymondloewy.com/) to offer a novel solution but acceptable to current consumers, to a more recent view on how to interpret the phenomenon of incremental versus radical innovations [8]. In a series of consumer studies, Hekkert et al. [9] found that consumers preferred novel designs but not so much novel as to hinder the typical use of it, implying a careful balancing act required by a designer between novelty and typicality. Similar findings are reported in a study of chair design where

the correlation between the level of novelty and aesthetic preference by people was observed as an inverted-U curve [10], implying a moderate level of novelty to be perceived best. More clearly categorising design activities by the *purpose of design* also comes into the picture: "design exploration" to find out what is possible and what would be desirable or ideal, as opposed to "design practice" to build a system that satisfies a specific group of users in a specific context [11]. These different kinds of design activities suggested can be seen as targeting to create applications at different points on the novelty spectrum. The transfer scenarios [12, 13] try to "combine the best of both worlds" of invention (idea generation) and inquiry (study of people) by studying the people with marginal or unusual practices and transferring the main features discovered to a different domain in order to design novel systems or services. Similarly, "matchmaking" method [14] tries to match the already-known, existing, and intended technology to a specific work domain that is not yet clearly defined or established.

Because it is difficult to suddenly come up with a novel activity or novel application that supports such an activity, there have been attempts to explore the methodological solutions to somehow balance between technologically oriented invention (right side of the spectrum) and grounded user study (left side of the spectrum). For example, a framework to align "blue-sky" research with real user interests [15], a playful participatory design to inspire new ideas [16], speed dating method to rapidly and cheaply compare design opportunities well before any prototyping effort is undertaken [17], "technology probe" [18] and other application studies that followed, a participatory envisioning and enactment to make the design-evaluation feedback cycle as dynamic and frequent as possible [19], and recent guidelines on when and how to use such a user enactment [20] are the examples in which the aspects of both users and technology were utilised in trying to come up with new applications on varying points on the novelty spectrum. Each of the methods as mentioned here will be better at creating novel applications on a different range or different points on the novelty spectrum. For example, those methods that involve participatory design approach will more likely end up creating novel applications on the left side, rather than right side, of the spectrum.

The novelty spectrum illustrated here is far from objective or accurate, but one of the aspects it highlights is that designing a novel interactive system can range from switching around the initial information access point (My Friends' Faces) to providing a value-added activity in conjunction with an existing activity (My Virtual Museum) to providing a completely novel activity that might currently be considered obsessive or even ridiculous (My Visual Diary). The spectrum can be used to roughly gauge any group of system or application development in terms of their level of novelty and to guide the kind of approach, tools, and overall mindset required to optimally engage in such development. For example, most of the demonstrator systems showcased at the recent Video Browser Showdown (Video Browser Showdown, at the 19th International Conference on Multimedia Modeling, 7–9 January 2013, available online at http://mmm2013 .org/Video_browser_showdown.htm) where all sorts of novel interactive video search systems had an open competition at a conference venue fall into the left side of the spectrum where the end-user need had been more or less clear from the beginning (quickly search for video clips) although the search features in the systems exploiting the computer vision and information retrieval techniques made them novel and innovative. On the other hand, many prototype systems exhibited at the laboratories such as MIT Media Lab and Interaction Research Studio at the University of London Goldsmiths try to experiment with new affordances that emerging technologies allow even when the result is not what people today have experience about (e.g., "History Tablecloth" [21] shows the trail of objects that had been on the table but moved away later. Nobody actually voiced that such a feature would be useful in our daily lives, but by being able to show such a history of where things had been on the table before, they are trying to discover or create a completely new, potentially beneficial use and need). We can locate this group of prototypes on the right side of the spectrum. Locating any of the developing systems by different research groups or communities on the spectrum provides a rough indication of their stance or agenda in exploring novel possibilities and the kind of weight they place between the knowledge on the end-user needs and the use of technology.

Another aspect the spectrum highlights is that, in general, the less novel is an application, the more useful it is in today's context and vice versa. As we strive to explore more novel applications (the right side of the spectrum), they will be obviously viewed as less useful in today's context because of the unknown nature of the need and activity that the application tries to support. Judging the value of a designed application purely based on its usefulness in today's context is thus not a particularly desirable way to think about future applications.

3.2. Exploiting a Promising but Immature Technology. In the three design examples, some emerging computational techniques served as the seed idea and starting point of the development process. This seems in stark contrast with the way conventional applications are supposed to be designed, but unlike supporting existing needs and known activities, identifying new needs and creating novel activities cannot solely depend on existing practices and known concepts, as implied in the previous section on the novelty spectrum. The design aim of these projects was to exploit a piece of emerging technological advancements as much as possible in the provision of new interaction features, instead of fitting the technology to an identified user need.

One difficulty in doing so is that the technological advancement to be exploited is, by definition, an immature and less-understood technology currently being researched in laboratories. A problematic issue with taking a premature piece of technology out of the lab and developing an application based on it is that it does not perform accurately, reliably or robustly. The developed novel application should be showcased and even user-tested to help explore more avenues for usage scenarios and interaction possibilities. However, when the very element that the design of the application tries to exploit does not function as expected, the value of the

application in the eyes of test users inevitably drops [22] as was the case with My Friends' Faces.

As the technological tools become more mature and accurate as R&D in these areas continues, there will be fewer such issues arising for that application. However, instead of simply expecting the technology to mature in a few years, a more constructive strategy is to design to support such inaccuracy. More and more computational technology research communities are realising that user interactions with the applications could support simple and easy manual correction mechanisms or other work-around solutions to alleviate this problem. For example, My Friends' Faces provides a simple manual name correction feature when the system predicts a person's name incorrectly; in My Virtual Museum, the user interface provides a drag-and-drop feature for a user to manually regroup the photos and a list of candidate photos from which the user can choose, for possible SIFT technique failures, and My Visual Diary has a minislider bar to adjust the number of events presented on the comic-book style panel if the system did not pick an important event initially. These interaction mechanisms have been designed in from the beginning of the development process and thus are seamlessly and gracefully incorporated as part of the overall interaction flow. Leveraging human users' intentional input by encouraging more user feedback and other types of emerging online crowdsourcing mechanisms such as Amazon Mechanical Turk (Amazon Mechanical Turk, artificial artificial intelligence, https://www.mturk.com/) can thus be understood as a way of compensating for the inaccuracy in fully automatic computations and is now increasingly featured in the demonstrators developed by computational technology communities. A unique situation the media technology community is facing today is that in trying to exploit computational tools initially intended to automate the labour-intensive tasks, they are beginning to bring back human users on the scene (or *behind* the scene, to be more accurate) in the form of a large number of anonymous human labours afforded by web connectivity, replacing or complementing the automatic methods.

3.3. Design Ideas Unfold as Project Progresses: Reflective Conversation with the Situation. There is a great deal of general design knowledge base that we can use to develop interaction features. Design principles, guidelines, and heuristics that have been generated, accumulated, and evolved over the past 20 years or so were adhered to in the design of the above examples and used to provide detailed interaction strategies, visual layout, sequencing, and emphasis which were correct and usable [23]. Emphasising the general design knowledge rather than the specific, contextual knowledge where the system will operate will lead to designing applications more "open to interpretation" in many ways [24]. By designing not to fit specific user needs or contexts that we do not know but instead to make the interactivity affordances clear, we have better chances to explore where the technical possibilities exploited in the application could further lead. This contrasts to how a system or an application is to be designed to support existing or conventional activities that people do today where a specific set of requirements and a specific context of usage should be targeted in order to satisfy a specific user needs.

However, using the general design knowledge base as the starting point for novel application design does not guarantee a successful execution of the project. In the three example design cases and indeed most other novel application design projects we have experienced, the absence of a user base and lack of information on the situations and contexts where an application is to operate forced us to take an approach that is strongly design disciplinary rather than scientific or problem solving. Having only vague initial visions on usage with stronger technical intentions (to exploit a particular technological tool), it was not possible to rigorously define and clarify the requirements that would typically drive a design in a mainstream design project. Rather, the earlier part of the design process proceeded mainly by filling in sensible or possible scenario elements by guessing, imagining, and framing; the latter part of the process proceeded by sketching the interaction and continuously revising by going through the sketches while receiving feedback from the members of the project providing the technical possibilities. The sketching activity was strongly helped by the general design knowledge base mentioned above to ensure general usability and clarity in its interaction affordances, but the crucial guidance of the design progress, especially in shaping the overall interaction strategies, occurred through seeing the sketches and critically reflecting on them to make revisions before reflecting again. In this sense, research through design [25] with its propositional, future-oriented and meaning-after-action approach of inquiry, is one of the ways to explain how these novel applications have been designed and experimented. Understanding the mechanisms of designing novel applications may well form an important body of case studies for formalising the Research through Design into a proper methodology as more theoretical and rigorous foundations are being shaped. A move towards "constructive design research" [26] where the construction of product, system or media itself takes the central place in accumulating knowledge will also contribute to shaping the agreed-upon foundation for understanding how novel applications are to be designed.

In our examples of novel applications, the design ideas, sketching, and ways to improve them unfolded and developed as the project progressed, becoming more concrete and detailed as the process continued. It can be said that the required knowledge was created bit by bit along the way, rather than available in large quantity at the beginning. It was impossible to collect all necessary information about the interaction at the beginning to set a definite "problem" and then to find the "solution." In most cases, we faced more elements of solutions readily available to us (technological tools that we wanted to exploit and general design principles and guidelines) than of problems (where the system will be used and what the users want to do in what context).

For My Visual Diary, for example, it was not even clear whether our future users would benefit from seeing a list of past events that were similar to a given event that happened today or, for that matter, whether they will want to review their days every evening. Having great uncertainty in the problem space and yet being fixated on finding solutions

regardless via continuous reflective conversation with the sketching [27] is a typical characteristic of design practise in domains such as architecture and industrial design [28, 29]. With regard to novel interactive application design, this design practise characteristic seems to be even more prominent and crucial. For example, the typical design characteristic of quickly generating possible solutions then putting efforts into refining them, instead of investing in fully understanding the problem first, renders itself well for novel application design situations where the weak initial information without definite and clear target contexts force the designer to dwell on the solution space rather than the problem space. In particular, design expertise exhibits the ability to work well with problems that do not lend themselves to exhaustive analysis [30], to consider different levels of abstraction at the same time [28, 29], and to innovate across disciplines [31]. Harnessing these design abilities into the methodological framework specifically tailored for designing novel applications allows more effective and successful technology-to-application transformations.

One implication of this shaky starting point in a novel application design (due to the lack of understanding of the eventual usage) and the continuous reflective exploration as the project progresses is that it is very difficult to prescribe a general step-by-step procedure which, when rigorously followed, will guarantee a successful creation of a novel application. The activity of designing a novel application requires a series of tentative exploration at the current situation with a limited information and understanding in order to unfold a more enlightened situation; the subsequent step is very much dependent on what has been found at the previous step and how to frame it for the next. However, reflecting on the example design projects as introduced in Section 2, a rough formation of the procedural aspect of this type of design project might take such steps as the following:

(1) identify a specific technological possibility afforded by a recently emerging computation or a combination of it;

(2) by discussing with the researcher or the group who developed that specific technology, find out the overall assumption or projection behind that piece of technology, however vague or far fetched;

(3) using the assumption revealed as the initial clue, start a series of sketching of possible usage scenarios scoping as generic and open as possible. The sketching sessions will be continuous feedback loops between the designer and the technology provider, making up the core creative stage of the design project. This stage will ask the technology provider on the characteristics and properties of the computational technology to be exploited and their implications for the end-user features (e.g., can the computation be real time; can it cope with different domain data; can it cope with small amount of input from the end users, and if so, what will be the minimum amount that could achieve an acceptable accuracy; can the computation run on the server or client; can it run on various interaction devices and gadgets available today or soon-to-be

available ones; can the accuracy be enhanced during the interaction by the end-user's manual input, etc.) and will intensively iterate between sketching and feedback. The result is a series of mockups or sketches of the application to demonstrate the concept and the power of the specific computation incorporated in the concept;

(4) implement a working version of the mockup in order to user-test its interactivity and obtain feedback from the end users.

Once a working prototype is available, then many conventional usability engineering methods currently practiced can be utilised to observe, monitor, and get the sense of the usage. As can be seen in these steps, the core of the methodology is in the art of exploiting the computation in concern in the suitable and innovative way (i.e., step 3) rather than in diligently adhering to a prescribed steps. Further prescribing a general procedure within step 3 may be less meaningful due to the many unpredictable factors at play in each specific project and the synthesis-oriented nature of the step perhaps more requiring the designer's inherent quality of trying to frame the situation from his or her experience and to match a portfolio of prior design solutions, thereby increasing the certainty for the next iteration. In this sense, recently proposed practical methodologies to support quick turnaround for innovative product design in business and industry such as O'Reilly's Lean UX [32] may be some early examples of how this design thinking-driven, iteration-heavy, and technology-inspired approach might eventually take a more procedural form.

3.4. Value of Novel Applications: Evaluation Criteria. For all three example applications described in Section 2, the motivation for conducting the user evaluation sessions was less about verifying whether the systems satisfied a set of identified requirements or supported the users' preconceived wishes but was more about witnessing how they perceived these systems to be beneficial to them and how they might see the novel interaction features could be adopted to their other existing tools and services or to their current lifestyle, although many detailed usability issues and widget-level problems on their user interfaces were also identified along the way as a side effect.

Greenberg and Buxton [33] warn against blindly following the evaluation doctrine available today, and Olsen Jr. [34] advises us to avoid the trap of only creating what a usability test today can measure. These are the points particularly relevant with regard to developing novel applications. Conventional application designs are driven by initially identified user needs and requirements, and thus their evaluation is also geared towards assessing whether the designed application satisfies user needs and requirements. The goal of designing novel applications, as demonstrated in this paper, is not so much to fit existing user needs and requirements. Therefore, there is a limitation when its evaluation is driven by the prevailing idea of how well the application satisfies the user needs and requirements.

People's initial reactions to a novel feature could be negative simply because it is not something with which they are familiar or had expected. For example, in My Friends' Faces, our test users' opinions about using the application were generally low simply because they expected concepts and styles similar to their familiar photo services. It is impossible to remove such a bias in conducting a one-off user evaluation and asking their opinions about novel features.

More appropriate criteria for the evaluation of this type of novel applications would include the following.

(i) How well does the application exploit and represent the back-end technique?

(ii) How well does the application exhibit the generic affordances as to how to interact with it?

(iii) How well does the application provoke brainstorming and discussion?

In other words, what should be evaluated is the role of the application in helping explore the connection between technical possibilities and novel usage, not the role of the eventual, situated application with its detailed feature provision to fit a specific usage context. Fitting the application to a specific context is a task that can be performed much later, after major technical possibilities and exploitation efforts have been explored. Once we draw a clearer distinction between design practise (context-driven, supporting real-world practise) and design exploration (idealistic, supporting invention of new artefacts) [11] in terms of the design methodology, then we will be able to devise and offer more specialised, more optimal, and more cost-effective design processes tailored for different kinds of design activities. There is no reason why the technology R&D community should try to create a perfect application in one go that exhibits novel functionalities *and* fulfills specific user needs at the same time.

4. Conclusion

This paper examined how some technology-oriented projects were conducted to design novel interactive applications as front-ends of technological systems in ways that differ from what the conventional usability engineering practise prescribes, yet they achieved highly desirable outcomes.

The paper highlighted the currently overlooked and undervalued activity of designing demonstrators in many technology laboratories, which are at the mercy of left-over resources at the end of projects and sometimes designed without the necessary design expertise. In particular, the prevailing mismatch between design approach and design purpose in these projects results in either wasted resources or under exploration of technological possibilities.

Through the example applications, we demonstrated that the "novelty" in novel applications can range from supporting a simple new access point in user interactivity, to expanding the scope of an existing activity, to a completely new activity which not many people would normally suggest. Also demonstrated in terms of incorporating emerging computational technologies as the core back end of a system was the shift from relying on full automation to "design for failure"—supporting the features for the users or group of users to easily cope with the imperfect system performance. In addition, testing the demonstrator systems featuring this type of error-coping features will help guide the research direction for the underlying computation and back end technology itself. Our novelty spectrum implied that sometimes less novel activities might have greater chance of benefiting from an initial user study or user research.

Interaction design has different purposes depending on the reason for designing a system, and from there, it follows that different design approaches and methodologies are required for different design purposes. Designing novel applications inspired by emerging technologies is an activity in which many R&D laboratories engage, and considering its huge potential influence in shaping our future interactivity with technology in the coming years, a more suitable and pragmatic methodological support is clearly needed for such a community today. We hope the discussions in this paper will push the methodological support to be sufficiently differentiated and tailored for the technology laboratories to more fully exploit the technological possibilities that they explore and thus to maximise their research output in the coming years.

Conflict of Interests

Author and coauthors of this paper do not have any form of relation, financial or otherwise, with company names or trademarks mentioned in this paper. This paper was written solely with an academic intention and to contribute to the knowledge in the field of human-computer interaction. The references to trademarks made in this paper are only in the context of how general public are familiar with some of the popular web services and the features provided by these services, in order to make a point of the way novel applications can be perceived by people.

Acknowledgment

The authors acknowledge the CLARITY: Centre for Sensor Web Technologies, Dublin City University, Ireland, for providing an excellent research environment where our interaction design activity continued for over a decade and from which the reflection and analysis in this paper is derived.

References

[1] C. G. M. Snoek, M. Worring, O. D. Rooij, K. E. A. van de Sande, R. Yan, and A. G. Hauptmann, "VideOlympics: real-time evaluation of multimedia retrieval systems," *IEEE Multimedia*, vol. 15, no. 1, pp. 86–91, 2008.

[2] D. A. Sadlier, H. Lee, C. Gurrin, A. F. Smeaton, and N. E. O'Connor, "User-feedback on a feature-rich photo organiser," in *Proceedings of the 9th International Workshop on Image Analysis for Multimedia Interactive Services (WIAMIS '08)*, pp. 215–218, City University, May 2008.

[3] D. G. Lowe, "Distinctive image features from scale-invariant keypoints," *International Journal of Computer Vision*, vol. 60, no. 2, pp. 91–110, 2004.

[4] M. Blighe, S. Sav, H. Lee, and N. O'Connor, "Mo Músaem Fíorúil: a web-based search and information service for museum visitors," in *Proceedings of International Conference on Image Analysis and Recognition (ICIAR '08)*, pp. 25–27, Povoa de Varzim, Portugal, June 2008.

[5] H. Lee, A. F. Smeaton, N. E. O'Connor et al., "Constructing a SenseCam visual diary as a media process," *Multimedia Systems*, vol. 14, no. 6, pp. 341–349, 2008.

[6] J. Boreczky, A. Girgensohn, G. Golovchinsky, and S. Uchihashi, "Interactive comic book presentation for exploring video," in *Proceedings of Conference on Human Factors in Computing Systems (CHI '00)*, pp. 185–192, ACM Press, April 2000.

[7] N. Caprani, A. R. Doherty, H. Lee, A. F. Smeaton, N. E. O'Connor, and C. Gurrin, "Designing a touch-screen SenseCam browser to support an aging population," in *Proceedings of the 28th Annual CHI Conference on Human Factors in Computing Systems (CHI '10)*, pp. 4291–4296, ACM Press, April 2010.

[8] D. Norman and R. Verganti, *Incremental and Radical Innovation: Design Research Versus Technology and Meaning Change*, Nielsen Norman Group, 2012, http://www.jnd.org/dn.mss/incremental_and_radi.html.

[9] P. Hekkert, D. Snelders, and P. C. W. van Wieringen, "'Most advanced, yet acceptable': typicality and novelty as joint predictors of aesthetic preference in industrial design," *British Journal of Psychology*, vol. 94, no. 1, pp. 111–124, 2003.

[10] W. K. Hung and L. L. Chen, "Effects of novelty and its dimensions on aesthetic preference in product design," *International Journal of Design*, vol. 6, no. 2, pp. 81–90, 2012.

[11] D. Fallman, "The interaction design research triangle of design practice, design studies, and design exploration," *Design Issues*, vol. 24, no. 3, pp. 4–18, 2008.

[12] S. Ljungblad and L. E. Holmquist, "Transfer scenarios: grounding innovation with marginal practices," in *Proceedings of the 25th SIGCHI Conference on Human Factors in Computing Systems (CHI '07)*, pp. 737–746, ACM, May 2007.

[13] L. E. Holmquist, *Grounded Innovation: Strategies for Creating Digital Products*, Morgan Kaufmann, Waltham, Mass, USA, 2012.

[14] S. Bly and E. Churchill, "Design through matchmaking: technology in search of users," *Interactions*, vol. 6, no. 2, pp. 23–31, 1999.

[15] Y. Rogers and V. Bellotti, "Grounding blue-sky research: how can ethnography help?" *Interactions*, vol. 4, no. 3, pp. 58–63, 1997.

[16] Y. Rogers, M. Scaife, E. Harris et al., "Things aren't what they seem to be: Innovation through technology inspiration," in *Proceedings of the 4th Conference on Designing Interactive Systems: Processes, Practices, Methods, and Techniques (DIS '02)*, pp. 373–378, ACM, June 2002.

[17] S. Davidoff, M. K. Lee, A. Dey, and J. Zimmerman, "Rapidly exploring application design through speed dating," in *Proceedings of the 9th International Conference on Ubiquitous Computing (UbiComp '07)*, J. Krumm et al., Ed., vol. 4717 of *Lecture Notes in Computer Science*, pp. 429–446, Springer.

[18] H. Hutchinson, W. Mackay, B. Westerlund et al., "Technology probes: inspiring design for and with families," in *Proceedings of the SIGCHI Conference on Human Factors in Computing Systems (CHI '03)*, pp. 17–24, Ft. Lauderdale, Fla, USA, April 2003.

[19] G. Iacucci, K. Kuutti, and M. Ranta, "On the move with a magic thing: Role playing in concept design of mobile services and

devices," in *Proceedings of the 3rd Conference on Designing Inter-active Systems: Processes, Practices, Methods, and Techniques*, pp. 193–202, Brooklyn, NY, USA, August 2000.

[20] W. Odom, J. Zimmerman, S. Davidoff, J. Forlizzi, A. Dey, and M. K. Lee, "A fieldwork of the future with user enactments," in *Proceedings of the Designing Interactive Systems Conference*, pp. 338–347, ACM, Newcastle, UK, June 2012.

[21] W. Gaver, J. Bowers, A. Boucher, A. Law, S. Pennington, and N. Villar, "The history tablecloth: Illuminating domestic activity," in *Proceedings of the Conference on Designing Interactive Systems (DIS '06)*, pp. 199–208, ACM, June 2006.

[22] H. Lee, "Issues in designing novel applications for emerging multimedia technologies," in *Proceeding of the 6th Symposium of the Workgroup Human-Computer Interaction and Usability Engineering (USAB '10)*, vol. 6389 of *Lecture Notes in Computer Science*, pp. 411–426, Klagenfurt, Austria, November 2010.

[23] H. Lee and A. F. Smeaton, "Establishing design knowledge for emerging interaction platforms," in *Proceeding of the 4th World Conference on Design Research (IASDR '11)*, pp. 1–11, Delft, The Netherlands, October-November 2011.

[24] P. Sengere and B. Gaver, "Staying open to interpretation: engaging multiple meanings in design and evaluation," in *Proceedings of the Conference on Designing Interactive Systems (DIS '06)*, pp. 99–108, ACM Press, University Park, Pa, USA, June 2006.

[25] J. Zimmerman, E. Stolterman, and J. Forlizzi, "An analysis and critique of research through design: Towards a formalization of a research approach," in *Proceedings of the 8th ACM Conference on Designing Interactive Systems (DIS '10)*, pp. 310–319, Aarhus, Denmark, August 2010.

[26] I. Koskinen, J. Zimmerman, T. Binder, J. Redstrom, and S. Wensveen, *Design Research through Practice: From the Lab, Field, and Showroom*, Morgan Kaufmann, Waltham, Mass, USA, 2011.

[27] D. Schon, *Reflective Practitioner: How Professionals Think in Action*, Basic Books, New York, NY, USA, 1984.

[28] N. Cross, "Designerly ways of knowing: design discipline versus design science," *Design Issues*, vol. 17, no. 3, pp. 49–55, 2006.

[29] B. Lawson, *How Designers Think: The Design Process Demystified*, Architectural Press, Burlington, Mass, USA, 4th edition, 2006.

[30] B. Lawson and K. Dorst, *Design Expertise*, Architectural Press, Oxford, UK, 2009.

[31] D. Norman, *The Design of Future Things*, Basic Books, New York, NY, USA, 2008.

[32] J. Gothelf and J. Seiden, *Lean UX: Applying Lean Principles to Improve User Experience*, O'Reilly Media, Cambridge, Mass, USA, 2013.

[33] S. Greenberg and B. Buxton, "Usability evaluation considered harmful (some of the time)," in *Proceedings of the 26th Annual CHI Conference on Human Factors in Computing Systems (CHI '08)*, pp. 111–120, ACM Press, April 2008.

[34] D. R. Olsen Jr., "Evaluating user interface systems research," in *Proceedings of the 20th Annual ACM Symposium on User Interface Software and Technology (UIST '07)*, pp. 251–258, ACM Press, Newport, RI, USA, October 2007.

17

Heart Rate Responses to Synthesized Affective Spoken Words

Mirja Ilves and Veikko Surakka

Research Group for Emotions, Sociality, and Computing, Tampere Unit for Computer-Human Interaction (TAUCHI),
School of Information Sciences, University of Tampere, Kanslerinrinne 1, FI-33014 University of Tampere, Finland

Correspondence should be addressed to Mirja Ilves, mirja.ilves@sis.uta.fi

Academic Editor: Eva Cerezo

The present study investigated the effects of brief synthesized spoken words with emotional content on the ratings of emotions and heart rate responses. Twenty participants' heart rate functioning was measured while they listened to a set of emotionally negative, neutral, and positive words produced by speech synthesizers. At the end of the experiment, ratings of emotional experiences were also collected. The results showed that the ratings of the words were in accordance with their valence. Heart rate deceleration was significantly the strongest and most prolonged to the negative stimuli. The findings are the first suggesting that brief spoken emotionally toned words evoke a similar heart rate response pattern found earlier for more sustained emotional stimuli.

1. Introduction

Verbal communication is unique to humans, and speech is an especially effective means to communicate ideas and emotions to other people [1]. McGregor [2] argued that spoken language is a more primary and more fundamental means of communication than written language. In speech, both verbal meaning and prosodic cues within the speech can communicate emotions; however, there is little research on the role of the verbal meaning of spoken words to human emotions. Although studies concerning the emotional processing of the verbal content of speech are rare, the scope of emotion studies has recently broadened from studying the reactions to the pictures of emotional scenes and human faces to visually presented linguistic stimuli. In a way, emotionally charged spoken stimuli uttered in a monotone or a neutral tone of voice partly parallels written text. By this, it is meant that only lexical contents of the stimuli offer knowledge about emotion, so the results about visually presented written words can provide some background references for studying reactions to spoken emotional words.

Studies using event related potential (ERP) measurements have repeatedly found that early cortical responses to visually presented words with emotional content are enhanced as compared to ERPs to neutral words. This suggests that the emotional content of a word is identified at an early lexical stage of processing (e.g., [3–5]). In addition, there is evidence that written emotionally negative words evoke larger activation of *corrugator supercilii* (i.e., frowning) facial muscle than positive words do [6–8]. There are also studies that have found larger startle reflex to unpleasant words than to neutral and positive words during shallow word processing [9, 10]. Further, there is some evidence that written words evoke autonomic nervous system responses. One study showed that heart rate decelerated more in response to unpleasant words than to other word types [11]. Based on these studies, physiological response patterns to emotional words seem to be quite consistent with the earlier findings about the reactions to emotional pictures and sounds.

Of course, the results of the responses to visually presented words are not directly applicable to spoken words, and more research is to be done to identify the role of the verbal content of spoken language in human emotional processing. In order to study purely the effects of the verbal content of spoken words to human emotion system, speech synthesizers offer good opportunities; this is because they offer good controllability over timing and prosodic cues related to the nonverbal expressions of emotions like loudness and the range of the fundamental frequency of voice. Controlling out the variation in nonverbal cues offers the possibility to study more purely the effects of the lexical meaning of spoken words. This results in a monotone tone of voice; however, there is evidence that such stimuli work well in the context of emotion research. A recent study investigated how spoken emotional stimuli pronounced by a monotone tone of synthesized voice activate the human emotional system. The findings showed that the verbal content of spoken sentences evoked emotion-relevant subjective and pupil responses in listeners [12]. Naturally, the knowledge about the effects of synthetically produced messages is also important in an application point of view; this is because interfaces that utilize speech synthesis have become increasingly popular.

Based on earlier research, heart rate measurement could provide new and valuable knowledge about the processing of spoken words; this is because previous studies have suggested that heart rate is sensitive to both cognitive (i.e., attention) and emotional aspects of stimulus processing. These studies have utilized the dimensional theory of emotions [13]. In earlier research, the most commonly used dimensions have been valence, reflecting the pleasantness of an emotional state, and arousal, which reflects the level of emotional activation. Lang et al. [14] have suggested that these dimensions relate to the functioning of the human motivational system, which guides us to approach or withdraw from objects. There is evidence that heart rate accelerates when people imagine emotional material [14] and decelerates during the perception of emotional information, such that the deceleration is largest and most prolonged to negative stimuli [15].

Based on these types of findings, Lang et al. [16] have suggested a special model known as the defense cascade model. This model suggests that a new stimulus in an environment causes an orienting response accompanied with a brief heart rate deceleration. Sustained heart rate deceleration relates to the increased and continued allocation of attentional resources towards somehow-threatening stimulus, which, however, does not require immediate action. If the stimulus is nonthreatening, the heart rate starts to recover back to the prestimulus onset level. Lang et al. [14] suggested that although the connection between valence and heart rate is evident, it is modest. Codispoti et al. [17] also suggested that a decelerating pattern of heart rate in visual contexts presumes sustained sensory stimulation. Research concerning heart rate responses to spoken stimuli can provide important knowledge about the meaning of speech, particularly verbal content, in emotional processing. It is noteworthy that the processing of emotion-related auditory information can have a significant role for human behavior because the hearing of vocally uttered sounds may have had a significant meaning for survival in many situations. Thus, the present study investigated the effects of brief emotionally negative, neutral, and positive synthesized spoken messages to heart rate and the ratings of emotions.

2. Method

2.1. Participants. Thirty-one volunteer students participated in the experiment. Data from eight participants were discarded from the analysis because of poor signal-to-noise ratio to guarantee the high quality of the analyzed heart rate data. In addition, data from three participants had to be rejected due to other equipment failures. Thus, data from 20 participants were used for the analysis (11 males, M_{age}: 27.8 years, range: 19–51 years). The participants were native speakers of Finnish and had normal hearing by their own report. All participants signed a written consent.

2.2. Equipment. The presentation of stimuli and rating scales were controlled by E-Prime [18] experiment generator software. The stimuli were audible via two loudspeakers placed in front of the participant. Continuous ballistocardiographic heart rate responses (beats/min) were measured with sampling rate of 500 Hz using the EMFi chair. The Quatech DAQP-16 card digitized the heart rate signal to a PC with a Windows XP operating system. The EMFi chair is a regular-looking office chair that has been developed and tested for unobtrusive measuring of heart rate changes [19–21]. The chair is embedded with electromechanical film (EMFi) sensors in its seat, backrest, and armrests. EMFi is a low-cost, cellular, electrically charged polypropylene film that senses changes in pressure and, thus, can be used to measure ballistocardiographic heart rate.

2.3. Stimuli. Stimuli consisted of 15 different affective words selected from the ANEW [22] based on their mean ratings in valence and arousal scales (ANEW stimuli numbers: 8, 37, 46, 227, 251, 266, 305, 494, 591, 613, 614, 759, 974, 1001, and 1015). Five stimuli were strongly positive and arousing, five were strongly negative and arousing, and five were neutral words. The words were translated in Finnish, and their lengths were matched across the categories.

The male voice of three Finnish speech synthesizers produced all the words. The used synthesis techniques were formant synthesis [23], diphone synthesis [24], and unit selection [25]. Each word was repeated three times, resulting in 45 stimulus words in total. Fundamental frequency of the voices was set to 100 Hz. The volume normalization was set at 75 dB using Wave Surfer 1.8.5 program, and the changes in intonation were set to zero, resulting in a monotone tone of voice.

2.4. Experimental Procedure. First, the electrically shielded and sound attenuated laboratory was introduced to the participant, and then the participant sat in the EMFi chair. The experimenter informed the participant that the aim was to study reactions to auditory stimuli and that the experiment would consist of a listening and a rating phase. The participant was to relax, sit still, and concentrate on listening to the set of words produced by speech synthesis. Then, in addition to the experimenter, speech synthesizer gave the instructions regarding the experimental task in order to get participant used to the monotone voice of the speech synthesizer. This synthesizer was not among the synthesizers used in the actual experiment. After giving the instructions, the experimenter left the room, and the stimulus presentation begun. After the experiment, the EMFi chair and the purpose of using it was explained to each participant.

Interstimulus interval was 15 seconds. A fixation-cross was in view five seconds before and after each stimulus presentation. After the fixation-cross disappeared, the question "Did you understand the word?" and the answer options "no" and "yes" appeared at the screen. The pressing of the left button of a response box indicated that she/he did not understand the word and the right button that she/he understood the word. The order of the stimulus presentation was fully randomized.

After the experimental phase, the participant heard the words again and rated her/his emotional experience during each stimulus on three dimensions: valence, arousal, and approachability. The ratings were given on nine-point bipolar scales. The valence scale ranged from unpleasant to pleasant, the arousal scale from calm to aroused, and the approachability scale from withdrawable to approachable. The center of all the scales represented neutral experience. Before the rating session, the scales were explained to the participant, and the giving of the ratings was rehearsed through two exercise stimuli. The stimuli were presented randomly, rating scales were presented on the display, and a keyboard was used to give the ratings. Finally, the participant was debriefed about the purpose of the study. None of the participants was aware that the chair was used to measure heart rate responses until after the experiment.

2.5. Data Analysis. First, artifacts caused, for example, by body movements were removed from the heart rate data with the algorithm described in Anttonen et al. [21]. Then, the data were baseline corrected using a one-second prestimulus baseline. The stimuli that included $\geq 50\%$ artifacts during the baseline period or during five seconds period from stimulus offset were discarded from further analysis (i.e., 19% of the data). Then, mean heart rate values both for the overall data and for second-by-second data five seconds from the stimulus offset were calculated. Finally, the data were categorized according to the stimulus categories.

The mean heart rate responses five seconds from the stimulus offset did not differ significantly between the stimuli that were understood and the stimuli that were not understood $t(19) = 1.550$, ns. Thus, the words that were judged difficult to understand were included in the analysis. It is likely that at least part of the words that participant judged as unclear were actually heard and understood, but he/she answered no when the word sounded dim. Further, there were no differences between the understandability of the negative and positive words $t(19) = 1.901$, ns. Instead, the neutral words were perceived as significantly more understandable than the negative $t(19) = 4.717$, $P < .001$, or positive $t(19) = 3.823$, $P < .01$ words. In addition, the heart rate responses did not differ significantly between the men and women $t(18) = 0.496$, ns.

The data were analyzed with repeated measures ANOVAs with Greenhouse-Geisser adjusted degrees of freedom when necessary. Multiple post hoc pairwise comparisons were Bonferroni corrected.

3. Results

3.1. Heart Rate. Figure 1 shows the mean heart rate responses, averaged over all synthesizers, to the different emotion categories during the period of five seconds after the stimulus offset. The left side shows grand averages during the period of 5 seconds from the stimulus offset. The right side shows responses on a second-by-second basis, both during the stimulation and five seconds from the stimulus offset. Figure 1 clearly shows that the heart rate responses to the different stimulus categories were diverse. Heart rate response seemed to be larger and more prolonged to the negative stimuli than to the positive or neutral stimuli. First, we tested the effect of the synthesizer on the heart rate responses. One-way ANOVA did not reveal a significant effect of the synthesizer to heart rate, $F(2,38) = 1,09$, ns.

One-sample t-test revealed a statistically significant deceleration from prestimulus baseline for the negative $(t(19) = 3.32, P < .01, d = .74)$ and neutral $(t(19) = 2.40, P < .05, d = .54)$ stimuli. Decrease after the positive stimuli was not statistically significant $(t(19) = 0.90, P > .05)$. Although one-way ANOVA with emotion content as a within subject factor was only nearly significant $(F(2, 38) = 3.12, P = .056, \eta^2 = .05)$, the linear trend between emotion categories was significant $(F(1, 19) = 4.95, P < .05)$. Thus, the deceleration was largest to the negative words.

The second-by-second analysis revealed a statistically significant effect of emotion category at the fifth second from the stimulus offset $(F(2, 38) = 4.80, P < .05, \eta^2 = .07)$; negative versus positive $(t(19) = 2.64, P < .05)$. Difference between the negative and neutral words or between the neutral and positive words was not significant. At that time point, the linear trend was also statistically significant $(F(1, 19) = 6.97, P < .05)$.

3.2. Subjective Ratings. Table 1 shows the results of the analysis of the subjective ratings. The statistical analysis showed a significant effect for the ratings of valence. Post hoc pairwise comparisons were all statistically significant. The positive words $(M = 5.71)$ evoked significantly more positive ratings of valence than the negative $(M = 3.75)$ or neutral words $(M = 4.89)$ did. The negative words evoked significantly more negative ratings of valence than the neutral words did. There was also a significant effect in the ratings of arousal. The negative words $(M = 5.95)$ were significantly more arousing than the neutral $(M = 5.21)$ or positive words $(M = 5.08)$. Further, there was a significant effect in the ratings of approachability. The positive words $(M = 5.47)$ were rated as significantly more approachable than the negative $(M = 3.44)$ or neutral words $(M = 4.82)$. The neutral words were rated as more approachable than the negative words.

4. Discussion

This study was the first showing significant heart rate changes to brief spoken emotionally toned words. The findings are of particular concern to responses to synthetically produced words. Heart rate deceleration five seconds from the stimulus

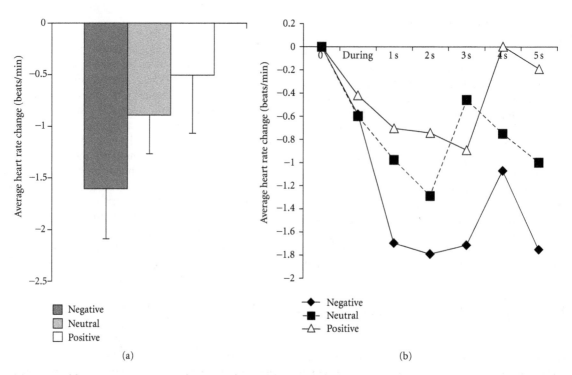

FIGURE 1: (a) Averaged heart rate responses and *SEM* to the negative, neutral, and positive words during the period of five seconds after the stimulus offset. (b) Averaged second-by-second heart rate changes by stimulus categories during the stimulus and five seconds after the stimulus offset.

TABLE 1: Statistical results of the ratings of valence, arousal, and approachability.

Rating scale	ANOVA	Effect size η^2	Pairwise comparisons
Valence	$F(2, 38) = 30.60, P < .001$	$\eta^2 = .54$	Negative < neutral $t(19) = 5.99, P < .001$ Negative < positive $t(19) = 5.67, P < .001$ Neutral < positive $t(19) = 4.44, P < .001$
Arousal	$F(2, 38) = 13.57, P < .001$	$\eta^2 = .19$	Negative > neutral $t(19) = 4.59, P < .001$ Negative > positive $t(19) = 4.30, P < .01$ Neutral versus positive $t(19) = 0.76$, ns
Approachability	$F(1, 23) = 29.30, P < .001$	$\eta^2 = .48$	Negative < neutral $t(19) = 7.94, P < .001$ Negative < positive $t(19) = 5.67, P < .001$ Neutral < positive $t(19) = 2.64, P < .05$

offset was largest to the negative stimuli. Further, the deceleration was the most prolonged to the negative stimuli, such that the difference between heart rate responses to the negative and positive stimuli was statistically significant at the fifth second from the stimulus offset. This was because at the fifth second from the offset of the positive stimulation heart rate had recovered nearly back to the baseline, while heart rate response to the negative stimulation remained decelerated. This finding is in line with the earlier studies that have investigated heart rate changes second-by-second (e.g., [19]). Many studies (e.g., [15, 17, 26]) have used other types of analysis, like analyzing only the averages over several seconds of stimulations, which do not reveal the second-by-second functioning of the heart. Overall, the current results showed that heart rate changes followed a triphasic form, which has been a typical pattern of response during

the perception of emotional stimulation [16]. This form is characterized by an initial deceleration, then an acceleration following a late deceleration so that heart rate deceleration is altogether stronger during negative than during positive stimulation. The ratings of the stimuli were in accordance with negative, neutral, and positive emotion categories.

Although the earlier findings of responses to emotional stimuli have been mainly consistent, Codispoti et al. [17] suggested that heart rate responses to briefly presented affective pictures are different from responses to longer stimuli. In their study, initial heart rate deceleration six seconds from the stimulus onset was minimal, and picture valence had no significant effect on heart rate responses. Thus, they concluded that a clear decelerating response to affective stimuli in visual contexts presumes more sustained sensory stimulation. In contrast to this, the present results suggest that the heart reacts differently to the spoken verbal material and that even very brief spoken words with lexical emotional content seem to evoke a corresponding decelerated heart rate response pattern as found earlier with longer emotional stimuli. Although there were some difficulties to understand some of the words, there were no significant differences between the understandability of the negative and positive words. Thus, the different heart rate responses to the negative and positive words reflect the differences in the emotional valence of the words, not the pronunciation quality of the word.

The current findings could be explained by differences in the processing of visual and auditory stimuli or in the processing of verbal and pictorial material. It is known that different senses process sensory information in different ways. For example, there are different sensory stores for each sense. There is evidence that auditory sensory information is available much longer (i.e., seconds) in a sensory storage than visual information (i.e., only a few hundred milliseconds). It has been proposed that auditory sensory store consists of two phases [27, 28]. In the initial phase, the stimulus is unanalyzed and it is stored for several hundred milliseconds. In the second phase, the information is stored for a few seconds and the content is partly analyzed. This means that while the auditory information is still available in the sensory store, the visual information has passed to the conscious processing of the working memory and has faded from the sensory store. Thus, it is possible that the hearing of brief lexical stimuli evokes similar heart rate responses to those to more continuous visual sensory stimulation.

Secondly, there is evidence that the processing of pictures and words activates the same brain areas [29]. However, studies with ERPs [30] and categorizing tasks [31] have shown that the processing time of words is slower than the processing time of pictures. This difference has been found by comparing the processing times between the visually presented words and pictures. Further, there is evidence that the processing of speech takes even a little longer than reading (see [32]). These differences may reflect the case that the processing of words and pictures is different. Following this, their effects seem to differ from each other. Because the processing time of spoken words is slower than the processing time of pictures, it may be also that listening binds the attentional resources longer than watching pictures does.

There is also some debate as to what extent the processing of emotional words affects physiological activation. Mainly, the findings about physiological responses to emotional words have been consistent with the earlier findings about the reactions to emotional pictures and sounds. However, it has also been suggested that the emotional content of written words does not automatically result in autonomic activation [33] or that the physiological responses are much smaller for words than for emotional pictures and sounds (e.g., [8]). Instead, the current (as well as some previous [12]) results suggest that perceiving the emotional content of the spoken words induces emotional reactions in the listeners even though the words were produced by the monotone voice of speech synthesis.

This may reflect the importance of speech and listening for humans. First, hearing has some advantages in comparison with other senses. For example, vision is limited to the position of the eyes while hearing is relatively independent from the position of the ears and the head. Thus, hearing is a primary system for receiving warnings from others [34]; consequently, people may be highly responsive to vocal emotional messages. Second, speech has a central role when people communicate each other and build social relationships [1]. Thus, humans have evolved to receive very effectively messages delivered through speech; perhaps for this reason the emotional words produced even by the flat, synthesized voice cause emotional responses in humans. In future research, it would be interesting to study whether there are any differences in emotional responses to synthesized and natural voices. There are some findings showing that increasing the human likeness of synthesized voice strengthens the emotional responses to voice messages [12, 35, 36]. On the other hand, the used synthesis technique did not affect heart rate responses in the present study. Thus, although it is possible that the emotional responses to human speech would be stronger as compared to synthetic voice, the present results together with the previous findings suggest that synthetic speech with emotional content also evokes emotional responses in humans.

In conclusion, the present results are the first to suggest that brief spoken words with emotional content can evoke the decelerated heart rate response pattern similar to those previously obtained only with longer stimuli. Further, the affective words evoked emotion-related responses in people, even though the words were produced by the artificial-sounding monotonous synthesized voices. Thus, it seems that the emotional expressions produced by a computer can evoke emotional responses in a human similar to responses to the emotional expressions of another human. The knowledge that speech-based computer systems can induce emotions in people is important for the field of human-computer interaction when creating and designing computerized interactive environments and devices.

Acknowledgments

The authors would like to thank all the participants of the study. This research was supported by the Doctoral Program in User-Centered Information Technology (UCIT) and a grant from the University of Tampere.

References

[1] G. A. de Laguna, *Speech: Its Function and Development*, Indiana University Press, Bloomington, Ind, USA, 1963.

[2] W. McGregor, *Linguistics: An Introduction*, Continuum International, New York, NY, USA, 2009.

[3] C. Herbert, M. Junghofer, and J. Kissler, "Event related potentials to emotional adjectives during reading," *Psychophysiology*, vol. 45, no. 3, pp. 487–498, 2008.

[4] J. Kissler, C. Herbert, P. Peyk, and M. Junghofer, "Buzzwords: early cortical responses to emotional words during reading:

research report," *Psychological Science*, vol. 18, no. 6, pp. 475–480, 2007.

[5] G. G. Scott, P. J. O'Donnell, H. Leuthold, and S. C. Sereno, "Early emotion word processing: evidence from event-related potentials," *Biological Psychology*, vol. 80, no. 1, pp. 95–104, 2009.

[6] M. Bayer, W. Sommer, and A. Schacht, "Reading emotional words within sentences: the impact of arousal and valence on event-related potentials," *International Journal of Psychophysiology*, vol. 78, no. 3, pp. 299–307, 2010.

[7] F. Foroni and G. R. Semin, "Language that puts you in touch with your bodily feelings: the multimodal responsiveness of affective expressions," *Psychological Science*, vol. 20, no. 8, pp. 974–980, 2009.

[8] J. T. Larsen, C. J. Norris, and J. T. Cacioppo, "Effects of positive and negative affect on electromyographic activity over zygomaticus major and corrugator supercilii," *Psychophysiology*, vol. 40, no. 5, pp. 776–785, 2003.

[9] C. Herbert, J. Kissler, M. Junghöfer, P. Peyk, and B. Rockstroh, "Processing of emotional adjectives: evidence from startle EMG and ERPs," *Psychophysiology*, vol. 43, no. 2, pp. 197–206, 2006.

[10] C. Herbert and J. Kissler, "Motivational priming and processing interrupt: startle reflex modulation during shallow and deep processing of emotional words," *International Journal of Psychophysiology*, vol. 76, no. 2, pp. 64–71, 2010.

[11] T. W. Buchanan, J. A. Etzel, R. Adolphs, and D. Tranel, "The influence of autonomic arousal and semantic relatedness on memory for emotional words," *International Journal of Psychophysiology*, vol. 61, no. 1, pp. 26–33, 2006.

[12] M. Ilves and V. Surakka, "Emotions, anthropomorphism of speech synthesis, and psychophysiology," in *Emotions in the Human Voice*, K. Izdebski, Ed., Culture and Perception, pp. 137–152, Plural, San Diego, Calif, USA, 2009.

[13] M. M. Bradley, "Measuring emotion: the self-assessment manikin and the semantic differential," *Journal of Behavior Therapy and Experimental Psychiatry*, vol. 25, no. 1, pp. 49–59, 1994.

[14] P. J. Lang, M. M. Bradley, and B. N. Cuthbert, "Emotion, attention, and the startle reflex," *Psychological Review*, vol. 97, no. 3, pp. 377–395, 1990.

[15] M. M. Bradley and P. J. Lang, "Affective reactions to acoustic stimuli," *Psychophysiology*, vol. 37, no. 2, pp. 204–215, 2000.

[16] P. J. Lang, M. M. Bradley, and B. N. Cuthbert, "Motivated attention: affect, activation, and action," in *Attention and Orienting—Sensory and Motivational Processes*, P. J. Lang, R. F. Simons, and M. T. Balaban, Eds., pp. 97–135, Erlbaum, Mahwah, NJ, USA, 1997.

[17] M. Codispoti, M. M. Bradley, and P. J. Lang, "Affective reactions to briefly presented pictures," *Psychophysiology*, vol. 38, no. 3, pp. 474–478, 2001.

[18] W. Schneider, A. Eschman, and A. Zuccolotto, *E-Prime User's Guide*, Psychology Software Tools, Pittsburgh, Pa, USA, 2002.

[19] J. Anttonen and V. Surakka, "Emotions and heart rate while sitting on a chair," in *Proceedings of the SIGCHI Conference on Human Factors in Computing Systems (CHI '05)*, pp. 491–499, April 2005.

[20] J. Anttonen and V. Surakka, "Music, heart rate, and emotions in the context of stimulating technologies," in *Proceedings of the 2nd International Conference on Affective Computing and Intelligent Interaction (ACII '07)*, pp. 290–301.

[21] J. Anttonen, V. Surakka, and M. Koivuluoma, "Ballistocardiographic responses to dynamic facial displays of emotion while

sitting on the EMFi chair," *Journal of Media Psychology*, vol. 21, no. 2, pp. 69–84, 2009.

[22] M. M. Bradley and P. J. Lang, "Affective norms for English words (ANEW): stimuli, instruction manual and affective ratings," Tech. Rep. C-1, University of Florida, Gainesville, Fla, USA, 1999.

[23] T. Saarni, *Segmental Durations of Speech [Doctoral Dissertation]*, University of Turku, Finland, 2010.

[24] Suopuhe [speech synthesizer], http://www.ling.helsinki.fi/suopuhe/english.shtml.

[25] Bitlips [speech synthesizer], http://www.bitlips.fi/index.en.html.

[26] O. Pollatos, B. M. Herbert, E. Matthias, and R. Schandry, "Heart rate response after emotional picture presentation is modulated by interoceptive awareness," *International Journal of Psychophysiology*, vol. 63, no. 1, pp. 117–124, 2007.

[27] N. Cowan, "On short and long auditory stores," *Psychological Bulletin*, vol. 96, no. 2, pp. 341–370, 1984.

[28] N. Cowan, "Evolving conceptions of memory storage, selective attention, and their mutual constraints within the human information-processing system," *Psychological Bulletin*, vol. 104, no. 2, pp. 163–191, 1988.

[29] P. Bright, H. Moss, and L. K. Tyler, "Unitary vs multiple semantics: PET studies of word and picture processing," *Brain and Language*, vol. 89, no. 3, pp. 417–432, 2004.

[30] A. Schacht and W. Sommer, "Emotions in word and face processing: early and late cortical responses," *Brain and Cognition*, vol. 69, no. 3, pp. 538–550, 2009.

[31] A. Roelofs, "Dynamic of the attentional control of word retrieval: analyses of response time distributions," *Journal of Experimental Psychology*, vol. 137, no. 2, pp. 303–323, 2008.

[32] K. Rayner and C. Clifton, "Language processing in reading and speech perception is fast and incremental: Implications for event-related potential research," *Biological Psychology*, vol. 80, no. 1, pp. 4–9, 2009.

[33] M. Bayer, W. Sommer, and A. Schacht, "Emotional words impact the mind but not the body: evidence from pupillary responses," *Psychophysiology*, vol. 48, no. 11, pp. 1553–1561, 2011.

[34] B. Scharf, "Auditory attention: the psychoacoustical approach," in *Attention*, H. Pashler, Ed., pp. 75–117, Psychology Press, Hove, UK, 1998.

[35] M. Ilves and V. Surakka, "Subjective and physiological responses to emotional content of synthesized speech," in *Proceedings of the International Conference on Computer Animation and Social Agents (CASA '04)*, N. Magnenat-Thalmann, C. Joslin, and H. Kim, Eds., pp. 19–26, Computer Graphics Society, Geneva, Switzerland, 2004.

[36] M. Ilves, V. Surakka, T. Vanhala et al., "The effects of emotionally worded synthesized speech on the ratings of emotions and voice quality," in *Proceedings of the 4th International Conference on Affective Computing and Intelligent Interaction (ACII '11), Part I*, S. D'Mello et al., Ed., vol. 6974 of *Lecture Notes in Computer Science*, pp. 588–598, Springer, 2011.

18

Assessment in and of Serious Games: An Overview

Francesco Bellotti,[1] Bill Kapralos,[2] Kiju Lee,[3] Pablo Moreno-Ger,[4] and Riccardo Berta[1]

[1] Department of Naval, Electric, Electronic and Telecommunications Engineering, University of Genoa,
Via all'Opera Pia 11/a, 16145 Genoa, Italy
[2] Faculty of Business and Information Technology, University of Ontario Institute of Technology, 2000 Simcoe Street North,
Oshawa, Canada L1H 7K4
[3] Department of Mechanical and Aerospace Engineering, Case Western Reserve University, 10900 Euclid Avenue,
Cleveland, OH 44106, USA
[4] Faculty of Computer Science, Universidad Complutense de Madrid, Ciudad Universitaria, 28040 Madrid, Spain

Correspondence should be addressed to Francesco Bellotti; franz@elios.unige.it

Academic Editor: Armando Bennet Barreto

There is a consensus that serious games have a significant potential as a tool for instruction. However, their effectiveness in terms of learning outcomes is still understudied mainly due to the complexity involved in assessing intangible measures. A systematic approach—based on established principles and guidelines—is necessary to enhance the design of serious games, and many studies lack a rigorous assessment. An important aspect in the evaluation of serious games, like other educational tools, is user performance assessment. This is an important area of exploration because serious games are intended to evaluate the learning progress as well as the outcomes. This also emphasizes the importance of providing appropriate feedback to the player. Moreover, performance assessment enables adaptivity and personalization to meet individual needs in various aspects, such as learning styles, information provision rates, feedback, and so forth. This paper first reviews related literature regarding the educational effectiveness of serious games. It then discusses how to assess the learning impact of serious games and methods for competence and skill assessment. Finally, it suggests two major directions for future research: characterization of the player's activity and better integration of assessment in games.

1. Introduction

Serious games are designed to have an impact on the target audience, which is beyond the pure entertainment aspect [1, 2]. One of the most important application domains is in the field of education given the acknowledged potential of serious games to meet the current need for educational enhancement [3, 4].

In this field, the purpose of a serious game is twofold: (i) to be fun and entertaining, and (ii) to be educational. A serious game is thus designed both to be attractive and appealing to a broad target audience, similar to commercial games, and to meet specific educational goals as well. Therefore, assessment of a serious game must consider both aspects of fun/enjoyment and educational impact.

In addition to considering fun and engagement, thus, serious games' assessment presents additional unique challenges, because learning is the primary goal. Therefore, there is also a need to explore how to evaluate the learning outcomes to identify which serious games are most suited for a given goal or domain, and how to design more effective serious games (e.g., what mechanics are most suited for a given pedagogical goal, etc.). In this sense, the evaluation of serious games should also cover player performance assessment. Performance assessment is important because serious games are designed to support knowledge acquisition and/or skill development. Thus, their underlying system must be able to evaluate the learning progress, since the rewards and the advancement in the game have to be carefully bound to it. This also stresses the importance of feedback to be consequentially provided to the player. Moreover, performance assessment enables adaptability and personalization in various aspects, for instance, definition, presentation, and scheduling of the contents to be provided to the player.

In summary, this paper intends to provide an overview of the two major aspects of assessment that concern serious games: (i) evaluation of serious games, and (ii) evaluation of player performance in serious games. The remainder of this paper is organized as it follows. Section 2 presents a literature review regarding the educational effectiveness of serious games. Section 3 discusses how to assess a serious game's learning impact. Section 4 reviews methods for competence and skill assessment, and Section 5 focuses on in-process assessment, which appears to be well suited for games. Concluding remarks and suggested directions for future research are given in Section 6.

2. General Context

Despite the a widespread consensus about the educational potential of video games, there is a shortage of studies that have methodically examined (assessed) learning via gameplay whether considering "entertainment" games or serious games, prompting some to challenge the usefulness of game-based learning (e.g., [5, 6]).

A number of studies have questioned the effectiveness of game-based learning (e.g., [7–9]). However, many of those reviews were conducted several years ago, and even in the last 10 years, there has been unprecedented development within the videogame field in general and educational games in particular. In contrast, more recently, Blunt [10] gathered evidence from three studies that had unquestionably achieved significantly better test results with students that had learned using games, compared to control groups who received typical instruction.

Furthermore, one cannot ignore the fact that simulations and serious games are a promising means for safely and cost-effectively acquiring skills and attitudes which are hard to get by rote learning [1] and that learning via gameplay may be longer lasting [11]. In addition, there are many examples of studies that have demonstrated that properly designed "learning games"—some examples are provided hereinafter—do produce learning, while engaging players [12].

One of the foundational reviews of the effectiveness of gaming was performed by Livingston et al. [13], when they evaluated seven years of research and over 150 studies to examine the effectiveness of gaming. Their results were later on mirrored by Chin et al. [14], and they concluded that "simulation games" are able to teach factual information although they are not necessarily more effective than other methods of instruction [13, 14]. However, it was observed that students preferred games and simulations over other classroom activities and participation in such "gamed simulations" can lead to changes in their the attitudes including attitudes toward education, career, marriage, and children although these effects could be short lived [13, 14].

More recently, Connolly et al. [15] have made an extensive literature study on computer games and serious games, identifying 129 papers reporting empirical evidence about the impacts and outcomes of games with respect to a variety of learning goals, including a critique of those cases where the research methods were not adequate. The findings revealed, however, that playing computer games is linked to a range of perceptual, cognitive, behavioural, affective, and motivational impacts and outcomes. The most frequently occurring outcomes and impacts were knowledge acquisition/content understanding and affective and motivational outcomes. Despite the diffused perception that games might be especially useful in promoting higher-order thinking and soft and social skills, the literature review provides limited evidence for this, also given the lack of adequate measurement tools for such skills.

Serious games look particularly effective in some specific application fields. One of the most relevant domains is healthcare, with different experiences that have provided positive results. The effectiveness of virtual reality and games in the treatment of phobias and in distracting patients in the process of burn treatment or chemotherapy has been scientifically validated with the use of functional Magnetic Resonance Imaging (fMRI) which has shown differences in brain activity in patients who were experiencing pain with and without the use of virtual reality and games [11]. An experiment with Re-Mission (a video game developed for adolescents and young adults with cancer) showed that the video-game intervention significantly improved treatment adherence and indicators of cancer-related self-efficacy and knowledge in adolescents and young adults who were undergoing cancer therapy [16]. More recently, Cole et al. [17] showed that activation of brain circuits involved in positive motivation during Re-Mission gameplay appears to be a key ingredient in influencing positive health behavior. Regarding behavioural change, the serious game *The Matrix*, developed to enhance self-esteem, was subject to rigorous scientific evaluation and was shown to increase self-esteem through classical conditioning [18].

Bellotti et al. [19] discuss the results of a lab user test aimed at verifying knowledge acquisition through minigames dedicated to cultural heritage. The implemented minigames were particularly suited for supporting image studying, which can be explained by the visual nature of games. Compared to text reading, the games seem to more strongly force the player to focus on problems, which favors knowledge acquisition and retention.

The aforementioned results show that serious games can be an effective tool to complement the educational instruments available to teachers, in particular for spurring user motivation [20] and for achieving learning goals at the lower levels in the Bloom's taxonomy [15]. The next section is dedicated to analyzing methods for assessing a serious game's learning impact.

3. Assessing a Serious Game's Effectiveness

Learning with serious games remains a goal-directed process aimed at clearly defined and measurable achievements and, therefore, must implement assessments to provide an indication of the learning progress and outcomes to both the learner and instructor [21] or as Michael and Chen [22] state "Serious games like every other tool of education must be able to show that the necessary learning has occurred." For serious games to be considered a viable educational tool, they must provide some means of testing and progress tracking and the testing must be recognizable within the context of the education or training they are attempting to impart.

Assessment describes the process of using data to demonstrate that stated learning goals and objectives are actually being met [14]. Assessment is a complement to purpose, and it is commonly employed by learning institutions, regardless the teaching methods used, whether or not their students actually learn [7]. However, learning is a complex construct making it difficult to measure, and determining whether a simulation or serious game is effective at achieving the intended learning goals is a complex, time consuming, expensive, and difficult process [8, 23]. Part of this difficulty stems from the open-ended nature inherent in video games making it difficult to collect data [14]. In other words, how do you show that students are learning what they should learn and how do you know what you are measuring is what you think you are measuring? [21].

Generally speaking, assessment can be described as either (i) *summative* whereby it is conducted at the end of a learning process and tests the overall achievements, and (ii) *formative* whereby it is implemented and present throughout the entire learning process and continuously monitors progress and failures [24]. With respect to serious games, it has been suggested that formative assessment is particularly useful and should be used particularly given that such assessments can be incorporated into the serious game becoming part of the experience [6], in particular through appropriate user feedback.

Considering the specific serious game domain, Michael and Chen [22] describe three primary types of assessment: (i) completion assessment, (ii) in-process assessment, and (iii) teacher assessment. The first two correspond to summative and formative assessments, respectively. Completion assessment is concerned with whether the player successfully completes the game. In a traditional teaching environment, this is equivalent to asking, "Did the student get the right answer?" and a simple criterion such as this could be the first indicator that the student sufficiently understands the subject taught albeit there are many problems using this measure alone. For instance, players could cheat and it is hard to determine whether the player actually learned the material or learned to complete the game [22]. Moreover, the game level upgrade barriers and score (as, in general, all the mechanics) must be designed so as to guarantee a proper balance between entertainment, motivation, and learning [25]. In-process assessment (we deal with it in detail in Section 5) examines how, when, and why a player made their choices and can be analogous to observations of the student by the educator as the student performs the task or takes the test in a traditional teaching environment. Teacher assessment focuses on the instructor's observations and judgments of the student "in action" (while they are playing the game) and typically aims at evaluating those factors that the functionalities/logic of the game are not able to capture.

Although various methods and techniques have been used to assess learning in serious games [26] and simulations in general, summative assessment is commonly accomplished with the use of pre- and posttesting, a common approach in educational research [27]. The pre- and posttest design is one of the most widely used experimental designs and is particularly popular in educational studies that aim to measure changes in educational outcomes after modifications to the learning process such as testing the effect of a new teaching method [28]. Within this design, participants are randomly allocated to either a "treatment" group (playing the serious game) or a "control" group (relying on other instructional techniques). Upon completion of the experiment, both groups complete a posttest, and significant differences across the test scores are attributed to the "treatment" (the serious game) [27]. The main problem with the pre- and posttest experimental design is that it is impossible to determine whether the act of pretesting has influenced any of the results. Another problem relates to the fact that it is almost impossible to completely isolate all of the participants (e.g., if two groups of child participants attend the same school, they will probably interact outside of lessons potentially influencing the results while if the child participants are taken from different schools to prevent this, then randomization is not possible) [29].

The most common method of postassessment currently consists in testing a players' knowledge about what they learned by way of a survey/test/questionnaire or teacher evaluation. This method is frequently employed because it is the simplest to implement, but it relies on the opinions of the player and does not depend on all of the information that can be collected regarding what happened within the game [6]. This method was used by Allen et al. [30] in the form of questionnaires before and after playing their game, Infiniteams Island game (TPLD). The goal of the game was for the players to learn about their team working abilities, and they were able to show through the questionnaires of 240 students that the players gained self-awareness about their skills through the game. ICURA is another example in which pre- and posttesting assessment was used to evaluate the knowledge learned through the game. Specifically, a role-playing game was used whereby students/players learned about Japanese culture in a role playing format. After playing the game, students completed a test to provide confirmation that they did indeed learn the intended material. The information learned about Japanese culture is more factual than for TPLD, so the measure of the person's performance through a test is a more objective assessment of the game.

Another summative assessment technique is given by the "level-up" protocol of testing, whereby players are divided into two groups with one of the groups beginning the game at the first level, for example, and the other beginning at the second level. If the group that started at the first level does significantly better than the other group, this is attributed to a successful game that is capable of imparting the intended instructional material (at least with respect to the first level) [27].

3.1. Indirect Measures of Learning. In addition to direct measures of learning achievable through targeted assessment, there are also other factors that can indirectly lead to learning. More specifically, serious games captivate and engage players/learners for a specific purpose such as to develop new knowledge or skills [31], and with respect to students, strong engagement has been associated with academic achievement [6], and thus the level of engagement may also be potentially used as an indicator to the learning a serious game is capable of imparting.

Various tools have been developed to provide a measure of engagement including the *Game Engagement Questionnaire* [32] and the *Game Experience Questionnaire* [33].

Another key characteristic of a game experience is given by flow—a user state characterized by a high level of enjoyment and fulfillment. The theory of flow is based on Csikszentmihalyi's foundational observations and concepts and consists of eight major components: a challenging activity requiring skill; a merging of action and awareness; clear goals; direct, immediate feedback; concentration on the task at hand; a sense of control; a loss of self-consciousness; and an altered sense of time [34]. Incorporating the concept of flow in computer games as a model for evaluating player enjoyment has been a focus of interesting studies [35, 36] and forms the basis of EGameFlow, a scale that was specifically developed to measure a learner's enjoyment of e-learning games [37]. EGameFlow is a questionnaire that contains 42 items allocated into eight dimensions: (i) concentration, (ii) goal clarity, (iii) feedback, (iv) challenge, (v) control, (vi) immersion, (vii) social interaction, and (viii) knowledge improvement.

In addition to subjective assessment, a growing area of assessment includes a branch of neuroscience that is investigating the correlation between user psychological states and the value of physiological signals. Several studies have shown that these measures can provide an indication of player engagement (see [38–41]) and flow [42]. Common physiological measures include the following [41, 43]:

(i) Facial electromyography (EMG) for measuring muscle activity through the detecting of electrical impulses generated by the muscles of the face when they contract. Such muscle contractions can provide an indication of emotional state and mood and can assess positive and negative emotional valence [40].

(ii) Cardiovascular measures such as the interbeat interval (the time between heart beats) and heart rate. Cardiac activity has been interpreted as an index to valence, arousal, and attention, cognitive effort, stress, and orientation reflex while viewing various media [40]. Although cardiac measures have been successfully used in a number of game studies, interpreting as described by Kivikangas et al. [40], interpreting the relevance of the resulting measurements within a game context is difficult and challenging.

(iii) Galvanic skin response (GSR), for measuring the electrical conductance of the skin, which varies with its moisture (sweat) level and since the sweat glands are controlled by the sympathetic nervous system skin can provide an indication of psychological or physiological(emotional) arousal.

(iv) Electroencephalography (EEG) for measuring the electrical activity along the scalp and, more specifically, measuring the voltage fluctuations resulting from current flows within the neurons of the brain. Depending on the actions performed by the player of a game, differences in the EEG can be detected. For example, Salminen and Ravaja [44] describe a study where the EEG of players plays a video game that involved them steering a monkey into a goal while collecting bananas for extra points while avoiding falling off the edge of the game board. They observed that each of the three events evoked differential EEG oscillatory changes leading the authors to suggest that EEG is a valuable tool when examining psychological responses to video game events. That being said, EEG is not widely used due of its complex analysis procedure [41].

Although there have been a large number of studies investigating the use of physiological responses within a game setting, plenty of work remains in providing a meaningful interpretation of the resulting data to facilitate design decisions for developers of serious games and e-learning application [43]. That being said, the area of physiological measurement within a game context is a promising field, and although a complete overview of the field is not provided here, excellent reviews are provided by Kivikangas et al. [40] and Nacke [41].

3.2. Audio/Visual Technologies to Support Assessment. In-process and teacher assessments can be accommodated by the use of recent technology. For example, it is now simple and cost-effective to obtain screen recordings of the player's gameplay, video recordings of the players while they are playing the game, and audio recordings to capture a players voice, for example, during thinking aloud processes which may happen unexpectedly or may also be encouraged. With today's technology, information from these recordings can also be obtained automatically (without the need for a camera operator, etc.) using a wide variety of available tools. The recordings and the information obtained from the recordings can also be used to facilitate debriefing sessions.

More recent assessment methods include "information trails" that consist of tracking a player's significant actions and events that may aid in analyzing and answering the what, how, when, who, and where in the game something happened. Although this cannot necessarily provide the reasons why a player selected a specific action or event as opposed to another one, it is suggested that this information be obtained from the players through debriefing (interview) session after they complete their gameplay session [23, 25, 45].

3.3. Assessing Entertainment. As mentioned in Section 1, a serious game has a twofold aim of entertainment and education, both of which must be considered in the assessment.

With respect to measuring fun and enjoyment, there are two possible directions: (i) quantitative approaches,

TABLE 1: Tools for e-Assessment.

Type	Short description	Sample tools
Assessment management systems	Tools to support instructors to create, administer, assess, and analyse tests	Assessment Tools for Teaching and Learning (e-asTTle), Questionmark Perception (QP), Assess By Computer (ABC)
Tools for natural language answer assessment	Tools that automatically assess answers written in free text	Short Answer Marking Engine (SAME), Intelligentassessment.com
Classroom response system	Interactive student response systems that enable teachers to instantly assess learning in class	CPS Student Response Systems, SMART Response, i>clicker, 2Know!, Audience Response System, Beyond Question

and (ii) qualitative approaches [46]. Qualitative approaches for modeling player enjoyment (e.g., the "entertainment" component) rely primarily on psychological observation, where a comprehensive review of the literature leads to the identification of two major lines: Malone's principles of intrinsic qualitative factors for engaging gameplay [47]— namely, challenge, curiosity, and fantasy—and the theory of flow, based on Csikszentmihalyi's foundational concepts [34]. Incorporating flow in computer games as a model for evaluating player enjoyment has been proposed and investigated in significant subsequent studies [35, 36].

In contrast, quantitative approaches attempt to formulate entertainment using mathematical models, which yield reliable numerical values for fun, entertainment, or excitement. However, such approaches are usually limited in their scope. For instance, Iida et al. [48] focus on variants of chess games, while Yannakakis and Hallam [46] focus on the player-opponent interaction, which they assume to be the most important entertainment feature in a computer game.

Therefore, there are different dimensions on which the player's experiences can be measured. A recent study has investigated the definition of these dimensions based on the actual players' experience [49]. That work exploited the Repertory Grid Technique (RGT) methodology [50], which includes qualitative and quantitative aspects. Within those studies, players were asked to use their own criteria in describing similarities and differences among video games. Analyzing the players' personal constructs, 23 major dimensions for game assessment were identified, among which the most relevant were (i) ability demand, (ii) dynamism, (iii) style, (iv) engagement, (v) emotional affect, and (vi) likelihood.

4. Techniques and Tools for Student Performance Assessment

Technology-assisted approaches have been employed for years for student performance assessment, thanks to their potential of streamlining the process of standardized tests and simplifying scoring and reporting. Recent studies have explored how technologies and tools can improve the quality of assessments by replacing certain tasks previously done by instructors, enabling customization of tests based on students' performance, allowing real-time bidirectional

communication between the instructor and students in classrooms, and adopting novel approaches for assessment.

A number of software products are available for online education testing and assessment [51]. Web-based assessments are useful because they decrease class time used for assessment and because multimedia can be integrated into the testing procedure. However, the deployment of such tools requires careful preparation, and the administrator/educator may lose control of the environment in which the test is taken.

Flynn et al. [52] recommend that pedagogic consideration should be given to the choice, variety, and level of difficulty of e-Assessments offered to students. Hewson [53] provides preliminary support for the validity of online assessment methods. Guzmán et al. [54] conducted empirical studies in a university setting demonstrating reliability for student knowledge diagnosis of a set of tools for constructing and administering adaptive tests via the Internet. In general, most of these tools are answering the growing needs for larger-scale education management. However, this approach also raises serious concerns about the quality of the outcomes.

Table 1 summarizes some tools for e-Assessment, which we describe hereinafter.

There are several computer-based systems available for designing tests and analyzing the results. Assessment Tools for Teaching and Learning (e-asTTle) is an online assessment tool, developed to assess students' achievement and progress in reading, mathematics, and writing. It was developed for students aged 8–16 in New Zealand schools and utilizes a computer program to create "paper pencil" tests designed to meet individual learning needs in reading, writing, and mathematics [55]. The system compiles a test based on specified entered characteristics as determined by teachers so that students' learning outcomes can be maximized and students can better understand their progress [56, 57]. e-asTTle allows instructors to create tests that are aligned to the teacher's and the classroom's requirements. It allows measuring student progress over time and provides rich interpretations and specific feedback that relate to student performance. e-asTTle presents the results in visual ways making it easier for teachers to discuss performance.

Similarly, Questionmark Perception (QP) is an assessment management system that enables trainers, educators, and testing professionals to author, schedule, deliver, and report on surveys, quizzes, tests, and exams. QP includes an authoring manager that allows for creation of surveys, quizzes, tests, and exams with a wide variety of question types and options for embedding media [58] and has been shown to be a successful learning and assessment tool [59, 60].

Assess By Computer (ABC) is also designed for flexible computer-based assessment using a variety of question formats [61]. It allows the administrator to design a test via an interactive user interface and then have the student take the test on a stand-alone computer or within a web browser. ABC has been designed to deliver and stimulate feedback through the mechanisms of formative assessment in a way that encourages self-regulated learning. The designers of ABC promote it as improving the appropriateness, effectiveness, and consistency of assessments [62].

Short Answer Marking Engine (SAME) is a software system that can automatically mark short answers in a free text form [63]. Short answers are responses to questions in the test takers' own words and therefore better reflect how well they understand the material since they have to provide their own response instead of choosing the most plausible of the alternatives, as with multiple choice questions [64]. Noorbehbahani and Kardan [65] have modified the BLEU algorithm so that it is suitable for assessing free text answers. To perform an assessment, it is necessary to establish a repository of reference answers written by course instructors or related experts. The system calculates a similarity score with respect to several reference answers for each question. As a commercial product, Intelligent Assessment Technologies provide technology to deploy online tests, assessments, and examinations. The technological suite also includes a module for automatically assessing short answers written in natural language.

A classroom response system (CRS) allows two-way communication between an instructor and their students using the instructor's computer and students' input devices [66]. CRS has been increasingly accepted in educational environments from K12 to higher education and also in informal learning environments [67]. Using CRS, the instructor poses questions and polls students' answers during the class enabling real-time two-way communications to occur. The system is also used to take class attendance, pace the lecture, provide formative and formal assessment, to enhance peer instruction, allow for just-in-time-teaching, and increase class interactivity [68]. Real-time interaction between students and instructors results in students paying greater attention and provides instructors with instant feedback on the students understanding of the tested subjects. Commercially available systems include the CPS Student Response Systems from e-Instruction, SMART Response interactive response systems from SMART Technologies, i>clicker, and 2Know! from Renaissance Learning, as well as the Audience Response System from Qwizdom, and Beyond Question from Smartroom Learning Solutions.

The IMS Question and Test Interoperability (QTI) is a standard interoperability format for representing assessment content and results, such as test questions, tests, and reports, so that they can be used by a variety of different development, assessment, and learning systems and be implemented using a variety of programming languages and modeling tools [69]. Specifically, it has a well-documented format for storing quiz and test items, allowing a wide range of systems to call on one

bank of items, and reports results in a consistent format. It is marketed as a way for creating a large bank of questions and answers that will be able to be used with different systems, now and in the future, and a method for information to be easily shared within and across institutions [70]. Applications can be created using XML (extensible markup language) or higher level development tools including virtual learning environments (e.g., Blackboard, JLE ESSI, and Oracle iLearning), commercial assessment tools (e.g., Can Studios, Calypso from Experient e-Learning Technologies, e-Test 3 from RIVA Technologies Inc, QuestionMark Perception, and QuizAuthor by Niall Barr), and R&D assessment tools (e.g., Ultimate Assessment Engine at Strathclyde University and E3AN).

An interesting application of web-based assessment is the assessment of the skills of potential hires. The goal here is to make sure that the candidates that the assessor companies choose to interview and hire have the desired skills for the job. For example, Codility Ltd. offers a service that provides online automated assessments of programming skills by having the test taker write snippets of code which are assessed for correctness and performance [71]. They sell their services to companies to test potential recruit's software skills and assess current employees. International Knowledge Measurement (IKM) is another web-based service that produces an objective and comprehensive profile of knowledge and skill of candidates and employees [72]. Both these services and others (Kenexa Prove It!, eSkill Corporation, etc.) have arisen in response to the desire to efficiently find employees that have desired skills for specific jobs. These methods could be adapted and used for testing before, inside, and after a serious game.

5. In-Game Assessment

Assessment of learning and training requires a systematic approach to determine a person's achievements and areas of difficulty. Standardized assessment methods often take less time and are easier to administer, and their results are readily interpretable [73]. However, there are limitations to such approaches including ineffective measurement of complex problem solving, communication, and reasoning skills [74, 75]. There is also a concern regarding whether the practice of "teaching to the test" has the potential to decrease a student's interest in learning and life-long learning [76, 77]. Furthermore, standardized tests lack the flexibility necessary to adjust or modify materials for certain groups, such as very high- or low-performing groups, and therefore may lead to loss of sensitivity for certain groups [77]. Although some standardized tests have added sections that move away from the concerning "fill-in the bubble approach", this decreases the efficiency of standardized tests.

Recent studies have explored how play-based assessment can provide more detailed and reliable assessment and emerging interests reflect the needs for an alternative or supplemental assessment tool to overcome limitations in the standardized approach [78, 79]. Play-based, or in-game, assessment can provide more detailed and reliable information, and the emerging interest in this field reflects the need for alternative and/or supplemental assessment tools to overcome limitations in the standard approaches [78, 79]. Traditionally, play-based assessment refers to analyzing how a person plays in order to assess their cognitive development, but here we focus on how play with supporting technology can be used as a vehicle to assess cognitive skills, or competences involved in the game, but not to assess the play itself. In particular, digital games have the advantage in this type of assessment that they can easily keep track of every move and decision a player makes [22].

As pointed out by Becker and Parker [27], serious games (and games in general) can and generally do contain in-game tests of effectiveness. More specifically, as players progress through the game, they accumulate points and experience, which enables facing new topics and higher difficulties in the next stages and levels. This is a very ecological and effective approach, since it integrates pedagogy and games, thus allowing provision of immediate feedback to the player and implementing user adaptivity [80, 81].

Incorporating in-game assessments takes us away from the predominant, classic form of assessment comprised of questionnaires, questions and answers, and so forth that usually interrupts and negatively affects the learning process [21] and is not very suited to verify knowledge transfer. Designing proper in-game assessment is a challenging and time-consuming activity. However, it should be a distinctive feature of any well-designed serious game, where all the mechanics (e.g., score, levels, leaderboards, bonuses, performance indicators, etc.) should be consistent with and inspired by the set pedagogical targets. The work of [21] provides a detailed survey and analysis of serious games, their components, and the related design techniques.

Still, "*many educational games do not properly translate knowledge, facts, and lessons into the language of games. This results in games that are often neither engaging nor educational*" [82]. The authors suggest that design should combine "*the fantasy elements and game play conventions of the real-time strategy (RTS) genre with numbers, resources and situations based on research about a real-world topic*", such as energy and agriculture. In this way, the player should be able to learn simply by trying to overcome the game's challenges.

In addition, in-game assessment provides the opportunity to take advantage of the medium itself and employ alternative, less intrusive, and less obvious forms of assessment which could (and should) become a game element itself [21]. Integrating the assessment such that the player is unaware of it forms the basis of what Shute et al. [6] describe as stealth assessment. In this way, the player can concentrate solely on the game [83]. This type of assessment incorporates the assessment in to the process of the game by designing it so that knowledge from previous sections will be necessary to move on in the game and the knowledge is not directly measured using a quiz or questionnaire [84].

Immune Attack is an example of a serious game that uses in-process assessment. It was designed with the goal of teaching students about the immune system in a fun environment, and while the game does not directly test the player, it does require that the player retains and learn new information about the immune system so that they can progress in the game [84]. In the game, the player must perform tasks such as training macrophages to identify allies versus enemies, identify if a blood vessel is infected, and countering increasingly more difficult attacks from bacteria [84].

CancerSpace is a game format that incorporates aspects of e-learning, adult-learning theory, and behaviorism theory in order to support learning, promote knowledge retention, and encourage behavior change [85]. CancerSpace's design encourages self-directed learning by presenting the players with real-world situations about which they must make decisions similar to those they would make in clinics. The targeted users are professionals working in community health centers. The gameplay is based on role-playing: the user has to help the clinical staff evaluate the clinical literature, integrate the evidence into their clinical decision-making, plan changes to cancer-screening delivery, and accrue points correlating to increased cancer-screening rates. The user takes decisions and observes whether the chosen course of action improves the cancer screening rates, which is the main indicator of performance. The game includes a small number of patient-provider interactions in which the decider must talk with a patient reluctant to get screened. The player's conversation choices are evaluated in preprogrammed decision trees, leading to success (the patient decides to get screened) or failure. Within this educational context, chance is considered an important entertainment and variability feature, which is implemented through wildcard events. To stimulate gameplay, CancerSpace has adapted an award system that motivates players to increase screening rates. The CancerSpace scenarios in which the decider guides the virtual clinical staff are based on research-tested interventions and best practices. Users receive points on the basis of their performance. At each game's conclusion, a summary screen indicates which decisions the player implemented and their effect on the clinic's screening rate.

In a Living World ad hoc designed for cultural training in Afghanistan [86], the main objective for a player is to successfully interpret the environment and achieve the desired attitude towards him by Nonplayer Characters (NPCs) that represent the local population. The entire living-world game space is fueled by the knowledge-engineering process that translates the essential elements of the culture into programmable behaviors and artifacts. For instance, "*In Afghan culture, older men have great influence over younger men, women, and children through local traditions and Islamic law*" or "*Ideologically, the guiding principles of Afghan culture are a sense of familial and tribal honor, gender segregation, and indirect communication*". All the NPCs in the game are modeled accordingly. Winning in the game "simply" requires successfully navigating cultural moves in the game space, thus achieving a good overall attitude of the village toward the player. Another key aspect is seriousness about assessment. The underlying 3D Asymmetric Domain Analysis and Training (3D ADAT) model, an ad hoc developed recursive platform for the realization and visualization of dynamic sociocultural models, specifically supports analysis of the cultural behavior exhibited by the player in the game.

Conversations and interactions between the NPCs and the player are recorded through a text log to provide game performance analysis. The assessment tool lists all the possible choices for player behavior and conversation, highlighting both the player's choice and the most culturally appropriate response. The tool provides scores on the opinion of the player at the NPC, faction, and village level. Additional comments can be provided that highlight the player's weaknesses, explaining why a particular response is most appropriate. Feedback is thus provided to improve future performance.

Business games, also known as business simulations, are another well-established category of serious games that are being used for many decades (originally in nondigital form—thus, they were not called serious games) in business schools [87, 88]. In SimVenture, the target of the player is to manage a company, dealing with four major types of issues: production, organization, sales and market, and finance. The player has a number of choices to perform in these domains. Their performance is expressed in terms of a parameter called "company value." But, as in the real world, the player has to maintain a number of factors, such as profit and loss, a balance sheet, and cash flow. Several other performance figures are also reported in the performance report. Each game session has a simulated time limit, expressed in months. The goal of the game—it can be fixed by the teacher or by the players themselves—can be the maximization of the profit or of cash flow (or any other parameter). Of course, players have to avoid bankruptcy within their time limit. Several predefined scenarios are available and can be loaded by players and classes, so that they can face some common critical cases (e.g., start up a company, managing growth, facing cashflow issues, etc.) at various levels of difficulty. Messages are displayed to the player, at the end of each month's simulation, highlighting the major issues encountered and to be faced. When defining a new game session, there is the possibility of introducing chance events. In the absence of chance events, the game session is deterministic, thus allowing a straightforward comparison of the performance of various players. SimVenture also includes complementary material for teachers and learners.

This material proposes also some additional activities, such as debriefing, answering questions, writing essays, and forecasting events and outcomes and business planning that are to be performed under the supervision and with the help of a teacher. This—in particular the presence of a teacher—is important in order to complement the operational knowledge and skills acquired through the gaming (problem-based learning, experiential learning, etc.) with reflection and verbal knowledge and exchange.

PIXELearning's Enterprise Game is a similar business game, with a major hyphenation on graphic quality and look and feel. Also in this case, defining a product meeting the market demand in terms of quality and price is the most important factor to make the business viable. Definition of a proper marketing strategy is a key as well. Here, the performance of competitor companies is also continuously displayed, so that the player is challenged to do better also with respect to them. Both SimVenture and The Enterprise Game are single player games, while a multiplayer web-based

environment would probably enhance the playability through online competition and collaboration.

6. Conclusions and Directions for Future Research

For serious games to be considered a viable educational tool, they must provide some means of testing and progress-tracking and the testing must be recognizable within the context of the education or training they are attempting to impart [22]. Various methods and techniques have been used to assess effectiveness of serious games, and various comprehensive reviews have been conducted to examine the overall validity of game-based learning. Results of these reviews seem to suggest that game-based learning is effective for motivating and for achieving learning goals at the lower levels in Bloom's taxonomy [15].

However, caution is still required with respect to many of the claims that have appeared in the literature about the "revolution" due to the use of serious games in education. Achieving more ambitious learning goals seems to require studying new types of games able to foster more accurate reasoning and reflection, stimulated through proper teacher guidance, allowing the player to efficiently structure the knowledge space. We also believe that comparison studies with other educational technologies should be carried out in order to better understand the serious games' effectiveness.

Assessing the user learning within a simulation or serious game is not a trivial matter, and further work and studies are required. With the advent of cheaper hardware and software, it has been possible to extend and enhance assessment by recording gameplay sessions and keeping track of players' in-game performance. In-game assessment appears to be particularly suited and useful given that it is integrated into the game logic and, therefore, does not break the player's game experience. Furthermore, it enables immediate provision of feedback and implementation of adaptability. In general, for assessment design, it must be stressed that clear goals must be set, followed by techniques to collect data that will be used to verify these goals.

As Kevin Corti of PIXELearning stated, "[Serious games] will not grow as an industry unless the learning experience is definable, quantifiable and measurable. Assessment is the future of serious games" [89]. This requires still a lot of research work. We see in particular two major research directions: characterization of the player's activity and better integration of assessment in games.

Characterization of the player's activities involves both task characterization (e.g., in terms of content, difficulty level, type of supported learning style, etc.) and user profiling [90]. It is necessary to identify the dimensions, relevant to learning, along which the users and the tasks are modeled. Then, the matching rules and modalities between users and tasks should be defined. The user profile should be portable across different games and even applications, particularly in the education field. Here, it is particularly important to consider also misconceptions and mistakes. In user profiling, analysis of neurophysiological signals is particularly promising, as it allows a continuous, in-depth, and quantitative monitoring of the user activity and state. Finally, proper user profiling is a key to enable adaptability and personalization.

Better integration of assessment in games is essentially a matter of definition of the proper mechanisms and conditions to activate them. It is important that these mechanisms should be general and modular, so to be seamlessly applicable in different games. This will increase efficiency in designing games and authoring contents, which is a key requirement for the serious game industry [20]. A strictly related topic concerns provision of feedback, which is a consequence of assessment and should be properly integrated in the game, in order not to distract the player while favoring performance enhancement.

Conflict of Interests

The authors hereby declare that they have no conflict of interests with the companies/commercial products cited in this paper.

Acknowledgments

The authors are grateful to the reviewers for their suggestions that have allowed us to significantly improve the quality of the paper. This work has been partially funded by the EC, through the GALA EU Network of Excellence in Serious Games (FP7-ICT-2009-5-258169). The financial support of the *Social Sciences and Humanities Research Council of Canada* (*SSHRC*) in support of the IMMERSE project that B. Kapralos is part of is gratefully acknowledged.

References

[1] J. P. Gee, *What Video Games Have to Teach Us about Learning and Literacy*, Palgrave MacMillan, New York, NY, USA, 2007.

[2] F. L. Greitzer, O. A. Kuchar, and K. Huston, "Cognitive science implications for enhancing training effectiveness in a serious gaming context," *ACM Journal on Educational Resources in Computing*, vol. 7, no. 3, article 2, 2007.

[3] F. De Grove, P. Mechant, and J. Van Looy, "Uncharted waters? Exploring experts' opinions on the opportunities and limitations of serious games for foreign language learning," in *Proceedings of the 3rd International Conference on Fun and Games*, pp. 107–115, Leuven, Belgium, September 2010.

[4] R. van Eck, "Digital game-based learning: it's not just the digital natives who are restless," *EDUCAUSE Review*, vol. 41, no. 2, pp. 16–30, 2006.

[5] J. Cannon-Bowers, "The state of gaming and simulation," in *Proceedings of the Training Conference and Expo*, Orlando, Fla, USA, March 2006.

[6] V. Shute, M. Ventura, M. Bauer, and D. Zapata-Rivera, "Melding the power of serious games and embedded assessment to monitor and foster learning: flow and grow," in *Serious Games: Mechanisms and Effects*, U. Ritterfeld, M. Cody, and P. Vorderer, Eds., pp. 295–321, Routledge, Taylor and Francis, Mahwah, NJ, USA, 2009.

[7] J. Gosen and J. Washbush, "A review of scholarship on assessing experiential learning effectiveness," *Simulation & Gaming*, vol. 35, no. 2, pp. 270–293, 2004.

[8] R. T. Hays, "The effectiveness of instructional games: a literature review and discussion," Tech. Rep. 2005-004, Naval Air Warfare Center, Training Systems Division, 2005.

[9] A. A. Kulik, "School mathematics and science programs benefit from instructional technology," United States National Science Foundation (NSF), National Center for Science and Engineering Statistics (NCSES), InfroBrief NSF-03-301, November 2002, http://www.nsf.gov/statistics/infbrief/nsf03301/.

[10] R. Blunt, "Do serious games work? Results from three studies," *eLearn Magazine*, vol. 2009, no. 12, 2009.

[11] B. Bergeron, *Developing Serious Games*, Thomson Delmar Learning, Hingham, Mass, USA, 2006.

[12] M. Prensky, *Don't Bother Me Mom—I'm Learning!*, Paragon House, 2006.

[13] S. Livingston, G. Fennessey, J. Coleman, K. Edwards, and S. Kidder, "The Hopkins games program: final report on seven years of research," Report No. 155, Johns Hopkins University, Center for Social Organization of Schools, Baltimore, Md, USA, 1973.

[14] J. Chin, R. Dukes, and W. Gamson, "Assessment in simulation and gaming: a review of the last 40 years," *Simulation & Gaming*, vol. 40, no. 4, pp. 553–568, 2009.

[15] T. M. Connolly, E. A. Boyle, E. MacArthur, T. Hainey, and J. M. Boyle, "A systematic literature review of the empirical evidence on computer games and serious games," *Computers and Education*, vol. 59, no. 2, pp. 661–686, 2012.

[16] P. M. Kato, S. W. Cole, A. S. Bradlyn, and B. H. Pollock, "A video game improves behavioral outcomes in adolescents and young adults with cancer: a randomized trial," *Pediatrics*, vol. 122, no. 2, pp. e305–e317, 2008.

[17] S. W. Cole, D. J. Yoo, and B. Knutson, "Interactivity and reward-related neural activation during a serious videogame," *PLoS ONE*, vol. 7, no. 3, Article ID e33909, 2012.

[18] S. D. Dandeneau and M. W. Baldwin, "The inhibition of socially rejecting information among people with high versus low self-esteem: the role of attentional bias and the effects of bias reduction training," *Journal of Social and Clinical Psychology*, vol. 23, no. 4, pp. 584–602, 2004.

[19] F. Bellotti, R. Berta, A. De Gloria, A. D'Ursi, and V. Fiore, "A serious game model for cultural heritage," *Journal on Computing and Cultural Heritage*, vol. 5, no. 4, pp. 1–27, 2012.

[20] F. Bellotti, R. Berta, and A. De Gloria, "Designing effective serious games: opportunities and challenges for research," *International Journal of Emerging Technologies in Learning*, vol. 5, pp. 22–35, 2010.

[21] G. Bente and J. Breuer, "Making the implicit explicit: embedded measurement in serious games," in *Serious Games: Mechanisms and Effects*, U. Ritterfield, M. J. Cody, and P. Vorderer, Eds., pp. 322–343, Routledge, New York, NY, USA, 2009.

[22] D. Michael and S. Chen, "Proof of learning: assessment in serious games," October 2005, http://www.gamasutra.com/view/feature/2433/proof_of_learning_assessment_in_.php.

[23] J. Enfield, R. D. Myers, M. Lara, and T. W. Frick, "Innovation diffusion: assessment of strategies within the diffusion simulation game," *Simulation & Gaming*, vol. 43, no. 2, pp. 188–214, 2012.

[24] C. Boston, "The concept of formative assessment," *Practical Assessment, Research & Evaluation*, vol. 8, no. 9, 2002.

[25] P. Moreno-Ger, D. Burgos, and J. Torrente, "Digital games in eLearning environments: current uses and emerging trends," *Simulation & Gaming*, vol. 40, no. 5, pp. 669–687, 2009.

[26] C. Sebastian, A. Anantachai, J. H. Byun, and J. Lenox, "Assessing what players learned in serious games: in-situ data collection, information trails, and quantitative analysis," in *Proceedings of the 10th International Conference on Computer Games: AI, Animation, Mobile, Educational and Serious Games*, pp. 10–19, 2007.

[27] K. Becker and J. R. Parker, *The Guide to Computer Simulations and Games*, John Wiley & Sons, Indianapolis, Ind, USA, 2011.

[28] P. Dugard and J. Todman, "Analysis of pre-test-post-test control group designs in educational research," *Educational Psychology*, vol. 15, no. 2, pp. 181–198, 1995.

[29] National Center for Technology Innovation (NCTI), "Experimental Study Design," 2012, http://www.nationaltechcenter.org/ http://www.nationaltechcenter.org/index.php/products/at-research-matters/experimental-study-design/.

[30] L. Allen, M. Seeney, L. Boyle, and F. Hancock, "The implementation of team based assessment in serious games," in *Proceedings of the 1st Conference in Games and Virtual Worlds for Serious Applications (VS-GAMES '09)*, pp. 28–35, Coventry, UK, March 2009.

[31] K. Corti, *Game-Based Learning: A Serious Business Application*, PIXELearning, Coventry, UK, 2006.

[32] J. H. Brockmyer, C. M. Fox, K. A. Curtiss, E. McBroom, K. M. Burkhart, and J. N. Pidruzny, "The development of the Game Engagement Questionnaire: a measure of engagement in video game-playing," *Journal of Experimental Social Psychology*, vol. 45, no. 4, pp. 624–634, 2009.

[33] W. A. IJsselsteijn, W. van de Hoogen, C. Klimmt et al., "Measuring the experience of digital game enjoyment," in *Proceedings of Measuring Behavior*, pp. 88–89, Maastricht, The Netherlands, August 2008.

[34] M. Csikszentmihalyi, *Flow: The Psychology of Optimal Experience*, Harper & Row, New York, NY, USA, 1990.

[35] B. Cowley, D. Charles, M. Black, and R. Hickey, "Toward an understanding of flow in video games," *Computers in Entertainment*, vol. 6, no. 2, pp. 1–28, 2008.

[36] P. Sweetser and P. Wyeth, "GameFlow: a model for evaluating player enjoyment in games," *ACM Computers in Entertainment*, vol. 3, no. 3, pp. 1–24, 2005.

[37] F. L. Fu, R. C. Su, and S. C. Yu, "EGameFlow: a scale to measure learners' enjoyment of e-learning games," *Computers and Education*, vol. 52, no. 1, pp. 101–112, 2009.

[38] S. H. Janicke and A. Ellis, "Psychological and physiological differences between the 3D and 2D gaming experience," in *Proceedings of the 3D Entertainment Summit*, Hollywood, Calif, USA, September, 2011.

[39] H. F. Jelinek, K. August, H. Imam, A. H. Khandoker, A. Koenig, and R. Riener, "Heart rate asymmetry and emotional response to robot assist task challenges in stroke patients," in *Proceedings of the Computing in Cardiology Conference*, Hangzhou, China, September 2011.

[40] J. M. Kivikangas, G. Chanel, B. Cowley et al., "A review of the use of psychophysiological methods in game research," *Journal of Gaming & Virtual Worlds*, vol. 3, no. 3, pp. 181–199, 2011.

[41] L. E. Nacke, *Affective ludology: scientific measurement of user experience in interactive entertainment [Ph.D. thesis]*, Blekinge Institute of Technology, Karlskrona, Sweden, 2009.

[42] A. Plotnikov, N. Stakheika, A. De Gloria et al., "Exploiting real-time EEG analysis for assessing flow in games," in *Workshop: "Game Based Learning for 21st Century Transferable Skills", at iCalt 2012*, Rome, Italy, June 2012.

[43] L. E. Nacke, "Physiological game interaction and psychophysiological evaluation in research and industry," Gamasutra Article, June 2011, http://www.gamasutra.com/blogs/ LennartNacke/20110628/7867/Physiological_Game_Interaction_ and_Psychophysiological_Evaluation_in_Research_and_Industry .php.

[44] M. Salminen and N. Ravaja, "Oscillatory brain responses evoked by video game events: the case of super monkey ball 2," *Cyberpsychology & Behavior*, vol. 10, no. 3, pp. 330–338, 2007.

[45] C. Loh, "Designing online games assessment as information trails," in *Games and Simulations in Online Learning: Research and Development Frameworks*, D. Gibson, C. Aldrich, and M. Prensky, Eds., pp. 323–348, Information Science Publishing, Hershey, Pa, USA, 2007.

[46] G. N. Yannakakis and J. Hallam, "Evolving opponents for interesting interactive computer games," in *Proceedings of the International Conference on Computer Games: Artificial Intelligence, Design and Education*, 2004.

[47] T. W. Malone, "Toward a theory of intrinsically motivating instruction," *Cognitive Science*, vol. 5, no. 4, pp. 333–369, 1981.

[48] H. Iida, N. Takeshita, and J. Yoshimura, "A metric for entertainment of boardgames: its implication for evolution of chess variants," in *Proceeding of: Entertainment Computing: Technologies and Applications, IFIP First International Workshop on Entertainment Computing (IWEC '02)*, R. Nakatsu and J. Hoshino, Eds., pp. 65–72, Kluwer Academic, Boston, Mass, USA, 2003.

[49] F. Bellotti, R. Berta, A. De Gloria, and L. Primavera, "Enhancing the educational value of video games," *Computers in Entertainment*, vol. 7, no. 2, pp. 23–41, 2009.

[50] M. Hassenzahl and R. Wessler, "Capturing design space from a user perspective: the repertory grid technique revisited," *International Journal of Human-Computer Interaction*, vol. 12, no. 3-4, pp. 441–459, 2000.

[51] N. Zoanetti, "Software for online testing and quizzes," 2011, http://www.assessmentfocus.com/online-testing.php.

[52] A. Flynn, F. Concannon, and M. Campbell, "An evaluation of undergraduate students' online assessment performances," *Advanced Technology for Learning*, vol. 3, no. 1, pp. 15–51, 2006.

[53] C. Hewson, "Can online course-based assessment methods be fair and equitable? Relationships between students' preferences and performance within online and offline assessments," *Journal of Computer Assisted Learning*, vol. 28, no. 5, pp. 488–498, 2001.

[54] E. Guzmán, R. Conejo, and J. L. Pérez-de-la-Cruz, "Improving student performance using self-assessment tests," *IEEE Intelligent Systems*, vol. 22, no. 4, pp. 46–52, 2007.

[55] J. Hattie and D. Masters, "asTTle—Assessment Tools for Teaching and Learning," HEFCE JISC, 2006, http://www.jisc.ac.uk/ media/documents/projects/asttle_casestudy.pdf.

[56] J. Hattie, G. Brown, P. Keegan et al., "Validation evidence of asTTle reading assessment results: norms and criteria," Asttle Tech. Rep. 22, University of Auckland/Ministry of Education, November 2003.

[57] J. Hattie, "Large-scale assessment of student competencies," in *Symposium: Working in Today's World of Testing and Measurement: Required Knowledge and Skills (Joint ITC/CPTA Symposium); the 26th International Congress of Applied Psychology*, Athens, Greece, July 2006.

[58] Questionmark Corporation, "Questionmark Perception Measure Knowledge, Skills and Attitudes Securely for Certification,

Regulatory Compliance and successful Learning Outcomes," 2012.

[59] J. Bull and D. Stephens, "The use of question mark software for formative and summative assessment in two universities," *Innovations in Education and Teaching International*, vol. 36, no. 2, pp. 128–135, 1999.

[60] G. M. Velan, R. K. Kumar, M. Dziegielewski, and D. Wakefield, "Web-based self-assessments in pathology with Questionmark Perception," *Pathology*, vol. 34, no. 3, pp. 282–284, 2002.

[61] HEFCE JISC, "Case study 5: making the most of a computer-assisted assessment system University of Manchester," 2010, http://www.jisc.ac.uk/media/documents/programmes/elearning/digiassess_makingthemost.pdf.

[62] M. Wood, *Human Computer Collaborative Assessment—Access by Computer (ABC)—University of Manchester*, HEFCE JISC, 2009.

[63] HEFCE JISC, "Short answer marking engines," 2009, http://www.jisc.ac.uk/media/documents/projects/shorttext.pdf.

[64] S. Jordan and T. Mitchell, "e-Assessment for learning? The potential of short-answer free-text questions with tailored feedback," *British Journal of Educational Technology*, vol. 40, no. 2, pp. 371–385, 2009.

[65] F. Noorbehbahani and A. A. Kardan, "The automatic assessment of free text answers using a modified BLEU algorithm," *Computers & Education*, vol. 56, no. 2, pp. 337–345, 2011.

[66] I. D. Beatty and W. J. Gerace, "Technology-enhanced formative assessment: a research-based pedagogy for teaching science with classroom response technology," *Journal of Science Education and Technology*, vol. 18, no. 2, pp. 146–162, 2009.

[67] C. Fies and J. Marshall, "Classroom response systems: a review of the literature," *Journal of Science Education and Technology*, vol. 15, no. 1, pp. 101–109, 2006.

[68] C. Fies and J. Marshall, "The C_3 framework: evaluating classroom response system interactions in university classrooms," *Journal of Science Education and Technology*, vol. 17, no. 5, pp. 483–499, 2008.

[69] IMS Global Learning Consortium, "IMS Question & Test Interoperability Specification (QTI)," 2012, http://www.imsglobal.org/question/.

[70] C. Smythe and P. Roberts, *An Overview of the IMS Question & Test Interoperability Specification*, Computer Aided Assessment, Leicestershire, UK, 2000.

[71] Codility Ltd., "Codility: WE TEST CODERS," 2009, http://codility.com/.

[72] About IKM, "Overview," 2011, http://www.ikmnet.com/about/overview.cfm.

[73] M. M. Clarke, G. F. Madaus, C. L. Horn, and M. A. Ramos, "Retrospective on educational testing and assessment in the 20th century," *Journal of Curriculum Studies*, vol. 32, no. 2, pp. 159–181, 2000.

[74] L. B. Resnick and D. P. Resnick, *Assessing the Thinking Curriculum: New Tools for Educational Reform*, Learning Research and Development Center: University of Pittsburgh and Carnegie Mellon University, Pittsburgh, Pa, USA, 1989.

[75] M. Lipman, "Some thoughts on the formation of reflective education," in *Teaching-Thinking Skills: Theory and Practice*, J. B. Baron and R. J. Sternberg, Eds., pp. 151–161, W. H. Freeman, New York, NY, USA, 1987.

[76] C. Tribune, "Standardized testing will limit students' future," April 2010, http://articles.chicagotribune.com/2010-04-21/news/chi-100421shafer_briefs_1standardized-test-scores-teacher-and-principal-evaluations.

[77] Fairtest, "What's Wrong with Standardized Tests?" May 2012, http://www.fairtest.org/facts/whatwron.htm.

[78] E. J. Short, M. Noeder, S. Gorovoy, M. J. Manos, and B. Lewis, "The importance of play in both the assessment and treatment of young children," in *An Evidence-Based Approach to Play in Intervention and Prevention: Integrating Developmental and Clinical Science*, S. Russ and L. Niec, Eds., Guilford, London, UK.

[79] A. S. Kaugars and S. W. Russ, "Assessing preschool children's pretend play: preliminary validation of the affect in play scale-preschool version," *Early Education and Development*, vol. 20, no. 5, pp. 733–755, 2009.

[80] F. Bellotti, R. Berta, A. De Gloria, and L. Primavera, "Adaptive experience engine for serious games," *IEEE Transactions on Computational Intelligence and AI in Games*, vol. 1, no. 4, pp. 264–280, 2009.

[81] C. H. Tan, K. C. Tan, and A. Tay, "Dynamic game difficulty scaling using adaptive behavior-based AI," *IEEE Transactions on Computational Intelligence and AI in Games*, vol. 3, no. 4, pp. 289–301, 2011.

[82] L. Doucet and V. Srinivasany, "Designing entertaining educational games using procedural rhetoric: a case study," in *Proceedings of the 5th ACM SIGGRAPH Symposium on Video Games*, pp. 5–10, Los Angeles, Calif, USA, July 2010.

[83] J. Froschauer, I. Seidel, M. Gärtner, H. Berger, and D. Merkl, "Design and evaluation of a serious game for immersive cultural training," in *Proceedings of the 16th International Conference on Virtual Systems and Multimedia (VSMM '10)*, pp. 253–260, IEEE CS Press, Seoul, Republic of Korea, October 2010.

[84] H. Kelly, K. Howell, E. Glinert et al., "How to build serious games," *Communications of the ACM*, vol. 50, no. 7, pp. 44–49, 2007.

[85] J. Swarz, A. Ousley, A. Magro et al., "CancerSpace: a simulation-based game for improving cancer-screening rates," *IEEE Computer Graphics and Applications*, vol. 30, no. 1, pp. 90–94, 2010.

[86] M. A. Zielke, M. J. Evans, F. Dufour et al., "Serious games for immersive cultural training: creating a living world," *IEEE Computer Graphics and Applications*, vol. 29, no. 2, pp. 49–60, 2009.

[87] M. King and R. Newman, "Evaluating business simulation software: approach, tools and pedagogy," *On the Horizon*, vol. 17, no. 4, pp. 368–377, 2009.

[88] A. J. Stainton, J. E. Johnson, and E. P. Borodzicz, "Educational validity of business gaming simulation: a research methodology framework," *Simulation & Gaming*, vol. 41, no. 5, pp. 705–723, 2010.

[89] U. Ritterfeld, M. Cody, and P. Vorderer, Eds., *Serious Games: Mechanisms and Effects*, Routledge, New York, NY, USA, 2009.

[90] F. Bellotti, R. Berta, A. De Gloria, and L. Primavera, "A task annotation model for SandBox Serious Games," in *Proceedings of IEEE Symposium on Computational Intelligence and Games (CIG '09)*, pp. 233–240, Milano, Italy, September 2009.

19

BCI Could Make Old Two-Player Games Even More Fun: A Proof of Concept with "Connect Four"

Emmanuel Maby, Margaux Perrin, Olivier Bertrand, Gaëtan Sanchez, and Jérémie Mattout

CRNL, Lyon Neuroscience Research Center, INSERM, CNRS, University Lyon 1, Dycog Team, 95 Bd Pinel, 69500 Bron, France

Correspondence should be addressed to Emmanuel Maby, manu.maby@inserm.fr

Academic Editor: Christoph Braun

We present a brain-computer interface (BCI) version of the famous "Connect Four". Target selection is based on brain event-related responses measured with nine EEG sensors. Two players compete against each other using their brain activity only. Importantly, we turned the general difficulty of producing a reliable BCI command into an advantage, by extending the game play and rules, in a way that adds fun to the game and might well prove to trigger up motivation in future studies. The principle of this new BCI is directly inspired from our own implementation of the classical P300 Speller (Maby et al. 2010, Perrin et al. 2011). We here establish a proof of principle that the same electrophysiological markers can be used to design an efficient two-player game. Experimental evaluation on two competing healthy subjects yielded an average accuracy of 82%, which is in line with our previous results on many participants and demonstrates that the BCI "Connect Four" can effectively be controlled. Interestingly, the duration of the game is not significantly affected by the usual slowness of BCI commands. This suggests that this kind of BCI games could be of interest to healthy players as well as to disabled people who cannot play with classical games.

1. Introduction

Driven by the needs of people with physical disabilities, researchers have begun to work on direct brain-computer interfaces (BCIs), in the aim of enabling them to communicate and move without resorting to the usual peripheral nervous and muscular pathways. In BCIs, users have to manipulate their brain activity to produce signals that control computers or machines directly. This is challenging for both users and researchers. The users often need to learn how to control the device, which is cumbersome if not impossible, while researchers have to deal with the difficulty of processing highly variable and noisy signals online. However, this research could have a profound impact in various pathologies, including those for which patients suffer from cognitive impairments and could possibly benefit from brain or neurofeedback training. Indeed, the latter also rests upon our ability to extract online the neurophysiological markers that should be fed back to the patients, so that they could learn how to control it and yield a cognitive or behavioral improvement [1].

The most practical and widely applicable BCI solutions are based on noninvasive electrophysiological recordings, namely, electroencephalography (EEG). As command signals, those BCI use event-related potentials (ERPs) like the P300 [2] or self-regulatory activities such as changes in cortical rhythms [3, 4].

Beyond medical applications [5–7], BCI has also a great potential for gaming, a domain where users are open to novelty and eager to face new challenges [8]. Besides, developing video games based on BCI could prove useful in some patients, by yielding a better efficiency and wider acceptance of BCI-based therapies. Indeed, since the number of training sessions required by neurological rehabilitation and training protocols is usually much larger than the one in BCI control applications, a motivational (more realistic and interactive) environment as encountered in computer games could be of great interest in that context [9, 10]. In particular, it has been argued that BCI games could well boost motivation and neurofeedback training performance [11]. Possible future investments of the gaming industry in BCI software and technologies might also stimulate the field and produce new devices, with engaging environments for future clinical applications like BCI-based stroke rehabilitation and neurofeedback therapies [12].

There are several examples of games that have been paired up with BCI systems yet, either by using imaginary movement-related markers [13], P300 responses [14, 15], or steady-state visual potentials [16]. However, only a few have been designed for multiple players, despite the fact that competition and socializing are among the strongest motivational factors reported by users of multiplayer games online [17].

A crucial limitation to the use of BCI in gaming is the highly unreliable nature of brain signals. The ensuing BCI commands are difficult to interpret and provide low degrees of freedom. In most applications, a reliable command can only be achieved by accumulating data over long time windows, at the expense of the primary interest of the game. Another drawback is the obvious one of having to put an EEG cap on, although the field has made tremendous progress in that respect in the last few years [18]. For all those reasons today, BCI hardly compete with traditional game effectors such as joysticks, mice, and keyboards, at least in healthy subjects. However, unreliable input control could be used to extend current video games and to create a motivating challenge for the users [19].

In this paper, we briefly report the online proof of concept of a new BCI game, based on the old and well-known "Connect Four". It is a very popular and easy game to play, which makes it attractive for a broad audience. The proposed BCI version has several advantages and our first online trial suggests it could overcome some of the current limitations of BCI applications to gaming. Interestingly,

(i) only brain signals are required to play the game;

(ii) two subjects play against each other;

(iii) the EEG setup has been limited to nine sensors per participant (compared to 32 in our previous experimental settings);

(iv) it exploits a well-established protocol and robust electrophysiological marker: the $N1$ (indeed, it has already been shown that the early visual evoked response plays a significant role in achieving higher accuracies in the classical P300 Speller paradigm. This strongly suggests that such BCIs thus highly rely on eye gaze or overt attention [20].) and P300 evoked response [21];

(v) it makes use of the unreliability of BCI commands in an elegant fashion, which extends the possibilities offered by the initial game;

(vi) its duration is comparable to the one of the traditional game play;

(vii) it holds promises for applications in patients, not only as an entertainment but possibly as an efficient tool for the training attention-related brain signals.

In the following, we introduce the traditional game "Connect Four" and its adaptation to a BCI version. We then describe our BCI implementation within the OpenViBE

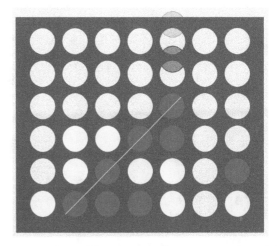

FIGURE 1: Traditional "Connect Four". Here, Red wins with four coins aligned diagonally (transparency has been added here to highlight the last command and winning command).

software environment. Finally, we report the results of a first online evaluation in two healthy subjects as a proof of concept to show that a BCI "Connect Four" can effectively be controlled.

1.1. Traditional "Connect Four". "Connect Four" is a two-player strategy game in which players interact through a vertical rectangular board made of 6×7 holes (6 rows and 7 columns). Each player starts with 21 coins, either all yellow or all red. Participants play in turn and place one coin at a time. They pick up a column and drop a coin which will fall down the board to the lowest available hole. The game ends when one participant first connects four coins, either horizontally, vertically, or diagonally. This participant is the winner of the game (see Figure 1).

1.2. BCI "Connect Four". In the BCI version of "Connect Four," we simply replace the manual drop of the coin by a P300-based selection of the target column. The column selection process follows the same principle as the item selection in the well-established P300 Speller paradigm. In the latter, a 6×6 matrix of symbols is usually displayed on a computer screen for spelling. The subject has to actively attend to the target symbol while rows and columns are being flashed alternatively, in a random fashion. Since the target events are rare and unpredictable, they elicit a typical EEG evoked response, the P300 whose detection allows us to identify the target symbol. In the "Connect Four" scenario, only columns matter and need to be proposed. This yields a simpler detection task and higher information transfer rate.

The P300 wave is a positive EEG deflection that occurs approximately 300 ms after stimulus onset (flash onset). It is typically recorded from central and parietal sensors. This response is evoked by paying attention to rare stimuli in a random sequence of irrelevant stimuli or distracters (the so-called oddball paradigm) [22]. Farwell and Donchin [23] were the first to show that the P300 component could be used to select items displayed on a computer screen [24]. From

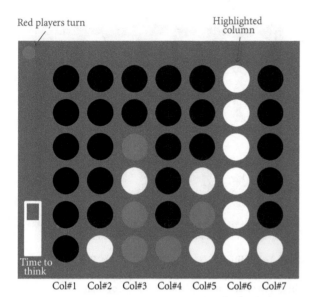

FIGURE 2: P300-based BCI "Connect Four". Black disks represent the empty places. Yellow and red disks correspond to player P1 and player P2 pieces, respectively. The column made of white disks represents a flashed column.

a cognitive perspective, the P300 can be seen as a measure of alertness and attention orientation, thus reflecting a subject's general level of arousal [25].

Importantly, we build on an existing BCI system that we extensively evaluated in previous studies [26, 27]. In particular, we showed that a similar setup could be reliably controlled by naive BCI subjects ($N = 42$), with very high spelling accuracy (85% correct letter selection on average, for 3 flashing sequences).

2. Material and Methods

2.1. Game Rules

2.1.1. Classic Mode. In turn, players choose an empty location based on their own strategy and aim at placing a coin in the corresponding column. To drop a coin in the right column, the player focuses her attention on that particular column (Figure 2) and is advised to count the number of times it is flashed, while avoiding to be distracted by the flashes occurring next to it. After all columns have been flashed (possibly several times), the most probable target according to real-time signal processing is selected. The player receives immediate feedback on her action. The game ends whenever one player has been successful in connecting four coins. Of course, each player should prevent the other player to complete a four-coin long connection. In the classic mode, this can only be done in turn.

2.1.2. Contest Mode. The principle is the same as for the classic mode, except that players can interfere with the outcome of the action of the other player. Players still act in turn. However, when player 1 is aiming at dropping a coin, player 2 has the possibility to modify the target column for this coin, and vice versa. To do so, she has to enter a kind

of mind competition and her choice will eventually prevail, provided that she could better focus her attention onto her preferred target column. The quantitative comparison between the attentional resources, respectively, allocated by the two players is based on the entropy of the posterior distribution of the target column for each player (see Section 2.3, paragraph *Classification*). In short, the winner is the one who produces the most accurate or less uncertain command. This mode allows for simultaneous competition between the two players and makes the interaction more challenging.

2.2. Experimental Setup. Two players, one female (P1) and one male (P2), aged 23 and 30 respectively, participated in this study. All subjects had normal or corrected to normal vision.

Players were seated 70 cm from the same 17″ computer screen. EEG was recorded from the two players using a single 32-channel ActiCap system with Ag/AgCl electrodes (Brain Products, Germany). Only nine sensors were used for each participant. The particular (centroparietal and occipital) electrode locations were chosen in order to optimize the signal to signal-plus-noise ratio (SSNR), according to one of our previous P300 Speller experiment [28]. We used the following sites from the extended 10-10 system: P7, P3, Pz, P4, P8, P09, O1, O2, and PO10. All electrodes were referenced to an electrode placed on the nose and impedances were kept below 5 kΩ for all sensors. Analog signals were amplified with BrainAmp amplifier (powered with a rechargeable battery, PowerPack) and digitized at a rate of 1000 Hz using the Brain Vision Recorder software (Brain Products, Germany).

To achieve good selection of one target column among seven, the two players were instructed not to move during stimulations, to stare at the targeted location, and to count how many times it was flashed.

Visual stimulations were handled by a C++/SDL software on a dedicated computer and sent to a CRT screen in random order. A trigger (labeled from 1 to 7, one per column) was also sent to the EEG amplifier via parallel port (jitter < 0.1 ms). The flash duration was set to 90 ms and the time between two flash onsets to 200 ms. We used two repetitions per shot, meaning that each column was highlighted twice per selection process.

Since the two players had never used such a P300-based BCI before, we had to start with a short and simultaneous session to calibrate the system. Subjects were given a sequence of 63 predetermined target columns to attend to. In practice, after each sequence of flashes for one target, the new target was indicated by a green frame. As in the forthcoming game, columns were flashed twice per trial during 90 ms, with a stimulus-onset asynchrony interval (SOA) of 200 ms. Based on those data, the feature selection and classification algorithms were trained for each subject, respectively.

After calibration, the two subjects performed three games in classic mode, followed by two games in contest mode. In each game, players had 10 s to choose a target before the columns started flashing. Finally and for each shot, each player was requested to write down her/his actual target number for future (offline) evaluation.

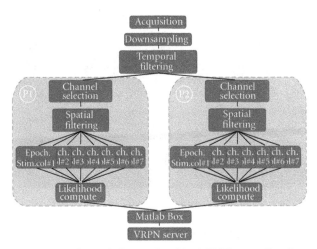

FIGURE 3: OpenViBE scenario of the BCI "Connect Four".

2.3. Online Processing. We implemented this BCI game scenario in OpenViBE (OV). OV is an open source platform to design, implement, and run BCI applications [29]. The dedicated online data processing stream consisted in a classical BCI pipeline made of successive modules in the following order: data acquisition, feature selection, feature classification, decision, and feedback (see Figure 3). Those modules operate as follows.

Acquisition. New chunks of raw EEG data are transmitted via TCP/IP every 20 ms. The data stream includes event markers. The Acquisition Server application converts those streams into OV format.

Downsampling. Data are sampled down to 100 Hz after being passed through an antialiasing filter.

Temporal Filtering. For each channel independently, downsampled data are then bandpass filtered between 1 and 20 Hz using a second-order Butterworth filter to remove very low frequencies and the higher frequency content of EMG.

Channel Selection. The channel selector limits the 32-channel data stream to two 9-channel data streams, one for each player.

Spatial Filtering. To extract the most relevant signal components and to increase the signal-to-noise ratio (SNR), we used the xDAWN algorithm which has been specifically developed for the P300 Speller [30]. Precisely, it optimizes orthogonal spatial filters (linear combinations of sensors) so as to maximize the signal to signal-plus-noise ratio. We used the first five filters (or virtual sensors) obtained from the calibration phase, for each subject.

Epoching. Epochs are generated upon reception of a given event marker. Seven stimulation-based epoching are performed in parallel, per player branch, each epoch type being associated with a different column. We considered 600 ms long epochs starting at flash onset.

Classification. The temporally and spatially filtered epoched data enter as features for subsequent classification. The aim of classification is to disentangle between target and nontarget events. Therefore, we adapted the Bayesian approach we used in a previous P300 Speller experiment [26]. The Bayesian procedure rests on computing the posterior probability $p(C \mid Y)$ that a given response Y pertains to the "target" or "nontarget" class type of event C. This conditional density is inferred from combining two antecedents: the prior probability $p(C)$ and the likelihood function $p(Y \mid C)$ which embeds a probabilistic model of the data to be observed. In the current scenario, we used a two-Gaussian mixture likelihood function. In a previous P300 Speller study, in twenty subjects, we had shown that this classifier was equivalent or even better than a classical LDA [26]. Moreover, it allows for the optimal and online updating of the posterior density, after each single new observation. Hence starting with a uniform prior over columns (each column is a possible target, with equal prior probability), the posterior density is computed based on the data likelihood and the given prior. If more data pertaining to the same shot are provided, the current posterior is taken as the new prior, in a Markovian fashion. In practice, online, this is performed in two OV steps as follows.

(i) *Likelihood compute*: this box computes the likelihood function for each class and each stimulus type. It provides the results in matrix form.

(ii) *Matlab Box*: it communicates with the Matlab Engine to perform matrix processing. In this scenario, it is used to combine the likelihood values and current priors to compute posteriors. It also makes the final decision by indicating the most probable target *a posteriori*, for each player *Pi*:

$$TC_{Pi} = \underset{k}{\mathrm{argmax}}(p(k = \mathrm{target} \mid Y_{Pi,k})), \qquad (1)$$

where $Y_{pi,k}$ indicates the observed features for player *Pi*.

Importantly, this Matlab Box provides a second measure which is the Shannon entropy of the posterior distribution for each player:

$$H_{Pi} = -\sum_{k} p_{Pi,k} \cdot \log(p_{Pi,k}), \qquad (2)$$

where $p_{Pi,k}$ is a short for $p(k = \mathrm{target} \mid Y_{pi,k})$.

Shannon entropy is used in contest mode only, as a measure of confidence in the machine's decision. We consider it as a proxy to the attentional resources devoted by the subject for a particular shot. Indeed, Shannon entropy can be compared between subjects. It is negative and bounded. The more informed the decision, the sharper the posterior probability distribution and the closer to zero the entropy. To summarize, the output of the Matlab Box depends on the game mode. In classic mode, the single output corresponds to the estimated target for the current player. In contest mode, the output is twofold and indicates both the winner of the contest and the target she or he most likely selected.

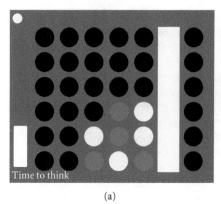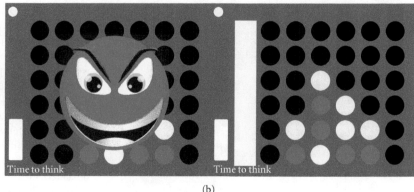

(a)   (b)

FIGURE 4: Visual feedback in classic (a) and contest modes (b).

VRPN Server. The final decision (the selected column) is sent via a VRPN (Virtual-Reality Peripheral Network) analog server to a VRPN client application host by the stimulator [31]. This information is used to provide the two players with visual feedback.

Feedback. In classic mode, a rectangle of the color of the current player is displayed to indicate the selected column (Figure 4(a)). In contest mode, a first feedback (red or yellow smiley) appears at the center of the screen to reveal the identity of the winner of the contest (left part of Figure 4(b)). A second feedback, similar to the one in classic mode, is finally provided and the coin is placed (right part of Figure 4(b)).

3. Results

3.1. Classic Mode. Player P2 (Red) won twice and P1 (Yellow) once. The average game duration was 4 min and 6 s, corresponding to an average of 7 shots per player. Figure 5 shows an outline of the third game.

In that game, players made almost no error (Figures 5(a) and 5(b)). In turn 7, Red made an error; he wanted to select the third column in order to thwart the other's player plan to connect four yellow coins (Figure 5(c)). Yellow won.

The average accuracy over all three games was 81.7%, which is way above chance level (14.3% for 7 classes) and corresponds to an information transfer rate of 35.3 bits/min. However, P2 (Red) reached a considerably higher accuracy than P1 (95.2% and 68.2%, resp., or 51.8 bits/min and 23.2 bits/min, resp.).

Table 1 shows the detailed results, separately for the two players and the three games in classic mode. This highlights the coherence between individual performance, in terms of accuracy, entropy, and the ensuing winner in each game.

3.2. Contest Mode. Each player won one game. The average game duration was 3 min and 37 s, corresponding to an average of 6 shots per player. Figure 6 shows an outline of the second game.

In this mode, both players compete to impose their own choice, whatever the color of the coin to be placed. An example is given in Figure 6. It was Yellow's turn (Figures 6(a1) and 6(a2)) but the Red player won the contest (Figure 6(a1)) and enforced the yellow coin to be placed in the second column instead of the fourth one, which keeps the opportunity for the Red player to win the game in the next turn (Figure 6(a2)). However, Yellow won the next contest (Figure 6(b1)) and prevented Red's victory by selecting the first column (Figure 6(b2)). In what follows, Yellow won again and placed the red coin in the first column, hence leaving the hole in the fourth column free (Figures 6(c1) and 6(c2)). Finally, Yellow won the last contest and hence the game by placing the coin in the fourth column (Figures 6(d1) and 6(d2)).

Over all games in contest mode, Player P1 won 48% of the contests. This indicates that both players were fully engaged in the game and close to each other in terms of devoted attentional resources.

Table 2 shows the detailed results, separately for the two players and the two games in contest mode. Interestingly, in contest mode, the player with the highest averaged accuracy is not necessarily the end winner of the game. Neither is the one who won most of the contests, since victory is the result of the complex interplay between accuracy, focus of attention, and strategy.

The average accuracy over all two games and players was 83.3%, or 37.0 bits/min. Precisely, P1 managed to increase accuracy by 18.8% compared to classic mode, reaching an average of 87.0% in contest mode, which corresponds to a bit-rate increase of 17.8 bits/min. To qualitatively evaluate this improvement, we compared the averaged features for "target" and "nontarget" stimuli, in both modes. We computed the Global Field Power (GFP) [32] over the five virtual sensors:

$$\text{GFP}(t) = \sum_{i=1}^{5} (Y_i(t))^2, \tag{3}$$

where $Y_i(t)$ is the value at the ith virtual channel, at time t.

Note, in Figure 7, that GFP increased around 200 ms and 500 ms peristimulus time, for target stimuli, in the contest

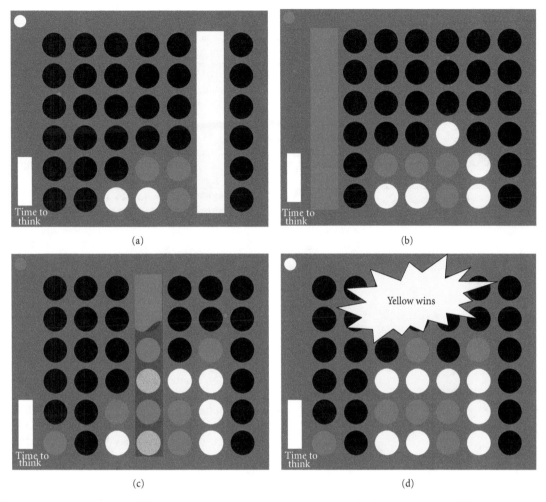

FIGURE 5: Third game in classic mode. Yellow won by connecting four coins horizontally. For the purpose of illustration, the red rectangle was made partially transparent to make all coins visible.

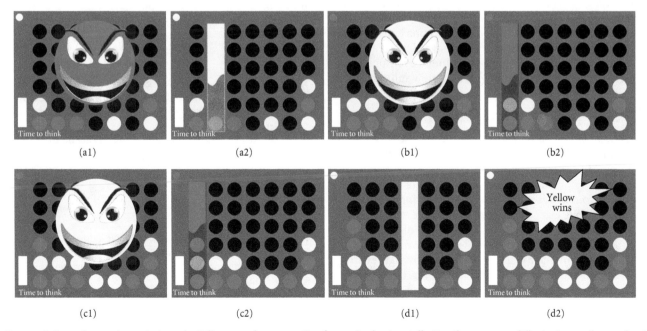

FIGURE 6: Second game in contest mode. Yellow won by connecting four coins horizontally. For the purpose of illustration, yellow and red rectangles are made partially transparent to make all coins visible.

TABLE 1: Detailed results for the three games in classic mode.

Run	Duration	Winner	Classification accuracy (%)		Entropy	
			Player 1	Player 2	Player 1	Player 2
1	5′10″	Player 2	55,6%	100,0%	$7,65E - 02$	$8,08E - 07$
2	3′07″	Player 2	60,0%	100,0%	$1,45E - 06$	$1,02E - 21$
3	4′01″	Player 1	87,5%	85,7%	$8,73E - 05$	$4,03E - 02$

TABLE 2: Detailed results for the two games in contest mode.

Run	Duration	Winner	Classification accuracy (%)		Entropy		Contest winner %	
			Player 1	Player 2	Player 1	Player 2	Player 1	Player 2
1	3′07″	Player 2	100,0%	90,0%	$4,98E - 07$	$1,01E - 03$	50,0	50,0
2	4′07″	Player 1	76,9%	73,3%	$1,29E - 02$	$9,09E - 03$	46,7	53,3

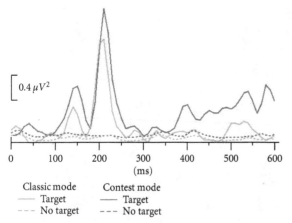

FIGURE 7: Global Field Power computed over five virtual channels for "target" and "nontarget" stimuli, in classic and contest modes (Player 1).

versus classic mode, although there is no specific difference in between the "nontarget" responses in the two modes. This might reflect the actual increase in classification accuracy and could well be a consequence of an enhanced motivation in contest mode because motivation was found to be positively correlated with the P300 amplitude in healthy subjects [33].

4. Discussion

BCIs were originally developed in the context of clinical research. In this study, we developed a P300-based BCI for gaming. Moreover, beyond most existing gaming applications of BCI, we instantiated a true online interaction, involving brain commands only, from two competing subjects, in an existing but extended gameplay ("Connect Four"). We showed that it is possible to take advantage of the variable nature of brain signals and of the cognitive challenge it takes to control their stability. This could make existing games more attractive and motivating, for both healthy players and patients. Through online evaluation, we observed that a simple setup, using nine EEG sensors, was sufficient to provide high performance comparable to our previous studies [26, 27], suggesting that BCI "Connect Four" can effectively be controlled, at a pace that compares to the one

of the traditional (manual) version of the game. Indeed, although motor execution remains faster than the 2.8 s that are needed in the present BCI implementation to select a command, the subjective perception of this additional cost might prove insignificant compared to the time allocated to the planning of the next move (of the order of 10 s). Moreover, following the hypothesis that the electrophysiological marker manipulated here, the P300, is known to reflect the orientation of attention, this BCI game or similar ones could prove useful in the near future, as part of a motivating system to train attention. This encouraging proof of concept calls for carefully designed experiments, involving a large number of subjects or patients, to study social interactions or effects on motivation of such an original and well-controlled BCI environment.

Acknowledgments

This work is supported by the French ANR project ANR-DEFIS 09-EMER-002 CoAdapt. Authors are grateful to Romain Bouet for technical support.

References

[1] N. Birbaumer, A. Ramos Murguialday, C. Weber, and P. Montoya, "Neurofeedback and brain-computer interface. Clinical applications," *International Review of Neurobiology*, vol. 86, pp. 107–117, 2009.

[2] L. A. Farwell and E. Donchin, "Talking off the top of your head: toward a mental prosthesis utilizing event-related brain potentials," *Electroencephalography and Clinical Neurophysiology*, vol. 70, no. 6, pp. 510–523, 1988.

[3] G. Pfurtscheller and C. Neuper, "Motor imagery direct communication," *Proceedings of the IEEE*, vol. 89, no. 7, pp. 1123–1134, 2001.

[4] J. R. Wolpaw, D. J. McFarland, G. W. Neat, and C. A. Forneris, "An EEG-based brain-computer interface for cursor control," *Electroencephalography and Clinical Neurophysiology*, vol. 78, no. 3, pp. 252–259, 1991.

[5] N. Birbaumer, N. Ghanayim, T. Hinterberger et al., "A spelling device for the paralysed," *Nature*, vol. 398, no. 6725, pp. 297–298, 1999.

[6] R. Leeb, D. Friedman, G. R. Müller-Putz, R. Scherer, M. Slater, and G. Pfurtscheller, "Self-paced (asynchronous) BCI control

of a wheelchair in virtual environments: a case study with a tetraplegic," *Computational Intelligence and Neuroscience*, vol. 2007, Article ID 79642, 8 pages, 2007.

[7] E. Maby, M. Perrin, D. Morlet et al., "Evaluation in a locked-in patient of the OpenViBE P300-speller," in *Proceedings of the 5th International Brain-Computer Interface Conference*, pp. 272–275, 2011.

[8] A. Nijholt, D. Tan, G. Pfurtscheller et al., "Brain-computer interfacing for intelligent systems," *IEEE Intelligent Systems*, vol. 23, no. 3, pp. 72–79, 2008.

[9] B. Graimann, B. Allison, and A. Gräser, "New applications for noninvasive Brain-Computer Interfaces and the need for engaging training environments," in *Brain-Computer Interfaces and Games Workshop at the International Conference on Advances in Computer Entertainment Technology*, pp. 25–28, 2007.

[10] R. Leeb, F. Lee, C. Keinrath, R. Scherer, H. Bischof, and G. Pfurtscheller, "Brain-computer communication: motivation, aim, and impact of exploring a virtual apartment," *IEEE Transactions on Neural Systems and Rehabilitation Engineering*, vol. 15, no. 4, pp. 473–482, 2007.

[11] J. van Aart, E. Klaver, C. Bartneck, L. Feijs, and P. Peters, "Neurofeedback gaming for wellbeing," in *Brain-Computer Interfaces and Games Workshop at the International Conference on Advances in Computer Entertainment Technology*, pp. 3–5, 2007.

[12] A. Nijholt, D. Oude Bos, and B. Reuderink, "Turning shortcomings into challenges: brain-computer interfaces for games," *Intelligent Technologies For Interactive Entertainment*, vol. 1, no. 2, pp. 153–168, 2009.

[13] B. A. S. Hasan and J. Q. Gan, "Hangman BCI: an unsupervised adaptive self-paced Brain-Computer Interface for playing games," *Computers in Biology and Medicine*, vol. 42, pp. 598–606, 2012.

[14] J. D. Bayliss, "Use of the evoked potential P3 component for control in a virtual apartment," *IEEE Transactions on Neural Systems and Rehabilitation Engineering*, vol. 11, no. 2, pp. 113–116, 2003.

[15] A. Finke, A. Lenhardt, and H. Ritter, "The MindGame: a P300-based brain-computer interface game," *Neural Networks*, vol. 22, no. 9, pp. 1329–1333, 2009.

[16] E. C. Lalor, S. P. Kelly, C. Finucane et al., "Steady-state VEP-based brain-computer interface control in an immersive 3D gaming environment," *Eurasip Journal on Applied Signal Processing*, vol. 2005, no. 19, pp. 3156–3164, 2005.

[17] N. Yee, "Motivations for play in online games," *Cyberpsychology and Behavior*, vol. 9, no. 6, pp. 772–775, 2006.

[18] C. Guger, G. Krausz, B. Z. Allison, and G. Edlinger, "Comparison of dry and gel based electrodes for P300 brain-computer interfaces," *Frontiers in Neuroscience*, vol. 6, article 60, 2012.

[19] F. Lotte, "Brain-computer interfaces for 3D games: hype or hope?" in *Proceedings of the Foundations of Digital Games (FDG '11)*, pp. 325–327, 2011.

[20] P. Brunner, S. Joshi, S. Briskin, J. R. Wolpaw, H. Bischof, and G. Schalk, "Does the 'P300' speller depend on eye gaze?" *Journal of Neural Engineering*, vol. 7, no. 5, Article ID 56013, 2010.

[21] M. S. Treder and B. Blankertz, "(C)overt attention and visual speller design in an ERP-based brain-computer interface," *Behavioral and Brain Functions*, vol. 6, article 28, 2010.

[22] M. Fabiani, D. Karis, and E. Donchin, "P300 and recall in an incidental memory paradigm," *Psychophysiology*, vol. 23, no. 3, pp. 298–308, 1986.

[23] L. A. Farwell and E. Donchin, "Talking off the top of your head: toward a mental prosthesis utilizing event-related brain potentials," *Electroencephalography and Clinical Neurophysiology*, vol. 70, no. 6, pp. 510–523, 1988.

[24] E. Donchin, K. M. Spencer, and R. Wijesinghe, "The mental prosthesis: assessing the speed of a P300-based brain-computer interface," *IEEE Transactions on Rehabilitation Engineering*, vol. 8, no. 2, pp. 174–179, 2000.

[25] A. Datta, R. Cusack, K. Hawkins et al., "The P300 as a marker of waning attention and error propensity," *Computational Intelligence and Neuroscience*, vol. 2007, Article ID 93968, 2007.

[26] E. Maby, G. Gibert, P. E. Aguera, M. Perrin, and O. Bertrand, "The OpenViBE P300-Speller scenario: a thorough online evaluation," in *Proceedings of the Human Brain Mapping Conference*, 2010.

[27] M. Perrin, E. Maby, R. Bouet, O. Bertrand, and J. Mattout, "Detecting and interpreting responses to feedback in BCI," in *Proceedings of the 5th International Brain-Computer Interface Conference*, pp. 116–119, 2011.

[28] H. Cecotti, B. Rivet, M. Congedo et al., "A robust sensor-selection method for P300 brain-computer interfaces," *Journal of Neural Engineering*, vol. 8, no. 1, Article ID 016001, 2011.

[29] Y. Renard, F. Lotte, G. Gibert et al., "OpenViBE: an open-source software platform to design, test, and use brain-computer interfaces in real and virtual environments," *Presence: Teleoperators and Virtual Environments*, vol. 19, no. 1, pp. 35–53, 2010.

[30] B. Rivet, A. Souloumiac, V. Attina, and G. Gibert, "xDAWN algorithm to enhance evoked potentials: application to brain-computer interface," *IEEE Transactions on Bio-Medical Engineering*, vol. 56, no. 8, pp. 2035–2043, 2009.

[31] R. M. Taylor, T. C. Hudson, A. Seeger, H. Weber, J. Juliano, and A. T. Helser, "VRPN: a device-independent, network-transparent VR peripheral system," in *Proceedings of the ACM Symposium on Virtual Reality Software and Technology (VRST '01)*, pp. 55–61, November 2001.

[32] D. Lehmann and W. Skrandies, "Reference-free identification of components of checkerboard-evoked multichannel potential fields," *Electroencephalography and Clinical Neurophysiology*, vol. 48, no. 6, pp. 609–621, 1980.

[33] S. C. Kleih, F. Nijboer, S. Halder, and A. Kübler, "Motivation modulates the P300 amplitude during brain-computer interface use," *Clinical Neurophysiology*, vol. 121, no. 7, pp. 1023–1031, 2010.

20

Static and Dynamic User Portraits

Ko-Hsun Huang,[1,2] **Yi-Shin Deng,**[3] **and Ming-Chuen Chuang**[1]

[1] *Institute of Applied Arts, National Chiao-Tung University, 1001 University Road, Hsinchu 300, Taiwan*
[2] *Madeira Interactive Technologies Institute, Caminho da Penteada, 9020-105 Funchal, Portugal*
[3] *Institute of Creative Industrial Design, National Cheng Kung University, 1 University Road, Tainan City 701, Taiwan*

Correspondence should be addressed to Ko-Hsun Huang, kohsun.huang@gmail.com

Academic Editor: Bill Kapralos

User modeling and profiling has been used to evaluate systems and predict user behaviors for a considerable time. Models and profiles are generally constructed based on studies of users' behavior patterns, cognitive characteristics, or demographic data and provide an efficient way to present users' preferences and interests. However, such modeling focuses on users' interactions with a system and cannot support complicated social interaction, which is the emerging focus of serious games, educational hypermedia systems, experience, and service design. On the other hand, personas are used to portray and represent different groups and types of users and help designers propose suitable solutions in iterative design processes. However, clear guidelines and research approaches for developing useful personas for large-scale and complex social networks have not been well established. In this research, we reflect on three different design studies related to social interaction, experience, and cross-platform service design to discuss multiple ways of identifying both direct users and invisible users in design research. In addition, research methods and attributes to portray users are discussed.

1. Introduction

Understanding target users is considered a basic step towards developing good products and services. In traditional industrial design, marketing, city planning, and environmental design, a wide range of research methods, including surveys, field studies, interviews, and focus groups, have been used with the clear purpose of identifying target audiences' preferences and needs [1–4]. In system and software development, usability evaluation and user-centered design methods, such participatory design, contextual inquiry, or ethnographic techniques, have also been well accepted and applied to better understand end users' knowledge background, behaviors, cognitive processes, and requirements [5–7].

To support rapid IT development and iterative design processes, it has become important to have clear images and models to represent end users: ideally models which can be reused and reapplied in the development of different products and services [8]. In software engineering, user modeling has focused on having an internal representation of users, which includes information such as background knowledge, preferences, and the ways that users interact with systems [9–11]. This type of user modeling or profiling can be used to design serious games, educational training, and learning systems or to evaluate systems by simulating different types of users [11–13]. Beyond traditional user cognitive models, much work has extended the modeling variables to cover users' previous computing experiences, personality traits, and background context for educational applications [11, 14]. Hothi and Hall [15] have addressed SaD (static and dynamic) user modeling, which focuses on both static information such as gender and age, and dynamic information such as diverse computing experiences and personality. They considered that such dynamic user data could be used to make a system dynamically adapt to an individual user. Karampiperis and Sampson [14] have highlighted two distinct submodels in adaptive educational hypermedia development: a frequently updated model to represent learners' knowledge space and a static model to represent learners' cognitive characteristics and learning preferences [11, 14, 16].

With a purpose similar to that of user modeling, personas have also been used to portray user types in serious games, adaptive training systems, communication, and experience design [17, 18]. The original concept of personas is to create fictional characters to represent different user and consumer types by describing their tastes, perceptions, possible reactions, and attitudes towards a certain product, service, or brand [18–20]. There are several significant benefits to having personas in the design process, such as providing all members of the development team a clear and common image of the target audience, evaluating if design solutions meet users' needs, and enhancing practitioners empathy on a certain type of user [18, 21]. For instance, Antle [22] has argued that most successful products for children are neither goal- nor task-oriented but meet specific needs of children in a particular age range. She has highlighted that child-personas of more experiential contexts can provide a way to incorporate concepts from developmental psychology into design and allow archetypical users to be presented throughout the design process for technology-enhanced educational systems [22–24]. To design roles and scenarios for serious games and game-based adaptive training systems, Raybourn [17] has also suggested using personas to guide the design process and to help game designers and game writers develop realistic or believable roles for players.

Although both user models and personas can offer various benefits in different phases of iterative design, including initial concept development, user testing, and redesign cycles, there are several problems associated with their application in complex designs of social interactions, experiences, and services. First, user-modeling methodology has been developed with a focus on human-computer interaction and centers on task-oriented analysis of behavior patterns, cognitive processes, and demographic data. The approaches and modeling can reveal detailed information about the ways that a user interacts with a system, but are incapable of taking large-scale social contexts into account [25–27]. Such modeling cannot account for subtle social interactions and communication between people, which is the emerging focus of serious games, adaptive hypermedia, and learning networks [28, 29]. Secondly, the information that a traditional persona offers is also limited to a few attributes. Although a person's sociocultural background and economic status may be considered, detailed information such as one's relationships with communities, products, and technologies, are generally absent. In addition, several researchers have criticized persona development for lacking scientific process and clear guidelines, which decrease the method's reliability and representability [30–33]. Both user modeling and personas restrict their scope by overlooking activity contexts; user modeling only focuses on direct users of systems, and personas mainly represent target and potential consumers, rather than capturing and revealing all participants involved in the activities of interest.

Much work has shown that having social perspectives and understanding nuanced social interaction will be the most challenging but necessary topic in today's experience and social media design [4, 7, 17]. In addition, much work has shown that enhancing social identity and applying social influence can help practitioners and designers develop systems for learning, behavior changing, and other social purposes [28, 34, 35]. Furthermore, design strategies such as applying CASA (Computer as Social Actor) in technology-enhanced education also require a thorough understanding of learners' sociocultural backgrounds [36, 37].

This paper discusses current methods, approaches, and frameworks applied in design research, including several user-centered approaches, design frameworks, and models developed for studying cultures. We highlight the strengths and shortcomings of these methods when applied to capture different levels of user information, from detailed interactions to sociocultural backgrounds [3–5]. Examples from user studies in three design projects are used to illustrate that the different levels of information help identify user types and build user portraits. In each case, multiple ethnographical techniques were applied, such as shadowing, in-depth interviews, grounded theory [38, 39], work modeling [40], and social activity modeling [4], to reveal the complicated involvement of different types of participants in social activities and product usage.

We reflect on the three case studies to recommend suitable user study methods for supporting large-scale services, adaptive systems, and development of serious games, as well as necessary information to gather when portraying users. By understanding participants' relationships and roles within a broader context, we also derive insights for identifying invisible users and potential users and the importance of understanding different users' motives and concerns.

2. Methods and Frameworks

Emerging areas of interest in IT development, such as serious games, adaptive systems, and experience design, are concerned with large complex communities and diverse generations. Large-scale services such as e-government and social media inevitably have to support people's social activities in the coming future. According to the central concept of ethnomethodology, people are intelligent and creative, and with ad hoc practices, they can apply their knowledge across domains and act in different contexts [41, 42]. It is the methods used by people to apply knowledge and their values and attitudes, which matter and can help scholars to predict further actions, reactions, and acceptance towards a certain system or service. Instead of looking into what people actually perform, understanding background motives is essential for developing more adaptive and flexible systems and services for greater social purposes in the future.

2.1. Models for Social and Cultural Studies. In social science, the strategies to study a culture include traditional anthropological approaches, such as participant observations with long-term involvement of the fields and interpretative approaches, in which researchers collect, conceptualize, and induce the concepts through diverse methods. For years, numerous discussions and debates have been held about ways to generate more solid and scientific results while applying these methods and approaches. Many researchers have focused on measurements and standards for improving the validity and reliability of qualitative research [43–45]. For instance, Glaser and Strauss [38] developed a grounded theory in which researchers analyze data and generate a theory repeatedly until they can thoroughly explain and describe the phenomenon. In this iterative process, Strauss placed emphasis on improving reliability and validation criteria in a systematic way [38, 39, 46]. However, in IT and product design practices, while designers and developers apply qualitative approaches, they tend to analyze the situations by using models as guidelines and check lists, and the research results generally only support short-term and inner group usages and have no impact on further related studies.

Applying the above-mentioned positivist or interpretivist approaches to gain knowledge about society and culture is very time consuming and requires experienced researchers to collect and analyze raw data. Therefore, to reduce the cost and to gain insights more efficiently, there are numerous theoretical frameworks and models developed in different domains. For instance, since the 1980s, researchers in management and leadership have discussed numerous models for understanding organizational cultures [47–51]. Most of these works have the same purpose, either to optimize the organizational process or to reduce internal conflicts within organizations.

In the fields of management and leadership, many scholars have taken similar approaches to identify cultures—firstly recognizing a culture's representative characteristics and then categorizing them into types. These researchers generally take an organizational point of view and focus on structures, power distribution, and divisions of labor [48, 52, 53]. The earliest work is Harrison's organization ideologies, in which there are four types of cultures highlighted by their typical features [52, 54]. This classification refers to power-, role-, task-, and person-oriented cultures, respectively, standing for centralized power, hierarchical structure, team support, and individual achievement [52, 55, 56]. Harrison's work has had a great impact on later studies of organizational culture, in which the power distribution and organizational formalization have become the basic criteria to locate a culture [52]. Furthermore, the ways that an organization or a community responds to outside influence and different situations, the flexibility and stability of organizational structures, and the forms of attention have also been widely discussed [48, 53, 57].

In contrast to categorizing cultures into types, many scholars focus on finding cultural concepts and patterns for intercultural studies. The earliest works are Hall's books, in which he identified two dimensions of culture, including the high- and low-context communication and polychromic versus monochromic time orientation [58, 59]. The high-low context concept is used to characterize information transaction and interpersonal communication in cultures, and the second concept is concerned with the way in which people structure their time, tasks, and schedules. Moreover, to deal with cross-national issues in the functioning of organizations, Hofstede [60] indicated

the differences between studying national cultures and organizational cultures where national cultures differ primarily in their values, but organizational cultures turn out to differ mainly in their practices. He identified six different dimensions of organizational cultures and claimed five other national cultural dimensions, including power distance, uncertainty avoidance, individualism versus collectivism, masculinity versus femininity, and long- versus short-term orientation [60, 61]. For understanding cultural diversity in global business, Trompenaars and Hampden-Turner [62] also developed a model of culture with seven dimensions, including universalism versus particularism, individualism versus collectivism, neutral versus emotional, and specific versus diffuse.

Instead of classifying existent international or organizational cultures into types, some researchers have focused on developing models for analyzing and understanding the culture of a particular group or organization. For instance, Schein [63] identified three fundamental levels at which culture manifests itself: observable artifacts, values, and basic underlying assumptions. Here, artifacts refer to physical layouts, manners, atmosphere, and phenomena that people can directly feel and observe, and values refer to members' norms, ideologies, and philosophies. The basic assumptions are those taken-for-granted, underlying and usually unconscious aspects that people have and share within groups, and they normally can determine people's perceptions, thought processes, and behaviors [63, 64]. Closely resembling Schein's three levels, Hofstede placed four manifestations of cultures at different levels of depth, namely symbols, heroes, rituals, and values [57, 60]. Rousseau [49] also detailed the nature of the cultural construct and its theoretical roots and layered these cultural elements according to subjectivity and accessibility. His five layers of culture, from outside in, are artifacts, patterns of behavior, behavioral norms, values, and unconscious fundamental assumptions. This type of layered cultural model also appears in many other researchers' works, in which basic assumptions and values are generally placed at the core layer(s), and then are encircled by beliefs, attitudes, rituals, behaviors, and then artifacts [65, 66].

There is one extreme example of the ambitious objective to combine all aforementioned concepts into one single model. Considering cultural impact on the implementation of enterprise resource planning (ERP), Krumbholz and Maiden [67] developed a metaschema for modeling culture. They integrated the surface and the deeper manifestations of culture into common business concepts such as processes, events, and information flows, and then developed a systematic framework to analyze culture for further explanation, prediction, and replanning of different corporate and national cultures. Their framework is based on Schein's three levels of culture and a wide range of social aspects (e.g., group norms, formal philosophy, and linguistic paradigms). Influenced by globalization trends and comparative studies, they also included Hofstede's and Trompenaars and Hampden-Turner's cultural dimensions in their work [16, 50, 62]. This enormous framework has more than twenty components in three main categories.

The first category covers common elements in business processes, such as agent, role, responsibility, and goal. The second category describes the core levels of culture, including hidden assumptions, beliefs, and values. The last category focuses on characteristics such as customs, symbols, and environments. Krumbholz and Maiden tried to cover all the important elements discussed in cultural studies. However, there are many unclear definitions and assumptions in this metaschema. For instance, social interaction is a significant component of the model, which influences and reflects one's beliefs and represents the types and ways people interact with each other. However, their work does not detail how to explain relationships between social actions, values, and beliefs nor does it suggest methodology to gain such an understanding.

The models of cultural types provide several ways to identify national or organizational cultures and have indicated the significant relationships between power structure and personal behaviors [48, 52–54]. However, there are two major reasons why it is difficult to apply these models directly as research frameworks in other domains. Firstly, the limited cultural types oversimplify the sociocultural issues and avoid the level of depth in cultural significance. In management and leadership cases, the classification approach provides a simple and quick way to identify the cultural characteristics, but due to a lack of clear essential definitions, these models are incapable of revealing the subtle relationships and influences between the cultural components. Second, most human behaviors, especially social activities, do not have a clear objective and can be analyzed into steps and processes. With a strong management and leadership purpose, these models purely focus on work processes and the ways that people achieve their goals and seldom take individuals' motives, attitudes, and perspectives into account. The similar tendency of work and goal orientation appealed in Hofstede's global-scale survey [60, 61], which he conducted to evaluate the work values of a specific company. Although Trompenaars and Hampden-Turner [62] discussed personal attitudes towards both leisure and work situations, their results related to underlying assumptions and values were very limited. Krumbholz and Maiden [67] have tried to combine both social science theories and psychological concepts into their metaschema, but their interview results did not reflect the richness and interaction among these cultural levels and components. In addition, the numerous components involved in different perspectives are all compressed into a single model, which makes this metaschema difficult to use as a research framework or as a format for representing the final output of the research.

In social interaction and experience design, issues which are related to individual attitudes and values can often be traced back to and better understood in the light of social norms or culture. However, studies of how society and culture act as constraints for design have very different goals than traditional broad studies of culture itself. They also differ from the above-mentioned models and measurements of culture which focus purely on work and whose purposes are either to enhance organizational performance or to improve management and leadership. Due to their strong task-orientation, the methodologies proposed for these studies focus on practical and behavioral views, environments, and symbols. They overlook several cultural aspects which are important in socially motivated interactions between people, technology, and services, such as people's motives for actions and their emotional needs.

2.2. Frameworks for Understanding Users and Usage Contexts. In the past decades, design research of information and system development has focused on interactions between humans and machines. Based on the introduction of cognitive psychology, most studies have concentrated on mental processes and information flows, with the scope being achieving a task or solving a problem. Taking an example of Donald Norman's seven stages of action, which have had a lasting impact on usability engineering and industrial design, the analysis of human action is concerned with a loop of forming the goal, forming the intention, specifying an action, executing the action, perceiving the state of the world, interpreting the state of the world, and evaluating the outcome [68]. Comparing these types of mental models with microsociological theories (e.g., symbolic interactionism and dramaturgy), they all focus on the interaction between individuals and environments and discuss how people perceive and interpret the outside signals, symbols and then take an action [69].

The scope of design research in technology development expanded during the 1990s from task analysis to more complex activity analysis. For understanding larger-scale usage contexts and supporting user experience design, many ethnographical research methods were introduced in design practices, such as interviews and long-term involvement observations [70–72]. In addition, to speed up design cycles, many analytic frameworks and models were introduced and developed to make user research more efficient, cheaper, and deeper. These frameworks, such as AEIOU (activity, environment, interaction, object, and user), POEMS (people, objects, environments, message, and services), Ax4 (atmosphere, actors, activities, and artifacts), activity theory, and contextual design methodology, have been discussed and applied in various domains with great success [40, 70, 73–75]. Most of the frameworks provide clear guidelines and dimensions for investigating the entire activity context, including practical behaviors and actions, related objects and environment settings, and information content, as well as taking into account relationships among people.

Among these research frameworks, contextual design methodology [40] and activity theory have their specific advantages for both system development and other design practices. Contextual design methodology was developed based on research techniques of ethnography and was influenced by the development of participatory design techniques in the 1980s and 1990s. It has a special purpose to help researchers and designers identify domain problems in rapid design cycles, especially for software and hardware redesign and usability evaluation. To help researchers and designers convey their domain knowledge, thoughts, and ideas, Beyer and Holtzblatt [40] developed five work models as a tangible representation for issues in different dimensions, including the flow model, cultural model, sequence model, artifact model, and physical model. Furthermore, for developing a successful system, which can "fit with the customer's culture, make conforming to policy easy and reduce friction and irritation in the workplace," Beyer and Holtzblatt [40] addressed the importance of understanding organizational culture. Their cultural model highlights cultural influences among individuals, groups, and the organization and also helps researchers identify invisible power, preferences, values, and emotions. Although the cultural model concentrates on representing organizational culture, it still shows individuals' opinions and attitudes to some extent.

Activity theory, with its roots in the 1930s Soviet cultural-historical psychology, was introduced and adapted into HCI and CSCW as a lens in ethnographic research [73, 76, 77]. To understand the mental capability of a single individual, activity theory considers a "goal-directed" activity as the unit of analysis and provides an analytical framework to describe activities with three hierarchical constructs: subject, object, and tool. In the theory, activities are described by how a single individual (subject) achieves a goal (object) through tools, and using tools reveals the details of both physical interactions and mental processes. Under this framework, a complex activity can be broken down into action or operation levels and can be analyzed from both behavioral and psychological viewpoints. To deal with multi-user systems and collaborative work, Engeström [73, 78] later proposed an extended schema for activity theory with additional constructs of community (people who share the same goal), rules, and division of labor. Engeström's schema makes activity theory very useful in groupware and social media design [79, 80].

With a strong intention to bridge the gap between subjective-to-objective and macro-to-micro concerns in design study, MultiLevel Social Activity Model (MLSAM) was proposed by Huang and Deng [4, 81]. There are two basic arguments behind the concepts. First, they argued that social behaviors are deeply localized and historical on the account of cultural background. They showed that the traditional customs perform a social function by creating cohesiveness in families and by offering a habitual practice that can be passed on from one generation to another. The social activity not only reflects norms and common values of the society, but also presents various inherent characteristics of the cultural context. Secondly, they argued that people have great agency and creativity to fulfill needs and achieve purposes in a variety of ways. Traditional field observations and user studies, which focus on a limited scope and settings, can only reveal partial results of how people perform to achieve their goals. Hence, their model emphasizes the necessity to identify people's motives and attitudes, which comparing to actual actions, are more permanent and static, and could be considered in further design for different platforms and services.

From an integrated sociological viewpoint, individuals' behaviors are not only encouraged, but also constrained by norms, religions, and sociocultural backgrounds. To well support hypermedia and adaptive systems for social purposes in the future, design research needs to extend from traditional usability evaluation and task-oriented studies to a larger-scale sociocultural scope. Therefore, an in-depth research approach is needed to answer to the complexity of social interactions. The following section presents three case studies of applying both contextual design [40] and multilevel social activity model [4, 81] in design practices and shows the benefits of applying multiple research methods to portray users.

3. Design Studies

To better support product and service design in the future, we applied multiple user study methods to uncover the complexity of participants' perspectives, interactions, and attitudes within different types of activities: a traditional ritual of a Taiwanese tea ceremony, Taiwanese teenagers' social activities, and technology use, and sports watching in Southern Europe. The first study is selected to show how well-accepted software design methods can be used together with the multilevel social activity model [4, 81], to capture more user information within a social event, a cultural tradition. The second case study is selected to discuss if this integrated approach can also be applied to investigate a complex physical and virtual social context. The third case study is a service design, in which the same approach is applied to identify different user types and help designers and practitioners make design decisions on developing adaptive and cross-platform systems. Contrary to what is common in traditional IT development, we identify different user types by using both the contextual design flow model [40] and the multilevel social activity model [4], to highlight participants' roles, relationships, motives, and sociocultural background.

3.1. A Traditional Social Ritual. The first case is a study of traditional tea ceremonies in Taiwan. These ceremonies have deep cultural roots and also contain complex forms of social interaction, which are typically ignored in most IT development and for which established research methodology is lacking [4]. We reflect on this case study because of its rich sociocultural backgrounds, which represent a good example to show complex social relationships and different user motives within an activity.

In this case study, we applied multiple user experience research methods, which include observations [3], contextual design work modeling [40], social activity modeling [4, 81], and in-depth interviews with grounded theory analysis [38, 39], to reveal different aspects of personal perceptions toward the overall sociocultural context of Taiwan's tea ceremony. In order to identify the value of the tea ceremony to participants from different generations, three subjects of different ages were recruited, together with their regular tea ceremony groups. The three subjects were all experts of tea ceremonies. The first subject was a forty-year-old parent with a twenty-year experience of tea ceremonies. The second subject was a retired senior citizen, with a seventeen-year experience and with an interest in learning techniques and knowledge of brewing tea from magazines and other connoisseurs. The third subject was a female graduate student, with a fourteen-year experience of tea ceremonies and with familiarity of the Internet and associated technologies. Each had taken part in tea ceremonies at least once per week in recent months. To observe the detailed social interaction within the activity, their family members and friends, who are regular members of the ceremonies, were also invited to participate in the sessions of observations and contextual inquiries. In total, we had ten participants.

The flow model in Figure 1(a) represents the different roles in the ceremony and their interactions. On the basis of the in-depth interviews and contextual inquiries, this flow model has been extended to portray all groups who directly or indirectly engage in a ceremony. Direct participants are the host (tea server), family members, and other friends, while indirect participants include hobbyists, tea sellers, tea producers (farmers in direct marketing), and tea connoisseurs. Although indirect participants do not actually attend ceremonies, they significantly impact the act through their close ties to the host. According to the study, the host of a ceremony is most likely a person of the middle-aged generation or the head of household. This person tends to actively exchange information and sentiments with other hobbyists and tea sellers, as well as seek out information from books, magazines, and newspapers.

While the flow model captures roles and interactions, the multilevel social activity model further reveals how participants' underlying motives and attitudes toward tea ceremony differ between generations. It also shows that attitudes and resulting behaviors are all strongly rooted in a cultural context. Both the younger generation and the elderly/middle-age generations (both groups in Figure 1(b)) are direct participants in tea ceremonies (marked in orange in Figure 1(a)). However, a comparison of the two models reveal that although the younger generation is interested in tea ceremonies and has inherited tea-drinking habits from their families, they are generally not consumers of the tea industry. They have neither contacted any other participants (i.e., tea sellers and tea farmers in direct marketing), nor do they receive information through magazines or newspapers. Instead, their primary sources of information about tea ceremonies are parents or grandparents.

The multilevel social activity model identifies different user groups by their attitudes towards activities and motives for participation. In addition to people's direct and immediate requirements, we consider that there are many hidden reasons for people to engage in a social activity that may be overlooked by methodologies that do not go deep enough. For instance, the social activity model reveals that the elderly have positive attitudes toward tea ceremonies potentially reflecting the awareness of Westernization, while the younger generation is more attracted by the health benefits associated with drinking tea.

An understanding of differences in user groups' cultural backgrounds and underlying motives can help designers make better decisions, in particular in design for social activities and communication. For instance, knowledge of cultural features, for example, pouring a cup of tea to convey esteem and respect during a tea ceremony, can further lead to more accurate portraits of users and better predictions of user behaviors. However, it is difficult to gain this knowledge using only activity- and usage-centered design methods. Instead, the case studies indicate that the knowledge can be gained from a historical and broader-context approach.

3.2. Virtual and Physical Social Networks. Crazy Vote was a social website in Taiwan that provided users with personal web space, such as weblogs and a message board. Due to its unique interface and features for voting on users' portraits, it became the biggest social website for Taiwanese teenagers in 2008, with more than 20,000 users of ages 15 to 19. To guide future application development, the company supported a two-month research project to fully understand their users' online activities and expectations of social media [82]. In the study, seven highly active users, who have their own fan clubs and hold social events, and two regular users, participated in both in-depth interviews and contextual inquiries, and the online logs of another 40 highly active users and 40 regular users were sampled at random to understand behavioral patterns in the platform. All qualitative data were analyzed by following grounded theory with Nvivo [83, 84]. At the same time, contextual design work models and the multilevel social activity model (MLSAM) were used as design research guidelines to capture information and present results [82].

By extending the research scope with both contextual inquires and in-depth interviews, the study shows that teenagers' common processes of making friends are complex, but flexible. In addition, the boundary between online social interaction and actual relationships is very blurred to Taiwanese teenaged online users. Their reason for making new friends on the Internet is simply to expand their interpersonal relationships in the real world. For instance, the interviewees mentioned that they preferred to make friends who live nearby to increase chances of meeting up in person, as society does not encourage teenagers to travel alone. Social issues that are associated with meeting online friends also make teenagers form unique networks to ensure that all members are using their real identities and to later develop real-life confidence in each other.

As shown in Figure 2, the multilevel social activity model also helped us identify three different user types among the website users. First, activity promoters, who were extremely confident and familiar with most social norms and manners on social media, voluntarily held gathering events, established clubs and recruited other users to join their own clubs. Second, followers were willing to participate in social events but had less interest to be a group leader or to organize activities. Third and finally, self-oriented users made up 90% of the user base, and their activities on the platform were more self-oriented, such as maintaining and updating blogs and photo albums. They seldom visited others' blogs or left messages to others. According to the in-depth interviews, we found that most self-oriented users were either introvert or lacked experience of interaction with unfamiliar people on the Internet. Therefore, we further separated these three

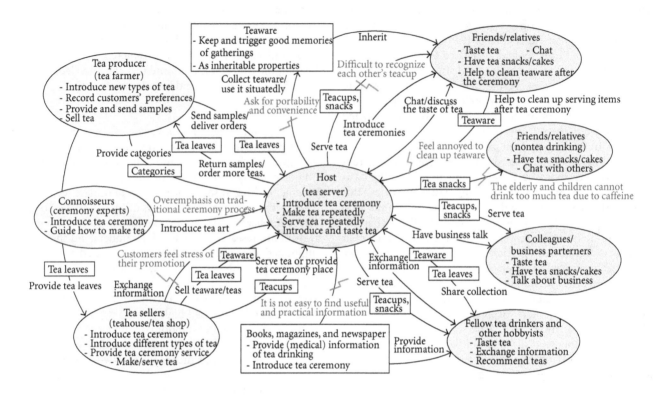

People who actually participate in tea ceremonies
People who are involved in tea ceremonies

(a) The flow model of tea ceremonies

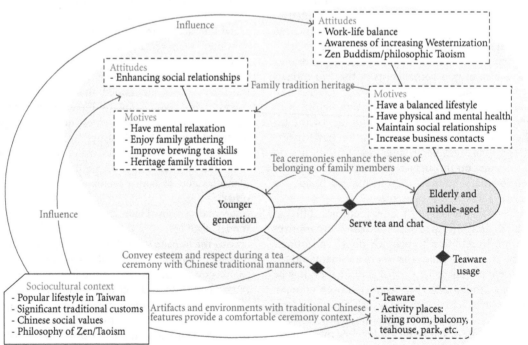

People who are direct consumers of teas and teaware
People who participate in tea ceremonies, but not consumers

(b) The multilevel social activity model of tea ceremonies

FIGURE 1: Different user types in tea ceremonies.

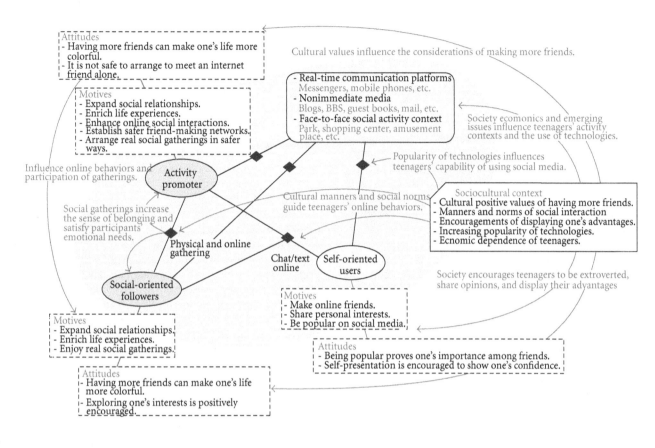

FIGURE 2: Diverse user types of social media.

type users, activity promoters, social-oriented followers, and self-oriented users, into to two groups, in which the first group users are more social-oriented (marked in orange in Figure 2) and the second group users are more self-oriented (marked in blue in Figure 2).

Some teen users had a common and well-defined procedure for making friends successfully and efficiently in the Crazy Vote platform, and most users in the social-oriented group were aware of and applied this process. First, nonverbal introductions would take place through the voting system or by sending emoticons to others. Communication would then be initiated by leaving a private message or by visiting and leaving public comments on each other's blogs. People who share similar interests and habits may then exchange other online contact information, such as MSN Messenger or Yahoo! Messenger accounts, and start communicating electronically outside of the Crazy Vote platform. In the end, these online friends may end up talking on mobile phones and meeting up face-to-face.

Rapid expansion of information and communication technology has made young people comfortable with using a wide range of communication platforms. Although taking place in an online environment, the observed process among Taiwanese teenagers for making friends is natural, mature and matches traditional Taiwanese social norms. For instance, the initial use of nonverbal emoticons and "likes" to make others aware of their presence was described in the interviews as a type of "reserved" introduction, similar to a head nod or eye gaze. Young users considered it too aggressive and impolite to suddenly show up and introduce themselves in front of strangers. However, according to both interviews and online tracing, users in the self-oriented group were unaware of this process and fell back on expanding their presentation of themselves in the system. Although both socially and self-oriented users initially shared the common goal of making new friends through the Crazy Vote website, the self-oriented users perceived a difficulty to initiate communication and greet strangers in proper ways, which later caused them to focus on their own blogs.

This study illustrates how more in-depth user research can lead to detailed interaction issues as well as an understanding of sociocultural contexts and their influences on users' motives and behaviors. Such knowledge can also be applied and reused in many different design projects. In addition, understanding users' expectations and abilities helps development teams make better decisions and predict user engagement. For instance, the social-oriented group's capabilities and successful strategies of making friends can be applied in social media design to help and guide the other types of users. However, current design research generally focuses on a single platform or a particular environment, which narrows down the research scope and overlooks people's great ability to manipulate different resources to achieve their goals.

3.3. Large-Scale Services and Cross-Platform Experiences. The third case study investigates people's sport watching experiences in Portugal. The design process began with interviews and observations of 20 active sports fans and people who had participated regularly in football watching activities, followed by modeling according to MLSAM [4] and contextual design [40] to understand their experiences, motives, and behaviors in sports watching. On the basis of the models, three personas and 30 different design concepts were then generated in a workshop, and 15 subjects were asked to do card sorting to rank the design concepts. In the design phase, several user experience and service design techniques were applied to define the details of the service system, including scenarios and storyboards, customer journey, use-case analysis, and service design blueprint [3, 17, 85, 86]. To gain overall feedback and to improve the systems, formal usability evaluation was conducted with five active football fans, by following collaborative usability inspection, rapid iterative testing, and evaluation and single-subject testing [87, 88].

The flow model in Figure 3(a) shows that football fans use laptops and other high-tech devices to enhance their football watching experience at home. Examples include accessing high quality streaming, using a projector, receiving statistical information from websites, and discussing referees and penalties with friends on the Internet. People watching the game at home do so either together with family members or with close friends. Figure 3(b) shows that a football watching activity in a sports bar involves several different types of people in addition to the football fans. This includes peddlers who sell team scarves and jerseys to sport bar customers, the staff, and owner of the bar, and the fans' friends, who despite not being present in the bar interact with bar customers through digital devices.

The multilevel social activity model (Figure 4) distinguishes several types of people by their different motives for participating in sport watching. Primary supporters enjoy watching games, with strong interests in details of the game and high-quality game play. Potential supporters consider football watching primarily as a social activity and their motives for participation are generally derived from primary supporters' interest (e.g., most of our male interviewees mentioned that their girlfriends, wives, and children try to understand the game rules so that they can be more involved in discussions of details together during the game). The other user types, such as bar owners and environment providers, participate in the events because of expectations of business opportunities.

Using the users types identified in the multilevel social activity model, we marked the primary supporters (football fans and community) in orange in Figures 3(a) and 3(b).

Entertainment and media companies have traditionally always targeted their products purely towards primary supporters. Groups marked in blue are not primarily attending the gathering to watch the game, but their greater interest in social interaction nonetheless makes them potential customers of a service. Although they are not the active sports fans, it is possible to include these groups as stakeholders in current or future service design processes to develop better services of greater scope. For instance, bar owners can be clients of media companies, if a service design aims to provide a social entertainment space with complete sport channels and other facilities.

Due to resource and time limitations in this academic project, only primary supporters were selected for the continued development. On the basis of the research findings, two personas were developed who, while both being primary supporters, have very different expectations of the IT product used. As shown in Figure 5, two user portraits were introduced to the development team in the session of brainstorming and decision-making. All project participants and sponsors agreed that the two user portraits were very representative of typical football fans in Portugal. The further customer activity journey, service architecture, scenario, and storyboard were also developed according to our personas' motives, usage of technology, and lifestyles.

Having a clear image of two user types also helped designers and engineers generate correct use cases [89] and prioritize important features in the later stages of prototyping and system development. For instance, the development team discussed different use cases and designed detailed interaction based on service design blueprints, which require correct selections of platforms (channels) for a certain type of users. During implementation, we noticed that our user portraits helped the development team focus on supporting the primary usage situations and helped reduce the complexity and conflicts while supporting cross-platform interactions. Moreover, the two user portraits were also used to plan the usability evaluation and to discuss our service values in user test sessions [87, 88].

4. Static and Dynamic User Portraits

In this section, we reflect on the three case studies and argue that two types of user information, the dynamic and static attributes, should be captured and included in design research. The suitable methods and techniques to capture this information will also be discussed.

4.1. Dynamic User Information. The cases indicate that there are two types of information that have not been highlighted in general user modeling, profiling, or persona description, yet are important for identifying potential users and predicting their behaviors. The first type of user information is dynamic attributes, such as knowledge space [14, 16], age, lifestyles, and IT consumption. The second type is permanent information, such as attitudes, preferences, customs, and appropriate behaviors.

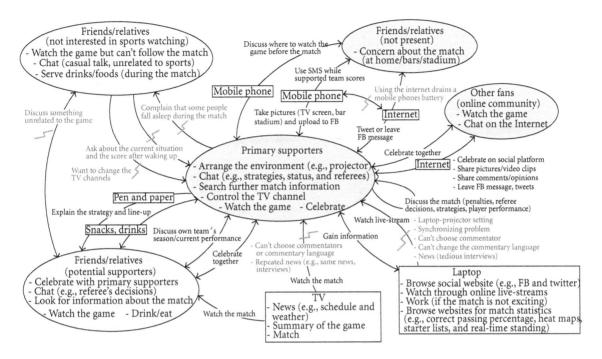

(a) The flow model of football watching at home

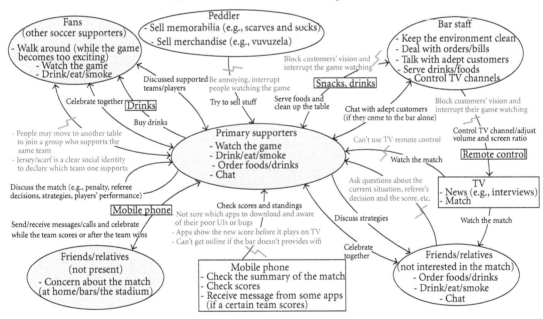

(b) The flow model of football watching at bars

FIGURE 3: The flow models of sport watching.

The importance of the first type of information emerged from both the case studies of tea ceremonies and of teenagers' social activities. As shown in Figure 1, tea ceremonies are a typical type of traditional social activity that enhances the sense of belonging of family members, and which is passed on from one generation to another. However, from marketing and usage-centered viewpoints, the youth involved in the ceremony are neither consumers nor end users. Due to differences in media usage, they generally receive no information from tea producers or direct-marketing farmers

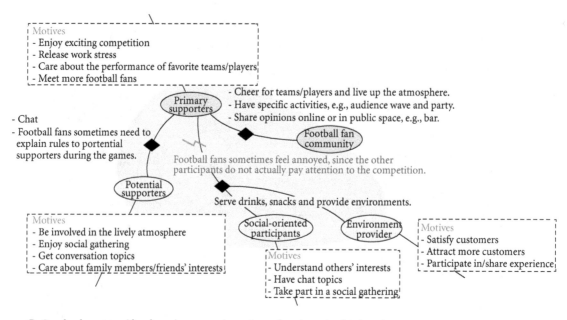

FIGURE 4: The multilevel social activity model of sport watching.

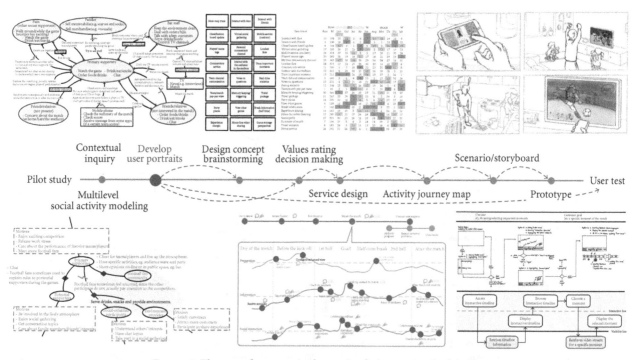

FIGURE 5: The uses of personas in the service design process (red dots).

(which is mainly accessible from magazines, newspaper advertisements, and yellow pages). However, the custom is still inherited, which means that within the predictable future, this young generation will grow to become the target audience of the tea ceremony. In other words, if service designers can identify this potential user group and provide information on the right platform, it is possible to support

this cultural inheritance and bridge the gap of media usage among different generations.

In the case study of teenagers' social activities, we found that although teenagers are willing to be active users of technology in their pursuit of new friends, their available modes of communication are often limited by their economic status. As teenagers generally have limited financial resources, most

IT products and media producers are unwilling to develop services for them. However, the older teenagers will see great improvements in their personal economy in only one or two years, and their great interest and reliance on the Internet will make them the target audience of smart phones, tablets, and other IT products in the near future. This type of information, predicting future audiences, is basic in marketing, but it is often overlooked in design research.

Different from most work in adaptive system development [15], we consider age and IT consumption to be dynamic attributes for user portraits. Traditional systems normally serve a specific type of users. For instance, most educational applications target a user group in a narrowed age range. However, for lifelong learning networks, large-scale services, and games with social purposes, the goal is to satisfy a large, diverse audience with long-run usage. Much work has highlighted several dynamic variables in development of technology enhanced learning systems and adaptive games, such as learners' knowledge space, skills, and capabilities [16, 90, 91]. However, we argue that user portraits, profiles, and models should also reflect how people's hypermedia experience, interests, and social behavior change with demographic transitions. Therefore, design research needs to consider predictable shifts in age, lifestyle, economic status, and IT consumption. To capture the dynamic information, surveys, self-documents, and focus groups can provide effective results.

4.2. Static User Information. More permanent and static information, including individuals' preferences, attitudes, and values, has been highlighted in some work of developing personas and user models [11, 14, 17, 28]. However, higher-level information such as norms, interpersonal relationships, and sociocultural backgrounds, are generally ignored in IT development.

According to multilevel social activity models and flow models of all the case studies, participants in a certain activity can have very similar behaviors, but their concerns, attitudes, and motives may still differ greatly. For instance, in the case study of football watching, we identified that participants' requirements and underlying motives varied, including seeking high-quality watching experiences (primary supporters), seeking detailed information (primary supporters), wanting to discuss the game with others, and enjoying each others' company (potential supporters). However, customer journey maps [92], which are used to describe an activity route of a user and to plan different touch points that characterize user's interactions within the service, cannot reveal such diversity of users' underlying motives and purposes of the activity. Moreover, due to lack of notation of different user types (e.g., differences in technology use), these models cannot fully support development teams when deciding suitable platforms (e.g., touch points and channels in service design). On the basis of our data gathered through multiple methods, we consider that the customer journey map has to be extended into an activity journey map (Figure 6), to reflect users' differing expectations. The map contains three types of customer journeys, representing different users' types and

their requirements. The awareness of the differences allows designers to develop reflective and reasonable scenarios and also helps development team prioritize use cases, decide appropriate platforms (channels), and plan user testing.

In addition, understanding of high-level information such as values, attitudes, and sociocultural background is easily taken for granted and therefore ignored in design research. Mulwa et al. [91] have listed twenty-one different user features for developing adaptive educational systems in the literature from 1996 to 2008, but none of these variables reflects values, social behaviors, and activity contexts. Most user experience design and HCI research methods can reveal detailed usage situations and users' cognitive characteristics, but have difficulty identifying meanings and norms behind activities. For instance, teenagers' friend-making processes on the Internet still follow the cultural manners that apply in their daily life. Additionally, in the case study of tea ceremonies some participants considered the ceremony to be part of East Asian culture and feel responsible to maintain this tradition.

4.3. Identify Invisible Users and Portray Users. On the basis of the studies of different social activities in different countries, we have discussed the strengths and weaknesses of different research methods. To better support rapid design research in most IT development, common user-centered design methods and frameworks provide a cheaper and more efficient way to account for the behaviors and interests of target users. However, in design for supporting communication, social purpose, and larger-scale services, we recommend to apply multiple research methods to gain deeper insights into the contexts and to identify potential and invisible users. Therefore, we propose the following process.

(1) Focus on a certain activity: as a pilot study, researchers can choose a representative activity and apply common context-, user-, or usage-centered research methods to capture events in great detail. In this stage, people who actually participated in the activity, objects, media, environmental circumstances, and interactions are identified.

(2) Extend the context: the goal of this stage is to identify the flow of information and find the social network that is related to the activity in the pilot study. Through an iterative process, researchers can identify how both central and peripheral events and people are connected with each other and associated with the main activity. To avoid missing important details, we suggest applying long-term ethnographic approaches, such as interviews, shadowing, behavior tracing, and self-documents.

(3) Recognize participants: in this stage, all people's goals, roles, interests, and participation in the target activity should be clarified. This information can help researchers to further distinguish different user types and identify potential users.

(4) Selection and focus: a workshop or a focus group in this stage can help development teams decide which

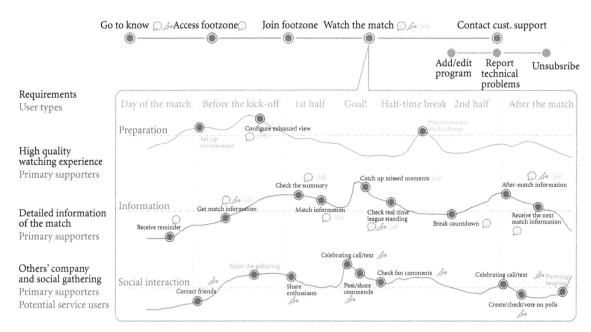

FIGURE 6: The activity journey map.

types of users should become the target audience and to set clear priorities for design development. Once the user types are selected, surveys and in-depth interviews can be used to capture in-depth information about these selected users.

To make the research results serve the same purpose as user models and personas, both dynamic and static information need to be highlighted while portraying the users. First, the portrait (it can be presented as a model or a document) should contain basic demographic information, such as gender, interests, and preferences. However, different from normal user profiling, we highly recommend that researchers also include dynamic user attributes that help predict how users' behaviors will change with shifts in their demographic data. For example, predictable increases in income are associated with transitions from a teenage life to maturity and result in changes in IT consumption and use. The second type, static information, is about higher-level concerns, including users' attitudes, motives, beliefs, and their sociocultural background. As mentioned above, this information is permanent and can enrich design solutions and can help evaluate designs in different phases of design cycles and in different projects.

5. Discussion

Through contextual design flow modeling, multilevel social activity modeling, and traditional ethnographic techniques, we have shown that there are different types of invisible users, who are involved in social activities, but are neither direct product users nor customers. In the case of a tea ceremony, the young generation, who has inherited tea-drinking habits from their parents, is not considered as a target audience of the traditional tea industry and can only access very limited

information. In the case of football watching, potential supporters represent a large group of people who participate in the activities regularly because their children, parents, friends, or colleagues are football fans, and they are willing to share these interests. However, most entertainment and media companies have only considered providing services for football fans. On the basis of what we learn from the three studies, it is argued that discovering all user types and presenting static and dynamic user portraits will bring many long-term benefits for systems and services.

(i) Identify potential users: in the three cases, we have shown that extending the research scope can help gain the necessary understanding of complex social interactions and social contexts and discover potential and indirect end users. We consider this to be significant understanding for serious games and technology enhanced education systems.

(ii) Support diverse and large user groups: development teams can predict new needs and expectations of future target audiences by identifying predictable changes in users' IT-product usage and economic status. Furthermore, identifying user types and motives can help designers propose more reasonable design solutions, satisfy users' different needs, and develop more adaptive systems.

(iii) Support multiple projects: compared to the outputs of usability and activity research, sociocultural information such as attitudes, values, and norms is more permanent in time and is valid across different media and physical spaces. Therefore, this type of knowledge can continuously be reused and reapplied in different projects. For instance, both the first and second studies have shown people's daily life and online activities are driven by norms and sociocultural values, which can always be considered in social media development.

As discussed in Section 2, most design research frameworks developed in HCI and related IT development generally do not focus on identifying user types or portraying users with the important dynamic and permanent attributes highlighted in the previous section. The design case studies have shown that ethnographic approaches, in-depth interviews, flow modeling, and multilevel social activity modeling can help development teams gain deeper insights, but that these methods are also time consuming and may require highly experienced researchers. Complex social media, service, and serious games development is challenging due to involving diverse user types, uncertain activity goals, and complex social interactions. Therefore, we argue that more comprehensive design research with a broader scope is needed to gain deeper insights, which can continue benefiting different phases in an iterative design cycle and help develop more adaptive and thoughtful systems.

6. Conclusion

Traditional user modeling mainly focuses on human-computer interaction. Although the traditional models reveal detailed information of the ways that people interact with systems, they are incapable of capturing many factors and contexts critical to design for social interaction, adaptive systems, and serious games. Personas, on the other hand, represent rich information about users' lifestyles and attitudes and bring various benefits to design practices. However, there is little consensus regarding suitable methodology for how to develop reliable and representative personas. Both user modeling and personas narrow down their audience groups by overlooking activity contexts. User modeling only focuses on direct users of systems, and personas mainly represent target consumers, rather than describing the many participants involved in the activities.

In this research, we compare the strengths and weaknesses of different design and research methods. We, first, present additional types of user information that were gained through application of multiple research methods. Second, we discuss the benefits of having this information in a design process, including being able to identify invisible users, increase awareness of different user types, and develop more informative and representative user portraits. We also suggest suitable research methods in each project phase and list the important information needed to develop user portraits. In addition, we provide many examples through our cases to illustrate how the knowledge of user types can be applied in a design process, in particular in the development of large-scale services, adaptive systems, and serious games. We are aware that the cost of applying long-term ethnographic approaches and multiple modeling strategies to gain these insights is high. However, following scientific approaches can contribute high-quality and reliable user portraits with significant dynamic and static user information, which can later be reused and reapplied in different future projects.

References

[1] K. Lynch, *The Image of the City*, Technology Press and Harvard University Press, Cambridge, Mass, USA, 1960.

[2] J. Zeisel, *Inquiry by Design: Tools for Environment-Behavior Research*, Cambridge University Press, 1984.

[3] B. Laure, Ed., *Design Research: Methods and Perspectives*, MIT Press, Cambridge, Mass, USA, 2003.

[4] K. H. Huang and Y. S. Deng, "Social interaction design in cultural context: a case study of a traditional social activity," *International Journal of Design*, vol. 2, no. 2, pp. 81–96, 2008.

[5] K. Holtzblatt and S. Jones, "Contextual inquiry: a participatory technique for system design," in *Participatory Design: Principles and Practices*, D. Schuler and A. Namioka, Eds., pp. 177–210, Lawrence Erlbaum Associates, Hillsdale, NJ, USA, 1993.

[6] F. Kensing and J. Blomberg, "Participatory design: issues and concerns," *Computer Supported Cooperative Work*, vol. 7, no. 3-4, pp. 167–185, 1998.

[7] J. Preece, Y. Rogers, and H. Sharp, *Interaction Design: Beyond Human-Computer Interaction*, John Wiley & Sons, New York, NY, USA, 2000.

[8] E. Arias, H. Eden, G. Fischer, A. Gorman, and E. Scharff, "Transcending the individual human mind: creating shared understanding through collaborative design," *ACM Transactions on Computer-Human Interaction*, vol. 7, no. 1, pp. 84–113, 2000.

[9] A. Kobsa, J. Koenemann, and W. Pohl, "Personalised hypermedia presentation techniques for improving online customer relationships," *The Knowledge Engineering Review*, vol. 16, no. 2, pp. 111–155, 2001.

[10] K. H. Huang, N. Nunes, L. Nobrega, L. Constantine, and M. Chen, "Hammering model: designing usable modeling tools," in *Human-Computer Interaction—INTERACT*, P. Campos et al., Ed., vol. 2011, pp. 537–554, Springer, 2011.

[11] P. Brusilovsky, "Adaptive hypermedia," *User Modelling and User-Adapted Interaction*, vol. 11, no. 1-2, pp. 87–110, 2001.

[12] G. Fischer, "User modeling in human-computer interaction," *User Modelling and User-Adapted Interaction*, vol. 11, no. 1-2, pp. 65–86, 2001.

[13] M. Montaner, B. López, and J. L. De La Rosa, "A taxonomy of recommender agents on the internet," *Artificial Intelligence Review*, vol. 19, no. 4, pp. 285–330, 2003.

[14] P. Karampiperis and D. Sampson, "Adaptive learning resources sequencing in educational hypermedia systems," *Educational Technology and Society*, vol. 8, no. 4, pp. 128–147, 2005.

[15] J. Hothi and W. Hall, "An evaluation of adapted hypermedia techniques using static user modeling," in *Proceedings of the 2nd Workshop on Adaptive Hypertext and Hypermedia*, pp. 45–50, Pittsburgh, Pa, USA, 1998.

[16] N. Henze and W. Nejdl, "A logical characterization of adaptive educational hypermedia," *New Review of Hypermedia and Multimedia*, vol. 10, no. 1, pp. 77–113, 2004.

[17] E. M. Raybourn, "Applying simulation experience design methods to creating serious game-based adaptive training systems," *Interacting with Computers*, vol. 19, no. 2, pp. 206–214, 2007.

[18] A. Cooper, *The Inmates are Running the Asylum*, SAMS, Transcending, Ind, USA, 2004.

[19] F. Long, "Real or imaginary: the effectiveness of using personas in product design," in *Proceedings of the Irish Ergonomics Society Annual Conference*, pp. 1–10, Dublin, Ireland, 2009.

[20] B. Pike, "Persona management," *Computer Fraud and Security*, vol. 2010, no. 11, pp. 11–15, 2010.

[21] T. Miaskiewicz and K. A. Kozar, "Personas and user-centered design: how can personas benefit product design processes?" *Design Studies*, vol. 32, no. 5, pp. 417–430, 2011.

[22] A. N. Antle, "Child-personas: fact or fiction?" in *Proceedings of the Conference on Designing Interactive Systems (DIS '06)*, pp. 22–30, New York, NY, USA, June 2006.

[23] A. N. Antle, "Child-based personas: need, ability and experience," *Cognition, Technology and Work*, vol. 10, no. 2, pp. 155–166, 2008.

[24] R. Chen and X. Wang, "Conceptualizing tangible augmented reality systems for design learning," in *Proceedings of the Design Computing and Cognition '08*, J. S. Gero and A. K. Goel, Eds., pp. 697–712, Springer, 2008.

[25] L. Suchman, *Plans and Situated Actions: The Problem of Human-Machine Communication*, Cambridge University Press, Cambridge, UK, 1987.

[26] M. S. Ackerman, "Intellectual challenge of CSCW: the gap between social requirements and technical feasibility," *Human-Computer Interaction*, vol. 15, no. 2-3, pp. 179–203, 2000.

[27] G. Fitzpatrick, *The Locales Framework*, Kluwer Academic Publishers, Amsterdam, The Netherlands, 2003.

[28] H. Drachsler, H. G. K. Hummel, and R. Koper, "Personal recommender systems for learners in lifelong learning networks: the requirements, techniques and model," *International Journal of Learning Technology*, vol. 3, no. 4, pp. 404–423, 2008.

[29] R. Koper and P. Sloep, *Learning Networks: Connecting People, Organizations, Autonomous Agents and Learning Resources to Establish the Emergence of Effective Lifelong Learning*, Heerlen, Open University of Netherlands, Amsterdam, The Netherlands.

[30] K. Rönkkö, "An empirical study demonstrating how different design constraints, project organization and contexts limited the utility of personas," in *Proceedings of the 38th Annual Hawaii International Conference on System Sciences*, p. 220, Washington, DC, USA, January 2005.

[31] C. N. Chapman and R. P. Milham, "The personas' new clothes: methodological and practical arguments against a popular method," in *Proceedings of the 50th Annual Meeting of the Human Factors and Ergonomics Society (HFES '06)*, pp. 634–636, October 2006.

[32] C. N. Chapman, E. Love, R. P. Milham, P. Elrif, and J. L. Alford, "Quantitative evaluation of personas as information," in *Proceedings of the 52nd Human Factors and Ergonomics Society Annual Meeting (HFES '08)*, pp. 1107–1111, September 2008.

[33] S. Portigal, "Persona non grata," *Interactions*, vol. 15, no. 1, pp. 72–73, 2008.

[34] K. H. Huang, C. H. Wuang, and H. L. Chong, "FootPal: build social rivalries around maintainable walking habits," in *Proceedings of the Extended Abstracts on Human Factors in Computing Systems (CHI '10)*, ACM, New York, NY, USA, 2010.

[35] C. H. Wu, T. F. Wu, Y. H. Chou et al., "HappyFeet! Influencing at the turning points: walking or scooter ride for short-distance journey?" in *Proceedings of the 12th International Conference on Human Computer Interaction with Mobile Devices and Services*, pp. 463–466, ACM, New York, NY, USA, 2010.

[36] F. W. Tung and Y. S. Deng, "Designing social presence in e-learning environments: testing the effect of interactivity on children," *Interactive Learning Environments*, vol. 14, no. 3, pp. 251–264, 2006.

[37] F. W. Tung and Y. S. Deng, "Increasing social presence of social actors in e-learning environments: effects of dynamic and static emoticons on children," *Displays*, vol. 28, no. 4-5, pp. 174–180, 2007.

[38] B. Glaser and A. Strauss, *The Discovery of Grounded Theory: Strategies of Qualitative Research*, Weidenfeld and Nicolson, 1967.

[39] A. Strauss and J. Corbin, *Basic of Qualitative Research: Grounded Theory Procedures and Techniques*, Sage, 1990.

[40] H. Beyer and K. Holtzblatt, *Contextual Design: Defining Customer-Centered Systems*, Morgan Kaufmann Publishers, 1998.

[41] H. Garfinkel, *Studies in Ethnomethodology*, Prentice-Hall, Englewood Cliffs, NJ, USA, 1967.

[42] J. Heritag, *Garfinkel and Ethnomethodology*, Polity Press, Cambridge, Mass, USA, 1984.

[43] M. D. LeCompte and J. P. Goetz, "Problems of reliability and validity in ethnographic research," *Review of Educational Research*, vol. 52, no. 1, pp. 31–60, 1982.

[44] E. G. Guba and Y. S. Lincoln, *Naturalistic Inquiry*, Sage, Newbury Park, Calif, USA, 1985.

[45] J. W. Creswell and D. L. Miller, "Determining validity in qualitative inquiry," *Theory into Practice*, vol. 39, no. 3, pp. 124–130, 2000.

[46] A. Strauss, *Qualitative Analysis for Social Scientists*, Cambridge, University Press, Cambridge, UK, 1987.

[47] L. Smircich, "Is the concept of culture a paradigm for understanding organizations and ourselves," in *Organizational Culture*, P. J. Frost, L. F. Moore, M. R. Louis, C. C. Lundberg, and J. Martin, Eds., pp. 55–72, Sage, Thousand Oaks, Calif, USA, 1985.

[48] R. E. Quinn and M. R. McGrath, "The transformation of organizational cultures: a competing values perspective," in *Organizational Culture*, P. J. Frost, L. F. Moore, M. R. Louis, C. C. Lundberg, and J. Martin, Eds., pp. 315–334, Sage, Thousand Oaks, Calif, USA, 1985.

[49] D. M. Rousseau, "Assessing organizational culture: the case for multiple methods," in *Organizational Climate and Culture*, B. Schneider, Ed., pp. 153–192, Jossey-Bass, San Francisco, Calif, USA, 1990.

[50] E. H. Schein, *Organisational Culture and Leadership*, Jossey-Bass, San Francisco, Calif, USA, 1992.

[51] M. Erez and E. Gati, "A dynamic, multi-level model of culture: from the micro level of the individual to the macro level of a global culture," *Applied Psychology*, vol. 53, no. 4, pp. 583–598, 2004.

[52] C. Handy, *Understanding Organizations*, Penguin, Harmondsworth, UK, 1976.

[53] D. Hellriegel and W. Slocum, *Organizational Behavior*, South-Western, 2007.

[54] R. Harrison, "Understanding your organization's character," *Harvard Business Review*, vol. 50, no. 3, pp. 119–128, 1972.

[55] L. Goodstein, T. N. Nolan, and J. W. Pfeiffer, *Applied Strategic Planning*, McGraw-Hill, New York, NY, USA, 1993.

[56] A. Brown, *Organisational Culture*, Pitman, London, UK, 1998.

[57] T. Deal and A. Kennedy, *Corporate Cultures: The Rites and Rituals of Corporate Life*, Penguin Books, London, UK, 1982.

[58] E. T. Hall, *The Hidden Dimension*, Doubleday & Company, New York, NY, USA, 1967.

[59] E. T. Hall, *Beyond Culture*, Anchor Books, New York, NY, USA, 1977.

[60] G. Hofstede, *Culture's Consequences: Comparing Values, Behaviors, Institutions and Organizations across Nations*, Sage, Thousand Oaks, Calif, USA, 2001.

[61] G. Hofstede, *Cultures and Organizations: Software of the Mind*, McGraw-Hill, New York, NY, USA, 1991.

[62] F. Trompenaars and C. Hampden-Turner, *Riding the Waves of Culture Understanding Cultural Diversity in Business*, Nicholas Brearley, London, UK, 1997.

[63] E. H. Schein, "Organizational culture," *American Psychologist*, vol. 45, no. 2, pp. 109–119, 1990.

[64] J. Martin and D. Meyerson, "Organizational cultures and the denial, channeling, and acknowledgement of ambiguity," in *Managing Ambiguity and Change*, L. R. Pondy, R. J. Boland, and H. Thomas, Eds., Wiley, New York, NY, USA, 1988.

[65] K. R. Thompson and F. Luthans, "Organizational culture: a behavioural perspective," in *Organizational Climate and Culture*, B. Schneider, Ed., Jessey-Bass, Oxford, UK, 1990.

[66] H. Spencer-Oatey, *Culturally Speaking: Managing Rapport Through Talk Across Cultures*, Continuum, London, UK, 2000.

[67] M. Krumbholz and N. Maiden, "How culture might impact on the implementation of enterprise resource planning packages," in *Advanced Information Systems Engineering*, B. Wangler and L. Bergman, Eds., pp. 279–293, Springer, 2000.

[68] D. A. Norman, *The Design of Everyday Things*, Basic Books, New York, NY, USA, 1988.

[69] G. Ritzer and D. Goodman, *Sociological Theory*, McGraw-Hill, London, UK, 2004.

[70] C. Wasson, "Ethnography in the field of design," *Human Organization*, vol. 59, no. 4, pp. 377–388, 2000.

[71] J. Whiteside, J. Bennett, and K. Holzblatt, "Usability engineering: our experience and evolution," in *Handbook of Human Computer Interaction*, M. Helander, Ed., North Holland, New York, NY, USA, 1998.

[72] D. Wixon, K. Holtzblatt, and S. Knox, "Contextual design: an emergent view of system design," in *Proceedings of the Conference of Human Factors in Computing Systems*, pp. 329–336, ACM, New York, NY, USA, 1990.

[73] Y. Engeström, "Activity theory as a framework for analyzing and redesigning work," *Ergonomics*, vol. 43, no. 7, pp. 960–974, 2000.

[74] P. D. Rothstein, "a (x 4): a user-centered method for designing experience," in *Proceedings of the Design Education. Industrial Designers Society of America (IDSA '01)*, 2001.

[75] V. Kumar and P. Whitney, "Faster, cheaper, deeper user research," *Design Management Journal*, vol. 14, no. 2, pp. 50–57, 2003.

[76] B. Nardi, "Studying context: a comparison of Activity Theory, situated action models, and distributed cognition," in *Context and Consciousness—Activity Theory and Human-Computer Interaction*, B. Nardi, Ed., MIT Press, Cambridge, Mass, USA, 1996.

[77] D. H. Jonassen and L. Rohrer-Murphy, "Activity theory as a framework for designing constructivist learning environments," *Educational Technology Research and Development*, vol. 47, no. 1, pp. 61–79, 1999.

[78] Y. Engeström, "Learning by Expanding. An Activity-theoretical approach to developmental research," 2011, http://communication.ucsd.edu/MCA/Paper/Engestrom/expanding/toc.htm.

[79] M. Fjeld, K. Lauche, M. Bichsel, F. Voorhorst, H. Krueger, and M. Rauterberg, "Physical and virtual tools: activity theory applied to the design of groupware," *Computer Supported Cooperative Work*, vol. 11, no. 1-2, pp. 153–180, 2002.

[80] S. L. Bryant, A. Forte, and A. Bruckman, "Becoming Wikipedian: transformation of participation in a collaborative online encyclopedia," in *Proceedings of the International ACM SIGGROUP Conference on Supporting Group Work (GROUP '05)*, pp. 1–10, November 2005.

[81] K. H. Huang, *An Integrated Research Approach for Social Interaction Design*, National Chiao Tung University, Hsinchu, Taiwan, 2012.

[82] K. H. Huang, H. C. You, and Y. S. Deng, "Clubs forming on CrazyVote—the blurred social boundary between online communities and the real world," *International Journal of Social and Human Sciences*, vol. 3, pp. 693–703, 2009.

[83] G. R. Gibbs, *Qualitative Data Analysis: Explorations with NVivo*, Buckingham, Philadelphia, Pa, USA, 2002.

[84] P. Bazeley, *Qualitative Data Analysis with NVivo*, Sage, London, UK, 2007.

[85] G. L. Shostack, "Designing services that deliver," *Harvard Business Review*, vol. 62, no. 1, pp. 133–139, 1984.

[86] M. J. Bitner, A. L. Ostrom, and F. N. Morgan, "Service blueprinting: a practical technique for service innovation," *California Management Review*, vol. 50, no. 3, pp. 66–94, 2008.

[87] J. Nielsen and R. L. Mack, Eds., *Usability Inspection Methods*, JohnWiley & Sons, 1994.

[88] L. Constantine, "Peer reviews for usability," *Cutter IT Journal*, vol. 18, no. 1, pp. 5–13, 2005.

[89] A. Cockburn, *Writing Effective Use Cases*, Addison-Wesley, 2001.

[90] D. Charles, M. McNeill, M. McAlister et al., "Player-centred game design: player modelling and adaptive digital games," in *Proceedings of the Conference Changing Views—Worlds in Play (DiGRA '05)*, pp. 285–298, British Columbia, 2005.

[91] C. Mulwa, S. Lawless, M. Sharp, I. Arnedillo-Sanchez, and V. Wade, "Adaptive educational hypermedia systems in technology enhanced learning: a literature review," in *Proceedings of the ACM Conference on Information Technology Education (SIGITE '10)*, pp. 73–84, January 2010.

[92] C. Voss and L. Zomerdijk, "Innovation in experiential services—an empirical view," in *Innovation in Services*, Department of Trade and Industry, Ed., pp. 97–134, DTI, London, UK, 2007.

Permissions

The contributors of this book come from diverse backgrounds, making this book a truly international effort. This book will bring forth new frontiers with its revolutionizing research information and detailed analysis of the nascent developments around the world.

We would like to thank all the contributing authors for lending their expertise to make the book truly unique. They have played a crucial role in the development of this book. Without their invaluable contributions this book wouldn't have been possible. They have made vital efforts to compile up to date information on the varied aspects of this subject to make this book a valuable addition to the collection of many professionals and students.

This book was conceptualized with the vision of imparting up-to-date information and advanced data in this field. To ensure the same, a matchless editorial board was set up. Every individual on the board went through rigorous rounds of assessment to prove their worth. After which they invested a large part of their time researching and compiling the most relevant data for our readers. Conferences and sessions were held from time to time between the editorial board and the contributing authors to present the data in the most comprehensible form. The editorial team has worked tirelessly to provide valuable and valid information to help people across the globe.

Every chapter published in this book has been scrutinized by our experts. Their significance has been extensively debated. The topics covered herein carry significant findings which will fuel the growth of the discipline. They may even be implemented as practical applications or may be referred to as a beginning point for another development. Chapters in this book were first published by Hindawi Publishing Corporation; hereby published with permission under the Creative Commons Attribution License or equivalent.

The editorial board has been involved in producing this book since its inception. They have spent rigorous hours researching and exploring the diverse topics which have resulted in the successful publishing of this book. They have passed on their knowledge of decades through this book. To expedite this challenging task, the publisher supported the team at every step. A small team of assistant editors was also appointed to further simplify the editing procedure and attain best results for the readers.

Our editorial team has been hand-picked from every corner of the world. Their multi-ethnicity adds dynamic inputs to the discussions which result in innovative outcomes. These outcomes are then further discussed with the researchers and contributors who give their valuable feedback and opinion regarding the same. The feedback is then collaborated with the researches and they are edited in a comprehensive manner to aid the understanding of the subject.

Apart from the editorial board, the designing team has also invested a significant amount of their time in understanding the subject and creating the most relevant covers. They scrutinized every image to scout for the most suitable representation of the subject and create an appropriate cover for the book.

The publishing team has been involved in this book since its early stages. They were actively engaged in every process, be it collecting the data, connecting with the contributors or procuring relevant information. The team has been an ardent support to the editorial, designing and production team. Their endless efforts to recruit the best for this project, has resulted in the accomplishment of this book. They are a veteran in the field of academics and their pool of knowledge is as vast as their experience in printing. Their expertise and guidance has proved useful at every step. Their uncompromising quality standards have made this book an exceptional effort. Their encouragement from time to time has been an inspiration for everyone.

The publisher and the editorial board hope that this book will prove to be a valuable piece of knowledge for researchers, students, practitioners and scholars across the globe.

List of Contributors

Alkinoos Athanasiou, Chrysa Lithari, Konstantina Kalogianni, Manousos A. Klados and Panagiotis D. Bamidis
Lab of Medical Informatics, Medical School, Aristotle University of Thessaloniki (AUTH), 54124 Thessaloniki, Greece

Brianna Potvin, Colin Swindells, Melanie Tory and Margaret-Anne Storey
Department of Computer Science, University of Victoria, Engineering/Computer Science Building (ECS), Room 504, P.O. Box 3055, STN CSC, Victoria, BC, Canada V8W 3P6

Joan De Boeck
Expertise Centre for Digital Media, transnational University Limburg, Hasselt University, Wetenschapspark 2, 3590 Diepenbeek, Belgium
ICT and Inclusion, K-Point, Katholieke Hogeschool Kempen, Kleinhoefstraat 4, 2440 Geel, Belgium

Lode Vanacken, Sofie Notelaers and Karin Coninx
Expertise Centre for Digital Media, transnational University Limburg, Hasselt University, Wetenschapspark 2, 3590 Diepenbeek, Belgium

Raheleh Mohammadi and Ali Mahloojifar
Department of Biomedical Engineering, Tarbiat Modares University, Tehran 14115194, Iran

Damien Coyle
Intelligent Systems Research Centre, University of Ulster, Derry BT48 7JL, UK

Kirsten Ellis and Jan Carlo Barca
Faculty of Information Technology, Monash University, Clayton Campus, VIC 3800, Australia

Outi Tuisku and Veikko Surakka
Research Group for Emotions, Sociality, and Computing, Tampere Unit for Computer-Human Interaction (TAUCHI), School of Information Sciences, University of Tampere, Kanslerinrinne 1, 33014 Tampere, Finland

Ville Rantanen and Jukka Lekkala
Sensor Technology and Biomeasurements, Department of Automation Science and Engineering, Tampere University of Technology, P.O. Box 692, 33101 Tampere, Finland

Toni Vanhala
Research Group for Emotions, Sociality, and Computing, Tampere Unit for Computer-Human Interaction (TAUCHI), School of Information Sciences, University of Tampere, Kanslerinrinne 1, 33014 Tampere, Finland
ICT for Health, VTT Technical Research Centre of Finland, Tekniikankatu 1, P.O. Box 1300, 33101 Tampere, Finland

Haipeng Mi, Tomoki Fujita and Masanori Sugimoto
Interaction Technology Laboratory, Department of Electrical Engineering and Information Systems, University of Tokyo, 7-3-1 Hongo, Bunkyo-ku, 113-8656 Tokyo, Japan

Aleksander Krzywinski
The Interaction Research Group, Department of Information Science and Media Studies, University of Bergen, Fosswinckelsgate 6, 5020 Bergen, Norway

Haiyue Yuan, Janko Calic and Ahmet Kondoz
I-Lab, Multimedia Communications Research, Centre for Vision, Speech and Signal Processing, University of Surrey, Guildford Gu2 7XH, UK

Pablo Moreno-Ger and Javier Torrente
Facultad de Informatica, Universidad Complutense de Madrid, 28040 Madrid, Spain

Yichuan Grace Hsieh and William T. Lester
Laboratory of Computer Science, Massachusetts General Hospital, Harvard Medical School, Boston, MA 02114, USA

Hazel Morton, Nancie Gunson and Mervyn Jack
Centre for Communication Interface Research, School of Engineering, University of Edinburgh, Edinburgh EH9 3JL, UK

Paulo Rogério de Almeida Ribeiro
Institute of Medical Psychology and Behavioral Neurobiology and MEG Center, University of Tubingen, Silcherstraße 5, 72076 Tubingen, Germany
Applied Neurotechnology Lab, Department of Psychiatry and Psychotherapy, University of Tubingen, Calwerstraße 14, 72076 Tubingen, Germany
International Max Planck Research School for Neural Information Processing, Osterbergstraße 3, 72074 Tubingen, Germany

Fabricio Lima Brasil
Institute of Medical Psychology and Behavioral Neurobiology and MEG Center, University of Tubingen, Silcherstraße 5, 72076 Tubingen, Germany
Applied Neurotechnology Lab, Department of Psychiatry and Psychotherapy, University of Tubingen, Calwerstraße 14, 72076 Tubingen, Germany
International Max Planck Research School for Neural & Behavioral Sciences, Osterbergstraße 3, 72074 Tubingen, Germany

Matthias Witkowski, Farid Shiman and Surjo Raphael Soekadar
Institute of Medical Psychology and Behavioral Neurobiology and MEG Center, University of Tubingen, Silcherstraße 5, 72076 Tubingen, Germany
Applied Neurotechnology Lab, Department of Psychiatry and Psychotherapy, University of Tubingen, Calwerstraße 14, 72076 Tubingen, Germany

Christian Cipriani, Nicola Vitiello and Maria Chiara Carrozza
The BioRobotics Institute, Scuola Superiore Sant'Anna, V.le R. Piaggio 34, 56025 Pontedera, Italy

Jana Appel, Astrid von der Putten and Nicole C. Kramer
Department of Social Psychology: Media and Communication, University of Duisburg-Essen, Forsthausweg 2, 47057 Duisburg, Germany

Jonathan Gratch
Institute for Creative Technologies, University of Southern California, 12015 Waterfront Drive Playa Vista, Los Angeles, CA 90094-2536, USA

Mats Liljedahl, Stefan Lindberg and Katarina Delsing
The Interactive Institute, Acusticum 4, 941 28 Pitea, Sweden

Mikko Polojarvi and Timo Saloranta
University of Oulu, PL 8000, Oulun Yliopisto, 90014 Oulu, Finland

Ismo Alakarppa
University of Lapland, P.O. Box 122, 96101 Rovaniemi, Finland

Alasdair G. Thin
School of Life Sciences, Heriot-Watt University, Edinburgh EH14 4AS, UK

Setare Amiri, Reza Fazel-Rezai and Vahid Asadpour
Biomedical Signal and Image Processing Laboratory, Department of Electrical Engineering, University of North Dakota, Grand Forks, ND, USA

Hyowon Lee
Singapore University of Technology and Design, 20 Dover Drive, Singapore 138682

Nazlena Mohamad Ali
Institute of Visual Informatics (IVI), Universiti Kebangsaan Malaysia, 43600 Bangi, Selangor, Malaysia

Lynda Hardman
Centrum Wiskunde & Informatica (CWI) and University of Amsterdam, Science Park 123, 1098 XG Amsterdam, The Netherlands

Mirja Ilves and Veikko Surakka
Research Group for Emotions, Sociality, and Computing, Tampere Unit for Computer-Human Interaction (TAUCHI), School of Information Sciences, University of Tampere, Kanslerinrinne 1, FI-33014 University of Tampere, Finland

Francesco Bellotti and Riccardo Berta
Department of Naval, Electric, Electronic and Telecommunications Engineering, University of Genoa, Via all'Opera Pia 11/a, 16145 Genoa, Italy

Bill Kapralos
Faculty of Business and Information Technology, University of Ontario Institute of Technology, 2000 Simcoe Street North, Oshawa, Canada L1H 7K4

Kiju Lee
Department of Mechanical and Aerospace Engineering, Case Western Reserve University, 10900 Euclid Avenue, Cleveland, OH 44106, USA

Pablo Moreno-Ger
Faculty of Computer Science, Universidad Complutense de Madrid, Ciudad Universitaria, 28040 Madrid, Spain

Emmanuel Maby, Margaux Perrin, Olivier Bertrand, Gaetan Sanchez and Jeremie Mattout
CRNL, Lyon Neuroscience Research Center, INSERM, CNRS, University Lyon 1, Dycog Team, 95 Bd Pinel, 69500 Bron, France

Ko-Hsun Huang
Institute of Applied Arts, National Chiao-Tung University, 1001 University Road, Hsinchu 300, Taiwan
Madeira Interactive Technologies Institute, Caminho da Penteada, 9020-105 Funchal, Portugal

Yi-Shin Deng
Institute of Creative Industrial Design, National Cheng Kung University, 1 University Road, Tainan City 701, Taiwan

Ming-Chuen Chuang
Institute of Applied Arts, National Chiao-Tung University, 1001 University Road, Hsinchu 300, Taiwan

Printed in the USA
CPSIA information can be obtained
at www.ICGtesting.com
JSHW051440221024
72173JS00006B/1527

9 781632 400246